BRONZE BY GOLD

BORDER CROSSINGS
VOLUME 3
GARLAND REFERENCE LIBRARY OF THE HUMANITIES
VOLUME 2061

Bronze by Gold
The Music of Joyce

Edited by
Sebastian D. G. Knowles

Garland Publishing, Inc.
A member of the Taylor & Francis Group
New York and London
1999

Library of Congress Cataloging-in-Publication Data

Bronze by gold : the music of Joyce / edited by Sebastian D. G. Knowles.
     p.   cm. — (Garland reference library of the humanities ;
v. 2061. Border crossings ; v. 3)
    Includes bibliographical references and index.
    ISBN 0-8153-2863-X (alk. paper)
    1. Joyce, James, 1882–1941—Knowledge—Music. 2. Music and litera-
ture—History—20th century. 3. Music—Ireland—History—20th century.
4. Ireland—In literature.   I. Knowles, Sebastian David Guy. II. Series:
Garland reference library of the humanities ; vol. 2061. III. Series: Garland
reference library of the humanities. Border crossings ; v. 3.
PR6019.09Z52633   1999
823'.912—dc21   98-49258
                                             CIP

Cover illustration: Tiziano Vecellio (1488/89–1576) (Titian). Concert Champêtre,
c. 1508, detail. Oil on canvas, approximately 43" × 54". Reprinted by permission
of the Louvre Museum © RMN. Also known as *Pastoral Symphony*, Fete
Champêtre. This painting, which has also been attributed to Giorgione, was the
inspiration for Pater's celebrated remark in "The School of Giorgione" that *"All
art constantly aspires towards the condition of music."*

Printed on acid-free, 250-year-life paper
Manufactured in the United States of America

For
Janette Marie Jelen Knowles

Bronze by gold heard the hoofirons, steelyringing.
(*U*, 11.1)

Contents

Contents

Abbreviations

The following abbreviations are used for references to these editions of Joyce's works throughout the volume.

CM   Joyce, James. *Chamber Music*. London: Jonathan Cape, 1971.

CW   Joyce, James. *The Critical Writings of James Joyce*. Eds. Ellsworth Mason and Richard Ellmann. New York: Viking Press, 1959.

D   Joyce, James. *Dubliners*. Ed. Robert Scholes in consultation with Richard Ellmann. New York: Viking Press, 1967.

E   Joyce, James. *Exiles*. New York: Penguin, 1973.

FW   Joyce, James. *Finnegans Wake*. New York: Viking Press, 1939.

GJ   Joyce, James. *Giacomo Joyce*. Ed. Richard Ellmann. New York: Viking Press, 1968.

JJA   Joyce, James. *The James Joyce Archive*. Eds. Michael Groden et al. New York: Garland Publishing, 1978–79.

L, I   Joyce, James. *Letters of James Joyce*. Vol. I. Ed. Stuart Gilbert. New York: Viking Press, 1957; reissued with corrections, 1966.

L, II   Joyce, James. *Letters of James Joyce*. Vol. II. Ed. Richard Ellmann. New York: Viking Press, 1966.

L, III   Joyce, James. *Letters of James Joyce*. Vol. III. Ed. Richard Ellmann. New York: Viking Press, 1966.

P   Joyce, James. *A Portrait of the Artist as a Young Man*. Ed. Richard Ellmann. New York: Viking Press, 1964.

SH   Joyce, James. *Stephen Hero*. New York: New Directions, 1963.

SL   Joyce, James. *Selected Letters of James Joyce*. Ed. Richard
      Ellmann. New York: Viking Press, 1975.
U   Joyce, James. *Ulysses*. Eds. Hans Walter Gabler et al. New
      York: Garland Publishing, 1984.

Editorial Conventions

All quotations from Joyce come from the above editions, unless particular interest is taken in a departure from them, in which case the different edition is listed in the Works Cited particular to the essay. All operas written in a foreign language are referred to by the title in their original language (*Die Zauberflöte*, *Le Nozze di Figaro*). Foreign words and phrases standing alone have been italicized (*nebeneinander*); quotations from texts in foreign languages and titles of opera arias have not ("M'appari"). Accents are not provided on capitalized letters of foreign words (*Etude*, *Ubermensch*). Italics have been used for emphasis throughout, except where a quotation includes italics, in which case underlining is used.

List of Figures

General Introduction to
Border Crossings
Daniel Albright

THE NEED FOR COMPARISONS AMONG THE ARTS

To study one artistic medium in isolation from others is to study an inadequacy. The twentieth century, so rich in literature, in music, and in the visual arts, has also been rich in criticism of these arts; but it's possible that some of the uglinesses and distortions in modern criticism have arisen from the consideration of each artistic medium as an autonomous field of development, fenced off from other media. It is hard for us to believe, but when, long ago, Horace said *Ut pictura poesis*—the poem should be like a picture—he meant it.

The twentieth century, perhaps more than any other age, demands a style of criticism in which the arts are considered as a whole. This is partly because the artists themselves insisted again and again upon inextricability of the arts. Ezra Pound, for one, believed that, in antiquity, "music and poetry had been in alliance [...] that the divorce of the two arts had been to the advantage of neither, and that melodic invention had declined simultaneously and progressively with their divergence. The rhythms of poetry grew stupider." He thought that it was the duty of the poet to learn music, and the duty of the musician to study poetry. But we must learn to challenge the boundaries among the arts, not only because the artists we study demanded it, but because our philosophy demands it as well. The linguistics of Ferdinand de Saussure and the philosophies of Ludwig Wittgenstein and Jacques Derrida tend to strip language of denotation, to make language a game of arbitrary signifiers; and as words lose connection to the world of hard objects, they become more and more like musical notes. Wittgenstein claimed, "To say that a word has meaning does not imply that it *stands for* or *represents* a thing. [...] The sign plus the rules of grammar applying to it is all we need [to make a language]. We need nothing further to make the connection with reality. If we did we should need something to connect that with reality, which would lead to an infinite regress." And, for Wittgenstein, the consequence of this disconnection was clear: "Understanding a sentence is much more akin to understanding a theme in music than one may think." To Horace, reading is like looking at a picture; to Wittgenstein, reading is like listening to music. The arts seem endlessly interpermeable, a set of fluid systems of construing and reinterpreting, in which the quest for meaning engages all our senses at once. Thinking is itself looking, hearing, touching, even tasting, since such words as *savoir* are forms of the Latin *sapere,* taste.

THE TERM *MODERNISM*

Modernism—like any unit of critical terminology—is a fiction, but an indispensable fiction. It is possible to argue (as Vladimir Nabokov did) that each work of art in the universe is unique and incommensurable; that there is no such thing as a school of artists; that an idea such as *influence* among artists arises from sheer intellectual laziness. This line of argument, however, contradicts our intuition that certain works of art look like one another; that, among many works of art produced at the same time or in the same place, there are family resemblances. Such terms as modernism need have no great prestige: they're simply critical inductions convenient for describing certain family resemblances.

Furthermore, these terms denote not only kinship-relations established by critics from outside, but also kinship-relations determined by artists from within. The term modernism had tremendous potency for the modernists themselves: when Ezra Pound first read a poem by T. S. Eliot, he was thunderstruck that Eliot had managed to *modernize* his poetry all by himself, without any contact with other poets. Pound regarded modernism itself as a huge group project: to this extent, modernism isn't just a label attached by students of a period, but a kind of tribal affiliation, one of thousands of examples of those arbitrary loyalty-groups that bedevil the human race. Nearly every early-twentieth-century artist felt the need to define himself or herself as a modernist or otherwise. When Stravinsky at last met Rachmaninov, in Hollywood, Stravinsky obviously greeted his colleague not simply as a fraternal fellow in the order of Russian expatriate composers, but as a (self-sacrificing) modernist condescending to a (rich and successful) romantic. The label *modernist* shaped the interactions of artists themselves: sometimes as a help, sometimes as a hindrance.

Of course, it's the task of criticism at the end of the twentieth century to offer a better account of modernism than the modernists themselves could. Stravinsky's ideas about Rachmaninov were wrong in several ways: not just because Rachmaninov's royalties weren't noticeably greater than Stravinsky's, but also because their music was somewhat more similar than Stravinsky would have liked to admit. For instance, compare the Easter finale from Rachmaninov's Suite for Two Pianos, op. 5, with the carillon evoked by the piano in Stravinsky's song *Spring,* op. 6/1: they inhabit the same aesthetic realm.

A theory of the modernist movement that might embrace both Rachmaninov and Stravinsky, or Picasso and Balthus, could be constructed along the following lines: modernism is a *testing of the limits of aesthetic construction.* According to this perspective, the modernists tried to find the ultimate bounds of certain artistic possibilities: volatility of emotion (expressionism); stability and inexpressiveness (the new objectivity); accuracy of representation (hyperrealism); absence of representation (abstractionism); purity of form (neoclassicism); formless energy (neobarbarism); cultivation of the technological present (futurism); cultivation of the prehistoric past (the mythic method). These extremes, of course, have been arranged in pairs, because aesthetic heresies, like theological ones, come in binary sets: each limit-point presupposes an opposite limit-point, a counterextreme toward which the artist can push. Much of the strangeness, the stridency, the exhilaration of modernist art can be explained by this strong thrust toward the verges of the aesthetic experience: after the nineteenth century had established a remarkably safe, intimate center where the artist and the audience could dwell, the twentieth century reaches out to the freakish circumferences of art. The extremes of the aesthetic experience tend to converge: in the modernist movement, the most barbaric art tends to be the most up-to-date and sophisticated. For example, when T. S. Eliot first heard Stravinsky's *The Rite of Spring,* he wrote that the music seemed to "transform the rhythm of the steppes into the scream of the motor-horn, the rattle of machinery, the grind of wheels, the beating of iron and steel, the roar of

the underground railway, and the other barbaric noises of modern life."
The Waste Land is itself written to the same recipe: the world of
London, with its grime, boredom, and abortifacient drugs, overlays the
antique world of primal rites for the rejuvenation of the land through
the dismemberment of a god. In the modernist movement, things tend
to coexist uncomfortably with their exact opposites.

Wallace Stevens referred to the story we tell ourselves about the
world, and about our presence in the world, and about how we attempt
to configure pleasant lives for ourselves, as a supreme fiction; and
similarly, critics live by various critical fictions, as they reconfigure the
domain of similarities and differences in the arts. Modernism is just
such a high critical fiction.

THE SPAN OF THE MODERNIST AGE

The use of a term such as modernism usually entails a certain
restriction to a period of time. Such a restriction is rarely easy, and
becomes immensely difficult for the interdisciplinary student: the
romantic movement, for example, will invariably mean one age for a
musicologist, another (perhaps scarcely overlapping) for a student of
British poetry. One might say that the modernist age begins around
1907–09, because in those years Picasso painted *Les Demoiselles
d'Avignon,* Schoenberg made his "atonal" breakthrough, and the
international careers of Stravinsky, Pound, Stein, and Cocteau were just
beginning or were not long to come. And one might choose 1951 for a
terminus, since in that year Cage started using the I Ching to compose
chance-determined music, and Samuel Beckett's trilogy and *Waiting
for Godot* were soon to establish an artistic world that would have
partly bewildered the early modernists. The modernists did not (as
Cage did) abdicate their artistic responsibilities to a pair of dice; the
modernists did not (as Beckett did) delight in artistic failure.
Modernism was a movement associated with scrupulous choice of
artistic materials, and with hard work in arranging them. Sometimes the
modernists deflected the domain of artistic selection to unusual states of
consciousness (trance, dream, etc.); but, except for a few dadaist
experiments, they didn't abandon artistic selection entirely, and even
Tristan Tzara, Kurt Schwitters, and the more radical dadaists usually
attempted a more impudent form of non-sense than aleatory procedures
can generate. The modernists *intended* modernism; the movement did
not come into existence randomly.

But the version of modernism outlined here—a triumphalist extension of the boundaries of the feasible in art—is only *a* version of modernism. There exist many modernisms, and each version is likely to describe a period with different terminal dates. It isn't hard to construct an argument showing that modernism began, say, around 1886 (the year of the last painting exhibition organized by the impressionists, at which Seurat made the first important show of his work): Nietzsche had privately published *Also Sprach Zarathustra* in 1885, and Mahler's first symphony would appear in 1889. And it is possible to construct arguments showing that modernism has only recently ended, since Beckett actualized certain potentialities in Joyce (concerning self-regarding language), and Cage followed closely after Schoenberg and Satie (Cage's *Cheap Imitation,* from 1969, is simply a note-by-note rewriting, with random pitch alterations, of the vocal line of Satie's 1918 *Socrate*).

And it is possible that modernism hasn't ended at all: the term *postmodernism* may simply be erroneous. Much of the music of Philip Glass is a straightforward recasting of musical surface according to models derived from visual surface, following a formula stated in 1936 by an earlier American composer, George Antheil, who wrote of the "filling out of a certain time canvas with musical abstractions and sound material composed and contrasted against one another with the thought of time values rather than tonal values [...] I used time as Picasso might have used the blank spaces of his canvas. I did not hesitate, for instance, to repeat one measure one hundred times." Most of the attributes we ascribe to postmodernism can easily be found, latently or actually, with the modernist movement: for another example, Brecht in the 1930s made such deconstructionist declarations as "*Realist* means: laying bare society's causal network / showing up the dominant viewpoint as the viewpoint of the dominators." It is arguable that, in the 1990s, we are still trying to digest the meal that the modernists ate.

If modernism can be said to reach out beyond the present moment, it is also true that modernism can be said to extend backward almost indefinitely. Wagner, especially the Wagner of *Tristan und Isolde,* has been a continual presence in twentieth-century art: Brecht and Weill continually railed against Wagnerian narcosis and tried to construct a music theater exactly opposed to Wagner's, but Virgil Thomson found much to admire and imitate in Wagner (even though Thomson's operas sound, at first hearing, even less Wagnerian than Kurt Weill's). In some

respects, the first modernist experiment in music theater might be said
to be the Kotzebue-Beethoven *The Ruins of Athens* (1811), in which the
goddess Minerva claps her hands over her ears at hearing the hideous
music of the dervishes' chorus (blaring tritones, Turkish percussion):
here is the conscious sensory assault, sensory overload, of
Schoenberg's first operas. Modernism is partly confined to the first half
of the twentieth century, but it tends to spill into earlier and later ages.
Modernism created its own precursors; it made the past new, as well as
the present.

THE QUESTION OF BOUNDARIES

The revolution of the information age began when physicists
discovered that silicon could be used either as a resistor or as a
conductor of electricity. Modernist art is also a kind of circuit board, a
pattern of yieldings and resistances, in which one art sometimes asserts
its distinct, inviolable nature, and sometimes yields itself, tries to
imitate some foreign aesthetic. Sometimes music and poetry coexist in
a state of extreme dissonance (as Brecht thought they should, in the
operas that he wrote with Weill); but on other occasions music tries to
become poetry, or poetry tries to *become* music. To change the
metaphor, one might say that modernism investigates a kind of
transvestism among the arts: what happens when one art stimulates
itself by temporarily pretending to be another species of art altogether.

Modernist art has existed in an almost continual state of crisis
concerning the boundaries between one art medium and another. Is a
painting worth a thousand words, or is it impossible to find a verbal
equivalent of an image, even if millions of words were used? Are music
and literature two different things, or two aspects of the same thing?
This is a question confronted by artists of every age; but the artists of
the modernist period found a special urgency here. The literature of the
period, with its dehydrated epics and other semantically supercharged
texts, certainly resembles, at least to a degree, the music of the period,
with its astonishing density of acoustic events. But some artists tried to
erase the boundaries among music and literature and the visual arts,
while other artists tried to build foot-thick walls.

Some of the modernists felt strongly that the purity of one artistic
medium must not be compromised by the encroachment of styles or
themes taken from other artistic media. Clement Greenberg, the great
modernist critic, defended abstractionism on the grounds that an

abstract painting is a pure painting: not subservient to literary themes, not enslaved to representations of the physical world, but a new autonomous object, not a copy of reality but an addition to reality. Such puritans among the modernists stressed the need for fidelity to the medium: the opacity and spectral precision of paint, or the scarified, slippery feel of metal, the exact sonority of the highest possible trombone note, the spondaic clumps in a poetic line with few unstressed syllables. As Greenberg wrote in 1940, "The history of avant-garde painting is that of a progressive surrender to the resistance of its medium; which resistance consists chiefly in the flat picture plane's denial of efforts to 'hole through' it for realistic perspectival space." To Greenberg, the medium has a message: canvas and paint have a recalcitrant will of their own, fight against the artists' attempts to pervert their function. He profoundly approved of the modernist art that learned to love paint for paint's sake, not for its capacity to create phantoms of solid objects.

But this puritan hatred of illusions, the appetite for an art that possesses the dignity of reality, is only part of the story of modernism. From another perspective, the hope that art can overcome its illusory character is itself an illusion: just because a sculpture is hacked out of rough granite doesn't mean that it is real in the same way that granite is real. The great musicologist Theodor Adorno was as much a puritan as Greenberg: Adorno hated what he called *pseudomorphism*, the confusion of one artistic medium with another. But Adorno, unlike Greenberg, thought that all art was dependent on illusion, that art couldn't attempt to compete with the real world; as he wrote in 1948, it is futile for composers to try to delete all ornament from music: "Since the work, after all, cannot be reality, the elimination of all illusory features accentuates all the more glaringly the illusory character of its existence."

But, while the puritans tried to isolate each medium from alien encroachment, other, more promiscuous modernists tried to create a kind of art in which the finite medium is almost irrelevant. For them, modernism was *about* the fluidity, the interchangeability, of artistic media themselves. Here we find single artists, each of whom often tried to become a whole artistic colony: we see, for example, a painter who wrote an opera libretto (Kokoschka), a poet who composed music (Pound), and a composer who painted pictures (Schoenberg). It is as if artistic talent were a kind of libido, an electricity that could discharge itself with equal success in a poem, a sonata, or a sculpture. Throughout the modernist movement, the major writers and composers both enforced and transgressed the boundaries among the various arts with unusual—at times almost savage—energy.

It is important to respect both the instincts for division and distinction among the arts, and their instincts for cooperation and unity. In the eighteenth century, Gotthold Lessing (in *Laokoon*) divided the arts into two camps, which he called the *nacheinander* (the temporal arts, such as poetry and music) and the *nebeneinander* (the spatial arts, such as painting and sculpture). A modernist *Laokoon* might restate the division of the arts as follows: not as a tension between the temporal arts and the spatial—this distinction is often thoroughly flouted in the twentieth century—but as a tension between arts that try to retain the propriety, the apartness, of their private media, and arts that try to lose themselves in some pan-aesthetic whole. On one hand, *nacheinander* and *nebeneinander* retain their distinctness; on the other hand, they collapse into a single spatiotemporal continuum, in which both duration and extension are arbitrary aspects. Photographs of pupillary movement have traced the patterns that the eye makes as it scans the parts of a picture, trying to apprehend the whole: a picture not only may suggest motion, but is constructed by the mind acting over time. Similarly, a piece of music may be heard so thoroughly that the whole thing coexists in the mind in a instant, as Karajan claimed to know Beethoven's fifth symphony.

There are, then, two huge contrary movements in twentieth-century experiments in bringing art media together: consonance among the arts, and dissonance among the arts. Modernism carries each to astonishing extremes. The dissonances are challenging; perhaps the consonances are even more challenging.

In the present series of books, each volume will examine some facet of these intriguing problems in the arts of modernism: the dissemblings and resistings, the smooth cooperations and the prickly challenges when the arts come together.

Acknowledgments

The editor would like to thank his contributors for their unflagging enthusiasm and far-ranging expertise, both characteristics of the Joyce community as a whole. The Joyce conferences in Zurich in 1996 and Toronto in 1997 made this book happen by bringing several of us together; many thanks to their organizers, Fritz Senn, Michael O'Shea, Garry Leonard, and Jennifer Levine. Without Maureen Stanton, my research assistant for 1997–98, this book would have been inaccurate, clumsy, and late. The help of Elva Griffith in the Ohio State University Rare Books Room was invaluable, and the eagle eye of Theron Ellinger, Medical Photographer for the Biomedical Communications Media Group, ensured the clarity of the figures. Thanks to the Réunion des Musées Nationaux, for making sense of my execrable French, to European American Music, for permission to print work by Luciano Berio, to Charles Amirkhanian, executor of the Antheil estate, and to Winnie Klotz, photographer for the Metropolitan Opera. Thanks to the Department of English at Ohio State, and particularly to its Chair, James Phelan, for graciously underwriting many of the costs associated with this project, and to Leo Balk and Richard Wallis, and the rest of the excellent staff at Garland Publishing. Murray Beja helped me considerably by having done everything I was learning to do, and Ned Sparrow and Adam Hayward were as supportive as friends and academics could ever be. In 1990, Zack Bowen agreed to be Don Giovanni to my Zerlina in Vancouver, beginning a collaboration of music, criticism, and comedy that was really the origin of my commitment to Joyce and music; since that time Zack has acquired three houses, the presidency of the James Joyce Foundation, and international fame, which makes me wonder what would have happened if I'd asked him to be Zerlina. Janette, my superstar, this book is for you.

Bronze by Gold:
The Music of Joyce

Sebastian D. G. Knowles

"Bronze by gold": the words are an invitation. Like the sirens they represent, they are themselves alluring. The "Sirens" episode of *Ulysses* begins with these seductive lines, and the episode is itself a seduction, drawing the reader into a world where text and music sound together, hinting at the possibility of a musical form. "Bronze" and "gold" are messengers of a multiple world, reinvented with each new context, each new chord. Bronze is the color of Lydia Douce's hair, the color of her sunburnt skin ("Miss bronze unbloused her neck" [*U,* 11.115]), the metal for statuary ("A haughty bronze replied" [*U,* 11.97]), and for bells ("they urged each each to peal after peal, ringing in changes, bronzegold, goldbronze" [*U,* 11.174–75]). Gold is the color of Mina Kennedy's hair, of sunlight ("Miss Kennedy sauntered sadly from bright light, twining a loose hair behind an ear. Sauntering sadly, gold no more" [*U,* 11.81–82]), of the mirror ("With grace of alacrity towards the mirror gilt Cantrell and Cochrane's she turned herself" [*U,* 11.214–15]), of whisky ("With grace she tapped a measure of gold whisky from her crystal keg" [*U,* 11.215–16]), and of laughter: "They threw young heads back, bronze gigglegold, to let freefly their laughter" (*U,* 11.159–60). Bronze and Gold are two of the Ages of Man: a third, Iron, is hidden in the sentence too. The phrase "Bronze by gold," falling under the weight of the several interpretations of its two signs, loses its lexical balance. Joyce, by overdetermining his opening phrase, is ensuring that it cannot be understood. Only then can it be heard; only then does the line approach the meaning of music.[1]

The "by" of "Bronze by gold" has multiple resonances as well. The preposition can be the "by" of location, of *nebeneinander,* or the "by" of the passing of time, of *nacheinander.* In the first sentence after the overture, it is one and then the other: "Bronze by gold, miss Douce's head by [*nebeneinander*] miss Kennedy's head over the crossblind of the Ormond bar heard the viceregal hoofs go by [*nacheinander*], ringing steel" (*U,* 11.64–65). The word "by" is literally multiple, in that it itself stands for the sign of multiplication. Bronze *x* gold; the two sirens are commutative ("bronzegold, goldbronze" [*U,* 11.175]), working together in an enharmonic modulation that allows each to take the other's place: "Yes, bronze from anear, by gold from afar" (*U,* 11.112), "Yes, gold from anear by bronze from afar" (*U,* 11.338). The opening lines of "Sirens" have been briefly prepared for in the viceregal cavalcade that ends "Wandering Rocks," but in that instance bronze and gold have switched positions: "Above the crossblind of the Ormond hotel, gold by bronze, Miss Kennedy's head by Miss Douce's head watched and admired" (*U,* 10.1197–99). The two are the mirror images of one another, as bronze is symmetrically reproduced in the gilt mirror of the bar:

> His spellbound eyes went after, after her gliding head as it went down the bar by mirrors, gilded arch for ginger ale, hock and claret glasses shimmering, a spiky shell, where it concerted, mirrored, bronze with sunnier bronze. (*U,* 11.420–23)

Bronze and gold are concerted and mirrored as music and words are concerted and mirrored in "Sirens": without the one you cannot have the other. These two things of opposite natures, like the imagined and the real for Wallace Stevens, seem to depend on one another, interdependent throughout Joyce.

Bronze is music, since Lydia Douce sings and Mina does not, trilling *"O, Idolores, queen of the eastern seas!"* (*U,* 11.226).[2] Gold is text, since Mina Kennedy reads and Lydia does not, reading at the same time as Lydia is singing: "Miss voice of Kennedy answered, a second teacup poised, her gaze upon a page" (*U,* 11.237–38). Mina reads in silence: "In drowsy silence gold bent on her page" (*U,* 11.312). Words can have as much a siren effect as music in this episode, and "Sirens" is as full of paper as it is of song. During the singing of "The Croppy Boy," as Bronze fondles the barpull, and "the music, air and words" (*U,* 11.1081) sink to the point of confession and betrayal, Bloom thinks of

writing on Lydia's face: "Write something on it: page" (*U,* 11.1086–
87). In "Sirens" he purchases "Two sheets cream vellum paper one
reserve two envelopes" (*U,* 11.295), requests pen and ink from Pat, and
writes to Martha as a lexical counterpoint to the singing from *Martha*
after the song is completed. The episode's final text is both gold and
bronze: a text, the last words of Robert Emmet, that Bloom reads in a
shop window, crossed with the music of Meyerbeer and the sounds of
the street. In "Sirens," the two worlds of words and music coexist, and
each world is represented in the opening two notes. These words,
bronze and gold, are haircolors, precious metals, and metonyms, but
they are also worlds, as Martha's confusion of "word" for "world"—"I
do not like that other world" (*U,* 5.245), which Bloom remembers in
"Sirens" (*U,* 11.871)—implies.

Words multiplied by music: modernism was fascinated with the
possibility. Joyce attempts to create a musical language, Aldous Huxley
searches for a literary equivalent to contrapuntal form in *Point Counter
Point,* Forster's characters attend a performance of Beethoven's
Symphony no. 5, Woolf's first heroine is a pianist, Stevens's speaker
plays a blue guitar, and Eliot's still point is the stillness of a violin.
Modernists aspire to the condition of music in their writing, following
Pater's lead in "The School of Giorgione," who in arguing for this
common aspiration defines that condition as one of a perfect marriage
between form and content, wherein form becomes obliterated and
meaning becomes untranslatable (Pater, 111). Since Pater, many critics
from Susanne Langer to Roland Barthes have tried to assess the
significance of music, and all have been able to say only that music has
a significance, but it is impossible to say what that significance is.[3] For
Langer, music is an "unconsummated symbol" (Langer, 240); for
Barthes, music disperses meaning into "a shimmering signifier," and
"this phenomenon of shimmering is called *signifying* [*signifiance*]"
(Barthes, 259). In *Swann's Way,* Swann is led by Vinteuil's sonata in F
sharp toward a state of happiness that he finds "unintelligible" (Proust,
228).[4] It is no surprise that the modernists, particularly, would aspire to
a language without words, an empty sign. There is a silence at the heart
of music. Eliot's "raid on the inarticulate," *Four Quartets,* is moving
toward this silence (Eliot, II.v). "Words move, music moves / Only in
time" (Eliot, I.v): but music moves faster. As Leonard Bernstein said in
a 1958 telecast, "An F sharp doesn't have to be considered in the mind;
it is a direct hit."[5] A word is impeded by its meaning; the necessary
contingency of language smothers the sound. Music becomes, for the

moderns, to a much greater extent than is now generally admitted, a paradigm for the literary arts, as a means of unimpeded expression, a sign without significance, an absence of meaning that is also the purest meaning of all.

This book is an attempt to examine the relation between bronze and gold, between music and literature, between the ear and the word. Music and literature are separate continents, each with its own territorial landscape, and a shared border between the two: it is this no-place between music and literature that "Sirens," particularly, inhabits. Joyce, more than any other modernist writer, has his ear to the ground, listening for catchphrases, musical tags, sound effects, verbal punning, and the rhythm of words. The rhythm of Joyce's cadences gives powerful evidence of the value of listening to Joyce. As Stephen says at the start of "Proteus," "Rhythm begins" (*U,* 3.23). Each of Joyce's celebrated climaxes has a separate rhythmical pulse, a heartbeat that is inseparable from the sense of the phrase: "Christ was a jew like me," "yes I said yes I will Yes," "*Baraabum!,*" "A way a lone a last a loved a long the," "my eyes burned with anguish and anger," "upon all the living and the dead." I'd like to take each of these in turn, listening for the music of the words.

Bloom's response to the citizen in the bar has the stresses of a waltz:

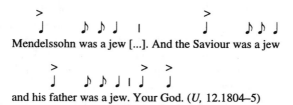
Mendelssohn was a jew [...]. And the Saviour was a jew

and his father was a jew. Your God. (*U,* 12.1804–5)

There is a second verse to this aria in 3/4 time:

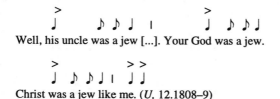
Well, his uncle was a jew [...]. Your God was a jew.

Christ was a jew like me. (*U,* 12.1808–9)

The rhythm of each verse is exactly parallel; three bars with a downbeat at the beginning of the bar, followed by a bar with two strong beats and a rest: "Your God," "like me." The first beat of each bar is progressively less cluttered with text ("Mendelssohn," "And the Saviour," "And his father," "Well, his uncle," "Your God"), until the final line, when the downbeat rings clear, with only one syllable ("Christ"), making the final line of the second stanza the cleanest articulation of the musical rhythm, as well as the cleanest verbal statement of Bloom's position. The first line of the first stanza has an ancillary line: the additional text reads "and Karl Marx and Mercadante and Spinoza" (*U,* 12.1804), and even that extra line is in 3/4 time, with three strong beats, one for each surname.

The provocation for Bloom's extraordinary outburst is the citizen's derisive call for "Three cheers for Israel!" (*U,* 12.1791), and Bloom has taken the number to heart, responding with three cheers in each verse (Mendelssohn, Saviour, father; uncle, God, Christ). As the three downbeats of the second verse suggest, the three cheers are for Holy Ghost, Father, and Son: though it is ironic that the Trinity would be invoked in a celebration of famous Jews in history, it makes the 3/4 rhythm that much more appropriate. And Bloom has been provoked into his aria in waltz time by music as well as words, for while the loafers are "calling for a speech" (*U,* 12.1799), a man with an eyepatch starts to sing *"If the man in the moon was a jew, jew, jew"* (*U,* 12.1801), which also insists on a thrice-repeated phrase.[6]

Ulysses ends with a waltz as well, at a faster tempo:

```
>                    >                 >
♩    ♩    ♩ |   ♩    ♩    ♩ |   ♩
yes   I   said  yes  I   will  Yes. (U, 18.1608–9)
```

As was the case for Bloom, Joyce's text as Molly reaches her climax can be given bar lines and a time signature: rhythm is the backbone of Joyce's cadences. The final three measures establish the 3/4 beat, allowing a back formation of the closing lines as follows:

```
>
yes and then he asked me would I
>
yes to say
```

>
yes my mountain flower and first I put my arms around him
>
yes and drew him down to me so he could feel my breasts all perfume
>
yes and his heart was going like mad and
>
yes I said
>
yes I will
>
Yes. (*U,* 18.1605–9)

The "yes" is always the downbeat: the measures are elastic, extended as "Mendelssohn" increases the number of syllables in the first downbeat of Bloom's aria to the citizen, extended as Molly holds the end of "Love's Old Sweet Song" ("comes loves sweet soooooooooooong" [*U,* 18.877]), extended as the B flat that is the climax of "M'appari" in "Sirens" is extended—"speeding, sustained, to come, don't spin it out too long long breath he breath long life" (*U,* 11.745–46)—while Bloom is extending the elastic band from the packet of stationery he bought at Wisdom Hely's around his hand ("Bloom wound a skein round four forkfingers, stretched it, relaxed, and wound it round his troubled double, fourfold, in octave" [*U,* 11.682–84]), an act that simulates the binding of Odysseus to the mast—"gyved them fast" (*U,* 11.684)—to allow him to listen to the Sirens' song. Molly's rhythms at the climax of her day are similar to her husband's at the climax of his: elastic at the start ("Mendelssohn," "yes and then he asked me would I"), but settling to its purest form at the end ("Christ was a jew I like me," "yes I said I yes I will I Yes").

The climax of Stephen's day is also in 3/4 time: when Stephen's mother appears in "Circe" she is accompanied by a waltz on the pianola:

THE PIANOLA

Best, best of all,
Baraabum! (*U,* 15.4105–7)

Recognizing the tune, Kitty leaps up to dance with Stephen; at the same time, "*A screaming bittern's harsh high whistle shrieks*" (*U,* 15.4111). "My Girl's a Yorkshire Girl" will become, as Stephen says, a "Dance of death" (*U,* 15.4139). But at the beginning it is merely a waltz:

THE PIANOLA

My girl's a Yorkshire girl.

ZOE

Yorkshire through and through. Come on all!

(*She seizes Florry and waltzes her.*)

STEPHEN

Pas seul!

(*He wheels Kitty into Lynch's arms, snatches up his ashplant from the table and takes the floor. All wheel whirl waltz twirl Bloombella Kittylynch Florryzoe jujuby women.* [...]) (*U,* 15.4114–23)

The waltz ends ("*Baraabum!*" [*U,* 15.4133]), the dancers call for a reprise ("Encore! Bis! Bravo! Encore!" [*U,* 15.4135]), and the pianola begins again, this time crossing the waltz with Stephen's free associations, and the rhythm of the words coincides with the rhythms in the chorus:[7]

(*Bang fresh barang bang of lacquey's bell, horse, nag, steer, piglings, Conmee on Christass, lame crutch and leg sailor in cockboat armfolded ropepulling hitching stamp hornpipe through and through. Baraabum! On nags hogs bellhorses Gadarene swine Corny in coffin steel shark stone onehandled Nelson two trickies Frauenzimmer plumstained from pram falling bawling. Gum he's a champion. Fuseblue peer from barrel rev. evensong Love on hackney jaunt Blazes blind coddoubled bicyclers Dilly with snowcake no fancy clothes. Then in last switchback lumbering up and down bump mashtub sort of viceroy and reine relish for tublumber bumpshire rose. Baraabum!* [...]) (*U,* 15.4140–50)

"*Bang fresh*" starts the chorus with the same strong beats of "My girl's," "*hitching stamp*" has the same rhythm as the phrase "Yorkshire girl," and "*hornpipe through and through*" mirrors "Yorkshire through and through." "*On nags*" reproduces the rhythm of "My girl's" again, and "*Gadarene swine*" replaces "Yorkshire girl" the second time around. "Eh! by gum, she's a champion!" is directly quoted in "*falling bawling. Gum he's a champion*," and the line "Though she's a fact'ry lass and wears no fancy clothes" can be teased out of "*Fuseblue peer* [...] *on hackney jaunt* [...] *with snowcake no fancy clothes.*" The last line of the chorus, "I've a sort of a Yorkshire Relish for my little Yorkshire Rose," is duplicated more precisely than any other line, with "*Then in* [...] *sort of a viceroy and reine relish for tublumber bumpshire rose.*"

Once again, the cadence is refined as it nears its close. With the completion of this rhythmical parody, Stephen's mother appears, and both the atmosphere and the rhythm change. The choir introduces a Gregorian chant, a rhythm borrowed by the apparition:

Liliata rutilantium te confessorum ... (*U*, 15.4164)

I was once the beautiful May Goulding. (*U*, 15.4173–74)

"I was once the" has the same rhythm as "Liliata"; the next words in both texts, "rutilantium" and "beautiful," begin with the same stressed vowel. And then, the once-beautiful May Goulding extends her arm slowly to Stephen's breast, an extension following the pattern of the extended elastic band and the sustained high note of "M'appari," in that the extension is mirrored in the protraction of the written line that describes it: "*she raises her blackened withered right arm slowly towards Stephen's breast with outstretched finger*" (*U*, 15.4218–19). The line is packed with trochaic qualifiers ("*blackened*," "*withered*," "*slowly*," "*outstretched*"), pulling the rhythm of the moment tauter and tauter until it snaps:

(*A green crab with malignant red eyes sticks deep its grinning claws in Stephen's heart.*) (*U*, 15.4220–21)

This snapping of the rhythmical elastic sends the text into a rigidly inelastic meter at the moment of crisis, when the inner world reaches out to the outer world and grabs its beating heart. The text screeches to a halt with "green crab" and "red eyes": the rhythm sticks its claws deep into the text, stopping its beat dead in its tracks.

From here until the close of "Circe" the rhythmic force of an allusion becomes its primary purpose. Each of the following lines has an immediately recognized meter:

> Theirs not to reason why. (*U*, 15.4397)

> My methods are new and are causing surprise. (*U*, 15.4478)

> But I love my country beyond the king. (*U*, 15.4535)

> O, won't we have a merry time, (*U*, 15.4563)

> The harlot's cry from street to street (*U*, 15.4641)

> Dublin's burning! Dublin's burning! On fire, on fire! (*U*, 15.4660)

"Circe" presents the breakdown of sense into rhythm, the reassertion of the primacy of rhythm in Joyce's musical language. By the end of the episode the meaning of the music disintegrates: Kelleher's song becomes "With my tooraloom tooraloom tooraloom tooraloom" (*U*, 15.4827–28), and the words of "Who Goes with Fergus" are lost, with only their beats remaining: "Who ... drive ... Fergus now" (*U*, 15.4932). Bloom's last lines, before the appearance of Rudy that acts as a counterpoise to the appearance of Stephen's mother, establish the importance of the rhythmic beat: "in the rough sands of the sea ... a cabletow's length from the shore .... where the tide ebbs .... and flows ....." (*U*, 15.4953–54). The flow of language is the "language of flow" (*U*, 11.298), as Bloom says in "Sirens," referring to the language of flowers, and perhaps to the language of Flotow, the composer of the text's central song, but primarily to the tides of language, the way that words ebb and flow, the cadence of the text.

The cadence always comes at the close, and at the close of *Finnegans Wake*, "Araby," and "The Dead," it is the music of the phrase that brings each piece to its watery end. "A way a lone a last a loved a long the" (*FW*, 628.15–16) waits for a downbeat that comes uneven and stuttering, as "Mendelssohn" did for Bloom, like an uncertain musical attack: "riverrun" (*FW*, 3.1) is a broken beat that sets the tone for the fractured language and rhythm that will follow. The neat precision of the end of "Araby," in exquisite contrast, establishes that these broken beats are deliberate: "Gazing up into the darkness I saw myself as a creature driven and derided by vanity; and my eyes burned with anguish and anger" (*D,* 35). "I saw myself" is mirrored in "my eyes burned," and "driven and derided" in "anguish and anger," and both "I saw myself" and "driven and derided" are themselves doubled, one through reflection, the other through alliteration: both the doubling and the mirroring serve to emphasize the boy's introspection. The sentence is a music box, tightly wound to bring "Araby" to a compact close.

At the end of "The Dead," Joyce finds the musical voice that sustains him through the rest of his career. The sentence is carefully measured, arranging itself into separate rhythmical units:

> His soul swooned slowly |
> as he heard the snow |
> falling faintly through the universe |
> and faintly falling, |
> like the descent of their last end, |
> upon all the living and the dead. | (*D,* 224)

There is a right way to read that sentence, as there is a right way to reproduce the rhythm of a musical phrase. Through the alliterative esses of "soul," "swooned," and "slowly," the sounds of falling snow can be heard with the character, then a pause for both "falling faintly" and "faintly falling," perfectly balanced phrases, as symmetrical as snowflakes, snowflakes that echo in their fall his soul's swoon, and then a third fall, descending to the two strong beats of "last end," an end, which like the Last End, isn't an end, for there is a final phrase, rising to the rocking rhythm of the cradle ("upon all the living") and returning to the grave ("and the dead"). The end, like the end of *Finnegans Wake,* the end of "Araby," and the end of "Penelope," is a return to the beginning of the text: in *Finnegans Wake* through the broken sentence, in "Araby" through the imagery of blindness, in "Penelope" by repetition of the opening word, and in "The Dead" through the closing restatement of the story's title.

Finally, there is the spondee, two long strokes that complete and cauterize a thought: "dead king!" (*P,* 39), "third stroke" (*D,* 9), "Tight boots?" (*U,* 13.771).[8] Each is a tragic completion, closing the coffin on an idea, whether the phrase sums up Simon's love for Parnell at the Christmas dinner, introduces the end of Father Flynn, or punctures the narrative fantasy of the first half of "Nausicaa." Each is a flat two-beat statement as terminal and emphatic as the pizzicati from the double basses that signify the fall of a guillotined head in Berlioz's *Symphonie fantastique*. In "Sirens" this spondaic voice follows Bloom wherever he goes, providing a ground, or bass part, for the fugue that the multilayered voicing of the episode outlines. This voice, hectoring, grave, comments on Bloom's situation through the association of the surface level of the episode—the conversation at the Ormond Bar—with Bloom's marital situation:

> —It's them has the fine times, sadly then she said.
> A man. (*U*, 11.84–85)

> —I won't listen, she cried.
> But Bloom? (*U*, 11.132–33)

> You're very simple, I don't think.
> He was. (*U*, 11.204–5)

Each time, Bloom's compromised position is brought into the picture through the spondaic line: "Of sin" (*U*, 11.157), "Not yet" (*U*, 11.352), "O'clock" (*U*, 11.386). The bass voice provides a ground for the other voices in the episode; in fact, the only way that "the eight regular parts of a *fuga per canonem*" (*SL*, 242) can be said to operate in "Sirens" is through such a separation of narrative voicing.

There are two four-part groups voiced in "Sirens": SATB (I) and SATB (II). In the bass of the first group (B_1), we hear the sullen spondees of "He had" (*U*, 11.262) and "There was" (*U*, 11.469). In the treble (S_1), the actual conversation in the bar: "Married to the greasy nose!" (*U*, 11.173). As alto (A_1) and tenor (T_1), the narrator and Bloom, often singing in duet, one picking up where the other leaves off: "By Bassi's blessed virgins Bloom's dark eyes went by. Bluerobed, white under, come to me. God they believe she is: or goddess" (*U*, 11.151–52). Sometimes these two voices overlap, sharing the same note; in the move from Bloom's thoughts of the poster at Wisdom Hely's to the narrator's description of his sight of Boylan, it is impossible to tell which voice "For Raoul" belongs to:

> Hair streaming: lovelorn. For some man. For Raoul. He eyed and saw
> afar on Essex bridge a gay hat riding on a jaunting car. (*U,* 11.301–2)

Then there are the musical effects, also in four parts. In the bass
(B_2), the leitmotifs, words reduced to the condition of music by being
divorced from their context in the opening overture, providing, as the
spondaic voice (B_1) does with the word-quartet, the ground for the
music-quartet. There are fifty-nine of them, each a separate note on a
musical keyboard. In the treble (S_2), the songs sung in the bar, like
"Love and War" and "The Croppy Boy." As alto (A_2), the musical
effects of a language spun like Mina Kennedy's hair into musical gold:
"Her wavyavyeavyheavyeavyevyevyhair un comb:'d" (*U,* 11.808–9).
And in the tenor (T_2), the actual sound effects: "Jingle" (*U,* 11.212),
"*La cloche!*" (*U,* 11.415), "Tap" (*U,* 11.933). Sometimes notes sound
together, as they did in the word-quartet: Bloom's fart sounds with the
tram, and the tap of the stripling's cane overlaps with the rap of the
knocker in Eccles Street.

So, in "Sirens," bronze and gold, words and music, come together.
Joyce's advertisement of the "*fuga per canonem*" in "Sirens" forces the
exploration of the connection between words and music; the phrase
itself has been a siren song for many critics drawn to the study of music
in Joyce. The following essays explore the territory between the two
worlds from each side of the border. All the writers in this collection
reassert the importance of the ear, insisting on the aurality of Joyce. As
with the voicing in "Sirens," there is overlap between the separate
inquiries, but for the most part the essays collected in the first half of
the book (Bronze) study music from a Joycean perspective, and the
essays in the second half (Gold) study Joyce's texts from a musical
perspective.[9]

Music first: Joyce's musical heritage has become more and more
the focus of critical study, as critics move toward a coherent catalogue
of his musical talents and affections. Seamus Reilly and John McCourt,
to that end, have dug into the archives of the musical worlds of Dublin
and Trieste during the years that Joyce lived in those cities, and allow
through their researches the substitution of facts and history for
assertion and mythology. Reilly provides a complete catalogue of the
operas produced in Dublin from 1888 to 1904; McCourt picks up the
musical narrative in studying the opera houses of prewar Trieste.
Joyce's affiliations with particular composers of his day are then
explored: Myra Russel relates the story of Joyce's connection with

Geoffrey Molyneux Palmer, whose settings of *Chamber Music* were sent to an admiring Joyce in 1909; Paul Martin traces the brief but stimulating collaboration between Joyce and Antheil in the 1920s; and I discuss Joyce's points of intersection with the Swiss composer Othmar Schoeck, whose cycle on live burial Joyce heard with great enthusiasm in 1935. Completing the cycle of music past, present, and future, two essays study Joyce's importance for music of the late twentieth century: Scott Klein finds Joyce everywhere in Cage, and demonstrates that the two artists share a common aesthetic; Murat Eyuboglu reveals Joycean elements in the "meta-music" of Peter Maxwell Davies and Luciano Berio, two composers who closely studied Joyce, setting his texts and further developing his ideas.

The book then begins again with a separate and parallel chronology, this time following the line of Joyce's own texts. Here, the primary focus of attention is on literature rather than music, concentrating more, as Mina Kennedy does, "upon a page" (*U,* 11.238). Allan Hepburn gives an authoritative reading of *Dubliners* that reasserts the centrality of music in the stories; Thomas Jackson Rice follows the sounds of Joyce's music from "The Dead" through *A Portrait of the Artist* and beyond, finding that both music and language are rooted in the system of mathematics. "Sirens" is the heart of the matter for any book on Joyce and music, and so three essays are devoted to that episode, each examining a different level of Joyce's musical language. Susan Mooney listens for the narrator, or "aurteur," of the episode, who arranges the acoustic fragments of "Sirens" to weave a richly reverberating structure of memory and desire. Andreas Fischer steps forward one level to examine the process of signification itself, and presents several ways that the episode can be read as a linguistic mapping of music. Margaret Rogers focuses still more narrowly on the letters of the episode, tracing a suggestive fugue, after the fashion of the Renaissance trope of *soggeto cavato,* carved into the words of the episode's opening. John Gordon's search for the actual sources of the hallucinations in "Circe" discovers an automated musical instrument called a Wonderlight in the brothel, and reveals the unmistakable presence of Ponchielli's *La Gioconda* at the episode's climax. Finally, two essays on *Finnegans Wake* explore "The Ballad of Persse O'Reilly" from first a literary and then a musical perspective: Zack Bowen and Alan Roughley read ambiguities into Joyce's musical setting of the ballad that suggest the impossibility of its performance; Dan Schiff then takes his reader, as if to corroborate the findings of

Bowen and Roughley, through the complexities and concessions of his own synthesized performance of the ballad, performed at the Zurich Symposium in 1996.

The compilation of these fifteen essays has been a delightful process of new discoveries. Fischer suggests that the sound of the blind stripling's cane changes from "Tap" (*U*, 11.1273) to "Tip" (*U*, 11.1281) as the surface changes from the street to the floor of the Ormond hotel. Mooney hears a golden world in the word "Ormond" that is both the world of the Other and the world of the Ear. Rice finds in Stephen's equations in *Portrait,* which Stephen compares to "stars" and "distant music" (*P*, 103), a reiteration of the classical quadrivium of music, algebra, geometry, and astronomy. Rogers discusses the twilight singing of "melody after melody" (*P*, 163) in *Portrait* as a biographical clue to the importance of music in Joyce's life; one of these melodies is clearly "Love's Old Sweet Song," not just because of the time the songs are sung, but because of the language of the moment: "till the last pale light died down," "they seemed weary already of the way" (*P*, 163–64). And then there is the idea that Joyce would carve music into his text, suggested by Rogers's analogy of the *soggeto cavato*. This musical carving is also found, I think, in "Scylla," where A. E. Russell's initials revolve in a lexical carousel:

> —People do not know how dangerous lovesongs can be, the auric egg
> of Russell warned occultly. The movements which work revolutions
> in the world are born out of the dreams and visions in a peasant's
> heart on the hillside. For them the earth is not an exploitable ground
> but the living mother. The rarefied air of the academy and the arena
> produce the sixshilling novel, the musichall song. France produces
> the finest flower of corruption in Mallarmé but the desirable life is
> revealed only to the poor of heart, the life of Homer's Phaeacians. (*U*,
> 9.103–10)

AE is soon to be involved in Joyce's joke of the vowels ("A. E. I. O. U." [*U*, 9.213]), and the riddle in the paragraph above is announced by the phrase "*a*uric *e*gg," with its readily identified acronym. The paragraph is a puzzle piece, with word after word playing a part: "d*a*ng*e*rous," "w*a*rn*e*d," "*are*," "dr*ea*ms," "h*ea*rt," "*ea*rth," "r*a*r*e*fied," "*are*na," "Fr*a*nce," "M*a*ll*a*rmé," "d*e*sir*a*ble," and "r*e*v*ea*led" are all coded words that conceal a carved purpose, to hide the initials of Russell's name. Joyce is engaging here in some occultism of his own:

the "movements which work revolutions" are at work in AE's own speech. The revolutions are not in the world, but in the word, making the same connection between world and word that Bloom notices in Martha's letter: for Joyce the word is alive, both "exploitable ground" and "living mother." The life of the word is clearly established in this playful game, bracketed by Eglinton, who has just spoken of Ireland as an "*e*mer*a*ld" (*U*, 9.102) and Mr. Best, whose next word will be "Mallarm*é*" (*U*, 9.112).

The joke, in its attempt to strip language down to its structure and remake it from within, is polyphonetic. For there is a critical three-letter word around which this riddling revolves: the word, of course, is Ear. The word anagrammatizes the initials of the author of a book on the origins of language; it is the organ for the central episode of *Ulysses;* it is, as AE's speech twice establishes, the h[ear]t's heart, both by orthographical coincidence, and because, as all of the essays that follow insist, it is the way to the heart of Joyce, the most direct way to reach an understanding of his work. The word is a world. Gold from an ear ("gold from anear"), Bronze from an ear ("bronze from anear"); Bronze and Gold, the worlds of music and literature, from both ears at once. "Miss Kennedy unplugged her ears to hear" (*U*, 11.136): so did Odysseus, and so has everyone who has ever been seduced by the music of Joyce.

NOTES

1. Several critics, including myself, have fallen prey to the attractions of this opening phrase. Charles Amirkhanian, the executor of the Antheil estate, hears in the phrase a "reverse alchemy." Heath Lees considers it to carry the tune of the main subject of Bach's *Art of the Fugue* (Lees, 47). Myra Russel, later in this volume, considers the "B" that begins the phrase and the episode to be the first note of hidden musical text. I liked to think of the "B" as the first letter of an anagrammatized acrostic that spelled out Bach's name ("*B*ronze," "*C*hips," "*H*orrid!," "*A* husky fifenote") (*U*, 11.1–5), before the establishing of "Imperthnthn thnthnthn" as a separate sentence between "Bronze" and "Chips" bitched the argument.

2. The fact that Lydia gets the words wrong, singing "Idolores" for "my Dolores," confirms the association of bronze with music. For the text to "The Shade of the Palm," see Bauerle, 360.

3. For more on recent critical developments in the study of meaning in music, see my "Muddying the Well: Contemporary Musicology and Absolute Music," *Music Reference Services Quarterly* 4, 3 (1996): 1–15.

4. This musical unintelligibility is mirrored by a related textual one: the pianist's aunt is so afraid of committing grammatical blunders in her speech that she deliberately makes herself incomprehensible, "with the result that her talk was a sort of continuous, blurred expectoration, out of which would emerge, at rare intervals, the few sounds and syllables of which she felt sure" (Proust, 222).

5. Cited in "An Affair to Remember," *Newsweek* 29 (October 1990): 80.

6. This song is an anachronism: Fred Fisher's "If the Man in the Moon Were a Coon," after which the man with the eyepatch's song is taken, was not published until 1905.

7. For the lyrics and score to the chorus of "My Girl's a Yorkshire Girl," see Bauerle, 351.

8. The "My" of Simon's line, like the "the" that introduces "third stroke" in "Sisters," is taken here as an upbeat to two prolonged notes.

9. Bronze and Gold do not mean to imply that music takes a lesser place in what Swann calls "the '*hierarchy*' of the arts" (Proust, 105). Contributors and musicians who feel slighted at being awarded a bronze medal to literature's gold are reminded of "the part that Paris played on another occasion," as Gabriel Conroy said on another occasion; to Gabriel, and to this editor, such a choice between equals "would be an invidious one" (*D*, 204).

WORKS CITED

Barthes, Roland. *The Responsibility of Forms: Critical Essays on Music, Art, and Representation.* Berkeley: University of California Press, 1991.

Bauerle, Ruth. *The James Joyce Songbook.* New York: Garland Publishing, 1982.

Eliot, T. S. *Four Quartets.* London: Harcourt Brace Jovanovich, 1971.

Langer, Susanne. *Philosophy in a New Key.* London: Oxford University Press, 1942.

Lees, Heath. "The Introduction to 'Sirens' and the *Fuga per Canonem.*" *James Joyce Quarterly* 22, 1 (1984): 39–54.

Pater, Walter. "The School of Giorgione." *The Renaissance.* New York: Modern Library, 1919. 107–27.

Proust, Marcel. *Swann's Way. Remembrance of Things Past.* Vol. I. Trans. C. K. Scott Moncrieff and Terence Kilmartin. New York: Random House, 1981.

PART I

Bronze: Music

Section 1: Joyce's Musical Background

CHAPTER 1

James Joyce and Dublin Opera, 1888–1904

Seamus Reilly

This essay combines two separate approaches to the question of James Joyce and Dublin music. First, I provide a complete catalogue of the operas produced in Dublin from 1888 to 1904, along with the names of the traveling companies that performed them. Second, I stress the importance of this musical context for an understanding of Joyce's texts. Recent studies have attempted, as Thomas Rice has pointed out, "to place James Joyce as a product of his contemporary culture" (Rice, xiii). Since music remained for Joyce a central part of his life and his fictions, it seems doubly important to "reground Joyce in his historical context" (Rice, xiv). Joyce remained a great fan of the opera and a champion of John Sullivan, the Franco-Irish tenor. As this essay demonstrates, that love for opera was learned not only at his father's knee (Bauerle and Hodgart, 3), but more than likely at the many opera performances available to Dublin audiences in the latter part of the nineteenth century. Here is provided concrete evidence of the musical culture in which Joyce lived and in which he participated as a performer, placing his texts in their historical-musical context.

Opera in Dublin was performed by a number of traveling operatic groups. The Carl Rosa and Rousbey companies, in particular, brought new operas to Dublin and maintained the operatic tradition. However, there were other groups that had brief tenures in the theaters of Dublin. The Moody-Manners Company was prominent toward the end of the nineteenth century, and the Neilson, Walsham, Valentine Smith, Grand English, F. S. Gilbert, and Royal Italian Opera (Covent Garden) companies all visited Dublin. In addition, the National Opera Company of Robert Cunningham had short-lived success. Sometimes these visits lasted three weeks, sometimes only a week. The seasons do not appear to have been rigidly fixed. The Rousbey Company usually performed starting St. Stephen's Day through the third week of January. Carl Rosa performed in August and September. Occasionally there were seasons around Easter time or brief seasons in October or November. The companies performed a mixture of popular operas but also introduced newer works. Carl Rosa seems to have been the main source of newer continental operas, but Rousbey quickly adapted whatever the more famous company was showing. Certain operas were perennial; *Faust, Il Trovatore, Maritana, The Bohemian Girl,* and *Carmen* were produced by every company that visited Dublin whether they were regularly engaged or not. The companies were also sensitive to the reaction of the audience. When the first performance of *La Bohème* was less than favorably received it was withdrawn the following week, presumably to give the cast time to refine the parts. Companies were quick to repeat operas that had been well received. Certain singers, especially Barton M'Guckin and Joseph O'Mara, were highlighted by the different companies. M'Guckin, for example, was specially engaged to sing with Carl Rosa and was renowned in the role of Don José in *Carmen*. Joseph O'Mara, who sang with the Royal Italian Opera, was advertised as the returning Irishman. The principal singers, moreover, were assigned to certain roles and operas to prevent the stress on the voice, and therefore audiences not only identified singers with roles but were assured of hearing relatively fresh voices for each performance.[1] Another singer, E. C. Hedmondt, replaced O'Mara as Don José, and was also famous for his Wagnerian roles.

Carl Rosa remained a prominent part of the Dublin musical season and was connected with the Gaiety Theatre, where it first performed in 1875. As Eric White remarks in *A History of English Opera,* the "London seasons were no longer regarded as the apex of the company's work" (370), and the company also moved away from the commissioning of new English operas and toward the production of new foreign operas in English. One such opera, Leoncavallo's *Pagliacci,* was first produced in Dublin in 1893. Irish audiences, therefore, were guaranteed a high quality of performance from professional touring companies.

The catalogue that follows not only fills in the gaps as far as the general musical scene is concerned, but also corrects earlier assumptions about operas more central to Joyce's writings. While

Stephen and Nona Watt, in Bauerle and Hodgart (319–22), include a brief listing of the operas performed in Dublin at the turn of the century, that list is incomplete. This catalogue provides for the first time a comprehensive list of all the operas performed in Dublin from 1888 to 1904, and includes information about the composers and performers. Such a list allows us to correct a number of misconceptions about opera in Dublin of the period. It has been assumed, for example, that Wagner's operas with a few exceptions were not produced in Dublin while Joyce was still living there.[2] Wagner had been produced in Dublin in the 1870s, but the opera annals showed no performances in the later years of the century.[3] This catalogue demonstrates that a greater number of Wagner's works than hitherto known were indeed produced in Dublin. Joyce, we know, was an early champion of Wagner, although his enthusiasm later cooled. The expanded list of Wagner operas produced while he lived in Dublin helps to explain both his interest and why he should have owned the libretti to Wagner's operas, which he had Stanislaus send to Paris in 1903: "send me *at once* (so that I may have it by Thursday night) my copy of Wagner's operas" (*L*, II, 25). It also explains the somewhat curious reference in *A Portrait of the Artist as a Young Man* to *Siegfried:* "They crossed the quadrangle together without speaking. The birdcall from *Siegfried* whistled softly followed them from the steps of the porch" (*P*, 237). Selections from Wagner were regularly performed in concerts in Dublin, but such a specific section from the opera would have been difficult to excerpt out of context. Normal practice has been to assume that Joyce would have heard it in concert or played the score, or else had silently and anachronistically inserted his knowledge of the opera from continental performances. A simpler solution to the puzzle is that the Carl Rosa Company produced the work for the first time in 1901, as part of a season that also included a first performance of *Tristan und Isolde*. In addition, works by Verdi, Donizetti, Puccini, and Mascagni were staged soon after their first performances on the continent and in London. In some cases, as I have indicated, Dublin premiered the opera.

The Gaiety Theatre, Leinster Hall, the Theatre Royal, and the Queen's Royal Theatre all had opera seasons. The Carl Rosa Company played exclusively in the Gaiety Theatre, while the Rousbey Company and the other traveling companies played at the Theatre Royal, Queen's Royal, or Leinster Hall. These theaters attracted large numbers to the various seasons and maintained a consistent ticket price through 1904, when it was still possible to attend the opera for sixpence. Dubliners were attracted by the operas themselves, but also by the number of international stars who came to the city as part of these companies. It would be impossible here to mention the many concerts and recitals held in Dublin in the sixteen years covered by this catalogue, but there is ample evidence that the Dublin audiences saw operas performed by quality, professional singers. There is proof, too, of the curious link between amateur and professional singers. Talented amateurs did appear in professional theaters in Dublin both in concerts and recitals, and also, in the case of O'Brien Butler's *Muirgheis,* as part of an opera company. Such opportunity for amateurs may well explain the opinion that has persisted about Joyce that he could easily have performed as a professional singer.

Immediately obvious from the catalogue is the number of different operas that were performed in Dublin in the period when Joyce was a boy and young man. It is known that operas with Irish themes, the so-called Irish Ring of *The Bohemian Girl, The Lily of Killarney,* and *Maritana,* were frequently produced in Dublin. The popularity and frequent repetition of these works have perhaps tarnished their image, but their popularity ensured the performance of these operas not only by Rousbey but by all the major operatic companies that visited the city. It is less well known that the operas produced in Dublin included the latest works from the continent. *La Bohème,* for example, was produced in Dublin before it was produced in New York. And Dublin audiences retained a love for the older operas such as *La Sonnambula,* which were part of the Joyce family mythology, and were produced often enough to allow one to understand how Joyce's father could refer to their aunt as "La Somnambula" [sic] without the reference seeming in the least esoteric or affected (S. Joyce, *The Dublin Diary,* 20). The opera, rarely performed today, was a perennial favorite of the Dublin houses. The famous scene recounted in Ellmann (276) when James and his father had a musical reconciliation in a village inn, where the elder Joyce played and sang from *La Traviata,* seems less remarkable when we consider the number of times the opera was produced in the city. Joyce's own selective operatic taste was refined and sharpened by his experience on the continent, especially in Trieste, but it was most surely molded and shaped by his experience of opera in Dublin.

The operas most commonly alluded to in Joyce's fictions are also the operas that were most frequently produced while he lived there. But for Joyce the experience of opera was more than theatergoing, and more even than the music: Joyce is also conscious of the way in which opera is centered on individual singers. The idea of the star, divo or diva, is extremely powerful as a way of enticing audiences or even creating a desire to simulate the appearance of the leading male or female singer. Joyce's fascination with singers and the ability of the voice to seduce an audience is prominent in varying degrees in "The Dead" and in "Sirens." Wayne Koestenbaum analyzes this relationship of audience and singer in erotic terms, since the audience member relates to the specific qualities of the singer's voice: "a timbre against which others would seem too full, too old, too ripe, too controlled" (20). Joyce depicts such individual vocal qualities in "Sirens" when Simon Dedalus's voice becomes separated from the actual performer. This separation enables the aficionado to be attracted to the singer in a manner that Koestenbaum describes as erotic, allowing the listener to delight in the sound of the voice without having a declared affection for the singer. It explains how Richie Goulding can be affected by Dedalus's voice even though they do not communicate. Molly Bloom likewise distinguishes between Simon's voice and his character, describing the voice in sensual terms: "Simon Dedalus too he was always turning up half screwed singing the second verse first [...] he had a delicious glorious voice" (*U,* 18.1290–94).

In "Sirens," of course, Joyce represents the phallic qualities of the voice, and in *Finnegans Wake* he describes the "upperotic" (*FW,* 439.25) qualities of Shaun's tenor, echoing the comment Bloom makes in "Sirens" that "Tenors get women by the score" (*U,* 11.686). It is, as Koestenbaum suggests, the high voices that prove the attraction, especially with regard to male voices. Joyce admired Sullivan's voice particularly because it was so powerful: "Don't you think the most important thing in a tenor is that he should sing *loud?*" (Bauerle and Hodgart, 84). This separation of voice from singer is used by Ruth Bauerle to describe Joyce's relation to Sullivan (Bauerle and Hodgart, 86–88).[4] However, the tenor who "had sung five encores to *Let Me Like a Soldier Fall,* introducing a high C every time" (*D,* 199), is almost certainly Ravelli, mentioned as one of the old singers in the story, who performed regularly in Dublin. A review of an Italian concert held on January 14, 1888, described how he was received by the audience "with deafening cheers" and performed "'In Terra si Divierso' and 'Let Me Like a Soldier Fall' in which at the end of the last operatic engagement, it may be remembered, he created a *furore*" (*Irish Times,* January 16, 1888).

   If singing represents real or simulated sexual or erotic behavior, the
theater itself is also a location of sexual activity. Molly Bloom
describes the uncomfortable feeling of being crushed in a theater
crowd, but also imagines that it must be used by certain of the patrons
for erotic purposes:

> [...] a lot of that touching must go on in theatres in the crush in the
> dark theyre always trying to wiggle up to you that fellow in the pit at
> the Gaiety for Beerbohm Tree in Trilby the last time Ill ever go there
> to be squashed like that for any Trilby or her barebum every two
> minutes tipping me there and looking away [...]. (*U,* 18.1039–44)

Molly has had her own experience with singers, including Bartell
D'Arcy who "commenced kissing me on the choir stairs after I sang
Gounods Ave Maria what are we waiting for O my heart kiss me
straight" (*U,* 18.274–75). However, Molly notes that the smallness of
his voice did not reduce his passion: "he was pretty hot for all his tinny
voice [...] I liked the way he used his mouth singing" (*U,* 18.276–78).
D'Arcy feels guilty since they were in a church at the time, but in
Finnegans Wake the linking of erotic, musical, and religious aptitudes
is a staple of Shaun's character. We remember too that Boylan's excuse
for visiting Molly is ostensibly to look over the music for the songs
they are to sing in the concert tour he is "getting up."
   Cheryl Herr stresses the importance of the theater as an institution
in understanding "Circe" since it reflects "the theater's rituals and
codes of expression" (97). The theater provides models or templates for
culture, not fixed as Herr points out, but a "version made general of that
society's theatrical experience" (98). The opera is a subset of the
general theatergoing experience, complete with its own influential
characteristics. Opera represented what Jacques Attali calls "the
supreme form of the representation by the bourgeoisie of its own order
and enactment of the political" (60). Lawrence Levine points out that
opera appealed to theatergoers across a wide political and social
spectrum, and represents in part what he calls the "Sacralization of
Culture" (84). If opera brought disparate social groups together, it also
supported different audience interpretations of what they saw:

> [...] opera was an art form that was *simultaneously* popular and elite.
> That is, it was attended both by large numbers of people who derived
> great pleasure from it and experienced it in the context of their

normal everyday culture, *and* by smaller socially and economically elite groups who derived both pleasure and social confirmation from it. (Levine, 86)

Moreover, the particular "theatrical experience" that resonates in Joyce's fictions is one in which the audience was willing to participate in the hurly-burly common to most nineteenth-century theaters, and was at the same time knowledgeable and highly critical of performers.

Several accounts of the culture of the late nineteenth and early twentieth centuries prove that Dublin audiences were familiar with a wide body of operatic works. T. J. Walsh's *Opera in Dublin 1705–1797* concludes with the following observation:

> Consequently, it is not difficult to imagine opera in Dublin during this period as little more than an appendage to the comic drama with music added. The only factor which occasionally raised it above the routine was the engagement of first-class singers. [...] These artists were the operatic shoots which would come to full flower amidst the vocal exuberance of the mid-nineteenth century, and which would leave a love of great singing inherent in Dublin for evermore. (312)

Opera survived into the nineteenth century largely through the touring companies that visited Dublin's main theaters. A wide variety of opera was presented, emphasizing a standard repertoire of works favored by the Irish audiences. They included many Irish singers who had moved to England to pursue their careers, and whose returns were eagerly anticipated. The Irish audiences identified strongly with the primary singers, and the leading tenors and sopranos were greeted with enthusiasm. The absence of a major domestic operatic company made the visiting companies even more of a social event, with their upcoming seasons advertised long in advance.[5] The opera, with its major stars and readily available translated sheet music and scores, was quickly adopted by the middle class as an important part of its entertainment.

Part of the attraction would have been the relatively stable ticket prices throughout the latter part of the nineteenth century. Although the poorer patrons were confined to the galleries at the highest part of the house, called the "gods," the distance from the stage did not blunt their enthusiasm. The love of opera was due to the love of music generally, but opera also represented a chance to hear serious music and remain culturally connected to the developments in European music. Newer operas were performed in Dublin soon after their performances in the major theaters of Europe, including new works by Verdi and Wagner. But at the same time there was a snob value associated with opera, its history of glamour and parties, the appearance of the more prominent members of society tiered together with the cheapest seats in the gallery. Charles Villiers Stanford's account of the audience breakdown at the old Theatre Royal, Dublin, in *Pages from an Unwritten Diary,* describes the structural arrangement of the theater and the behavior of the audience:

> There were no stalls, the pit filling the whole floor, and there were four tiers. The occupants of the top gallery, where wit and humour were concentrated, had a kind of hereditary feud with the pittites, chaffing them everlastingly and at times objurgating them so loudly that wise men preferred to get as near the middle of the house as possible in order to insure comparative safety from a possible orange or other less savoury missile from above. (87)

This theater structure seems to correspond with Lawrence Levine's account in *Highbrow/Lowbrow* of the hierarchy that existed in the American theaters, with its "tripartite seating arrangement: the pit (orchestra), the boxes, and the gallery (balcony)" (24); the behavior of the "gallery gods" is remarkably consistent. Like American audiences, the Dubliners commented loudly and often on both the performers and the fellow members of the audience. This warring was probably, as Levine suggests, a direct result of the hierarchical seating arrangement (61). There is an emphasis, though, in Stanford's description on the fact that Irish audiences were extremely knowledgeable about opera in general and singers in particular. He suggests a slightly different characteristic of the Irish "gods" when he describes their knowledge and affection for the music of the opera:

> As the "gods" were in possession long before the "Quality" arrived, they used to while away the time partly by singing airs, more often than not belonging to the opera which they had come to hear, quite as well as or better than they were afterwards given on the stage. (Stanford, 87–88)

Stanford's account points up two interesting aspects of Dublin music. First, the music was so regularly performed, either by professionals or by amateurs, that the audience as a group could perform impromptu versions. In fact, some members of the audience were as talented as the performers they had come to see. This is certainly in keeping with the view that James and Stanislaus give of John Joyce, a talented amateur with professional vocal qualities, and also the view that we have of James Joyce. "Sirens," particularly, plays on this aspect of Dublin musical life.

Second, Stanford points to an appreciation of opera across class lines. Although audience members might criticize their counterparts or the quality of the performance, their interest was centered in the music. Stanford underscores this commitment to high musical standards by indicating that the behavior of the "gods" was not simply uproarious behavior, but was linked instead to a keen sense of musical appreciation. He gives some examples of the commentary on performers: "A tenor whose voice was somewhat thin, and who trusted for his final high note to *falsetto*, had the mortification of hearing Micky on one side of the gallery ask a friend opposite 'Jim! was that the gas?'" (Stanford, 88). Stanford also indicates the disputes that took place between the performers in the "gods" and the gentry in the pit:

> The gods had internecine quarrels also, mostly the sham battles of the rival singers and their friends aloft, whereat their old enemies, the pit, would rise *en masse* and turn round with a roar of protest, drowning all the proceedings on the stage the while. It was during one of these demonstrations that the well-known dialogue occurred: "Throw him over! Throw him over!" "Don't was(h)te him, kill a fiddler wid him!" (88)

However, most of these exchanges "took place in the entr'actes, or when an inferior artist had irritated the deities" (Stanford, 88). When the performance was of a high quality, "there was a silence that might be felt" (Stanford, 88). Stanford's account suggests that the less-well-off were knowledgeable concerning the performances and that their rowdiness was the result of inferior performance as much as irritability with their social betters seated below them.

Joseph O'Brien's *Dear Dirty Dublin* depicts the decline in importance of the Irish capital, and in particular the falling-off of entertainment standards. This was apparently true of the theater:

Places of entertainment were few, so few in fact that a select
committee in 1892 was astounded to learn that Ireland contained only
7 or 8 theatres in all, 2 of them (the Gaiety and the Queen's) being in
Dublin:

Q. As a matter of fact, I suppose the Irish are not great theatre
goers?
A. They are.
Q. But there are only two theatres in Dublin.
A. Yes.

London alone boasted about 40 theatres and as many large music
halls. (O'Brien, 44)[6]

O'Brien's view is slightly misleading. For one thing it is unfair to
compare London and Dublin, since the populations varied considerably.
Dublin certainly could not boast the same number of theaters as
London, but that was because of demographics and not cultural taste.
As the commentator in the *History of the Theatre Royal* notes, the
theaters were large and the theatergoing population small. O'Brien is
critical of the scarcity of orchestral and chamber recitals, underscored
by the fact that Dublin did not possess a recital hall. His criticism
reflects a hierarchical reading of music as "high" and "low," and the
fact that theaters doubled for both "serious" and "light" entertainment
seems to bolster his argument that entertainment in Dublin was of a
somewhat sketchy and "low class" variety. The building of new
theaters throughout the nineteenth century was a somewhat risky
venture,[7] given the burgeoning entertainment industry that now
provided organized sports such as football, rugby, and cricket in
addition to variety houses and music halls, not to mention the
beginnings of the motion picture industry, which was showing
myrioramas in Dublin as early as 1890, one of which Molly Bloom
remembers attending in *Ulysses* (*U,* 18.40).[8]

The argument that only two theaters existed in Dublin in 1892 is
principally misleading since the small number of actual theaters did not
mean a lack of locations that featured musical performances.[9] Operas
were performed at the Gaiety, Queen's, and Leinster Hall throughout
the year. Leinster Hall was also a venue for concerts as were the
Antient Concert Rooms, Metropolitan Hall (which in February 1892
featured an African native choir), Molesworth Hall, Earlsfort Terrace,
the Royal Dublin Society, and the Rotunda. These venues are only
those within the city center and include neither performances held

outside in the surrounding suburbs including Kingstown (Dun Laoghaire), which frequently had an operatic season of its own, nor the many churches where concerts and recitals were given. The choice of music included operas from the Carl Rosa Company as well as the Rousbey Company. There were performances of Mendelssohn's *Elijah,* and recitals by the English tenor Ben Davies, and sopranos Lillian Nordica and Nellie Melba. There were military concerts, and even a performance given by the Masonic Female Orphan School organized by the Lodge of Israel #126. Dan Lowry's Star Theatre boasted Miss Maud Distin, a female baritone, and provided an array of entertainments for Dublin audiences,[10] as did the Bijou theater; occasional events were also held at the Coffee Palace Hotel.

The Parliamentary Committee of 1892 reveals an attempt to control entertainment and institutionalize a hierarchy of "high" and "low" art, and also perhaps explains why Dublin is portrayed as having relatively few theaters. Francis Wolfe's 1898 pamphlet, "Theatres in Ireland," reacted to the advertisement in the Dublin papers in January 1898 on "behalf of the Patentees of the Gaiety Theatre, Theatre Royal, and Queen's Royal Theatre" (3), which gave notice of their intent to sue anyone attempting to perform any sort of public entertainment in Dublin. Their arguments were based on an old law that related the granting of theater licenses to the theater owners in order to protect the houses from strolling players. Wolfe points out that the 1892 Parliamentary Committee "did not ask some of the public bodies or some private individuals in Ireland to give evidence relative to theatres" (19). In fact, "the only two persons from Ireland who were examined by the Committee of the House of Commons were Mr. Phipps, the architect of the Gaiety Theatre, and Mr. Gunn, the proprietor" (Wolfe, 19). Not surprisingly, they found nothing wrong with the system of theaters in Ireland. In reply to the questions on whether the theatergoing public of Dublin had its needs satisfied, Gunn replied, "I think thoroughly satisfied" (Wolfe, 20). Wolfe observes: "Mr. Gunn, of course, is quite satisfied with the present law; it gives him a monopoly, and the authorities appear likely to continue it, unless public opinion can be brought to bear" (20).

That Joyce, like his compatriot George Bernard Shaw, benefited from the breadth and variety of the musical performances and performers, is verified by the letters and biographies of friends and relatives, as well as by his own memories. It is evident too from the hundreds of references to music in his fictions. Joyce's own family underwent a decline of its own that saw it slip from a position of relative prosperity to among the poorer sections of the lower middle class. It meant that the young Joyce was to know more about the cheap musical productions in Dublin than he was to know about the more polished ones. That this influenced his musical tastes in later life is reflected in his fictions. That it was formed by his experience as a young man in the theaters and music halls of Dublin is reflected in the history of the musical productions there in his most formative years. Joyce was aware of the larger thematic elements of the opera, as witnessed by his use of the Wandering Jew legend used by Wagner (Martin, *Joyce and Wagner,* 54–77), but was more interested in the local and symbolic connections he could make with his characters in the context of their own situations. When opera is alluded to in Joyce's texts we are made aware of the institutions of the theater and the opera, but also of a dramatic moment of enactment on a stage. Opera combines the dramatic effect that music has on the auditor—passing "over the fantastic fabrics of [the] mind, dissolving them painlessly and noiselessly" (*P,* 160)—and an institutionalization of codes of social behavior by establishing dramatic scenes that characters consciously or unconsciously reenact. There are frequent references in Joyce's fictions to the experience of visiting the theater.[11] The conversation around the dinner table in "The Dead" turns to specific performances that the characters have attended, and even, in the case of Mary Jane, would like to attend: "O, I'd give anything to hear Caruso sing" (*D,* 199). Stephen Dedalus's mother remembers hearing "old Royce sing in the pantomime of *Turko the Terrible* and laughed with others when he sang" (*U,* 1.257–59). Molly Bloom remembers her experience of going to the theater (*U,* 18.1040), and Leopold Bloom wonders if he can manage to get a free pass to the Gaiety (*U,* 6.187–88).

Joyce's use of opera draws attention to its sophisticated cultural codes. Opera is linked to the institutional structure of the theater, and is also a cultural institution in itself. Opera connects a specific person with a work or aria, thus encapsulating the memory not only of a song or piece of music, but of a dramatic enactment of the music by a single performer. It provides a star system that in turn attracts an audience to the institution, such as Enrico Caruso and John McCormack did for certain audience members. Joyce himself liked to listen to the operas that John Sullivan appeared in, and went to see the singer's performance rather than the complete operatic work. The catalogue that follows lists those performances he would have been likely to see.

A COMPLETE CATALOGUE OF THE OPERAS PRODUCED IN DUBLIN FROM 1888 TO 1904

Note: The catalogue below lists the operas together with the companies that performed them. Most of the information was taken from the *Irish Times,* which advertised and reviewed the operatic performances and the many other musical shows available to Dublin audiences. Only operas have been included: the D'Oyly Carte Company appeared annually in the Gaiety Theatre to perform Gilbert and Sullivan, and other operettas such as *Dorothy, La Cigale,* and *Marjorie* were familiar to Dublin audiences. The Carl Rosa Company later became the Royal Carl Rosa Operatic Company as a result of a command performance given for Queen Victoria in 1892; other companies frequently changed their names. The Royal Italian Opera Company was based in Covent Garden, and the Shamus O'Brien Opera Company Limited was formed as a limited stock company specifically to perform Stanford's opera for the Gaiety Theatre's anniversary. The month given indicates the start of the run: companies that started their season in August usually ran over into September, and the Rousbey Company, when it started in December, usually went on into January. I have included the names of some of the singers who appeared in the operas. Characters like Barton M'Guckin, Georgina Burns, and Joseph O'Mara were stars of the Dublin musical scene and remembered by Joyce in his fictions.

1888

Aïda (Verdi). Gaiety Theatre, Royal Italian Opera, November.
The Bohemian Girl (Balfe). Gaiety Theatre, Carl Rosa, August. Fanny Moody, Leslie Crotty.
Carmen (Bizet). Gaiety Theatre, Carl Rosa, August.
———. Gaiety Theatre, Royal Italian Opera, November.
Don Giovanni (Mozart). Gaiety Theatre, Carl Rosa, August. Payne Clarke.
Ernani (Verdi). Gaiety Theatre, Royal Italian Opera, November.
Esmeralda (Dargomizhsky). Gaiety Theatre, Carl Rosa, August.
Faust (Gounod). Gaiety Theatre, Carl Rosa, August. Barton M'Guckin.
———. Gaiety Theatre, Royal Italian Opera, November.
Les Huguenots (Meyerbeer). Gaiety Theatre, Royal Italian Opera, November.
Lohengrin (Wagner). Gaiety Theatre, Royal Italian Opera, November.
Lucia di Lammermoor (Donizetti). Gaiety Theatre, Royal Italian Opera, November.
Maritana (Wallace). Gaiety Theatre, Carl Rosa, August.

Mignon (Thomas). Gaiety Theatre, Carl Rosa, August. Georgina Burns, John Child, F. H. Celli, Wilfred Esmond, O. Campbell, Jenny Dickerson.

The Puritan's Daughter (Balfe). Gaiety Theatre, Carl Rosa, August. Dublin premiere.

Robert le Diable (Meyerbeer). Gaiety Theatre, Carl Rosa, August.

Il Trovatore (Verdi). Gaiety Theatre, Carl Rosa, August.

Die Zauberflöte (Mozart). Gaiety Theatre, Royal Italian Opera, November.

1889

The Bohemian Girl (Balfe). Gaiety Theatre, Carl Rosa, August.

Carmen (Bizet). Gaiety Theatre, Carl Rosa, August. Barton M'Guckin.

L'Etoile du Nord (Meyerbeer). Gaiety Theatre, Carl Rosa, August.

Faust (Gounod). Gaiety Theatre, Carl Rosa, August.

La Juive (Halévy). Gaiety Theatre, Carl Rosa, August.

Lucia di Lammermoor (Donizetti). Gaiety Theatre, Carl Rosa, August.

Maritana (Wallace). Gaiety Theatre, Carl Rosa, August.

Mignon (Thomas). Gaiety Theatre, Carl Rosa, August.

Robert le Diable (Meyerbeer). Gaiety Theatre, Carl Rosa, August.

Il Trovatore (Verdi). Gaiety Theatre, Carl Rosa, August.

1890

Belphegor (Jones). Leinster Hall, Rousbey, January.

The Bohemian Girl (Balfe). Leinster Hall, Rousbey, January.

————. Town Hall, Kingstown (Dun Laoghaire), Walsham, July.

————. Gaiety Theatre, Carl Rosa, August.

Carmen (Bizet). Carl Rosa, August. Barton M'Guckin.

La Damnation de Faust (Berlioz). Royal University Building, Dublin Musical Society, May. Ireland premiere.

Don Giovanni (Mozart). Leinster Hall, Rousbey, January.

L'Etoile du Nord (Meyerbeer). Gaiety Theatre, Carl Rosa, August.

Faust (Gounod). Town Hall, Kingstown (Dun Laoghaire), Walsham, July.

————. Gaiety Theatre, Carl Rosa, August.

The Lily of Killarney (Benedict). Gaiety Theatre, Carl Rosa, August.

Lurline (Wallace). Gaiety Theatre, Carl Rosa, August.

Maritana (Wallace). Leinster Hall, Rousbey, January.

————. Gaiety Theatre, Carl Rosa, August.

Martha (Flotow). Town Hall, Kingstown (Dun Laoghaire), Walsham, July.

Le Nozze di Figaro (Mozart). Leinster Hall, Rousbey, January.

Roméo et Juliette (Gounod). Gaiety Theatre, Carl Rosa, August. Dublin premiere.

The Rose of Castille (Balfe). Leinster Hall, Rousbey, January. Vadini, Sass, Julia Lennox, M. W. Campbell, Arthur Rousbey.

La Traviata (Verdi). Gaiety Theatre, Carl Rosa, August.

Il Trovatore (Verdi). Town Hall, Kingstown (Dun Laoghaire), Walsham, July.

The Waterman (Dibdin). Town Hall, Kingstown (Dun Laoghaire), Walsham, July.

1891

Il Barbiere di Siviglia (Rossini). Rotunda, Mr. Valentine Smith, December.

Blanche de Nevers (Balfe). Rotunda, Mr. Valentine Smith, December. Ireland premiere.

The Bohemian Girl (Balfe). Leinster Hall, Rousbey, January.

————. Queen's Royal, Grand English Opera, July.

————. Rotunda, Mr. Valentine Smith, December.

Carmen (Bizet). Gaiety Theatre, Carl Rosa, August.

Don Giovanni (Mozart). Leinster Hall, Rousbey, January.

Faust (Gounod). Leinster Hall, Rousbey, January.

————. Gaiety Theatre, Carl Rosa, August.

La Fille du Régiment (Donizetti). Gaiety Theatre, Carl Rosa, August.

Fra Diavolo (Auber). Town Hall, Kingstown (Dun Laoghaire), Walsham, February.

————. Gaiety Theatre, Carl Rosa, August.

Les Huguenots (Meyerbeer). Gaiety Theatre, Carl Rosa, August.

The Lily of Killarney (Benedict). Leinster Hall, Rousbey, January.

————. Gaiety Theatre, Carl Rosa, August.

Lucia di Lammermoor (Donizetti). Leinster Hall, Rousbey, January.

————. Town Hall, Kingstown (Dun Laoghaire), Walsham, February.

Maritana (Wallace). Leinster Hall, Rousbey, January.

————. Queen's Royal, Grand English Opera, July.

————. Gaiety Theatre, Carl Rosa, August.

————. Rotunda, Mr. Valentine Smith, December.

Martha (Flotow). Leinster Hall, Rousbey, January.

Norma (Bellini). Town Hall, Kingstown (Dun Laoghaire), Walsham, February.

————. Rotunda, Mr. Valentine Smith, December.

Le Nozze di Figaro (Mozart). Rotunda, Mr. Valentine Smith, December.

Rigoletto (Verdi). Leinster Hall, Rousbey, January.

Roméo et Juliette (Gounod). Gaiety Theatre, Carl Rosa, August.

The Rose of Castille (Balfe). Leinster Hall, Rousbey, January.
————. Rotunda, Mr. Valentine Smith, December.
La Sonnambula (Bellini). Town Hall, Kingstown (Dun Laoghaire), Walsham, February.
The Talisman (Balfe). Gaiety Theatre, Carl Rosa, August.
La Traviata (Verdi). Gaiety Theatre, Carl Rosa, August.
Il Trovatore (Verdi). Leinster Hall, Rousbey, January.
————. Queen's Royal, Grand English Opera, July.
————. Gaiety Theatre, Carl Rosa, August.
————. Rotunda, Mr. Valentine Smith, December.

1892

Aïda (Verdi). Gaiety Theatre, Carl Rosa, August. English language premiere.
L'Amico Fritz (Mascagni). Gaiety Theatre, Carl Rosa, August. Dublin premiere.
Un Ballo in Maschera (Verdi). Leinster Hall, Rousbey, January.
The Bohemian Girl (Balfe). Leinster Hall, Rousbey, January.
————. Gaiety Theatre, Carl Rosa, August.
Carmen (Bizet). Gaiety Theatre, Carl Rosa, August. E. C. Hedmondt.
Cavalleria Rusticana (Mascagni). Gaiety Theatre, Carl Rosa, August. Dublin premiere.
Djamileh (Bizet). Gaiety Theatre, Carl Rosa, August.
Don Giovanni (Mozart). Leinster Hall, Rousbey, January.
Faust (Gounod). Gaiety Theatre, Carl Rosa, August.
La Fille du Régiment (Donizetti). Gaiety Theatre, Carl Rosa, August.
The Lily of Killarney (Benedict). Leinster Hall, Rousbey, January.
Lucia di Lammermoor (Donizetti). Leinster Hall, Rousbey, January.
Maritana (Wallace). Leinster Hall, Rousbey, January.
————. Gaiety Theatre, Carl Rosa, August.
Martha (Flotow). Leinster Hall, Rousbey, January.
Le Nozze di Figaro (Mozart). Leinster Hall, Rousbey, January.
Le Prophète (Meyerbeer). Gaiety Theatre, Carl Rosa, August.
Rigoletto (Verdi). Leinster Hall, Rousbey, January.
The Rose of Castille (Balfe). Leinster Hall, Rousbey, January.
Il Trovatore (Verdi). Leinster Hall, Rousbey, January.
————. Gaiety Theatre, Carl Rosa, August.

1893

L'Amico Fritz (Mascagni). Gaiety Theatre, Carl Rosa, August.

————. Gaiety Theatre, Royal Italian Opera, October. Royal Italian Opera company artistes included Morello, Guetary, Joseph O'Mara, Corsi, Ravoglia, Gherlsen Dagmar, Florenza Bianioli.

Un Ballo in Maschera (Verdi). Leinster Hall, Rousbey, January.

The Bohemian Girl (Balfe). Leinster Hall, Rousbey, January.

————. Gaiety Theatre, Carl Rosa, August.

Carmen (Bizet). Gaiety Theatre, Carl Rosa, August.

————. Gaiety Theatre, Royal Italian Opera, October.

Cavalleria Rusticana (Mascagni). Leinster Hall, Rousbey, January.

————. Gaiety Theatre, Carl Rosa, August.

————. Gaiety Theatre, Royal Italian Opera, October.

Don Giovanni (Mozart). Leinster Hall, Rousbey, January.

Faust (Gounod). Leinster Hall, Rousbey, January.

————. Gaiety Theatre, Carl Rosa, August.

————. Gaiety Theatre, Royal Italian Opera, October.

La Fille du Régiment (Donizetti). Leinster Hall, Rousbey, January.

————. Gaiety Theatre, Carl Rosa, August.

The Golden Web (Goring Thomas). Gaiety Theatre, Carl Rosa, August.

Lohengrin (Wagner). Gaiety Theatre, Royal Italian Opera, October.

Maritana (Wallace). Leinster Hall, Rousbey, January.

Orfeo ed Euridice (Gluck). Gaiety Theatre, Carl Rosa, August. Company premiere.

————. Gaiety Theatre, Royal Italian Opera, October.

Otello (Verdi / English version Hueffer). Gaiety Theatre, Carl Rosa, September.

Pagliacci (Leoncavallo). Gaiety Theatre, Carl Rosa, August. Company premiere.

————. Gaiety Theatre, Royal Italian Opera, October.

Philémon et Baucis (Gounod). Gaiety Theatre, Royal Italian Opera, October.

Le Postillon de Lonjumeau (Adam). Gaiety Theatre, Carl Rosa, August. Dublin Company premiere.

I Rantzau (Mascagni). Gaiety Theatre, Royal Italian Opera, October.

The Rose of Castille (Balfe). Leinster Hall, Rousbey, January.

Tannhäuser (Wagner). Gaiety Theatre, Carl Rosa, August.

La Traviata (Verdi). Leinster Hall, Rousbey, January.

Il Trovatore (Verdi). Leinster Hall, Rousbey, January.

————. Gaiety Theatre, Carl Rosa, August.

1894

L'Amico Fritz (Mascagni). Gaiety Theatre, Carl Rosa, August.

At Santa Lucia (Tasca). Gaiety Theatre, Carl Rosa, August. United Kingdom
   premiere.
The Bohemian Girl (Balfe). Leinster Hall, Rousbey, January.
———. Gaiety Theatre, Carl Rosa, August.
Carmen (Bizet). Gaiety Theatre, Carl Rosa, August.
———. Gaiety Theatre, Royal Italian Opera, October.
Cavalleria Rusticana (Mascagni). Leinster Hall, Rousbey, January.
———. Gaiety Theatre, Carl Rosa, August.
———. Gaiety Theatre, Royal Italian Opera, October.
La Damnation de Faust (Berlioz). Gaiety Theatre, Carl Rosa, August.
   Abramoff.
Don Giovanni (Mozart). Leinster Hall, Rousbey, January.
Esmeralda (Goring Thomas). Gaiety Theatre, Carl Rosa, August.
Falstaff (Verdi). Gaiety Theatre, Royal Italian Opera, October.
Faust (Gounod). Leinster Hall, Rousbey, January.
———. Gaiety Theatre, Carl Rosa, August.
———. Gaiety Theatre, Royal Italian Opera, October.
La Fille du Régiment (Donizetti). Leinster Hall, Rousbey, January.
———. Gaiety Theatre, Carl Rosa, August.
Fra Diavolo (Auber). Leinster Hall, Rousbey, January.
Galathée (Massé). Leinster Hall, Rousbey, January.
Les Huguenots (Meyerbeer). Gaiety Theatre, Royal Italian Opera, October.
The Lily of Killarney (Benedict). Leinster Hall, Rousbey, January.
Lohengrin (Wagner). Gaiety Theatre, Carl Rosa, August.
———. Gaiety Theatre, Royal Italian Opera, October. Joseph O'Mara.
Lucia di Lammermoor (Donizetti). Gaiety Theatre, Carl Rosa, August. Barton
   M'Guckin.
Maritana (Wallace). Leinster Hall, Rousbey, January.
———. Gaiety Theatre, Carl Rosa, August.
———. Queen's Royal, Grand English Opera, November.
Martha (Flotow). Leinster Hall, Rousbey, January.
Massaroni (Buculossi). Leinster Hall, Rousbey, January. World premiere.
Die Meistersinger (Wagner). Gaiety Theatre, Royal Italian Opera, October.
La Navarraisse (Massenet). Gaiety Theatre, Royal Italian Opera, October.
Orfeo ed Euridice (Gluck). Gaiety Theatre, Royal Italian Opera, October.
———. Gaiety Theatre, Carl Rosa, August.
Pagliacci (Leoncavallo). Leinster Hall, Rousbey, January.
———. Gaiety Theatre, Carl Rosa, August.
———. Gaiety Theatre, Royal Italian Opera, October.
Rienzi (Wagner). Gaiety Theatre, Carl Rosa, August.

Roméo et Juliette (Gounod). Gaiety Theatre, Carl Rosa, August. E. C. Hedmondt, Esty, Abramoff.

Tannhäuser (Wagner). Gaiety Theatre, Carl Rosa, August.

————. Gaiety Theatre, Royal Italian Opera, October.

La Traviata (Verdi). Leinster Hall, Rousbey, January.

Il Trovatore (Verdi). Leinster Hall, Rousbey, January.

————. Gaiety Theatre, Carl Rosa, August.

1895

Bastien et Bastienne (Mozart). Gaiety Theatre, Carl Rosa, August.

The Bohemian Girl (Balfe). Leinster Hall, Rousbey, January.

Carmen (Bizet). Gaiety Theatre, Carl Rosa, August.

Cavalleria Rusticana (Mascagni). Leinster Hall, Rousbey, January.

————. Gaiety Theatre, Carl Rosa, August.

Don Giovanni (Mozart). Leinster Hall, Rousbey, January.

Ernani (Verdi). Leinster Hall, Rousbey, January. Dublin English language premiere.

Faust (Gounod). Leinster Hall, Rousbey, January.

————. Gaiety Theatre, Carl Rosa, August.

Il Figliuol Prodigo (Ponchielli). Gaiety Theatre, Carl Rosa, August.

La Fille du Régiment (Donizetti). Leinster Hall, Rousbey, January.

————. Gaiety Theatre, Carl Rosa, August.

Der Fliegende Holländer (Wagner). Gaiety Theatre, Carl Rosa, August.

Fra Diavolo (Auber). Leinster Hall, Rousbey, January.

Der Freischütz (Weber). Gaiety Theatre, Carl Rosa, August.

Galathée (Massé). Leinster Hall, Rousbey, January.

Hänsel und Gretel (Humperdinck). Gaiety Theatre, Carl Rosa, August.

Ivanhoe (Sullivan). Gaiety Theatre, Carl Rosa, August.

Jeanie Deans (MacCunn). Gaiety Theatre, Carl Rosa, August.

The Lily of Killarney (Benedict). Leinster Hall, Rousbey, January.

Lohengrin (Wagner). Gaiety Theatre, Carl Rosa, August.

Maritana (Wallace). Leinster Hall, Rousbey, January.

Martha (Flotow). Leinster Hall, Rousbey, January.

Le Nozze di Figaro (Mozart). Leinster Hall, Rousbey, January.

Petruccio. Leinster Hall, Moody-Manners, October.

Rigoletto (Verdi). Leinster Hall, Rousbey, January.

La Sonnambula (Bellini). Leinster Hall, Rousbey, January.

Tannhäuser (Wagner). Gaiety Theatre, Carl Rosa, August.

La Traviata (Verdi). Leinster Hall, Rousbey, January.

Il Trovatore (Verdi). Leinster Hall, Rousbey, January.
————. Gaiety Theatre, Carl Rosa, August.

1896

The Bohemian Girl (Balfe). Leinster Hall, Rousbey, January.
————. Queen's Royal, Neilson, June.
————. Leinster Hall, Neilson, September.
Carmen (Bizet). Gaiety Theatre, Carl Rosa, August.
Cavalleria Rusticana (Mascagni). Leinster Hall, Rousbey, January.
————. Queen's Royal, Neilson, June.
————. Gaiety Theatre, Carl Rosa, August.
————. Leinster Hall, Neilson, August.
Le Chalet (Adam). Leinster Hall, Rousbey, January. Dublin premiere.
Don Giovanni (Mozart). Leinster Hall, Rousbey, January.
————. Gaiety Theatre, Carl Rosa, August.
Faust (Gounod). Leinster Hall, Rousbey, January.
————. Queen's Royal, Neilson, June.
————. Gaiety Theatre, Carl Rosa, August.
————. Leinster Hall, Neilson, September.
La Fille du Régiment (Donizetti). Leinster Hall, Rousbey, January.
————. Queen's Royal, Neilson, June.
————. Leinster Hall, Neilson, September.
Der Fliegende Holländer (Wagner). Gaiety Theatre, Carl Rosa, August.
Fra Diavolo (Auber). Leinster Hall, Rousbey, January.
————. Leinster Hall, Neilson, September.
Galathée (Massé). Leinster Hall, Rousbey, January.
The Lily of Killarney (Benedict). Leinster Hall, Rousbey, January.
————. Leinster Hall, Neilson, September.
Lohengrin (Wagner). Gaiety Theatre, Carl Rosa, August.
Lucia di Lammermoor (Donizetti). Leinster Hall, Rousbey, January.
Maritana (Wallace). Leinster Hall, Rousbey, January.
————. Queen's Royal, Neilson, June.
————. Gaiety Theatre, Carl Rosa, August.
————. Leinster Hall, Neilson, September.
Martha (Flotow). Leinster Hall, Rousbey, January.
Die Meistersinger (Wagner). Gaiety Theatre, Carl Rosa, August.
Mercedes. Leinster Hall, Rousbey, January. World premiere.
Mignon (Thomas). Gaiety Theatre, Carl Rosa, August.
Le Nozze di Figaro (Mozart). Leinster Hall, Rousbey, January.

Pagliacci (Leoncavallo). Leinster Hall, Rousbey, January.
———. Gaiety Theatre, Carl Rosa, August.
Rigoletto (Verdi). Leinster Hall, Rousbey, January.
Roméo et Juliette (Gounod). Gaiety Theatre, Carl Rosa, August.
Shamus O'Brien (Stanford). Gaiety Theatre, Shamus O'Brien, November.
La Sonnambula (Bellini). Leinster Hall, Rousbey, January.
Tannhäuser (Wagner). Gaiety Theatre, Carl Rosa, August.
Il Trovatore (Verdi). Leinster Hall, Rousbey, January.
———. Queen's Royal, Neilson, June.
———. Leinster Hall, Neilson, September.
La Viandière. Gaiety Theatre, Carl Rosa, August. Dublin premiere.

1897

La Bohème (Puccini). Gaiety Theatre, Carl Rosa, August.
The Bohemian Girl (Balfe). Leinster Hall, Rousbey, January.
———. Gaiety Theatre, Carl Rosa, August.
Carmen (Bizet). Gaiety Theatre, Carl Rosa, August.
Don Giovanni (Mozart). Leinster Hall, Rousbey, January.
Faust (Gounod). Gaiety Theatre, Carl Rosa, August.
La Fille du Régiment (Donizetti). Leinster Hall, Rousbey, January.
Fra Diavolo (Auber). Leinster Hall, Rousbey, January.
The Lily of Killarney (Benedict). Leinster Hall, Rousbey, January.
Lucia di Lammermoor (Donizetti). Leinster Hall, Rousbey, January.
Maritana (Wallace). Leinster Hall, Rousbey, January.
———. Gaiety Theatre, Carl Rosa, August.
Martha (Flotow). Leinster Hall, Rousbey, January.
Mignon (Thomas). Gaiety Theatre, Carl Rosa, August.
Le Nozze di Figaro (Mozart). Leinster Hall, Rousbey, January.
Rigoletto (Verdi). Leinster Hall, Rousbey, January.
Roméo et Juliette (Gounod). Gaiety Theatre, Carl Rosa, August.
La Sonnambula (Bellini). Leinster Hall, Rousbey, January.
Tannhäuser (Wagner). Leinster Hall, Rousbey, January. Henry Beaumont.
    Company premiere.
———. Gaiety Theatre, Carl Rosa, August.
La Traviata (Verdi). Leinster Hall, Rousbey, January.
Il Trovatore (Verdi). Leinster Hall, Rousbey, January.
———. Gaiety Theatre, Carl Rosa, August.

1898

Un Ballo in Maschera (Verdi). Theatre Royal, Rousbey, January.
The Bohemian Girl (Balfe). Theatre Royal, Rousbey, January.
————. Gaiety Theatre, Carl Rosa, August.
————. Theatre Royal, Grand English Opera, November.
Carmen (Bizet). Gaiety Theatre, Carl Rosa, August.
Cavalleria Rusticana (Mascagni). Theatre Royal, Rousbey, January.
————. Gaiety Theatre, Carl Rosa, August.
Don Giovanni (Mozart). Theatre Royal, Rousbey, January.
Faust (Gounod). Theatre Royal, Rousbey, January. Esty.
————. Gaiety Theatre, Carl Rosa, August.
————. Theatre Royal, Grand English Opera, November.
La Fille du Régiment (Donizetti). Theatre Royal, Rousbey, January.
————. Theatre Royal, Carl Rosa, November.
The Lily of Killarney (Benedict). Theatre Royal, Rousbey, January.
————. Theatre Royal, Grand English Opera, November.
Lohengrin (Wagner). Gaiety Theatre, Carl Rosa, August.
Lucia di Lammermoor (Donizetti). Theatre Royal, Rousbey, January. Barton
    M'Guckin.
Maritana (Wallace). Theatre Royal, Rousbey, January.
————. Gaiety Theatre, Carl Rosa, August.
————. Theatre Royal, Grand English Opera, November.
Martha (Flotow). Theatre Royal, Rousbey, January.
Martyr of Antioch (Sullivan). Gaiety Theatre, Carl Rosa, August.
Pagliacci (Leoncavallo). Theatre Royal, Rousbey, January.
————. Gaiety Theatre, Carl Rosa, August.
The Puritan's Daughter (Balfe). Theatre Royal, Grand English Opera,
    November.
The Rose of Castille (Balfe). Theatre Royal, Rousbey, January.
La Sonnambula (Bellini). Theatre Royal, Rousbey, January.
Tannhäuser (Wagner). Theatre Royal, Rousbey, January.
————. Gaiety Theatre, Carl Rosa, August.
Il Trovatore (Verdi). Theatre Royal, Rousbey, January.
————. Gaiety Theatre, Carl Rosa, August.

1899

The Amber Witch (Wallace). Theatre Royal, Moody-Manners, October.
The Bohemian Girl (Balfe). Gaiety Theatre, Robert Cunningham, January.
————. Theatre Royal, Rousbey, April.

————. Queen's Royal, F. S. Gilbert, July.

Cavalleria Rusticana (Mascagni). Gaiety Theatre, Robert Cunningham, January.

Don Giovanni (Mozart). Gaiety Theatre, Robert Cunningham, January.

————. Theatre Royal, Rousbey, April.

Faust (Gounod). Gaiety Theatre, Robert Cunningham, January.

————. Theatre Royal, Rousbey, April.

————. Queen's Royal, F. S. Gilbert, July.

————. Theatre Royal, Moody-Manners, October.

La Fille du Régiment (Donizetti). Queen's Royal, F. S. Gilbert, July.

Fra Diavolo (Auber). Queen's Royal, F. S. Gilbert, July.

Hänsel und Gretel (Humperdinck). Gaiety Theatre, Robert Cunningham, January.

The Lily of Killarney (Benedict). Gaiety Theatre, Robert Cunningham, January.

————. Theatre Royal, Rousbey, April.

————. Queen's Royal, F. S. Gilbert, July.

————. Theatre Royal, Moody-Manners, October.

Lohengrin (Wagner). Gaiety Theatre, Robert Cunningham, January.

————. Theatre Royal, Moody-Manners, October.

Lucia di Lammermoor (Donizetti). Theatre Royal, Rousbey, April.

Maritana (Wallace). Gaiety Theatre, Robert Cunningham, January.

————. Theatre Royal, Rousbey, April.

————. Queen's Royal, F. S. Gilbert, July.

Masaniello (Auber). Theatre Royal, Moody-Manners, October.

The Prentice Pillar (Somerville). Gaiety Theatre, Robert Cunningham, January.

The Puritan's Daughter (Balfe). Theatre Royal, Moody-Manners, October.

Rigoletto (Verdi). Theatre Royal, Rousbey, April.

Tannhäuser (Wagner). Gaiety Theatre, Robert Cunningham, January.

————. Theatre Royal, Rousbey, April.

La Traviata (Verdi). Theatre Royal, Rousbey, April.

Il Trovatore (Verdi). Gaiety Theatre, Robert Cunningham, January.

————. Theatre Royal, Rousbey, April.

————. Queen's Royal, F. S. Gilbert, July.

————. Theatre Royal, Moody-Manners, October.

1900

The Amber Witch (Wallace). Theatre Royal, Moody-Manners, April.

At the Harbour Side. Gaiety Theatre, Carl Rosa, September.

The Bohemian Girl (Balfe). Theatre Royal, Moody-Manners, April, November.

Carmen (Bizet). Theatre Royal, Moody-Manners, April, November.
————. Gaiety Theatre, Carl Rosa, September.
Faust (Gounod). Theatre Royal, Moody-Manners, April, November.
————. Gaiety Theatre, Carl Rosa, September.
La Juive (Halévy). Theatre Royal, Moody-Manners, November.
The Lily of Killarney (Benedict). Theatre Royal, Moody-Manners, April.
Lohengrin (Wagner). Theatre Royal, Moody-Manners, April, November.
————. Gaiety Theatre, Carl Rosa, September.
Maritana (Wallace). Theatre Royal, Moody-Manners, April. November.
————. Gaiety Theatre, Carl Rosa, September.
The Puritan's Daughter (Balfe). Theatre Royal, Moody-Manners, April.
Tannhäuser (Wagner). Theatre Royal, Moody-Manners, April, November.
————. Gaiety Theatre, Carl Rosa, September.
Il Trovatore (Verdi). Theatre Royal, Moody-Manners, April.

1901

The Beauty Stone (Sullivan). Gaiety Theatre, Carl Rosa, November.
The Bohemian Girl (Balfe). Queen's Royal, F. S. Gilbert, August.
————. Gaiety Theatre, Carl Rosa, November.
Cinq-Mars (Gounod). Gaiety Theatre, Carl Rosa, November. Ireland premiere.
The Emerald Isle (Sullivan). Queen's Royal, Savoy Theatre, November. Sir
    Arthur Sullivan's last opera.
Faust (Gounod). Gaiety Theatre, Carl Rosa, November.
La Fille du Régiment (Donizetti). Queen's Royal, F. S. Gilbert, August.
Lohengrin (Wagner). Gaiety Theatre, Carl Rosa, November.
Maritana (Wallace). Queen's Royal, F. S. Gilbert, August.
————. Gaiety Theatre, Carl Rosa, November.
————. Theatre Royal, Moody-Manners, December.
Satanella (Balfe). Queen's Royal, F. S. Gilbert, August. First production in
    thirty years.
Siegfried (Wagner). Gaiety Theatre, Carl Rosa, November. Ireland premiere.
Tannhäuser (Wagner). Gaiety Theatre, Carl Rosa, November.
Tristan und Isolde (Wagner). Gaiety Theatre, Carl Rosa, November. Dublin
    premiere.
Il Trovatore (Verdi). Queen's Royal, F. S. Gilbert, August.

1902

The Bohemian Girl (Balfe). Theatre Royal, Moody-Manners, January.
Carmen (Bizet). Theatre Royal, Moody-Manners, January.

————. Gaiety Theatre, Carl Rosa, September.

Cinq-Mars (Gounod). Gaiety Theatre, Carl Rosa, September.

L'Etoile du Nord (Meyerbeer). Theatre Royal, Moody-Manners, January.

Faust (Gounod). Theatre Royal, Moody-Manners, January.

————. Gaiety Theatre, Carl Rosa, September.

The Lily of Killarney (Benedict). Theatre Royal, Moody-Manners, January.

Maritana (Wallace). Gaiety Theatre, Carl Rosa, September.

Martha (Flotow). Theatre Royal, Moody-Manners, January.

Much Ado About Nothing (Stanford). Theatre Royal, Moody-Manners, January. Ireland premiere.

Le Nozze di Figaro (Mozart). Gaiety Theatre, Carl Rosa, September.

Tannhäuser (Wagner). Theatre Royal, Moody-Manners, January.

————. Gaiety Theatre, Carl Rosa, September. E. C. Hedmondt.

Tristan und Isolde (Wagner). Gaiety Theatre, Carl Rosa, September.

Il Trovatore (Verdi). Theatre Royal, Moody-Manners, January.

1903

The Bohemian Girl (Balfe). Theatre Royal, Moody-Manners, January. Blanche Marchesi, Joseph O'Mara, Marie Alexander, William Dever.

————. Theatre Royal, Moody-Manners, April.

————. Queen's Royal, F. S. Gilbert, July.

Carmen (Bizet). Theatre Royal, Moody-Manners, January, December.

————. Gaiety Theatre, Carl Rosa, September.

Cavalleria Rusticana (Mascagni). Theatre Royal, Moody-Manners, January, April.

————. Gaiety Theatre, Carl Rosa, September.

Faust (Gounod). Theatre Royal, Moody-Manners, April.

————. Queen's Royal, F. S. Gilbert, July.

————. Gaiety Theatre, Carl Rosa, September.

La Fille du Régiment (Donizetti). Queen's Royal, F. S. Gilbert, July.

Fra Diavolo (Auber). Queen's Royal, F. S. Gilbert, July.

La Gioconda (Ponchielli). Theatre Royal, Moody-Manners, April. Ireland premiere.

The Lily of Killarney (Benedict). Theatre Royal, Moody-Manners, January, April.

Lohengrin (Wagner). Theatre Royal, Moody-Manners, January.

————. Gaiety Theatre, Carl Rosa, September.

Maritana (Wallace). Theatre Royal, Moody-Manners, April.

————. Queen's Royal, F. S. Gilbert, July.

————. Gaiety Theatre, Carl Rosa, September.

Muirgheis (O'Brien Butler). Theatre Royal, December. World premiere.

Le Nozze di Figaro (Mozart). Gaiety Theatre, Carl Rosa, September.

Pagliacci (Leoncavallo). Theatre Royal, Moody-Manners, January, April.

————. Gaiety Theatre, Carl Rosa, September.

Roméo et Juliette (Gounod). Theatre Royal, Moody-Manners, April.

Satanella (Balfe). Queen's Royal, F. S. Gilbert, July.

Tannhäuser (Wagner). Gaiety Theatre, Carl Rosa, September. Julius Walther.

Il Trovatore (Verdi). Theatre Royal, Moody-Manners, January, April.

————. Queen's Royal, F. S. Gilbert, July.

1904

The Bohemian Girl (Balfe). Theatre Royal, Moody-Manners, January.

————. Queen's Royal, Elster Grimes, June.

Faust (Gounod). Theatre Royal, Moody-Manners, January.

————. Queen's Royal, Elster Grimes, June.

La Fille du Régiment (Donizetti). Theatre Royal, Moody-Manners, January.

————. Queen's Royal, Elster Grimes, June.

The Lily of Killarney (Benedict). Theatre Royal, Moody-Manners, January.

————. Queen's Royal, Elster Grimes, June.

Lohengrin (Wagner). Theatre Royal, Moody-Manners, January.

Maritana (Wallace). Theatre Royal, Moody-Manners, January.

————. Queen's Royal, Elster Grimes, June.

Martha (Flotow). Theatre Royal, Moody-Manners, January.

Mignon (Thomas). Theatre Royal, Moody-Manners, January.

Roméo et Juliette (Gounod). Theatre Royal, Moody-Manners, January.

Il Trovatore (Verdi). Theatre Royal, Moody-Manners, January.

————. Queen's Royal, Elster Grimes, June.

NOTES

1. Stephen Watt suggests that the opera season would have stretched the vocal limits of singers, particularly tenors (Bauerle and Hodgart, 319), but this appears unlikely to have been the case.

2. Timothy Martin in "Joyce and Literary Wagnerism" claims: "Joyce's first important encounters with Wagner, in fact, were not in the opera house; for in Dublin the scale and, in Joyce's time, the dubious morality of the operas would have limited opportunities to hear the composer to excerpts played in concerts" (Bauerle, ed., 109).

3. Timothy Martin cites Alfred Loewenberg's *Annals of Opera* to demonstrate that only *Lohengrin* and *Der Fliegende Holländer* were performed in Dublin, in 1875 and 1877 respectively. Stephen Watt's catalogue in *Joyce's Grand Operoar* adds *Tannhäuser* to the list, and mentions that *Tristan und Isolde* was also performed there, but in December 1904 when Joyce had already left Ireland.

4. Bauerle also describes the enthusiasm with which divos and divas were greeted in Dublin, as seen in the drawing of Therese Tietjens's carriage back to her hotel by her fans (Bauerle and Hodgart, 25), a moment recorded in "The Dead" (*D*, 199).

5. Charles Villiers Stanford notes that "The opera company of Her Majesty's Theatre used to pay a prolonged visit to Dublin every autumn. Many standard works now relegated in this country to the scrap-heap, were given in first-rate style to one of the most appreciative audiences to be found anywhere" (85). Changing musical taste in the later part of the century may have accounted for the dismissal of these earlier works and performances.

6. This surprising information attracted the attention of Hugh Kenner, who quotes the passage in the foreword to O'Brien's book without clarification or inquiry.

7. There was also growing concern for the safety of the theater-going public:

> [...] between the years 1866 and 1892, no less than ten London theatres had been totally destroyed by fire, and during the same period fourteen music halls had been also wholly destroyed, and there were ninety-eight partial destruction[s] of theatres and numerous partial destructions of music halls in the same period. (Wolfe, 9)

In the previous seventy-three years, the total losses had amounted to seventeen.

8. The show was held at Leinster Hall on June 30, 1890, and was titled "Stanley's Travels in Africa" (*Irish Times*). A "myriorama," according to Gifford, is "a large picture or painting composed of several smaller ones that can be combined in a variety of ways" (610).

9. In fact, Francis Wolfe in his pamphlet "Theatres in Ireland" mentions that the 1892 Parliamentary Committee found there were three theaters, the Theatre Royal being an operatic and concert venue throughout the latter part of the century.

10. Lowry's theater included musical and sensational items. My own favorites include his January 16, 1888, advertisement "Lions, Tigers, Panthers, and Bears!" and the unbeatable "13 Performing Wolves," offered on March 5, 1888.

11. Joyce himself was a frequent theatergoer, often going to see all the performances given of a single opera. When separated from Nora in 1909, he asked her to attend a performance of *Madama Butterfly* so that as she listened to "Un bel dì" she would understand how he longed to be there with her (*L,* II, 256). John McCourt will speak of this letter in the next essay.

WORKS CITED

Attali, Jacques. *Noise.* Trans. Brian Massumi. Minneapolis: University of Minnesota Press, 1985.

Bauerle, Ruth, ed. *Picking Up Airs: Hearing the Music in Joyce's Text.* Urbana: University of Illinois Press, 1993.

Bauerle, Ruth and Matthew Hodgart. *Joyce's Grand Operoar: Opera in Finnegans Wake.* Urbana: University of Illinois Press, 1997.

Ellmann, Richard. *James Joyce.* Rev. ed. Oxford: Oxford University Press, 1982.

Gifford, Don. Ulysses *Annotated.* Rev. ed. Berkeley: University of California Press, 1988.

Herr, Cheryl. *Joyce's Anatomy of Culture.* Urbana: University of Illinois Press, 1986.

History of the Theatre Royal. Dublin: Ponsonby, 1870.

Irish Times. 1888–1904.

Joyce, Stanislaus. *The Dublin Diary.* Ed. George Harris Healey. Ithaca, N.Y.: Cornell University Press, 1962.

———. *My Brother's Keeper.* Ed. Richard Ellmann. London: Faber & Faber, 1958.

Koestenbaum, Wayne. *The Queen's Throat: Opera, Homosexuality, and the Mystery of Desire.* New York: Vintage, 1994.

Levine, Lawrence. *Highbrow/Lowbrow.* Cambridge, Mass.: Harvard University Press, 1988.

Martin, Timothy. "Joyce and Literary Wagnerism." *Picking Up Airs: Hearing the Music in Joyce's Text.* Ed. Ruth Bauerle. Urbana: University of Illinois Press, 1993. 105–27.

———. *Joyce and Wagner.* Cambridge: Cambridge University Press, 1991.

O'Brien, Joseph. *Dear Dirty Dublin.* Berkeley: University of California Press, 1982.

Rice, Thomas. *Joyce, Chaos, and Complexity.* Urbana: University of Illinois Press, 1997.

Stanford, Charles Villiers. *Pages from an Unwritten Diary.* London: Edward Arnold, 1924.

Walsh, T. J. *Opera in Dublin 1705–1797*. Dublin: Allen Figgis, 1973.

White, Eric. *A History of English Opera*. London: Faber & Faber, 1983.

Wolfe, Francis. "Theatres in Ireland." Pamphlet. Dublin: 1898.

CHAPTER 2

Joyce's Trieste:
Città Musicalissima

John McCourt

The aim of this essay is to draw attention to the role of Trieste—*città musicalissima*—in the musical formation of James Joyce. I will attempt to illustrate some of the important musical elements in the turn-of-the-century emporium and to put some of the musical allusions in Joyce's writings into a Triestine context. Given Trieste's prominence as a musical city, given the fundamental role music played in the city's culture—on the streets, in the bars, in the drawing rooms, concert halls, theaters, and opera houses—and given the extent to which Joyce's works are saturated with similar elements, it is surprising that so little attention has been paid to Trieste as a musical source in the many volumes devoted to Joyce and music. If one takes a look, for instance, at Ruth Bauerle's valuable and informative *Picking Up Airs: Hearing the Music in Joyce's Text,* one finds no reference to Trieste. Indeed, when attempting to establish that Joyce was acquainted with Puccini's *La Bohème,* Bauerle mentions productions in forty cities, the vast majority of which Joyce never set foot in, from Antwerp to Athens, Port Said to Warsaw, but there is no mention of Trieste. This essay is an attempt to place Trieste on Joyce's musical map.

As Herbert Gorman showed and as Richard Ellmann did not, James Joyce's life in the city of Trieste was not simply a dull gross effort at survival. The multicultural and multilinguistic emporium that was Joyce's Trieste provided the writer and his brother, Stanislaus, with a variety of stimuli and played a major role in informing Joyce as a novelist. Writing of Joyce's early years in Trieste, Gorman records that Joyce

dove into the variegated life of Trieste with the pleasure of a dolphin
diving in familiar waters. Every aspect of the city seemed to please
him, the picturesque life along the quays, the diverse ways of the
Città Vecchia with their wine-shops and cheap restaurants, [...] the
huge powdered beadle at the Opera who bawled for carriages and the
three opera seasons themselves—the Christmas and Carnival season
at the Teatro Communale and the summer season in the open-air
theatre and the autumn season at the Politeama, the excited jabber of
buyers and sellers in the markets for there were no set prices, the
smell of fish and the sight of sea spiders cooked in their shells, the
innumerable taverns bearing Christian names and, above all, the
Triestines, charitable, witty, irreligious, sceptical, fond of cakes and
the black wine of Istria and the fortified *vin rosé*—the Opollo from
Lissa. Even the 'bora,' that dreadful wind that blew so fiercely
through the town that ropes had to be stretched across the streets to
aid pedestrians, fascinated him as one of the irresistible phenomena
of nature. (142–43)

Even allowing for the overblown lyricism of this description
(sanctioned and approved by Joyce himself), it cannot be denied that
Trieste afforded the Joyce brothers with various ways of amusing
themselves and that these various forms of entertainment provided rich
material for Joyce's writing. The Joyces helped the time pass in a
variety of rather pleasant ways: by going for long walks along the coast
or in the Carso hills; by going to the cinematograph (which would
inspire Joyce to become the first person to open one in Dublin); by
going out to eat or simply to drink *ottavi* of wine in restaurants and
bars; perhaps by going to the variety theaters to see performers such as
the famous Italian transformist Leopoldo Fregoli or by going to the
Ippodromo (founded by their Greek friend, the Count Sordina) to watch
the horseracing or to see Buffalo Bill; by going to the Viennese-style
coffee shops or the *cafés chantants;* by simply hanging round the
streets and soaking up the atmosphere; by attending lectures organized
by the innumerable *circoli culturali;* and by going regularly to the
theater and the opera.

The bars and the opera were Joyce's favored forms of
entertainment. He liked to drink "absinthe, whisky, wine, slivovic, a
liquor like whisky, made with prune alcohol" (Francini Bruni,
[Interview], 1954) in the *città vecchia*—the old city—a home from
home teeming with sailors and dockers, drinkers, layabouts. What

Bloom says of Dublin—"Good puzzle would be cross Dublin without passing a pub" (*U*, 4.129–30)—was equally true of Trieste and so it was with good reason that Stanislaus, writing of Joyce's early years in Trieste, gave evidence of his brother's intermittently heavy drinking: "Jim went out at night until one or two o'clock, ranging from one smoky pothouse or low bar to another, and then came falling in about the place, or I went out to look for him" (S. Joyce, Letter, [1910]). Italo Svevo's daughter, Letizia Fonda Savio, confirmed that Joyce "was a peculiar type. He drank a lot. He said that Trieste reminded him of Dublin. The *osterie* reminded him of the pubs of his native city" (cited in Mo, November 21, 1987). Although Joyce already had plenty of experience to draw on from Dublin, it seems likely that this environment cannot but have helped him create *Ulysses,* and in particular to write the latter part of "Oxen of the Sun," as well as "Circe" with its loud confusion of drunken navvies, prostitutes, policemen, loiterers, and hangers-on. He reveled in this confusion and felt no pressure to adhere to the quiet and orderly world that was so deeply important to the middle classes and to Stanislaus, who, with Joyce's friend and colleague Francini Bruni, tried to rein him in.

The *osterie* were places where musical performance was not simply tolerated but even appreciated. In his Triestine *Book of Days,* Stanislaus Joyce recalled taking lunch in the Viola restaurant when a dozen Slavs suddenly broke into song. They sang "in harmony together with as good expression as a trained choir [...] There must be music in the nature of this people if 12 labourers can all at once break into such good song" (S. Joyce, *Book of Days,* April 3, 1908). The music was not always so harmonious. On some nights Joyce liked to join the revelers who spilled out of the bars onto the streets and continued to sing arias such as "La Vergine degli angeli" from Verdi's opera *La Forza del Destino* (Rismondo de Smecchia, 6).[1] More often the choice of songs was not so highbrow and local songs in dialect were very popular, as Francini Bruni noted:

> I had to accept the situation and smell Joyce's alcoholic breath, while in chorus with the other drunkards he roared a high-pitched, out of tune,
>
> Ancora un litro di quel bon [...]. ("Joyce Stripped Naked," 32)

As the following article, "The Night Singers," published in the Triestine daily, *Il Piccolo della Sera,* shows, Francini Bruni was not the only one who disapproved:

> Many citizens have complained to us that they are not able to sleep on Saturday, Sunday or very often on Monday nights. On every street where there are a couple of *Osterie* (and what street in Trieste does not have them?), at a certain hour of the night there is always someone who has the vocation to try to be *Tamagno:* sometimes two or three feel the desire, and when the noise is at its worst, it is not rare that some *Bellincioni* or some *Patti* joins in. The programme does not change much [...] nor are the musical effects very varied, all of them are out of tune. Nonetheless this monotony is not even capable of inducing sleep, and if these "divi" of the little streets would stay quiet a moment, they would probably hear their listeners hissing in their beds like vipers. It would be better if the police asked these errant swans to respect the night peace, which, at least two nights a week is violated in Trieste as in no other city on this earth. (*Il Piccolo della Sera,* May 9, 1905)[2]

More than occasionally Joyce was out with these violators of the city's peace, but at the same time he was delighted to have the opportunity to choose more genteel entertainment by taking his place in the *loggione* (the upper gallery) of the Teatro Comunale Giuseppe Verdi. Occasionally Francini Bruni would give him a free ticket that he would have procured as a journalist for *Il Piccolo della Sera,* but, even if Bruni did not, tickets to the *loggione* were cheap. Joyce was most at home here in the *loggione,* a democratic zone frequented by the less-well-off but also by the musical *intenditores* who chose to sit there because it was considered the best place from which to appreciate the voices. From there, he could watch the opera and, at the same time, enviously eye his rich pupils in the best seats down below. Later in *Giacomo Joyce,* he left a D'Annunzian impression of the scene:

> Loggione. The sodden walls ooze a steamy damp. A symphony of smells fuses the mass of huddled human forms: sour reek of armpits, nozzled oranges, melting breast ointments, mastick water, the breath of suppers of sulphurous garlic, phosphorescent farts, opoponax, the frank sweat of marriageable and married womankind, the soapy stink of men. (*GJ,* 12)

The Teatro Verdi was just one cog in a rich musical machine in Trieste. Indeed the city was the envy of many for its superb collection of theaters. The Verdi was the most prestigious, but also popular was its sister theater next door, La Sala della Filarmonica Drammatica, which was used for lectures, commemorations, and plays. With a capacity of a thousand people, it was the most comfortable and elegant theater in Trieste and had the best acoustics. The biggest theater, Il Teatro Politeama Rossetti, opened as a three thousand seater in 1878 and was used as a space for plays, operas, public meetings, and lectures (including the famous Futurist evening held there in January 1913, probably in Joyce's presence). Il Teatro Goldoni, so named in 1902, was built in 1852 as the Teatro Armonia and was home to a host of visiting dramatic companies. Il Teatro Fenice in via Stadion was the stage of plays, opera, operetta, and variety shows, while La Sala del Casino Schiller on Piazza Grande specialized in choral and orchestral concerts. Trieste also had a two-thousand-seat open-air theater, the Anfiteatro Minerva, where operas were mounted in summer. It opened for the first time on June 8, 1905, with Apolloni's opera *L'Ebreo (The Jew)*,[3] which was followed by Petrella's *La Contessa d'Amalfi* and Verdi's *I Due Fosrari*. It offered a rich summer season of opera, not unlike that offered in the Arena of Verona today, which Joyce and Stanislaus often attended. The 1908 season included Mascagni's *Cavalleria Rusticana,* Leoncavallo's *Pagliacci,* Donizetti's *Lucia di Lammermoor* and *L'Elisir d'Amore,* Verdi's *Rigoletto,* and Rossini's *Il Barbiere di Siviglia;* perhaps of most interest to Joyce was a production of Sidney Jones's operetta *La Geisha* (libretto by Harry Greenbank), which had a character called Miss Molly and from which Joyce later quoted in the "Hades" episode of *Ulysses*.[4]

The city attracted international singers (Caruso sang in *L'Elisir d'Amore* in 1901 and in *Rigoletto* in 1902 at the Teatro Politeama Rossetti) and was far more than what Brenda Maddox terms "a convenient stopover on the route between Milan and Vienna" (82). Isabel Burton, wife and biographer of the great explorer Captain Sir Richard Burton, himself the author of *A Plain and Literal Translation of the Arabian Nights' Entertainments* as well as *His Britannic Majesty's Consul for Dalmatia, Carniola and the Austrian Littoral,* vividly described the atmosphere and quality of the opera in Trieste in the 1870s and 1880s as being second only to what was available at Milan's La Scala:

I always think of a *prima donna* at Trieste, with regard to the
public. We import our operas from Milan two years before they
appear in London. We have an excellent Opera house [...] and the
Triestines are so severe and so critical that artistes become extremely
nervous; they know if they can pass Trieste they can sing anywhere.
One evening, a very plain, but first rate, *prima donna* appeared on the
stage. She had not yet opened her mouth; they all began to hiss and
hoot. She advanced with great resolution to the footlights, and said:
"*Cari Triestini,* I know I am frightful, but I did not come to be looked
at, I came to sing. Hear me before you hiss." There was a dead
silence. She opened her mouth, and before she had finished the first
few bars, the applause was deafening and prolonged. She remained a
favourite ever after. (12)

Politically part of the Austro-Hungarian empire but patriotically
drawn to Italy, Trieste attracted many immigrants from both places.
The more refined merchant class that settled brought with it the culture,
literature, and music of a cultivated central-European bourgeois class.
Music was perhaps the most comprehensively central-European aspect
of the city's culture. In this respect the city was like a small version of
the Vienna of the eighteenth and nineteenth centuries. Figures such as
Toscanini, Martucci, Nikisch, Siegfried Wagner, and Mahler conducted
there between 1905 and 1910. But the musical life of the city was also
increasingly influenced by politics—by the competing pulls of Italy and
Germany, exemplified by Verdi and Wagner, both of whom enjoyed
great prominence.

In this atmosphere, Joyce and Stanislaus went as often as possible
to the opera and, when money problems prevented them, they attended
some of the free concerts, including one that, much to Stanislaus's
amusement, featured a selection from Wallace's *Maritana:*

By the hokey! They played a selection from "Maritana" plump in the
middle of Piazza Grande. I disliked the opera sufficiently never to go
to it in Dublin; it came kindly to my ears now, badly as it was played.
(S. Joyce, *Book of Days,* January 26, 1908)

The wealth of choice entertainment that Trieste offered is well
illustrated by the clash, on December 5, 1905, of "La Duse" with
Gustav Mahler, who came to conduct the Orchestrale Triestina in a
concert that comprised works by Mozart, Beethoven and his own

Symphony no. 5[5] and was organized by an acquaintance of Joyce's, a certain Enrico Schott.[6] Mahler was impressed by Trieste and wrote to his wife:

> The people are terribly nice. [...] The orchestra is really quite good, excellently prepared and full of zeal and of fire. I'm hoping for a good performance. All the seats have been sold. (169)

He would have also found a well-prepared and critical audience. Many Triestines studied at the city's Conservatory of Music and others learned at least one instrument from a private teacher.[7] The newspapers all had serious music critics who gave unusually long and detailed accounts of plays, music, and performance. Hilda Brunner, a student of Joyce's, later remembered: "My family did not bring me to the concerts or the opera if I had not read the libretto, and, when I was older, learned the scores" (35), and this approach was typical. Joyce also bought the scores in order to prepare himself to see the operas even if, once again, they were beyond his means. In fact, on October 15, 1913, *Il tribunale civile* (the city court) wrote to Joyce's employers in the Scuola Revoltella telling them that he had not paid a sum of money owed to the Stabilemento Musicali Giuseppe Verdi, a music shop in Trieste. Joyce had bought music costing sixty-two crowns on May 2, 1913, and had "forgotten" to pay. The court now sought to have the amount deducted on a monthly basis from his salary.

Although Dublin had a rich musical tradition, Trieste was a step or two ahead when it came to opera and to symphonic concerts and Joyce felt he was somewhat behind the times. His comments, after seeing Catalani's *La Wally* for the first time in 1908, bear testimony to this, as shown in Stanislaus Joyce's Triestine *Book of Days:*

> This evening he (Joyce) went to *Wally* by Catalani and I met him outside the theatre at close on midnight. [...] He admitted that a musician is generally a decade ahead of his audience and that he was probably a decade behind half the audience. (*Book of Days,* October 8, 1908)

But Joyce was not put off by musical innovation, and, within a couple of days, returned to see *La Wally* a second time:

> While I was out for the second time, with Jim, he told me that he was
> coming again tonight to *Wally.* Altogether the opera costs us today,
> poor as we are, close on 3 crowns, and this week and last week about
> 6 crowns each. Meanwhile the pane of glass remains broken in the
> next room and the baby has no proper boots. I went a little after seven
> to the top Gallery and kept a place in the front row where Jim could
> follow it later on. About the opera I shall say nothing because I have
> seen it only once; but I liked Romboli, the baritone, I liked Cervi-
> Caroli, the soprano, Wally's melodious, expressive voice and really
> good acting. (S. Joyce, *Book of Days,* October 11, 1908)

Cervi-Caroli was, along with Gemma Bellincioni, one of the most
accomplished sopranos and most appreciated performers on the
Triestine stages and was a favorite with the public and critics alike, as
this quotation from a review of *La Traviata* at the Teatro Politeama
Rossetti in 1910 shows: "Signora Cervi-Caroli showed off all her
artistic treasures, the splendour of her voice, the feeling, the passionate
warm phrasing, all her real intellectually powerful individuality in this
Traviata" (*L'Indipendente,* October 16, 1910). Bellincioni took the
leading role in 1909 in the Triestine premiere of Strauss's *Salome,* an
event that aroused huge interest and was probably the musical highlight
that year, being remembered as "a landmark in modernism previously
considered utopian and incapable of realization" (Hermet, 228). Each of
the newspapers devoted long articles to Strauss's work and practically
all reviewed it glowingly. *L'Adriatico* reported as follows:

> Strauss's opera which has always aroused enormous curiosity,
> from its very first production in Dresden, to the Italian productions in
> Turin and Milan, to the most recent in Lisbon, and has also enjoyed
> great success everywhere, attracted a packed and distinguished
> audience to our best theatre yesterday evening. All of Trieste's
> artistic notorieties, all of its music-lovers and connoisseurs and an
> enormous gaily-coloured crowd of ladies filled every single seat in
> the stalls and crammed the galleries. The tense, nervous silence in the
> audience as the play began was not broken until the very end, except
> for a round of applause for Bellincioni's first entrance. [...] At the end
> the applause thundered and the success was consecrated with a dozen
> enthusiastic curtain-calls.
>
> On the whole it was an indisputable success, the like of which
> no other new production in our theatre has enjoyed this year. The

beautiful white-gloved hands of the innumerable ladies of the elite
gave their approval which will perhaps be the nicest thing to be
reported back to the far-off author of genius. The final comments and
animated discussions among the musicians, the amateurs as they left
the theatre were a proof of the seriousness of the success.
(*L'Adriatico,* March 25, 1909)

This production provided Joyce with a journalistic opportunity and
indeed he played an important role in highlighting Wilde's text as the
basis for Strauss's *Salome* in his article "Oscar Wilde: Il Poeta di
'Salome,'" which was published in *Il Piccolo della Sera* of March 24,
the day the opera opened in Trieste. Joyce's is basically a biographical
piece, which sketches Wilde's life, his successes, and his ultimate fall.

Another production in the 1908–09 season that would have
presented a challenge to Joyce's traditional musical tastes was the
return to Trieste of Antonio Smareglia's *Nozze Istriane.* Joyce would
later become a neighbor and friend of Smareglia when they both lived
on via Bramante in the years leading up to the First World War.
Although Smareglia was by then almost blind (indeed they attended the
same eye specialist), he would have made interesting company for
Joyce as he was probably Trieste's only artist of recognized European
standing. Smareglia is a somewhat forgotten figure today, but in
Joyce's time his works were heard in some of the world's most famous
opera houses—the Teatro Fenice in Venice, the Teatro dal Verme in
Milan, the Imperial Theatre in Vienna—and were warmly praised by
Gounod, Verdi, Puccini, Ricordi, Brahms, and D'Annunzio. In 1895 his
most famous work, the *Nozze Istriane,* premiered at the Teatro Verdi in
Trieste and was later put on in Venice where it was applauded by
Puccini. In 1897 his opera *La Falena* (libretto by Joyce's friend Silvio
Benco) opened and earned Verdi's praise, while in 1903 Toscanini
conducted the premiere at La Scala in Milan of his *Oceàna.*

Not long after settling in Trieste, Joyce felt increasingly drawn to
the operatic stage and decided to set about becoming a professional
tenor. According to Ellmann, he began to take singing lessons with
Giuseppe Sinico, the illustrious Triestine composer, famous for having
composed the city's anthem *L'Inno di San Giusto* (199). But this could
not have been the case, for in 1905 Giuseppe Sinico was in such bad
health that he had already retired from his teaching commitments, and,
in fact, died just two years later. Joyce was taught by Sinico's son
Francesco Riccardo (1869–1949), who praised Joyce's voice but told

him he would need two years to train it properly. Predictably, neither Joyce nor Stanislaus had enough money to enable him to persevere, but for as long as the lessons lasted he was lucky to be taught by the heir to a musical dynasty that had been teaching music in Trieste for three generations. Indeed Francesco Sinico, the most distinguished singing teacher of his time in Trieste, the principal music teacher in the Scuola Popolare and the choirmaster of the Greek and Serbian Orthodox churches as well as of the second Jewish synagogue, made such an impression on Joyce that he took the unusual step of using the musician's name for Captain and Emily Sinico in "A Painful Case."

Joyce's interest in becoming a tenor did not wane, as Stanislaus noted in 1907, after they had attended a production at the Anfiteatro Minerva of *Cavalleria Rusticana* together:

> There is no doubt that Italy is the country for tenors. There were four good tenors on the cast, and one of them—Tegonini—had a tenor of the very purest type. Jim wanted to know if he had a better trained voice than Tegonini. I decided he hadn't. He is still "thinking" of having his voice trained. He has too many futures. (*Book of Days,* July 5, 1907)

Joyce's fascination with tenors was enduring, but it induced him to be rather unflattering with regard to other singers:

> Talking about the raptures of the critics over the new soprano Madam Tetrazzini, Jim said he could not understand such talk. He thought most sopranos simply screeched. For the best of them, Calvé or Melba, he felt inclined to say: "Good woman, Well done". As for baritones, whenever they came on the stage, his sentiments were: "Oh, here's this bloody fellow again going to make a noise"; he listened to them with absolute displeasure, and, of course, no one ever knew what the hell a bass was singing. The only voice that had any sense of meaning in it for him was a tenor. (S. Joyce, *Book of Days,* November 6, 1907)

Perhaps Joyce agreed with Bloom's opinion: "Tenors get women by the score. Increase their flow. Throw flower at his feet" (*U,* 11.686–87). This quotation, as Ruth Bauerle has pointed out, recalls the opera *Carmen* (one of Stanislaus's favorites) and Don José's "La fleur que tu m'avais jetée." The opera *Carmen* also reappears in "Scylla and Charybdis" when Stephen says "Lover of an ideal or a perversion, like José he kills the real Carmen" (*U,* 9.1022), and later in "Circe" Bella Cohen is described cooling herself *"flirting a black horn fan like Minnie Hauck in* Carmen" (*U,* 15.2745). Incidentally, the Joyces would have had many opportunities to see *Carmen,* since it was put on at the Teatro Politeama Rossetti in 1904, 1907, and 1912, at the Teatro Verdi in 1914, and at the Teatro Fenice in 1907, 1908, and 1911.

Joyce's interest in singers in general and tenors in particular also spilled over into "The Dead," which he was writing at exactly this time, that is, in the summer of 1907. In that story we find a detailed discussion of opera companies and singers:

> Mr Browne could go back farther still, to the old Italian companies that used to come to Dublin—Tietjens, Ilma de Murzka, Campanini, the great Trebelli, Giuglini, Ravelli, Aramburo. Those were the days, he said, when there was something like singing to be heard in Dublin. He told too of how the top gallery of the old Royal used to be packed night after night, of how one night an Italian tenor had sung five encores to *Let Me Like a Soldier Fall,* introducing a high C every time, and of how the gallery boys would sometimes in their enthusiasm unyoke the horses from the carriage of some great *prima donna* and pull her themselves through the streets to her hotel. Why did they never play the grand old operas now, he asked, *Dinorah, Lucrezia Borgia?* Because they could not get the voices to sing them: that was why.
> —O, well, said Mr Bartell D'Arcy, I presume there are as good singers to-day as there were then.
> —Where are they? asked Mr Browne defiantly.
> —In London, Paris, Milan, said Mr Bartell D'Arcy warmly. I suppose Caruso, for example, is quite as good, if not better than any of the men you have mentioned. (*D,* 199)[8]

Joyce returned to the idea of starting a career as a tenor in 1908. As Stanislaus's Triestine *Book of Days* shows, this was a period in which Joyce attended the opera three or four times a week, chiefly to hear the different tenors:

> He has gone to so many operas in order to hear various tenors and compare his voice to theirs. [...] We came to discuss, then,

whether Jim had a sufficiently musical temperament to express himself by singing, as to which I have my doubts in view of the fact that he has so long expressed himself otherwise and that he rejected a singer's life that was offered to him because he looked down on it. (*Book of Days,* October 4, 1908)

Be all that as it may or may not, just a day after talking of Joyce's possible career as a tenor, Stanislaus noted his brother's decision to have his voice trained:

Stretching on the sofa today Jim announced that he had retired from public life and that for the present he was going to devote his attention to getting rid of his rheumatism, having his voice trained and fattening himself. (*Book of Days,* October 5, 1908)

Joyce's second Triestine singing teacher was the distinguished Romeo Bartoli, teacher at the Conservatorio Musicale di Trieste and resident choirmaster of both the Politeama Rossetti and the Teatro Verdi. Bartoli was also director of the city's highly regarded Madrigal choir and a renowned expert in old music.[9] Joyce's lessons with Bartoli took place in 1908 and 1909 and evidently they got along well together, perhaps drawn together by a common indifference to financial responsibilities. Joyce was enthusiastic and rapidly made progress. Soon after starting, he went out and put down fifteen crowns on a piano so that he could practice at home. Bartoli was enthusiastic about Joyce's voice, as Stanislaus noted: "Run-down and weakened as his voice is, Jim still has B natural, continental pitch, (about B flat English pitch) on his voice" (*Book of Days,* October 16, 1908).

Later, when Joyce was in Dublin from October to December 1909, Stanislaus took his place with Bartoli, but Joyce continued to show interest in his music teacher's successes, asking Stanislaus in a letter of November 8, 1909: "Did Bartoli conduct well L'EdiA [*L'Elisir d'Amore*]. How is your barreltone tenor getting on?" (*L,* II, 260).[10] Evidently, Stanislaus was upset when Bartoli was not particularly impressed with his voice, but Joyce encouraged him to continue: "I hope you go on with Bartoli. Don't be discouraged by his sleepy manner. He has heard a lot of tenors in his day and that, added to his natural fat, makes him unenthusiastic. I know he will teach you no vices" (*L,* II, 262). In *Finnegans Wake,* Joyce refers to Shaun's abilities as a singer, possibly with Stanislaus's Triestine singing lessons in mind:

> [...] I heard a voice, the voce of Shaun, vote of the Irish, voise from afar (and cert no purer puer palestrine e'er chanted panangelical mid the clouds of Tu es Petrus, not Michaeleen Kelly, not Mara O'Mario, and sure, what more numerose Italicuss ever rawsucked frish uov in urinal?) [...]. (*FW*, 407.13–17)

The "panangelical," perhaps the "Panis Angelicus," is more likely to have been sung by Joyce himself in his cups. Indeed, Francini Bruni noted: "Joyce had an inclination for liturgical chant. He had a tenor voice that seemed naturally suited to this kind of music. We frequently listened in astonishment as he sang parts in the traditional Gregorian style" ("Recollections," 41). Silvio Benco confirmed that Joyce "sang church music" (58).

Joyce returned to this topic later in *Finnegans Wake,* again mixing Irish musical elements, such as the Athlone-born John McCormack and Benedict's *The Lily of Killarney*, with Italian musical notation such as "bemolly"—from the Italian "bemolle" (flat)—and "jiesis"—very close to the Italian "diesis" (sharp)—and Italian singers such as the tenors, Tamagno "lamagnage" and Mario "Nomario":

> [...] I'd gamut my twittynice Dorian blackbudds chthonic solphia off my singasongapiccolo to pipe musicall airs on numberous fairyaciodes. [...] I may have no mind to lamagnage the forte bits like the pianage but you can't cadge me off the key. I've a voicical lilt too true. Nomario! And bemolly and jiesis! For I sport a whatyoumacormack in the latcher part of my throughers. And the lark that I let fly (olala!) is as cockful of funantics as it's tune to my fork. Naturale you might lower register me as diserecordant, but I'm athlone in the lillabilling of killarnies. That's flat. (*FW*, 450.17–29)

The "whatyoumacormack" is put in for good reason. Joyce had known and indeed sung with McCormack back in Dublin at the "Grand Gaelic Concert" in August 1904 under the banner "Kindly Irish of the Irish / Neither Saxon nor Italian,"[11] and continued to follow his progress with interest from Trieste. On April 25 Stanislaus noted the great tenor's progress as reported in the *London Standard:* "Mr McCormack has been engaged for the whole series of next season's seven London ballad concerts. He has also been engaged to sing in Paris, Berlin, Dresden, and Vienna during the autumn, besides singing in Liverpool, Manchester, Birmingham, Leeds, Sheffield, York, Glasgow, Edinburgh, and Dublin. Due to the great demand for his service in England Mr McCormack has been obliged to refuse several flattering offers from America" (*Book of Days,* April 25, 1908). A few lines later Stanislaus continues:

> He (Joyce) is glad he withdrew early from competition with McCormack, first because he would have been beaten in it, and secondly because a singer's life would in no way have suited him. It must be a damnable thing he thought to have to practice scales for two hours every morning and go about nursing a throat for fear of colds. (*Book of Days,* April 25, 1908)

Neither Joyce nor Stanislaus made it onto the stage as professional singers, although sometime in 1909 Joyce did sing in the quintet from *Die Meistersinger.*[12] The circumstances of this concert are unknown although Stanislaus does mention in his diary that "Jim has been asked to sing at a concert next January by a pupil who takes lessons here and heard him practising in the next room" (*Book of Days,* October 23, 1908). As no record of it survives in Trieste's "Schmidl" music museum, which has a vast collection of posters, fliers, tickets, and programs for concerts during this period, it is probable that it was a free concert given by Bartoli's students. But the choice of *Die Meistersinger* was significant because it was closer to the Italian bel canto tradition, so loved by Joyce, than any other Wagnerian opera.[13] Joyce was already well acquainted with the contents of Wagner's works before he came to Trieste, but it was here that he had opportunities to see and hear them, to see their complex techniques come alive in the orchestra and on the stage.

The highlight of the 1907 spring concert season at the Teatro Comunale Giuseppe Verdi was the concert on April 4 conducted by Mahler. Under his direction the orchestra played the prelude to Wagner's *Die Meistersinger,* Beethoven's Symphony no. 5, and his own Symphony no. 1. On April 18 and 20, the orchestra and singers under Giuseppe Martucci performed excerpts from Wagner's *Parsifal.* In a hugely successful concert given on June 18, 1908, at the Teatro Politeama Rossetti, Pietro Mascagni conducted the prelude to Act I of *Die Meistersinger,* along with the overture to Verdi's *Les Vêpres*

Siciliennes, Goldmark's second symphony, and the overtures to his own *Le Maschere* and to Rossini's *Guillaume Tell.* At Christmas 1908, Wagner's *Die Meistersinger* was produced at the Teatro Verdi and followed in the spring by *Siegfried* and *Das Rheingold.* Winter 1910 brought *Götterdämmerung* and spring 1913 his *Walküre.* One of the featured singers was the great Italian tenor Tito Schipa. The winter season of 1913–14 brought Wagner's *Tristan und Isolde,* but the real highlight came on January 20 with the first full Italian production of Wagner's *Parsifal,* which, unusually for Trieste, received rave reviews. Francini Bruni remembered this event clearly: "The first production of *Parsifal* was in Trieste; Joyce went like everyone else, but Joyce went 3 or 4 times more. It was very long, given in two parts, one started at 4 and the other at 8. [...] Joyce would sing 'L'enchantement du fée' from *Parsifal*" ([Interview], 1954).

The reception of Wagner's works in Trieste was generally less enthusiastic than in other Italian cities but far more knowledgeable, and Wagner's view of himself as not only a composer but also a poet would certainly have been up for regular discussion. The literary Wagner, the man of ideas who had such an influence on Joyce, was the subject of much local newspaper interest during Joyce's years in the city. All this would have helped Joyce later to put Wagner's theories about a *Gesamtkunstwerk* into effect, by merging countless literary and musical genres into *Ulysses,* as well as providing Joyce with a blueprint for the leitmotif technique.

But even if Wagner's popularity grew during Joyce's years in Trieste, the city's favorite composer was undoubtedly Giuseppe Verdi. No operatic season passed without revivals of several of his operas. Verdi's centenary fell on October 10, 1913, and this occasion provided the Triestines with a particular reason to celebrate this ultra-Italian artist, who had, after all, visited the city several times and allowed the world premiere of his opera *Stiffelio,* part of which he had written in Trieste, to be held at the city's Teatro Grande (later Teatro Verdi).[14]

In February 1913 *Rigoletto* was performed and was closely followed by a production of *Nabucco.* If Verdi had written operas like *Nabucco* to recall the unhappy state of Italy in the 1840s, it now served to remind turn-of-the-century Trieste of its unhappy state under Austria. Just as Joyce would come to link the Irish and the Jews—two peoples deprived of their homelands—so too did the Irredentists in Trieste look to the Jews as having much in common with themselves. Verdi's *Nabucco* symbolized this for them and allowed them an opportunity to bemoan their lot as a subject people under Austria and at the same time celebrate the triumphs of the Italian *risorgimento*. To prepare the public for this production of *Nabucco, Il Piccolo della Sera* published a series of articles to introduce it:

> The Nabucco or Nabucodonosor of the opera is not the one-dimensional Asian tyrant described by history. The biblical legends insist that the God of the Jews punished Nabucodonosor for the crime of having destroyed the Jewish kingdom by having him eat grass like a poor cow for seven years. But history shows that he in fact ruled his vast Assyrian Kingdom for 43 years and was probably without remorse for the conquest of Israel, for the massacres of the Jews, for the blinding of King Sedcia and for having reduced the Jews to slavery. (*Il Piccolo della Sera,* January 28, 1913)

With great irony Joyce would later name "Ichabudonosor" (*U,* 15.1862) as one of Bloom's ancestors. According to Gifford, this name at least partly derives from "Nebuchadnezzar, king of Babylon," who "besieged and reduced Jerusalem and carried the Israelites captive into Babylon" (482).[15] Taking the Italian spelling "Nabucodonosor," which is so much closer to Joyce's spelling, this link seems even more likely. He certainly would not have missed this important production in Trieste and was surely impressed by it, not least because his former singing teacher Romeo Bartoli prepared the chorus for it:

> The chorus, which in "Nabucco" has the lion's share, trained with love by Maestro Bartoli, gave an excellent performance, particularly in the "Va Pensiero" which was the highlight of the evening. [...] We have already said that the opera was an enormous success [...] with delirious applause [the audience] demanded an encore of the famous chorus of the Hebrew slaves. (*Il Piccolo della Sera,* January 29, 1913)

In the autumn the city was swamped with Verdi celebrations, and the Teatro Politeama Rossetti organized a Verdi season that featured *Il Trovatore* in late September, *Rigoletto* in October, *La Traviata* and *Aïda* in November. On the day of Verdi's centenary an enormous statue of the composer was unveiled in Piazza San Giovanni and four separate concerts were organized for the afternoon. The biggest, held in Piazza Grande, was turned into a huge Irredentist demonstration attended by some thirty thousand protesters who sang the banned "Va Pensiero." The Irredentist papers devoted three and four full pages to these events, going into minute details about the participants, and giving blow-by-blow accounts in an attempt to outdo one another in fervid enthusiasm,[16] as this extract from another Triestine daily, the rather highbrow *L'Indipendente,* shows:

> The authorities decided to ban the chorus from "Nabucco," the "Va Pensiero su l'ali...," but the enormous crowd, with their souls drawn towards thoughts that can only be reached at with wings, began to sing the harmonious chorus. Starting with single groups of young people the chorus gradually spread until the whole square was in song and the phrase "O mia Patria sì bella..." rose to the sky from those thousands and thousands of breasts all in unison and inspired by a deep feeling which united them [...]. (*L'Indipendente,* October 13, 1913)

The rhetorical excess combined with a focus on detail is suggestive of Joyce's ironic descriptions in the "Cyclops" episode of "the picturesque foreign delegation known as the Friends of the Emerald Isle" (*U,* 12.554) and of Robert Emmet's hanging. What is heroic in Trieste becomes mock-heroic in *Ulysses:*

> The arrival of the worldrenowned headsman was greeted by a roar of acclamation from the huge concourse, the viceregal ladies waving their handkerchiefs in their excitement while the even more excitable foreign delegates cheered vociferously in a medley of cries, *hoch, banzai, eljen, zivio, chinchin, polla kronia, hiphip, vive, Allah,* amid which the ringing *evviva* of the delegate of the land of song (a high double F recalling those piercingly lovely notes with which the eunuch Catalani beglamoured our greatgreatgrandmothers) was easily distinguishable. (*U,* 12.596–604)

Joyce later sprinkled *Finnegans Wake* with allusions to Verdi's works. *Il Trovatore* turns up many times, for example in the famous lines "And trieste, ah trieste ate I my liver! *Se non é vero son trovatore*" (*FW,* 301.16–17). Two lines later we find "He was a sadfellow, steifel!," which recalls Verdi's *Stiffelio.* Later we have an almost direct translation of the Conte di Luna's line in *Il Trovatore,* "Il Trovator! Io fremo," which Joyce slavicized, a fact that certainly would not have gone down well in Trieste, into "The balacleivka! Trovatorovitch! I trumble!" (*FW,* 341.9).

In more general terms, there are other parallels to be drawn between Joyce and Verdi. Both were concerned in their art to address the plights of their respective countries; both were fascinated by Shakespeare and adapted his works to their own artistic ends. As they progressed through their careers both wrote bigger and ever more complicated works. Verdi declared in 1853: "Ten years ago I would not have dared to tackle *Rigoletto* [...] Today I would refuse subjects of the kind of *Nabucco, Foscari,* etc. [...] They harp on one chord, elevated, if you like, but monotonous" (cited in Sadie, XIX, 641). Joyce's creative arc reached in a similar direction. Less happily, both Verdi and Joyce were the victims of political and ecclesiastical censorship, and both might be termed "unbelievers" antagonistic to the Church, yet quite capable of drawing on its rituals in the works. Verdi remembered having been kicked by a priest when he was serving mass as an altar boy. The priest cursed him, saying "Dio t'manda na sajetta!" ("May God strike you with lightning"). Later the archbishop deplored Verdi's use of the sacrament of baptism in *I Lombardi,* while the composer later had to change the witches in his *Macbeth* to gypsies, not from "another world" but "another country."

Joyce was also impressed by Verdi's great successor, Giacomo Puccini, to the extent that having purchased and studied the libretto of his *La Bohème* (written by Giuseppe Giacosa, whom he later admired in his notes for *Exiles,* and Luigi Illica), Joyce attended the second Triestine production of the opera eight times in the first two weeks of October 1908.[17] This led Stanislaus to comment in his diary, "He will hear of no opera but *Bohème,* which he says is perfect" (*Book of Days,* October 22, 1908). Stanislaus also went—twice—and very much enjoyed the opera:

> No opera that I have seen since *Carmen* has moved or pleased me so much as *Bohème.* [...] The first act pleased me, the second act amused me, the third act moved me, the fourth act gave me a momentary despair - what more can an opera do? The music is at several times sprightly. Finally the script is impetuous, very tender, sad. The book alone is worth the reading and the music is always cleverly set to it. I think I shall never tire of the Third act; to mention one air alone which I, the first night I heard the opera, passed unnoticed, Coline's farewell [...]: "Addio Vecchia Zimarra." It has as beautiful a bass

melody as any I have heard. If Verdi could have invented it, had given it to a father parting with a son or daughter, it would have brought down the house, but when *Bohème* was announced the critics here turned up their noses at it as I might have at *Trovatore, Maritana* or *The Bohemian Girl;* add to this, that it was excellently sung and acted all round. (*Book of Days,* October 22, 1908)

Stanislaus is correct in saying that Puccini was underrated in Trieste, but Joyce certainly was enthusiastic about his operas. What might have attracted Joyce to Puccini? His only comment about him is contained in a letter of October 27, 1909, to Nora, shortly after he had taken her to see *Madama Butterfly,* which was enjoying a successful Trieste premiere (with the public if not with the critics). Unfortunately their evening was overshadowed by a row:

The night we went to *Madame Butterfly* together you treated me most rudely. I simply wanted to hear that beautiful delicate music in your company. I wanted to feel your soul swaying with languor and longing as mine did when she sings the romance of her hope in the second act *Un bel di*: 'One day, one day, we shall see a spire of smoke rising on the furthest verge of the sea: and then the ship appears'. I am a little disappointed in you. (*L,* II, 255–56)

In critical terms, Joyce's comments are rather basic and comprehend only the emotional power of Puccini's works. But behind that emotion was a very carefully worked-out musical and dramatic technique. Following Wagner's influence, Puccini sought to use all the elements at his disposal—costumes, lighting, scenery, movement, acting, facial expression, and of course singing—to create as complete an effect as possible. All these he regulated with complex stage directions. Puccini, who paid an almost Joycean attention to detail, also favored simple stories that often observe the classical unities of action, time, and space and urged his librettists to be as sparing as possible with words. His subjects were not on the grand scale of Verdi, and especially in his early works he was concerned for "'le cose piccole,' the little things in the lives of little, unimportant people, and for 'grande dolore in piccole anime'" (Sadie, XV, 437). These factors must have appealed to Joyce, creator of Little Chandler and Leopold Bloom.

Wagner, Verdi, and Puccini, and many more composers including Mozart (but not his *Don Giovanni*), Tchaikovsky, Beethoven, Grieg,

Rossini, Bellini, Catalani, Massenet, Bizet, Donizetti, and Strauss were heard and appreciated by Joyce in Trieste and some found their way into *Finnegans Wake*. In one glorious passage, we find a collection of great composers cluttered together just as Joyce had found them in the rich musical world of Trieste. Among the many who appear in the following passage are Bach, Beethoven, Bellini, Bizet, Field, Gluck, Mercadante, Meyerbeer, Mozart, Pergolesi, Tchaikovsky (his *Nutcracker Suite* is suggested in the "Nutsky"), possibly Verdi (perhaps "Questa o quella" from *Rigoletto*), as well as some Wagnerians ("wheckfoolthenairyans"):

> Let everie sound of a pitch keep still in resonance, jemcrow, jackdaw, prime and secund with their terce that whoe betwides them, now full theorbe, now dulcifair, and when we press of pedal (sof!) pick out and vowelise your name. A mum. You pere Golazy, you mere Bare and you Bill Heeny, and you Smirky Dainty and, more beethoken, you wheckfoolthenairyans with all your badchthumpered peanas! We are gluck-glucky in our being so far fortunate that, bark and bay duol with Man Goodfox inchimings having ceased to the moment, so allow the clinkars of our nocturnefield, night's sweetmoztheart, their Carmen Sylvae, my quest, my queen. Lou must wail to cool me airly! Coil me curly, warbler dear! May song it flourish (in the underwood), in chorush, long make it flourish (in the Nut, in the Nutsky) till thorush! Secret Hookup. (*FW,* 360.3–17)

It might seem odd, given Joyce's knowledge and appreciation of so many great composers, that he chose to intersperse *Ulysses,* not with one or many of their works but with an operetta written by a mediocre German composer as a leitmotif, particularly in the "Sirens" episode. I am referring to Friedrich von Flotow's *Martha* and in particular to Lionel's aria "M'appari."[18] But of course it is not odd at all. Rather it is a sign of Joyce's ability to suspend his own personal choices and pick the correct aria from the correct opera for his 1904 Dublin. He chose "M'appari" precisely because it was popular in Dublin at the time and suited his thematic needs but also because Flotow provided him with a link between Bloom's central-European ancestry and his Irishness. Perhaps Joyce also appreciated that Flotow (a bit like himself) was not above a little "stolentelling," or borrowing from other composers whatever suited him: in the case of *Martha,* Thomas Moore's "'Tis the

Last Rose of Summer," which Joyce also draws liberally from in *Ulysses*.

None of Joyce's Triestine or even European sources was of any use to him if he could not stitch the music into the rich Irish fabric of his work. This is true of *Ulysses,* where "The Croppy Boy" can be heard as a close transposition of the "Death March" from Handel's *Saul,* itself directly mentioned in the "Hades" and "Circe" episodes, and of *Finnegans Wake,* where side by side we find Kerry quadrilles and Listowel lancers linked with Wagnerian mastersinging. No matter how much Joyce trawled in Dublin, Zurich, or Paris, the range and variety of musical references in his final two books are all the greater by virtue of his long sojourn in Trieste, *città musicalissima.*

NOTES

1. Joyce attended *La Forza del Destino* at the Teatro Politeama Rossetti in Trieste on October 16, 1908.

2. Francesco Tamagno was an Italian tenor famous for being the first to play the leading role in Verdi's *Otello;* Gemma Bellincioni was a particular favorite of the old Verdi and the first Santuzza in *Cavalleria Rusticana.* Joyce saw her singing the leading role in Strauss's *Salome* at the Teatro Verdi in 1909. Adelina Patti was another renowned Italian opera singer.

3. The plot, written in 1850, concerns Ferdinand of Aragon and Isabella of Castile's siege of Granada, the Moors' last bastion in Spain.

4.   *And they call me the jewel of Asia,*
      Of Asia,
      The geisha. (U, 6.355–57)

5. Ellmann is mistaken in dating Mahler's concerts in Trieste to 1904 and 1906 (*SL,* 168).

6. In *L'Indipendente* of December 6, 1905, the critic was enthusiastic about the concert and found space to praise Schott: "All the lovers of music must thank Mr. Enrico Schott who, with the disinterest of a patron in love with the beautiful art of sounds, made possible a concert of such rich importance, and is preparing others." Schott was an older brother of Edoardo Schott, Joyce's best Triestine student and later one of his friends in Zurich. The Schott family were important for Joyce and provided him with many links to literary and musical culture in Trieste. Joyce may have met Enrico Schott through Leopoldo Popper. Joyce mentions him in a letter of September 5, 1909, to Nora from Dublin: "But I will send on a copy of *Chamber Music* from London. Tell

Stannie to take it to my binder and have it done exactly like the one for Schott [...]" (*L*, II, 247–48).

7. *La Guida di Trieste* of 1907 lists well over one hundred fifty private music teachers working in the city, compared with forty-five private language teachers.

8. Giacomo Meyerbeer's *Dinorah* was more recently produced in Trieste than in Dublin. It was put on at the Teatro Verdi in 1888 and at the Teatro Fenice in 1900. Gaetano Donizetti's *Lucrezia Borgia* was produced at the Teatro Politeama Rossetti in 1878 and at the Teatro Verdi in 1887.

9. *Il Piccolo della Sera* of February 13, 1936, remembered Bartoli fondly when he died in that year:

> This magnificent man of music was born on 1 January 1875. [...] Romeo was very precocious in his musical abilities: at four years of age, without a teacher he played the piano; at eight he was brought to the opera, and, as soon as he got back home, he began to play by ear all the music he had heard. But he was given no formal musical training and he remained an autodidact; [...] he went to university to study mathematics and during his holidays he conducted a small orchestra of friends. His family suffered financial ruin and he was forced to abandon university and thus began a long precarious bohemian existence. His bills were famous and so was the serene indifference which allowed him to live without any money; equally famous was his musical temperament, his superb musical taste. At that time he met *il Maestro Smareglia,* who quickly spotted the young man's genius. Bartoli thus became his inseparable companion for several years, and he learned composition and singing teaching from him. Soon, Bartoli was invited to work as choirmaster in our theatres; in 1899 he was conductor for the opera season in the *Politeama Rossetti,* in which Flotow's *"L'Ombra"* and other works were performed.

The writer went on to praise his work at the Teatro Verdi, as the creator of the Madrigal choir and as a music teacher.

10. Joyce here anticipates Ben Dollard's "base barreltone" (*U,* 11.559) in "Sirens."

11. See the advertisement in the *United Irishman* of August 1904, repr. in Jackson, 122.

12. No record of this concert exists. Joyce does seem to rather exaggerate his musical links (in his letters), referring to John McCormack as "a friend of mine" (*L,* I, 66). Perhaps he was just trying to impress his correspondent. Just

what Joyce thought of *Die Meistersinger* is not clear. In a letter of July 19, 1909, to G. Molyneux Palmer, the Irish composer who in 1909 set to music some of the poems of *Chamber Music,* Joyce wrote that he thought the opera was "pretentious stuff" (*L,* I, 67). Georges Borach said that Joyce referred to it as "my favorite Wagner opera" (72).

13. See Martin, *Joyce and Wagner,* and also his essay "Joyce, Wagner, and Literary Wagnerism" in *Picking Up Airs,* 105–27.

14. The overture from this opera was performed at the Teatro Politeama Rossetti in 1913.

15. Joyce also explicitly mentions Nabucodonosor (again with the Italian spelling) in *Finnegans Wake:* "Nomad may roam with Nabuch but let naaman laugh at Jordan! For we, we have taken our sheet upon her stones where we have hanged our hearts in her trees; and we list, as he bibs us, by the waters of babalong" (*FW,* 103.9–12).

16. See, for example, *Il Piccolo della Sera, L'Indipendente,* and *L'Adriatico* of October 13 and 14, 1913.

17. The first Triestine production was staged at the Teatro Fenice in 1903.

18. This opera does not appear to have been produced in Trieste later than the 1889 production at the Teatro Fenice.

WORKS CITED

L'Adriatico. 1909–13.

Bauerle, Ruth, ed. *Picking Up Airs: Hearing the Music in Joyce's Text.* Urbana: University of Illinois Press, 1993.

Benco, Silvio. "James Joyce in Trieste." *Portraits of the Artist in Exile: Recollections of James Joyce by Europeans.* Ed. Willard Potts. New York: Harcourt Brace Jovanovich, 1979. 49–58.

Borach, Georges. "Conversations with James Joyce." *Portraits of the Artist in Exile: Recollections of James Joyce by Europeans.* Ed. Willard Potts. New York: Harcourt Brace Jovanovich, 1979. 69–72.

Brunner, Hilda. "Breve Saga dei Brunner." Private Collection, Trieste.

Burton, Isabel. *AEI—Arabia Egypt India, A Narrative of Travel.* London and Belfast: Mullan, 1879.

Francini Bruni, Alessandro. Interview with Richard Ellmann, July 1954. Richard Ellmann Collection, McFarlin Library, University of Tulsa, Box 5.

———. "Joyce Stripped Naked in the Piazza." *Portraits of the Artist in Exile: Recollections of James Joyce by Europeans.* Ed. Willard Potts. New York: Harcourt Brace Jovanovich, 1979. 7–39.

————. "Recollections of Joyce." *Portraits of the Artist in Exile: Recollections of James Joyce by Europeans.* Ed. Willard Potts. New York: Harcourt Brace Jovanovich, 1979. 39–46.

Gifford, Don. Ulysses *Annotated.* Rev. ed. Berkeley: University of California Press, 1988.

Gorman, Herbert. *James Joyce.* New York: Farrar & Rinehart, 1939.

Hermet, Guido. "La Vita Musicale a Trieste (1801–1944), con speciale riferimento alla musica vocale." *Archeografo Triestino* (1947).

L'Indipendente. 1910–13.

Jackson, John Wyse and Bernard McGinley, eds. *James Joyce's* Dubliners: *An Illustrated Edition with Annotations.* London: Sinclair-Stevenson, 1993.

Joyce, Stanislaus. *Book of Days* (1907–1909). Richard Ellmann Collection, McFarlin Library, University of Tulsa.

————. Letter to John Stanislaus Joyce, [1910]. Typescript by Richard Ellmann. Richard Ellmann Collection, McFarlin Library, University of Tulsa, Box 77.

Maddox, Brenda. *Nora: A Biography of Nora Joyce.* London: Hamish Hamilton, 1988.

Mahler, Alma. *Gustav Mahler.* Ed. L. Rognoni. Trans. L. Dallapiccola. Milano: Il Saggiatore, 1960.

Martin, Timothy. *Joyce and Wagner: A Study of Influence.* Cambridge: Cambridge University Press, 1991.

Mo, Ettore. "Quando Svevo e Joyce litigavano." *Il Corriere della Sera*, November 21, 1987.

Il Piccolo della Sera. 1905–13.

Rismondo de Smecchia, Giuseppe. "James e Stanislaus Joyce a Trieste." Unpublished lecture, Associazione Italo-Britannico, March 20, 1996.

Sadie, Stanley, ed. *New Grove Dictionary of Music and Musicians.* New York: Macmillan, 1980.

Section 2: Joyce and His Contemporaries

CHAPTER 3

Chamber Music: Words and Music Lovingly Coupled

Myra T. Russel

> I have chiefly aimed to couple my words and notes lovingly together,
> which will be much for him to do that hath not power over both.
> (Campion, *Second Book of Airs,* "To the Reader")

James Joyce ... as *Poet?* ... as *Lyricist?* ... as *Composer?* The answer to all three questions, of course, is a resounding *Yes.* His very first book to be published was the little volume of thirty-six poems entitled *Chamber Music.* The legendary problems that were to plague almost all of Joyce's books began here, including the loss of the manuscript by one publisher who then rejected the second copy, followed by negative responses from three others. Finally Elkin Mathews accepted the book and it was published in May 1907. Even before the poems appeared in print, Joyce expressed ambivalence about them, protesting to his brother Stanislaus that he was "no love 'pote'" and did not wish "to stand behind his own insincerity and fakery," but the rejoinder that the publication of this book "with all its dishonesty" might enable him to publish "his other books with all their honesty" persuaded Joyce not to withdraw *Chamber Music* (Ellmann, 260). He had argued earlier about a name for the collection, declaring "I should prefer a title which to a certain extent repudiated the book, without altogether disparaging it" (*L,* II, 182). Another letter to Stanislaus, written after the proofs arrived, illustrates Joyce's conflicting attitudes even more clearly:

> I don't like the book but wish it were published and be damned to it.
> However, it is a young man's book. I felt like that. It is not a book of

love-verses at all, I perceive. But [...] they are not pretentious and
have a certain grace. (*L,* II, 219)

Richard Ellmann indicates that Joyce "exaggerated his own
indifference" (232) to the fate of his little verses. At the same time he
realized that the poems were a genuine expression of himself; perhaps
the approval of W. B. Yeats and the subsequent enthusiasm of Ezra
Pound aided the process of recognition.

Certainly there can be no dispute about Joyce's inclination and
talent as a lyricist. To begin with, he often referred to the poems as
"songs," using the terms interchangeably. In a letter to Geoffrey
Molyneux Palmer, whose musical settings of *Chamber Music* remained
Joyce's lifelong favorites, he indicated that the poems were meant to be
set to music and expressed the hope that the composer would
eventually set all of them: "The book is in fact a suite of songs," Joyce
wrote, "and if I were a musician I suppose I should have set them
myself" (*L,* I, 67). Pound insisted that the lyrics were so musical "that
the musician's work [was] very nearly done for him" (414), but that did
not prevent the poems from acting as a magnet for a variety of
composers. Joyce knew of nearly forty during his lifetime; by 1993 the
list numbered one hundred forty-one and is still growing.[1]

There is only one song, published several years after his death, to
substantiate the claim that James Joyce was also a composer, but it is
sufficient. The haunting melody he composed for "Bid Adieu" (XI)[2] is
simply beautiful (in conversations with me, tenor Robert White calls it
"gorgeous"), and the piano accompaniment by Edmund Pendleton, an
expatriate American musician in Paris, is exactly right. With its faithful
rendering of music to words, its eloquent shifts of mood and tempo, and
its sophisticated modulations, the song affords a moving experience for
singer, pianist, and listener. It is quite unforgettable.

THE WORDS OF JOYCE

Many who have read, or even better, have recited the *Chamber Music*
poems enjoy their delicacy and gracefulness, finding them not only
pleasurable but delightful. Critics, however, with very few exceptions,
have been far less accepting, judging the book as unworthy of a genius;
their disapproval has ranged from embarrassment to outright ridicule or
contempt. While the musical quality of Joyce's language is generally
acknowledged, rarely has the vital importance of music to the poems

been recognized. Horace Gregory insists that when it comes to the poems, the critics are essentially "tone-deaf," belonging to a generation that "accepted the flaws of Pound, Eliot, and Auden as standards of excellence in writing verse and grew to admire flat lines and tone-deaf phrasing. Joyce's gift was nine-tenths auditory" (163).

Why has Joyce's earliest book so seldom been accorded its due? Why has this little collection of verses suffered flagrant misinterpretation, distortion, and even, at times, disdain? One obvious explanation is that after the brilliant innovations, symbolic complexity, layered meanings, and playful, often earthy humor of his major works, the tiny poems were overshadowed and diminished. Far more damaging, however, was the tendency to search for hidden meanings or similar techniques, using hindsight. Subsequent efforts compared and correlated particulars in the lyrics to *Ulysses,* for example, or proclaimed the presence of symbols where none exists. Such misreadings were not only unfair and inappropriate, but led to false conclusions and sometimes wild excess.

Still, distortions and misinterpretations cannot fully account for the negative reactions to *Chamber Music.* The problem actually originates with the title. Its famous association with an under-the-bed vessel generated the atmosphere of a joke that, however entertaining, trivializes the book's contents. Begun by Oliver Gogarty, a sometime friend and rival, then propagated by Herbert Gorman in his early biography of Joyce, and generally "much distorted" according to Ellmann (154), the waggish, off-color story easily assumed an air of authenticity. There can be no doubt that Joyce enjoyed the joke too, since he used it in *Ulysses:*

> Chamber Music. Could make a kind of pun on that. It is a kind of music I often thought that when she. Acoustics that is. Tinkling. (*U,* 11.979–81)

But this is hardly proof that Joyce meant the title as a bit of foreshadowing, or that he originally intended the double meaning. The joke became so popular that little attention was paid to Stanislaus's indignant protest:

> I had already suggested and Jim had accepted the title *Chamber Music* [...]. [Gorman's story], which seems to have tickled the fancy

of some American critics [...] is false, whatever its source. (S. Joyce,
Keeper, 209–10)

Actually, the rationale offered by Stanislaus for choosing that title well
demonstrates both his sensitivity to his gifted brother and the soundness
of his critical judgment. Given what he saw as "the analogy with
musical composition in these little songs" (S. Joyce, *Keeper,* 209)—and
the association of chamber music as a small and intimate setting for a
limited group of performers does seem fitting—that title "seemed to me
suitable to the *passionless love themes* and *studious grace* of the songs"
(S. Joyce, *Keeper,* 175; emphasis added). This statement has always
impressed me as one of the most accurate and most insightful attempts
to characterize the poems.

 Chamber Music attracted little attention in the ensuing years,
except from musicians. Three composers submitted musical settings to
Joyce within three years of the volume's 1907 publication: W. B.
Reynolds, music critic for *The Belfast Telegraph* (whose songs are
lost); Herbert Hughes, folk song collector and later close friend of
Joyce (lost); and Geoffrey Molyneux Palmer (whose manuscripts were
recently found and published). Adolph Mann had the distinction of
being the first to have a Joyce song appear in print; his setting of
"Donnycarney" was published in 1910, prompting a polite letter of
thanks from the author. A review of *Chamber Music* appeared in the
Freeman's Journal in June 1907, written by one of Joyce's Dublin
friends, Thomas Kettle, who liked the poems but regretted the lack of
Celtic lore or nationalist references. But that same month in the *Nation,*
Arthur Symons—the first major critic to review any book by Joyce—
admired the lyrics, praising them as "tiny evanescent things," "the very
dew of roses," "slight as a drawing of Whistler is slight," "a whispering
clavichord of ghostly tunes" (Symons, June 22, 1907). Of course
Symons had the tremendous advantage of seeing the poems and
evaluating them long before they were dwarfed by Joyce's major
works. About the only hint of the Joyce-to-come is in the portmanteau
words: *lookingglass* (XXIV), *songconfessed* (XXV), *poisondart*
(XXVII).

 Virtually everything about *Chamber Music*—its style, subject
matter, language, structure, and spirit—suggests not a twentieth-century
author, but instead a much earlier period in the history of literature.[3] To
comprehend fully and precisely what Joyce was doing, and to
appreciate the extent to which he succeeded, it is necessary to examine

somewhat less familiar material. Once it becomes clear that the lyrics are a deliberate intellectual endeavor to reproduce "ayres" of the Elizabethan period, to find that wonderful balance of words and music so elegantly captured by Renaissance poets and composers, then Joyce's songs acquire a new stature, what Stanislaus called "studious grace."

The seeds were planted in 1893 when James Joyce was still a boy, during his two years at Belvedere College. Kevin Sullivan's illuminating book, *Joyce among the Jesuits,* describes the school's thorough and exacting approach to classical literature: the rigorous, almost linguistic methods applied to poetry, along with the probing analysis and demanding exercises that accompanied each text (71–83). The young Joyce absorbed lessons in poetics that would influence and direct his own talents. Translation, memorization, and *emulatio* were standard features of Jesuit pedagogy, and not surprisingly, Joyce was an unusually apt pupil. His translation of an ode by Horace effectively conveys flowing fountains, demonstrating the "skill, grace, and accuracy that reveals [...] a sense of language that was to mature into genius" (Sullivan, 76).

That Joyce always loved old English songs and as a young man spent long hours in the National Library of Ireland copying out Elizabethan airs is widely known. Stanislaus mentions only John Dowland and Henry VIII, but Joyce certainly knew the songs of Thomas Campion and was familiar with Ben Jonson, Thomas Morley, William Byrd, and others. The contents of Renaissance songbooks provided not only a congenial spirit and style, but had a challenging intellectual appeal. After all, this was the Golden Age of English poetry and music; musical understanding, taste, and appreciation were widespread and expected of a gentleman, along with an ability to sight-read and sing. The royal court set a high value on music: Queen Elizabeth maintained a regular establishment of sixty to seventy wind and string players, with lutenists holding the highest rank since they composed their own songs, played as well as sang, and arranged music for consort. The nobility emulated the court and kept a staff of instrumentalists and singers who performed and gave lessons to family members. Many composers earned their living this way, including Dowland, who was famous as a virtuoso lutenist. Given the vital importance of music, it is hardly surprising that standards were so high and the quality of the music so extraordinary.[4]

James Joyce also emerged from a background where music played a prominent role in everyday life and was highly esteemed. Turn-of-the-century Dublin was alive with song as well as talk about singers and opera; families gathered around the parlor piano in the evening to enjoy familiar melodies. Joyce grew up surrounded by music: his father, who had sung as a child on the concert stage in Cork, was known for his fine voice, his mother played the piano, and the family, according to Ellmann, regarded literature as "an aberration from the proper art of music" (*Songs*). Proud of his sweet tenor voice, Joyce delighted in entertaining friends and family with Irish and English folk songs, ballads, barroom ditties, French songs, and always, old sentimental songs. For him, the singing voice, preferably tenor, was the highest form of music. But song also had the power to console, to dispel pain and gloom: he composed a melody or chant to Yeats's melancholy "Who Goes with Fergus," which he sang for his youngest brother, and a year later for his mother, when each lay dying.

Often, touching remembrances of music and its capacity to affect family life appear in Joyce's works, where it can reflect, create, or lighten a mood. During one of the family's all-too-frequent moves in the autobiographical *Stephen Hero,* even the care-worn mother feels "light-hearted" as they carry the precious ancestral portraits in a procession led by the father along the sea-wall, when

> through the clear air Stephen heard his father's voice like a muffled
> flute singing a love-song. He made his mother stop to listen and they
> both leaned on the heavy picture frames and listened [...]. (*SH*, 160)

In a more melancholy mood, tormented by self-doubt and an awareness of the decay and hopelessness surrounding him, Stephen sits at the piano as the day fades:

> He desisted from his chords and waited, bending upon the keyboard
> in silence: and his soul commingled itself with the assailing,
> inarticulate dusk. (*SH*, 162)

This scene is reminiscent of *Chamber Music*'s poem II, where the young girl also bends over the keys of the old piano at twilight.[5]

One of the most poignant of all musical recollections in Joyce occurs in *A Portrait of the Artist,* when Stephen Dedalus returns home, similarly at twilight—"the sad quiet greyblue glow of the dying day"(*P*,

163)—to find his parents once again out hunting for cheaper living quarters to avoid being evicted. His brothers and sisters are sitting around a table made dismal with watered tea, discarded crusts, and lumps of sugared bread. After a pang of remorse at the more favorable circumstances he had enjoyed as the eldest, Stephen listens as their sadness finds voice in song:

> The voice of his youngest brother from the farther side of the fireplace began to sing the air *Oft in the Stilly Night*. One by one the others took up the air until a full choir of voices was singing. They would sing so for hours, melody after melody, glee after glee, till the last pale light died down on the horizon, till the first dark nightclouds came forth and night fell.
>
> He waited for some moments, listening, before he too took up the air with them. He was listening with pain of spirit to the overtone of weariness behind their frail fresh innocent voices. Even before they set out on life's journey they seemed weary already of the way. (*P*, 163–64)

These passages reveal more than the power of music to convey a mood, or to elevate the spirits. They inform us about Joyce's complex relationship with his family, the extent to which he is both a part of them and apart from them. While he can join his siblings in their singing, he is painfully conscious of their bleak future, and extends his pity to "endless generations of children" whose voices will carry echoes of "weariness and pain," who are destined to be "weary of life even before entering upon it" (*P*, 164). And lurking underneath is the absolute certainty that he—son, brother, and author—must flee to escape their fate.

Still another illuminating factor is Joyce's exceptional inclination and ability to *listen*. Undoubtedly this auditory skill is related to, and probably stems from, his love of music, especially vocal music. His uncanny sense of hearing is apparent in the musical quality of his earliest poems, and will assume even greater proportions as his eyesight deteriorates. Listening to music is one of the major themes of "The Dead," where its functions are manifold: music is described, it is a topic of conversation, it is sung, danced to, and performed at the piano (allowing the narrator to indulge in some music criticism); it reaches its highest point of significance with "The Lass of Aughrim," which then haunts everything that follows, transforming moods, determining situation and plot, and ultimately revealing character. Every reader of *Ulysses* and *Finnegans Wake* must be aware of Joyce's ubiquitous and innovative use of operatic arias and the abundant variety of songs (see Bauerle); the sound of language is paramount. As Harry Levin has pointed out, "ultimately it is the sense of hearing that dominates and modulates his prose" (Russel, ed., xii). That special ability to listen and absorb what is heard is part of his genius.

So it seems altogether congruent that Joyce should have found Elizabethan airs so enchanting and stimulating; their wonderfully skillful blending of words and music spoke to his own talent for musical language. Having mastered the techniques of translation and imitation, as well as the rules of prosody, he was now free to test his own virtuosity by confronting the challenge of the past.[6] He even investigated the possibility of having a lute made for him so that he might "coast the south of England from Falmouth to Margate singing old English songs" (*L,* I, 54). But the London instrument maker, who had made a psaltery for Yeats, informed Joyce that lutes were very expensive to make and very difficult to play; he advised a harpsichord. That Joyce's fascination with this past age motivated and lay beneath *Chamber Music* is reinforced by his reference to its "feudal terminology" (Ellmann, 260) and his remarks to Stanislaus:

> It is not a book of love-verses at all, I perceive. But some of them are pretty enough to be put to music. I hope some-one will do so, someone who knows old English music such as I like. Besides they are not pretentious and have a certain grace. (*L,* II, 219)

Unfortunately no one ever did set them in the old English style, inasmuch as no one was aware of his desire. Perhaps some future composer will.

The greatest irony relating to *Chamber Music* is that the very factors that mark Joyce's success in achieving the style of a former age are precisely those that have been the target of the most scathing criticism. "Archaic" and "artificial" are terms frequently used to denigrate the poems. William York Tindall actually chides Joyce for his excessive use of "sweet" and "soft," contending that they help to "give *Chamber Music* its reputation for triviality, emptiness, and sentiment" (218). Surely this professor of literature must have known that these two words were staples of Elizabethan poetry. A line from

Ben Jonson's "Celebration of Charis" that exclaims "O so white! O so soft! O so sweet!" (124) is typical.

One of the most persistent and damning charges leveled against Joyce's little book of verses has been that it lacks substance. However, Renaissance poets, whose goal was delicacy and gracefulness, plus a certain cleverness with words and musical effects, would have regarded "lack of substance" favorably as "lightness," something to be desired. On the question of substance, W. H. Auden offers an enlightening comment:

> [...] the only element taken from the world of everyday reality is the English language. Since words, unlike musical notes, are denotative, his songs have to be "*about*" some topic like love [...] but *the topic is not itself important*. (11; emphasis added)

In support of this analysis, Auden quotes C. S. Lewis:

> His poetry is as nearly passionless as great poetry can be. There are passions somewhere in the background, but a passion, like a metre, is [...] only a starting point [...]. By the time he has finished, the original, the merely actual, passion hardly survives as such. (cited in Auden, 11)

No, it is not James Joyce about whom these discerning remarks are being written—although they might well be—but Thomas Campion, the most outstanding Elizabethan poet-composer. And how delightful that *passionless* is used to describe the lyrics when that is the identical term chosen by Stanislaus to characterize Joyce's! Not only does the explanation of substance in the poetry of Campion apply equally to *Chamber Music,* thus providing a valuable insight, but it also establishes still another link between Joyce and his predecessors.

What exactly are Joyce's poems "about"? While various aspects of music serve as a dominant theme and while nature is often invoked, the major theme is, of course, love: a universal theme through the ages, but dealt with quite differently by the Elizabethans and much later by Joyce. Their treatment of love is distinctive in its emphasis on and exclusive concern with the feelings and moods of the hero-narrator, whose object of love and desire remains simply an object or a sounding board. He pines, he serenades, he pursues a fair maiden; she listens, she trips lightly, she may react with scorn or possibly a willingness to surrender. The poetic conventions of the earlier age and the fact that Elizabethan songs were performed for a live audience placed certain restrictions: content had to be unpretentious and easily understood, emotions were diffused, lovers generalized, images and language relatively familiar and simple, although not without sophistication. Love in the old anthologies and songbooks is often so abstract, consisting as it does of invocations to joy, desire, and fulfillment, that the suitors appear to be directing their entreaties to a mere pronoun or concept rather than a human lover. Joyce's images of the beloved are similarly vague, even featureless, with only a rare glimpse of "Goldenhair" (V). Because Joyce arranged his poems into a suite, he could create the semblance of a plot as another of the connecting links: the narrator progresses from wooing and winning to gradual disillusion and, toward the end, from sadness to desolation. Even so, what most substantially unites the portrayal of love across the centuries is the suggestion of artifice, the idea that love is a game, after all, a circumscribed ritual for a lovesick hero in search of an ideal.

Certainly *Chamber Music* is "about" love, although hardly within "the world of everyday reality." In a letter he sent to Nora in 1909, Joyce is unusually revealing about his state of mind and his outlook on love when he was writing the poems:

> When I wrote them I was a strange lonely boy, walking about by myself at night and thinking that some day a girl would love me. But I never could speak to the girls I used to meet [...]. Then you came to me. You were not in a sense the girl for whom I had dreamed and written the verses you now find so enchanting. She was perhaps (as I saw her in my imagination) *a girl fashioned into a curious grave beauty by the culture of generations before her,* the woman for whom I wrote poems like 'Gentle lady' or 'Thou leanest to the shell of night'. (*L,* II, 236–37; emphasis added)

Ellmann says that three poems—"O Sweetheart, Hear You" (XVIII), "I Would in That Sweet Bosom Be" (VI), and "My Love Is in a Light Attire" (VII)—were "probably" (165) written for Nora, although Stanislaus rather tartly remarks that when his brother actually fell in love, he stopped writing love poems. As a Christmas present for her, Joyce copied his manuscripts of all the verses by hand in India ink on parchment, with their initials intertwined on the cover. He was delighted that she loved the poems, and on another occasion had a special necklace made for her, inscribed with the words "Love is unhappy when love is away," the last line of "Winds of May" (IX). However imaginary or idealized the love motif may have been, it could be taken seriously when it applied.

Even without that significant clue—"a girl fashioned into a curious grave beauty by the culture of generations before her"—the imaginary sweetheart of *Chamber Music* is portrayed in simple, traditional terms as "young and fair" (VIII), "Gentle" (XXVIII), "shy" (IV), and before yielding to her lover, "virginal" (VIII). Yet there are those who cannot countenance simplicity in Joyce and go to fantastic extremes in their quest for hidden meaning and symbols. Thus to one critic she becomes "the indefinite archetype, like Jung's anima, of all that man supposes, suggesting by turns the mistress, the mother, the church, Ireland, and maybe the soul itself" (Tindall, 81). Another critic broadens and inflates that already excessive view of the girl in *Chamber Music* by highlighting her image with allusions to Eve, the Queen of Sheba, the Virgin Mary, Dante's Beatrice, sensual Zoe, and the "witchery" of Circe or Titania, while the "malice" of poem XXVII further suggests Cleopatra, Hester Prynne, and Molly Bloom (Boyle, 24, 28–29). Combining a multitude of dissimilar traits (passionate-cold, shy-determined, sensitive-selfish, talented, lovely, resentful, guilt-ridden, and possessive), "Joyce's woman" emerges for Boyle not only as "a woman of infinite variety" but also "a clear Irish figure" (28). Truly, some critical pronouncements can confound common sense. Surely no one can take seriously Tindall's notion that "I Would in That Sweet Bosom Be" (VI) indicates "a regression to a maternal fantasy" (188). And by what strange logic can the lines of poem VII, "My love goes lightly, holding up / Her dress with dainty hand," be contorted into giving the earth "something of her substance" (Tindall, 74)? Perhaps this silly comment is intended as a reminder of the chamberpot joke. In any event, such misreadings are a disservice to the poems; they falsify and ridicule Joyce's achievement.

The opening lyric of *Chamber Music* clearly illustrates the efficacy of Joyce's many uses of simplicity.

> Strings in the earth and air
>   Make music sweet;
> Strings by the river where
>   The willows meet.

There's music along the river
　　For Love wanders there,
Pale flowers on his mantle,
　　Dark leaves on his hair.

All softly playing,
　　With head to the music bent,
And fingers straying
　　Upon an instrument. (I)

The words flow gently, the mood is cheerful, the pace leisurely, which is probably one reason this poem has been set to music more frequently than any other. Themes are introduced and smoothly blended, as music and nature pay homage to love. Elizabethan resemblances are immediately apparent: the word "air," which is to become so significant; the adjective "pale," which shares Chaucer's meaning of *lovesick* and fits Shakespeare's description of Benedick as "pale with love" (*Much Ado,* I.i.233), which should not mean "funereal" or "deathly," as has been claimed; and certainly the use of those recurrent words, "sweet" and "soft." Furthermore, the phrase "to music bent" comes directly from Campion, whose *Two Bookes of Ayres* includes a song that begins with "To Musicke Bent" (Campion, *Selected Songs,* 56). Far from disapproving of "borrowing," the Elizabethans freely appropriated whatever suited their purpose. John Hollander says that composers often "raided miscellanies [...] as well as published books and poems in manuscript" (16), sometimes even altering them to fit a musical setting. Poets too commonly borrowed words or phrases or an unusual rhyme from each other without censure; in poem XXVII Joyce transforms Dowland's "poison'd dart" into a portmanteau word (Dowland, 8). Poem XXXV of *Chamber Music,* linked by Joyce to the final poem as "a tailpiece" and usually attributed to the influence of Verlaine, also is indebted to Dowland for its uncommon structure and rhyme scheme.[7] His *Fifty Songs* includes a poem with these lines:

I'll go to the woods,
And alone,
Make my moan, (Dowland, 30–31)

which bear more than a passing resemblance to Joyce's

All day I hear the noise of waters
    Making moan
Sad as the seabird is when going
    Forth alone
He hears the winds cry to the waters'
    Monotone. (XXXV)

But unfortunately, Joyce commentators have been less attentive to the many Elizabethan connections—particularly those apparent in poem I—preferring to call attention to the dubious proposition that the last stanza with "fingers straying / Upon an instrument" signifies masturbation.[8] Certainly there can be no doubt that sexual activities and earthiness are integral to *Ulysses,* but just as surely they are quite alien to *Chamber Music,* where even the consummation of love is delicately represented by "dewy dreams" and "veils / Of grey and golden gossamer" (XV). To twist Joyce's poetic phrases (or the title) into risqué or scatological double entendres goes beyond mere humor or mockery; it belittles particular poems and violates the spirit of the entire collection.

Love may be the dominant theme, the driving force that gives movement and coherence to Joyce's suite of songs, but it is "music sweet" (I) that surrounds the lovers and animates the scene. Poem II introduces the young woman as she "bends upon the yellow keys" of the old piano; in the lyric that follows, "sweet" and "invisible" harps are "playing unto Love" (III). Throughout, other instruments and other sounds can be heard: "The bugles of the cherubim" (XI), "flowery bells of morn" (XV), "piping poets" (XXVII), as well as the call of thrushes (XVI), the hum of wild bees (X), and "choirs of faery" (XV). Song is indispensable to both courtship and the demise of love; the narrator woos her with singing and she, Goldenhair, responds with "a merry air" (V). The end of love is also expressed in song:

Gentle lady, do not sing
    Sad songs about the end of love;
Lay aside sadness and sing
    How love that passes is enough. (XXVIII)

Even the ubiquitous winds are musical, whistling "merrily" (XXXIII) or weaving "a music of sighs" (XIV). Truly music is everywhere, and

its flavor is distinctly Elizabethan. As Campion advises in one of his
songs in *The Lord's Maske:*

> Courtship and Musicke suite with love,
>   They both are workes of passion;
> Happie is he whose words can move,
>   Yet sweete notes helpe perswasion.
> Mixe your words with Musicke then [...].[9]
> (Campion, *Selected Songs,* 130)

Nature also plays a significant role in the poems of both ages: as
theme, as metaphor, or simply as background. Images of sky, sea, trees,
sunrise, or moonlight are traditional. Weather too is conspicuous: all
the poets seem to agree that sunlight is "sweet," but Joyce's elements
include rain that evokes memories and versatile winds that range from
gentle to wild or desolate. References to the seasons recur frequently in
Elizabethan poetry, and here Joyce gains an advantage with his cyclical
arrangement: his seasons can unfold chronologically, from merry
springtime through the heat of summer, then from "The year, the year is
gathering" (XXXIII) to "The voice of the winter / Is heard at the door"
(XXXIV). Time of day, though not in sequence, is specified in many of
the verses, often with some of Joyce's most colorful imagery: "The
twilight turns from amethyst / To deep and deeper blue" (II); the lovers
lie "In deep cool shadow / At noon of day" (XX); there is "starlight"
(XII) and "nightdew" (XIV), as well as a "hooded moon" (XII); and
"Eastward the gradual dawn prevails / Where softly burning fires
appear" (XV).

In matters of prosody Joyce is a diligent student, following his
predecessors closely. Stanzaic structure, rhyme scheme, metric feet,
and number of stresses to a line are strikingly similar, with only
occasional variations. Most verses are brief, with anywhere from one to
four stanzas, although the number of lines within each stanza may vary.
As for rhyme, twenty-eight of Joyce's lyrics conform to the most
common pattern of the Elizabethans, *abba* or *abab,* with or without the
final *cc* couplet. Several of his poems have an *abcb* rhyme scheme,
abbab if the stanza has five lines, and examples of these can also be
found in the old songbooks. Sixteenth- and seventeenth-century poets,
for all their adroitness at adhering to the rules, easily tolerated
irregularities. But even they might have been puzzled by the strange
disorder of poem XIV, the one with echoes from the Song of Solomon,

which Joyce considered central to the book. Its opening stanza is only slightly deviant with *abbb,* but the pattern shifts to *cbba,* then *deef,* and finally to the unclassifiable *bfeb.* Was he experimenting with flouting the conventions? After all, Campion had warned against forced or superfluous rhyme. Or was Joyce drawing aside, for a moment, the curtain of this idealized neo-Elizabethan world to permit a glimpse of the modern? In actuality, the chaotic rhyming of "My dove" becomes insignificant, virtually irrelevant, inasmuch as the predominance of the *b* rhyme in *arise, lies, eyes,* and *sighs,* occurring ten times, readily suffices to supply continuity and focus. As for meter, Joyce shares with Dowland a fondness for the trochee, which lends itself to the resonant one-syllable verbs so favored in *Chamber Music:* "lean," "bend," "sleep," and so forth. The trochee virtually takes over in the highly stylized "Lightly Come or Lightly Go" (XXV), just as it does in Campion's metrically unusual poem XI (Campion, *Selected Songs,* 46). A more uncommon metrical foot, the spondee, which in a 1606 song proclaimed emphatically, "Down, Down, Proud Mind" (Corkine), is used effectively by Joyce in "Gentle lady, do not sing / *Sad songs* about the end of love," and again in the second stanza, "Sing about the long *deep sleep* / Of lovers that are dead" (XXVIII; emphasis added).

Altogether, the counterparts and correspondences between Joyce's lyrics and those of the Renaissance appear to be as deliberate as they are numerous, and far more extensive than former critics have allowed. The only significant departure from tradition is *Chamber Music*'s format, which Joyce fashioned into a suite or song cycle. With its conventional but flexible story linking the poems, the love motif serves as "a starting point"; it is what the lyrics are "about." The many references to music and the repetition of key words and phrases furnish another bond. Then Joyce creates a cyclical effect with the change of seasons and by rotating the various times of day. But his most striking innovation was the clever way he threaded the word "air" through the verses. That sound, along with its rhyming counterparts, occurs fittingly as a motif twenty-four times as an end rhyme and many other times within the lines of the first twenty-five poems. In addition to frequently using "fair," "where," and "hair," Joyce calls attention to the word "air" by featuring it in all its multiple connotations. The melody sung by Goldenhair or played on the piano is one kind of "air." But there is also celestial "air" surrounding the earth, as well as breezy "air" blown by the wind. Quite different is the suggestion of "many a pretty air" (XXIV), signifying demeanor, with an additional implication of "putting on airs." And, of course, all of these are to be found in a book of "airs" called *Chamber Music*. Just to have captured the essence of the Golden Age of poetry and music would itself be a remarkable achievement, but Joyce has gone beyond, adding yet another touch of artistry and serendipity. The applause of Campion, Dowland, and all the others seems to echo down the centuries.

THE MUSIC OF PALMER

If, as Joyce indicated, the poems were meant to be set to music, and if, indeed, music is the element without which the lyrics are incomplete, then composer Geoffrey Molyneux Palmer is of paramount importance. His musical settings so faithfully translate every nuance of Joyce's little verses, very often augmenting and highlighting each text, that *Chamber Music* is both illuminated and transformed. Joyce always valued this composer's songs above all others, though he saw only ten of Palmer's thirty-two settings.[10] An extraordinary number of composers have recognized the musical qualities and possibilities of the poems: most settings are for voice and piano, though occasionally for a guitar or other instrument, and the music ranges from traditional to contemporary. Some songs are beautiful, but many are not; some fit the words admirably, while others overpower the delicate verses with heavy chords, or an avalanche of arpeggios, or graceless and jarring dissonances. Some are simply uninteresting or undistinguished, while still others show such a disparity between words and music that Joyce's lines seem to serve merely as a springboard, thus rendering the poem negligible. But the eight settings Palmer sent in 1909—a group of five in February and three more in July—met with immediate approval. Joyce, whose knowledge of music, especially vocal music, was considerable, evidently recognized at once that these graceful and lovely melodies with their fitting piano parts were eminently suited to his lyrics. In his earliest replies to the composer, he expressed his pleasure along with his praise. Joyce also mentioned that he had shown the songs to his singing teacher, who "admires them very much" (*L,* I, 66); a few months later he wrote "All the persons to whom I showed your music think it very distinguished" (*L,* I, 67), and in another letter, "I think your music is very elegant and would like it to be sung" (*L,* I, 70). And many years later, long after their correspondence had ended, Joyce wrote to his son, who was in New York preparing for an audition, urging him to sing his three Palmer favorites ("Gentle Lady,"

"At That Hour," "Donnycarney"), describing them as "better than any of the subsequent ones" (*L*, III, 348).

The first indication of the young and as yet unknown G. Molyneux Palmer, as he usually signed his name, and the only available source of information about their relationship, is found in the letters and notes they exchanged. Joyce's side of the correspondence, which spanned a period of twenty-four years from 1907 to 1931, is always clear and consistent. Palmer, on the other hand, emerges as a somewhat shadowy figure: reticent, often pessimistic, occasionally contradictory, and on the whole rather formal. Although his replies seem candid and straightforward, his startling failure to respond to Joyce's urgent messages about a realistic plan to "bring [...] out" the songs (cited in Russel, ed., 7)—revealed in a series of notes unpublished until recently—remains an enigma.[11] Nevertheless, the letters contain valuable and rewarding material, even if the view of Palmer is spare. He seems to have been the only one, apart from Stanislaus, with whom Joyce discussed his intent or revealed his judgment and preferences concerning the music for the *Chamber Music* poems.

Certain facts about Palmer are known.[12] As a minor composer of two operas and three cantatas based on Irish folklore, a few instrumental pieces, and many songs based on other poets (twenty-eight of them in the British Library), he won several prizes at Dublin's Feis Ceoil; he also merited a brief biography in *Grove's Dictionary of Music and Musicians* from the third to the fifth editions, and in other publications listing composers. Nowhere was there any mention of Joyce songs, which, as it was later revealed, he kept secret from family and friends. Few in the musical circles of London or Dublin even remembered his name, and tracking him down required methods not unlike those in a detective story; travel, several key interviews, and a variety of investigative paths eventually yielded pertinent information. Palmer's father, a clergyman whose ancestry went back to a Reverend Palmer of County Kerry who had taken part in the 1688 battle of Killowen, served as vicar in parishes in and around London. His mother, a descendant of former Lord Mayor Hone of Dublin, was the author of several didactic books for boys; it was she who gave Palmer the gift of *Chamber Music* when it first appeared. Although born and educated in England, Palmer made it clear in a letter to Joyce dated March 25, 1909, that he considered himself an Irishman: "I am an Irishman myself though I have lived nearly all my life in England" (Palmer MS., Cornell). At Oxford he had the distinction at nineteen of being the youngest recipient of a Music Baccalaureate ever, but in his final year he was stricken with multiple sclerosis. The illness would recur periodically throughout his life, eventually making him a total invalid, though he lived to be seventy-five. After a few years of semiretirement, during which he was choirmaster and organist in his father's church, he entered the Royal College of Music in London. There he studied with Charles Villiers Stanford, a composer whose influence on many British musicians was considerable, and whose predilection for Brahms can sometimes be detected in the music of Palmer. It was during his last month as a student that he wrote his first letter to Joyce on July 13, 1907, requesting permission to set the poems.

Having decided by 1910 to settle in Ireland, where he lived until his death in 1957, Palmer apparently felt enough at ease to seek advice from Joyce about where and how to find affordable lodgings. The reply was kindly and generous, offering practical recommendations about how much to pay and where to advertise, volunteering possible contacts, and also suggesting that the composer apply directly to the Irish Church in Dublin, stating his qualifications, which "are surely *too* good!" (*L,* I, 69). It was in this same letter that Joyce said, "I fancy by your name that you are a protestant." Palmer did secure a post as organist at the Protestant church in Mallow, County Cork, where for the first time he was able to live independently; his 1913 letter was unusually cheerful and loquacious. The years that followed were productive musically, and he became part of the intellectual life of Dublin, even taking an interest in the Gaelic movement and learning the language. The National Library's manuscript room contains letters from various musicians, as well as from such known figures as Douglas Hyde, Alfred Graves, and Patrick Tuohy (who had just returned after painting Joyce's portrait), along with some from the widow of William Allingham, whose poems Palmer had set to music. A message of March 20, 1918, from Grattan Flood, music historian and author of the write-up in *Grove,* exclaims, "You are embalmed now among the immortals! And so am I!" (Palmer MS., Ireland). Out of these benign and promising years came the last two songs sent to Joyce in 1921.

But by then the illness had been worsening, and Palmer was compelled to move into the home of his sisters, now in Sandycove, who took care of him for the rest of his long life. (The house is on Marine Parade fronting the bay, and by still another coincidence, unnoted or unremarked by Joyce, is within obvious sight of Joyce's famous Martello tower.) Evidently Palmer was quite reticent about his infirmity, mentioning it only in his last letter extant (July 14, 1919) when he wrote, "My leg makes me quite a cripple now" (Palmer MS., Cornell). His stoicism in the face of growing paralysis brought praise and sympathy from the prestigious Hamilton Harty, best remembered as conductor of Manchester's Hallé Orchestra:

> I was distressed and sorry to read your letter [...]. I had no idea you were so much troubled in your life [...]. I felt that your cheerful acceptance of ill-fortune was a very fine thing [...].
>
> Another thing—quite apart from what I have been talking about, may I say that I have great respect for your musical gifts, and will be happy if I could find a work of yours suitable for production here. (Palmer MS., Ireland)

From the very beginning in 1909, Joyce expressed far more than a passing interest in Palmer's songs; he wrote that he was "much honoured" by them and went on to "admire" the music of the parenthesis in "I Would in That Sweet Bosom Be," as well as "the way you reproduce the changes of stress" in "O Cool Is the Valley" (*L*, II, 227). Not identified, unfortunately, is "the last song (which pleases me best)" (*L*, II, 227); any one of the remaining three might qualify.[13] Joyce also added the perceptive comment: "I hope you will find a good singer for them as your music needs to be well sung" (*L*, II, 227). No doubt his own experience as a singer enabled him to realize that the seeming simplicity of many Palmer settings is deceptive, often masking sophisticated and innovative musical touches that only a performer might recognize. Palmer agreed to Joyce's request to "kindly let me know of their success" (*L*, II, 228) in the event that they were sung, adding a pessimistic note: "I fear the music is not likely to be popular" (Palmer MS., March 25, 1909, Cornell). The second group of settings, sent a few months later, became Joyce's personal favorites for the rest of his life and prompted an even more enthusiastic reply:

> The second three songs please me better than the first five. The setting of the first ["Donnycarney"] is very delicate and the effect is finely sustained in the third ["Gentle Lady"]. The rendering of 'Play on, invisible harps, &c' ["At That Hour"] follows the change of the verse splendidly. (*L*, I, 67)

The strenuous and persistent efforts made by Joyce to promote the Palmer settings, to have them "brought out," began that same year, continued intermittently, and would reach a dramatic climax nearly two decades later. During his brief visit to Dublin, shortly after receiving the second group, Joyce tried several approaches. He persuaded the secretary of Feis Ceoil to write to the composer requesting the eight songs completed (Joyce indicated that the entire collection was being set, as indeed he had urged Palmer to do) so that singers could try them and perhaps perform them at a Feis concert. However, when two months brought no reply (possibly a harbinger of what was to come), Joyce wrote, asking "Have you done anything in the matter?" (*L*, II, 261). If Palmer lacked enthusiasm for a wider audience, certainly Joyce did not. He consulted the manager of Maunsel & Company, where *Dubliners* was under consideration, about the possibility of printing the songs in conjunction with a music press. In addition, having somehow learned that the proprietor, Maunsel Hone, was related to the Palmer family, Joyce suggested that the composer try that approach. After hearing one of the four songs they had published by an Irish composer named Charlotte Milligan Fox, Joyce assured Palmer that "your music is much finer" (*L*, II, 261). A postcard sent to Stanislaus, now in Trieste, during this period asks him to send the eight songs, "carefully registered" (*L*, II, 271), to a singer identified only as W. Sheean.

Many years later in Paris, Joyce spoke to John McCormack, with whom he was on friendly terms, about Palmer's settings, and in two separate letters (December 1920 and January 1921), pressed the composer to send his three favorites, "keyed up to tenor pitch" (*L*, III, 38), to the famous singer. However unsuccessful Joyce may have been in his strenuous efforts to gain for this "delicate music [...] the appreciation which it deserves" (*L*, III, 35), he continued to search for ways to publicize the songs. His efforts were to become even more insistent during the final and most dramatically revealing phase of their relationship, when what he had hoped for and had sought for so many years became a reality. At last he found someone in Paris who was willing to publish the settings: a Polish impresario named Jan Slivinsky, whose press was called Au Sacre du Printemps. The mounting urgency of a series of six notes sent to Palmer between October 29, 1927, and February 5, 1928, is conclusive evidence of Joyce's commitment. Despite a message to a friend in Dublin that he was "painfully ill" and "suffered the worst Xmas and New Year I can remember" (*L*, III, 168), Joyce pursued the Palmer matter with energy and intensity. After a request for six settings "up to A flat or G natural," and obviously referring to a question from the composer, the second of Joyce's six notes to Palmer, dated December 4, 1927, reads: "Yes. Please send your Ms to that address and print me a list of the songs you are offering so that I may try to arrange a Zurich version to be printed too." (This is the first of five notes that were recently published in Russel, ed., 9–10.) The next postcard is dated January 1, 1928: "Best wishes for the New Year. Your ms came and I took it to Slivinsky. As soon as I hear from him I will let you know." By January 10 a plan had been formulated:

> Herewith is Slivinsky's estimate. Can you pay this amount. Total 2800 frs (£22) of which 1200 (£10 about) now and rest on publication. Sale price 27 frs a copy (5p about). The nos of the songs refer to *Chamber Music* not to your MS. If you took 200 copies I think the other 100 could be sold here.

Apparently worried by Palmer's failure to respond, Joyce sent another note one week later (January 17), dramatically reducing the cost:

> You may count out my fees. If Cape (my present publisher) says anything I will say you paid them all years ago through Mathews, who is dead. [...] He [Slivinsky] and I will go thirds with you, if you like, i.e. 900 francs each. If this suits you, please remit him [...] 450 francs and the work will be put in hand. The other 450 is payable on publication. 300 copies at 4/-. I think they will sell for you here and in London, if you are known there. The Dublin sales are unimportant.

Even this generous offer elicited no reply, although Joyce made one more and equally futile attempt on February 5:

> On basis outlined Slivinsky would give you free one-third of edition, i.e., 168 copies to dispose of as you please. If this will do please let me know. He is not much interested in any but very modern music, Antheil, Stravinsky, etc. If not, I will try the 2 song proposal.

Now all plans had to be dropped, and the correspondence seemed to have ended. However, a brief exchange took place in 1931 when Joyce received a letter from the composer asking if he had heard a program of Palmer's other music, broadcast on Radio Eirann; Joyce had not.

Whether the letter contained any explanation or apology for his silence
is not known, since this is one of the missing notes, but it is unlikely.
Nevertheless, Joyce's response, written with eloquent simplicity and
restraint, is a testimony to his kindness and magnanimity:

> It is a great pity you were not able to proceed with the publication I
> had arranged with Slivinsky in Paris some years ago. Still I hope you
> will find a publisher in England for the songs. If I can do anything to
> that end let me know as I liked them very much. (*L*, I, 304)

Any attempt to explain Palmer's strange reluctance to publish his
Joyce songs, particularly his wordless and cryptic withdrawal when the
project was about to be realized, can only be speculative. Lack of funds
was the reason offered by Palmer's nephew (son of the only one of
Palmer's four sisters who married), but he hardly knew his uncle,
recalling only a quiet, "very Irish" man in a wheelchair whom he had
visited occasionally. While all possibilities must be considered, surely
Palmer had coped with writers' fees before, although his income, at
best, must have been negligible. To what extent his illness might have
been a factor remains unknown. Was he not flattered to be so highly
esteemed by a famous author? And did he not appreciate Joyce's efforts
and the financial sacrifice involved in the final proposal to publish the
songs?

There are two other plausible and far-reaching explanations:
Palmer's secrecy about his Joyce settings and his total dependency on
his sisters. To begin with, no one in those years before or during the
Paris undertaking knew anything about his connection with Joyce or
Chamber Music. A close friend, Rhoda Coghill, for whom Palmer had
written several piano pieces—an elderly and dignified woman, a
concert pianist who had also won Feis prizes and was still performing
on Radio Eirann in 1981—was indignant at the very idea, insisting that
if Geoffrey had composed Joyce songs, he would have told her about it.
And had a Chicago Joyce collector not written to the sisters after he
learned about the composer's death, urging them to search for anything
relating to Joyce, the manuscripts might never have come to light.

The reason for Palmer's secrecy becomes clearer once his family
situation and background are understood. His eldest sister had left
England in 1919, crossing the Irish Sea to found and become
headmistress for the next thirty years of a very proper and conservative
English-style school for wealthy Irish girls, called Hillcrest (now

Rathdown). Shortly after, another sister followed to teach at the private school, and a third came to help take care of their brother, serving also as a part-time instructor. They were highly respected and the library was later dedicated to their memory; obviously, respectability was essential to the Palmer name.[14] The truth of this observation was unexpectedly confirmed during my fortuitous encounter at the Martello tower with two former students of the school: they reacted with considerable shock to the idea that *any* Palmer—even the remote brother of their venerated "Miss Gladys" and "Miss Phyllis," whom they had known well—might have had any connection with James Joyce! Since respectability and caution were probably intrinsic to the upbringing of a vicar's family, it is also possible that Geoffrey, too, was proper and conservative. Brian Boydell, a professor of music at Trinity College, remembered Palmer vaguely as "a nineteenth-century gentleman" (Russel, ed., 11).

In any event, the fact that his sisters supported him and took care of him for all those years had to be an important factor in accounting for his silence. After all, when the correspondence began long ago in 1907, Joyce was simply a little-known poet, author of a "beautiful little collection" called *Chamber Music*. But *Dubliners* had caused considerable wrangling in Ireland, while *A Portrait of the Artist as a Young Man* and later *Ulysses* escalated the controversy into outrage. Therefore, when all the circumstances are weighed—the Palmers' prudence and sense of propriety, the composer's disabling illness and total dependency on his sisters, along with the clamor and censure surrounding Joyce's works (even more extreme in Ireland)—it seems inevitable that ambivalence, withdrawal, and silence would supplant the gratification of having a famous but controversial author as patron and champion.

WORDS AND MUSIC TOGETHER: PALMER'S SETTINGS OF JOYCE

What matters most, of course, is the remarkable legacy of Geoffrey Molyneux Palmer: his songs. That Joyce, an experienced singer himself, recognized their merit immediately and never wavered from his original judgment that the settings were elegant and distinguished— the finest of the many that he was familiar with—is a tribute to his musical taste and understanding, as well as to Palmer's artistry. No doubt the composer's admiration and appreciation of the lyrics, expressed when he wrote, "I have been reading with the greatest of pleasure your beautiful collection of poems" (Palmer MS., July 13, 1907, Cornell), contributed to the unerring "rightness" of his settings. The music that Palmer composed for all but four of the thirty-six verses not only follows the structure of the poems, but consistently and often brilliantly captures the graceful spirit of each lyric. Always attentive to meaning, the sound of the words, and every shift in mood, he faithfully observes rhythm, meter, and stress, along with each caesura or enjambment. He remains true to Joyce's concept of a suite of songs by establishing continuity with thematic relationships, rhythmic patterns, and occasional repetition, thus creating a musical cycle. While his music belongs essentially to the tradition of early twentieth-century British art songs—filled with flowing melodies, shifts from major to minor, recurring accidentals, and brief modulations—hints of Brahms's architectural richness and Schubert's lyricism can also be heard. Yet somehow Palmer retains a distinctive voice of his own. Even his mildly innovative touches, such as uncommon intervals, dissonant chords, or endings in a different key, are blended with older techniques of ornamentation. Except for the dissimilar music of the final poem, "I Hear an Army" (XXXVI), with its powerful effects and dramatic recitative, Palmer's settings are subtle rather than obvious, elegant rather than emphatic. This music interprets as it surrounds and merges with the text, integrating words with melody and accompaniment, reinforcing the poem; it also augments and transforms many of the verses, making words and music as inseparable, for example, as "Greensleeves" or "Danny Boy." Altogether, Palmer's sensitivity to every aspect of the style, substance, and internal music of *Chamber Music* is truly extraordinary.

Even a small sampling of Palmer's songs will demonstrate the range and diversity of his music, aspects of his style and methods of composition, and most notably, the wondrous skill and sensitivity he brings to Joyce's lyrics. The simple opening poem sets the stage and introduces the themes: sweet-sounding music and images of nature surround the personification of love (Figure 3–1).[15] So faithfully does Palmer translate those themes into music that his setting, too, sounds simple, though it is not. Running eighth-note triplets evoke the flow of the river, the shimmer of the willows, and the continual presence of music, while love reaches up to the singer's highest note. The composer creates "a sensuous musical arch," says Robert White, with "soaring melodic phrases" that "would not seem out of place in a Puccini aria"

(39–40).[16] The three short stanzas are through-composed (i.e., new music for each), achieving cohesiveness by means of similar melodic passages and the repetition of rhythmical configurations. Since the opening couplets start with the same word and have identical meters, Palmer uses the same melody; even the resolution of each couplet is almost the same, so that "willows meet" echoes "music sweet." While the four lines rhyme perfectly, "air" requires a stress and is held with a quarter note tied to an eighth, while the corresponding "where," which needs no accent, is enjambed with the running notes that push forward to the phrase's end. Simple, light, and exactly right. The two stanzas that follow, however varied in melodic line and rhythmic patterns, are closely related both to each other and to the beginning. Also noteworthy is Palmer's masterly use of word painting on "straying," a technique he will employ very dramatically in song III. Finally, the staccato effects of the piano at the end of the song—with the word "instrument" and in the brief solo passage after—add a sprightly and wonderfully imaginative touch with their suggestion of pizzicato strings.

"Gentle Lady" (XXVIII), the song from the group of three favorites that Joyce described as "finely sustained," is one of the most poignant and richly textured settings. The interweaving of major and minor modes and the profusion of accidentals add color, as the piano enriches with deeply resonant chords in a lovely solo passage between stanzas and again just before the delayed ending, "Love is aweary now." Just as Joyce repeats certain key words—love, sing, and sleep— so Palmer repeats his three-measure motif, with only slight rhythmic variations to accommodate the words. So smoothly and euphoniously does this elegant music encompass the poem that "Gentle lady" ranks as one of everybody's favorites.

Also from the group of three, "At That Hour" (III) is based on a poem that differs from the others in many respects; it is complex and presents several challenges. More ambitious, more grandiose, and less light or Elizabethan than most, this lyric is almost rhapsodic in its celebration of "invisible harps" and "The pale gates of sunrise." One of the longer poems, its prosody—so uniform elsewhere, with the usual four or five stresses to a line—is decidedly irregular, lacking consistency. The only traditional metrical pattern seems to be the three stresses in the final line of each stanza, and although four or five stresses may predominate in the main body of the text, they do so without alternating or revealing any predictable pattern. Moreover, two lines appear to have six accents, depending on how the words are scanned. However problematic these irregularities may be for a composer, Palmer not only succeeds in overcoming them, but reconciles them brilliantly; the result is one of his most beautiful songs.

To highlight at once the dramatic essence of Joyce's poem, Palmer begins the song with an octave leap, repeats it at the start of the second line, and still again at the opening of the second stanza. The elaborate word painting of sixteenth notes "playing unto Love" compels the singer, according to tenor Robert White, "to be both the strings and the strummer of those harps, all the while leading up to a voice-carried break of dawn on the word 'sunrise'" (40). But it is precisely that strumming that disguises the problem of those two lines, "Of harps playing unto Love to unclose / The pale gates of sunrise?" Here is a rare but inescapable instance of awkwardness in Joyce's diction. Even the smooth enjambment of "The pale gates" cannot conceal the gracelessness of "unto Love to unclose." But the music can and does. Palmer cleverly emphasizes the playfulness of those sixteenth notes on "playing," then slows down their pace with quarter notes in reverse order, and what's more, adds to the spirit of play by using the same three notes—E flat, C, and F—for five full measures from "night wind" to the brink of "sunrise," a novel strategy for Palmer and not without risk. But this passage does serve to divert attention away from the short-lived awkwardness, and whether the composer did it intentionally or instinctively hardly matters. These same measures also function as a pause, an interlude suspended in time, to heighten the dramatic moment when the sun rises on G, modulating into a bright C major. Ensconced between exhilarating leaps and musical radiance, the repetitious passage is saved from the danger of monotony.

Another problem, the irregularities of meter in the opening line of each stanza, is rendered inconsequential by the music. Palmer gives four stresses to the first (*hour, all, things,* re-*pose*), three strong accents (*all,* re-*pose,* a-*lone*), and two weak (*things, you*), but in the last stanza where the mood shifts from contemplative to joyous, both "Play" and "on" require stress, so only the singer's interpretation of "unto" will determine whether the line has five or six accents. However, metrical inconsistency becomes trivial, particularly in the majestic final stanza where the sudden and exuberant change of mood and key—described by Joyce as "follow[ing] the change of verse splendidly"—expresses a stately grandeur. To find a fitting conclusion for this imposing and complex poem, Joyce went back to his opening lyric, rearranging its key words into "Soft sweet music in the air above / And in the earth below," establishing one of the many connections linking the poems. Palmer follows suit with a melody reminiscent of his earlier setting, calling attention to the borrowing by having the piano recapitulate that song's final motif, complete with staccato effects. Altogether, the music transcends and transforms a difficult and challenging text; the setting is not only one of Joyce's favorites, as well as one of the most impressive and outstanding of the collection, but it is also a testimony to Palmer's great talent.

Another gem is "Donnycarney" (XXXI), which portrays a cheerful remembrance of love: no longer ardent or sad, but nostalgic now that it has settled into the past tense. Palmer's captivating and lyrical melody has the flavor of an Irish love song, perhaps a response to Joyce's only mention of Ireland; Donnycarney was a rural area outside Dublin where lovers frequently strolled at dusk. Since twilight is when bats customarily emerge, the function of the bat that "flew from tree to tree" is clearly to signify the time of day. Inasmuch as the lovers continue to walk and talk peacefully, without any sign of distress, it is also obvious that this bat is benign, not threatening.[17] Palmer captures its swoop with a dramatic, almost modal leap from F up to D flat. Although the second stanza starts out with the same lovely melody that begins the song, nothing in the words can justify a repeat of that exciting jump; instead, with great ingenuity, the composer provides an echo of the leap in the vocal space between "murmuring" and the jubilant "O, happily!"; this time the singer must reach for an even higher interval, a diminished seventh to E flat. Word painting is also part of the charm of this setting; the piano has been "murmuring" all along and the singer adds another touch on the actual word. After the music gently modulates into A flat and then returns to the original key of F major, the song ends with still another leap, this time an octave down. Finally, fragments of that haunting melody are heard at the piano, resonating through the air and into memory, to conclude the piece. Every aspect of this setting, including its *molto espressivo* directive, contributes to its outstanding musical quality. That this song was Joyce's particular favorite comes as no surprise, for it is truly a jewel of the collection.

Many other varieties of style and method distinguish Palmer's settings. The brief and frolicsome "Lean Out of the Window" (V) and "Winds of May" (IX) delight as they scamper by; "Lightly Come or Lightly Go" (XXV) displays similar gaiety and charm, though it is longer and ends on a note of sadness. "Goldenhair" is particularly enchanting because of its imaginative evocation of the fairy tale of Rapunzel, a mere suggestion in the poem, but amplified in the exuberant setting:

> The high tessitura of the last six measures has the singer up in the stratosphere of the beloved's tower-window retreat. Just as in the children's tale, Palmer suddenly brings the golden "ladder," as it were, tumbling to earth on the downward octave leap of those last two words, "golden hair!" (White, 40)

Totally dissimilar in style and mood is poem XVII, where the theme of betrayal by a friend (a situation that recurs in several of Joyce's works) is offered without color or the embellishment of an adjective. For this poem, musical treatment might seem unlikely, yet in twelve short bars Palmer's setting conveys the pain of a broken friendship. Although the song segues in G major from the preceding and far happier "O Cool Is the Valley" (XVI), and then ends in D major, the key signature seems unsettled in between. Hints of a minor mode, diminished chords, and accidentals provide color, but in a somewhat darkened hue; the repetition of the slow, stately melody for each line of the verse adds to the melancholy tone. The solid chords may very well represent the lover's only solace: the reassuring presence of his beloved. Not only is the setting remarkably true to the words and spirit of Joyce's poem, but the overall effect of the music is arresting, almost spellbinding.

In many ways "Sleep Now" (XXXIV)—originally intended to close the cycle, until Joyce and his brother decided to add two more in what they called a tailpiece—is one of the most unusual and distinctive of all the poems. With its stark contrast between the peacefulness of sleep inside and the threatening voice of winter outside, this lyric creates a new dimension. Sleep, the tranquillity it can bring, and the warning of death in "Sleep no more!" are fundamental to human experience, and by giving them expression in simple but lyrical form, Joyce imbued *Chamber Music* with a moment of profundity. The plain and often-repeated words that recur within the lines, across the stanzas, and as part of the rhyme scheme have a soothing, almost hypnotic effect, and the steady two-beat rhythm also helps to bind all the elements into a compelling unity. Palmer's beautiful setting is equally distinguished; every aspect of the music is completely in harmony with the poem. The simple and very slow melody, always softly but insistently rendered, is extremely powerful and moving. Each repetition of the phrase "Sleep now"—and the corresponding "peace now" of the second stanza—is set to a descending interval, the first time a third, and the ones that follow, a fourth. The "voice of the winter" summons a different melodic phrase and introduces a brief touch of the minor, after which the final stanza goes back to the original motifs of the beginning. Also striking are the solid basic chords of the piano, for they add depth and a dynamic force as they softly support and enrich the prolonged, stressed vowels; frequently they appear on an off-beat, between the sung notes, making them more emphatic. Although Joyce received this setting (one of the last two sent in 1921) and sent a letter in response, he made no mention of the music.

A very long time was to elapse before Palmer's settings were discovered; they had always been assumed missing or lost, and Joyce's copies had never turned up. Several years before his death in 1957, the composer evidently had a change of heart, indicating that he was now willing to publish the songs, but no publisher was interested. The Joyce collector who purchased them from Palmer's sisters in 1958 offered the modest sum of £20 (then worth about $56) for the thirty-two holographs, which had been divided and bound into two volumes. The sisters, now elderly and retired, having no idea what price to expect, agreed. He, in turn, bequeathed them to the Morris Library at the University of Southern Illinois at Carbondale, where they were housed in the Croessmann Collection of James Joyce. According to the librarian there, I was the first person ever to ask for them in the twenty-two years since they were acquired. What matters now is that the songs are available, Joyce's hopes have been realized, and Palmer's remarkable achievement is gaining recognition and appreciation.

Apart from the wondrous power of many if not most of Palmer's songs to enchant the listener, the full significance of this composer goes beyond his ability to create music so admirably and felicitously attuned to each poem. What his accomplishment proves is the essentiality of music to Joyce's *Chamber Music;* it substantiates the judgment that without music, *Chamber Music* is missing a vital ingredient. And based on this conclusion, Joyce's little volume of poems can now take its place in the time-honored tradition of the lyric: not only back to the Elizabethan period when it flowered, but back to the ancient Greeks where the union of poetry and music was taken for granted. A true lyric (as distinct from lyrical poetry) is defined with great simplicity by C. Day Lewis: it is "a poem written for music" (3). The lyric is characterized by "brevity, simplicity," and what he terms "impersonality" or the "lack of personal flavour"; music imposes "discipline" on the lyric and "is at the service of [its] tradition" (Lewis, 5–9). Every aspect of that definition fits Joyce's verses, with Palmer's musical settings filling in the missing piece.

James Joyce and Geoffrey Molyneux Palmer never met, yet their letters give evidence of a strong bond between the two men, a harmonious relationship based on mutual respect and admiration. Just as the young composer was attracted and inspired after "reading with the greatest of pleasure your beautiful collection of poems" (Palmer MS., Cornell), so the young Joyce responded enthusiastically to the musical settings, calling them "elegant," "distinguished," "the finest," and "the best." Together, they succeeded in achieving what Campion describes so eloquently as his goal in the preface to his *Second Book of Ayres:* "to couple my words and notes lovingly together." Joyce's place in literary history is assured; Palmer's musical importance is to be highlighted by his reinstatement into the Millenium edition of *Grove's Dictionary of Music and Musicians,* after having been dropped from editions since 1955. Joyce never abandoned his desire to see the songs in print, confident that they would be highly valued and acclaimed. In a letter to Palmer in 1920, he wrote: "I shall be glad to hear from you and to know that your delicate music is meeting at last with the appreciation which it deserves" (*L,* III, 35). Perhaps now that hope will be fully realized.

NOTES

Parts of this essay have appeared before in Myra T. Russel, *James Joyce's Chamber Music: The Lost Song Settings* (Bloomington: Indiana University Press, 1993). Reprinted by permission of Myra T. Russel. The author would like to thank the Morris Library at the University of Southern Illinois at Carbondale, the home of the Palmer settings, for their help in this project's research.

1. See the appendix to Russel, ed., *Song Settings,* 113–14.

2. All Roman numerals refer to poems within *Chamber Music.*

3. There is no way the final poem, "I Hear an Army" (XXXVI), with its aura of nightmare and anguish, can belong to any century but our own (which may explain why it is often singled out for praise). This essay applies, therefore, only to the other thirty-five lyrics of *Chamber Music.*

4. For more about the role of music during this period, see Russel, "The Elizabethan Connection," 134–36.

5. Although her music is "Sedate and slow and gay," altering the mood.

6. Stanislaus often observes and pinpoints Elizabethan influences on Joyce's early life and poetry. Several months after his brother's death in 1941, he wrote "Recollections of James Joyce" for an Italian journal, and remarks, commenting on Joyce's move to Trieste: "Thus ended his attempt to live in Dublin in the merry Elizabethan manner, and *Chamber Music* can be considered the poetic expression of that attempt" (*Recollections*).

7. The authorship of the texts of Dowland's songs is often unknown; here the composer is allowed to stand in for the anonymous poet.

8. Of course this association might have flitted across the mind of the young Joyce, but its unfitness would have been obvious.

9. There is even a hint of Shakespeare's *Richard II* in "Sad songs about the end of love": "For God's sake, let us sit upon the ground / And tell sad stories of the death of kings" (III.ii.153–56).

10. The four that Palmer did not set are: "What Counsel Has the Hooded Moon" (XII), "Be Not Sad" (XIX), "Rain Has Fallen" (XXXII), and "Now, O Now, in This Brown Land" (XXXIII). Except for "Rain," these are not among Joyce's best.

11. The six notes are in the manuscript room of the National Library of Ireland. Only the first appeared in the *Letters* (III, 167); the others were judged "trivial" (*L,* II, xxix), along with miscellaneous communications. Now the remaining five notes have been published, for the first time, in Russel, ed., 9–10.

12. Palmer was born in 1882, the same year as Joyce, a coincidence that would have pleased Joyce had he been aware of it.

13. Most likely "Strings in the Earth and Air" (I), but possibly "Winds of May" (IX) or even "Who Goes amid the Green Wood" (VIII).

14. Evidence that Palmer was concerned about his sisters' good name can be found in a letter to him dated October 25, 1921, from a Gaelic League member (sister of poet Tom MacDonagh, executed as one of the leaders of the Easter rebellion) in which she discusses Palmer's wish to dedicate his opera "Sruth na Maoile," or "Sea of Moyle," to Eamon de Valera (then a rebel, in and out of prison) and donate the rights to the Gaelic League:

> As for the dedication. All I can say is that "respectable people"
> are an atrocious nuisance. I am always having to keep dark about
> many things I do on account of my "respectable" school. Would it be

any protection to your sisters if you used only the Irish form of your
name in connection with it?

Of course, they cannot in any case be responsible for what their
"wild" brother chooses to do, but there is certainly a great risk.
Perhaps by the time the opera appears in public, De Valera may be
the most respectable person in the country. (Palmer MS., Ireland)

So the headmistress of a conservative school had to be shielded from radical
politics as well as from the shock of Joyce.

15. The figure, "Strings in the Earth and Air," is taken from Russel, ed.
The other settings discussed in detail in this section can also be found in that
volume.

16. Robert White has performed Palmer's songs in many recitals here and
abroad, including a performance at the 1990 International James Joyce
Symposium in Monaco. Indiana University Press has also issued a cassette
tape, as a companion to the book *James Joyce's* Chamber Music: *The Lost Song
Settings,* where this noted tenor and the pianist Samuel Sanders perform all
thirty-two settings.

17. Tindall insists on seeing bats as "female vampires," a reading that
simply does not apply to *Chamber Music.*

WORKS CITED

Auden, W. H., preface. *Selected Songs of Thomas Campion.* Ed. and introd.
John Hollander. Boston: David Godine, 1973.

Bauerle, Ruth. *The James Joyce Songbook.* New York: Garland Publishing,
1982.

Boyle, Robert, S. J. "The Woman Hidden in James Joyce's *Chamber Music.*"
Women in Joyce. Eds. Suzette Henke and Elaine Unkeless. Urbana:
University of Illinois Press, 1982. 3–30.

Campion, Thomas. *Second Book of Ayres.* London: Stainer & Bell, 1922.

———. *Selected Songs of Thomas Campion.* Pref. W. H. Auden. Ed. and
introd. John Hollander. Boston: David Godine, 1973.

Corkine, William. *Second Book of Ayres.* Menston, U.K.: Scolar Press, 1970.

Dowland, John. *Fifty Songs.* Book II. Selected and ed. Edmund Fellowes.
London: Stainer & Bell, 1971.

Ellmann, Richard. *James Joyce.* Rev. ed. Oxford: Oxford University Press,
1982.

———. Liner notes. *Songs to Texts by James Joyce.* Lyrichord LL 83.

Gregory, Horace. *The Dying Gladiators.* New York: Grove Press, 1961.

Hollander, John, ed. and introd. *Selected Songs of Thomas Campion.* Pref. W. H. Auden. Boston: David Godine, 1973.

Jonson, Ben. *Complete Poetry of Ben Jonson.* Ed. William Hunter, Jr. New York: Norton, 1963.

Joyce, Stanislaus. *My Brother's Keeper.* New York: Viking Press, 1958.

———. *Recollections of James Joyce.* Trans. Ellsworth Mason. New York: James Joyce Society, 1950.

Lewis, C. Day. *The Lyric Impulse.* Cambridge, Mass.: Harvard University Press, 1965.

Palmer, Geoffrey Molyneux. Manuscript file. National Library of Ireland.

———. Manuscript file. Rare Book Room, Cornell University Library.

Pound, Ezra. *Literary Essays of Ezra Pound.* London: Faber & Faber, 1985.

Russel, Myra. "The Elizabethan Connection: The Missing Score of James Joyce's *Chamber Music.*" *James Joyce Quarterly* 18, 2 (1981): 133–45.

Russel, Myra, ed. and introd. *James Joyce's* Chamber Music: *The Lost Song Settings.* Foreword by Harry Levin. Bloomington: Indiana University Press, 1993.

Sullivan, Kevin. *Joyce among the Jesuits.* New York: Columbia University Press, 1957.

Symons, Arthur. *The Nation,* LXXIII, June 22, 1907.

Tindall, William York. *Chamber Music.* New York: Columbia University Press, 1954.

White, Robert, foreword. *James Joyce's* Chamber Music: *The Lost Song Settings.* Ed. and introd. Myra Russel. Bloomington: Indiana University Press, 1993.

Figure 3–1. Geoffrey Molyneux Palmer, *Chamber Music.* Song I, "Strings in the Earth and Air" (Russel, 44–45). Reprinted from Myra Russel, ed. and introd., *James Joyce's* Chamber Music: *The Lost Song Settings* (Bloomington: Indiana University Press, 1993), by permission of Myra T. Russel.

CHAPTER 4

"Mr. Bloom and the Cyclops": Joyce and Antheil's Unfinished "Opéra Mécanique"

Paul Martin

Anyone who has read about the artistic community in Paris during the 1920s will be familiar with the name of George Antheil, composer of the infamous *Ballet Mécanique.* Joyceans will also recognize him as a friend of the Joyces, one of the composers who set a poem from *Chamber Music* for *The Joyce Book,* and as an occupant for some time of the apartment directly above Shakespeare and Company. Almost everyone who has written even briefly about Antheil's friendship with Joyce mentions that the composer and the author often discussed the possibility of collaborating on an opera. The most common account of this possible creative union is that, although Joyce was eager to proceed, Antheil was unable to commit to the project and so the opera never made it past the planning stage. Further investigation, however, reveals that this was not the case; Antheil actually did begin work on an opera based on the "Cyclops" episode of *Ulysses* and a small fragment of that work still exists today. My own recording of "Mr. Bloom and the Cyclops" was played at the 1996 International James Joyce Symposium, marking not only the first public performance of this piece, but also the first time it had ever been heard by anyone, including Antheil.[1] It was recorded with an orchestration closely approximating what the composer had envisioned. The recording clearly demonstrates that this fragment is so brief that, ultimately, it is of marginal interest as a piece of music. Nevertheless, we can still learn a great deal from the score itself, including perhaps why, in the end, this highly anticipated "collaboration" never saw the light of day.

Born in 1900 in Trenton, New Jersey, George Antheil began studying piano at the age of six and turned to composition in his midteens. In 1919, under the tutelage of the great American composer and teacher Ernest Bloch, Antheil began composing his first symphony, which, significantly, was his attempt to portray in music the industrial town of his childhood. Having ended his lessons with Bloch in 1921, Antheil spent several months in Bernardsville as the guest of Margaret Anderson who, as the founder and editor of *The Little Review,* would later be instrumental in ensuring Antheil's introduction to all the important people in the Paris artistic community. After he returned to Philadelphia, where he had once studied with Constantin von Sternberg, Antheil was able to secure the patronage of Mary Louise Bok, who, despite disapproving of his style of composition, provided him with a monthly stipend for most of the 1920s.

In 1922, Antheil decided he would more quickly attain his financial and artistic goals—he wanted to be both rich *and* famous—by becoming a concert pianist. After months of intense practice and with the financial backing of Mrs. Bok, Antheil left America for a European concert tour in which he would perform pieces by composers such as Chopin and Debussy as well as several of his own works. These compositions, however, were not of the more classical style of his first symphony but were, to borrow one of Antheil's favorite terms to describe his work, "ultramodern," cacophonous compositions such as his 1921 *Airplane Sonata.* After settling in Berlin later that year, Antheil attended the world premiere of his first symphony, gave a successful concert tour of Eastern Europe, and composed his most avant-garde piano music yet. Pieces like the "Sonata Sauvage," "Death of Machines," and "Mechanisms" were so provocative, in fact, that they caused riots at nearly every one of his concerts. The artistic and commercial achievements Antheil made during this time set the stage for him to leave Berlin for Paris in June of 1923.

Once in Paris, Antheil was introduced by Margaret Anderson to many of the most important figures in the expatriate artist community, including Joyce, Pound, Hemingway, and Picasso. Word of Antheil's radical style and riot-causing concerts quickly spread, and he was soon given the opportunity to present a recital at the Théâtre Champs Elysées before a performance of the Ballet Suédois. That October 1923 concert, which was attended by many of the most important artistic figures of the time, was marked by another violent riot in the audience. This time, though, the riot was not caused entirely by Antheil's music. Without the knowledge of many audience members and of Antheil himself, the uprising was partially staged by the actress Georgette Leblanc, who stacked the audience with rioters so that Marcel L'Herbier could film the crowd's reaction for a scene in his 1924 film *L'Inhumaine*. In his memoirs, *La Tête qui Tourne*, L'Herbier writes that Antheil's music was ideal for provoking in the audience the realistic frenzy he wanted for the scene:

> Pendant ce temps-là, pour maintenir l'excitation à son comble, Georges Antheil, pianiste américain de choc, surexcitait les nerfs de ces figurants d'un jour en les baignant dans l'acidité de ces rythmes sauvages. Parfaits détonateurs pour séquence explosive. (104)

> (During this time, to maintain the excitement at its peak, George Antheil, the American shock pianist, overexcited the nerves of these momentary film extras, immersing them in the acidity of the savage rhythms. Perfect detonators for an explosive sequence.)

Antheil claimed that he did not learn of the filming of the riot until the following year, when he happened to see *L'Inhumaine*. Maintaining that the film's riot "is no fake one," he notes with pride that "you can if you wish see a vast rioting public, including such illustrious figures as James Joyce, Picasso, Les Six, the Polignacs, the Prince of Monaco, the surrealist group, and Man Ray—although a good many of these remain seated" (Antheil, *Bad Boy,* 136).

Notwithstanding the dubious authenticity of the riot at the Théâtre Champs Elysées, news of the concert firmly established Antheil's reputation as the enfant terrible of the Paris music scene, at least as far as nonmusicians were concerned. Antheil was eager to capitalize on this new publicity and announced several days later that he was about to begin the composition of an even more revolutionary work: the *Ballet Mécanique*. During the two and a half years between his first Paris performance and the highly anticipated premiere of his *Ballet Mécanique,* George Antheil became one of the most talked-about figures on the Parisian cultural landscape. His name appeared in almost every important literary periodical of the time, including *Criterion, transition,* and *The Little Review,* and both Ernest Walsh's *This Quarter* and Ford Madox Ford's *Transatlantic Review* featured excerpts of

Antheil's scores in special musical supplements. Antheil's own opinion came to matter a great deal and thus these same journals were eager to publish articles by Antheil about his own works and those of others. This period also marked the height of Antheil's friendship with Joyce.

It was a shared love of music rather than complementary personalities that caused James Joyce and George Antheil to become friends. As Antheil wrote in his autobiography, *Bad Boy of Music:*

> Conversation with Joyce was always deeply interesting. He had an encyclopedic knowledge of music, this of all times and climes. Occasional conversations on music often extended far into the night and developed many new ideas. He would have special knowledge, for instance, about many a rare music manuscript secreted away in some almost unknown museum of Paris, and I often took advantage of his knowledge. (*Bad Boy,* 153–54)

Although there has yet to be any definitive evidence to support Antheil's claim that Joyce wrote "several articles in French magazines upon my music" (*Bad Boy,* 151), it is clear that Joyce was very interested in his friend's compositions. As well as being present at Antheil's infamous 1923 performance at the Ballet Suédois, Joyce was also one of twelve guests invited to a private premiere of the pianola parts from the *Ballet Mécanique.* As Bravig Imbs recounts in his memoir, *Confessions of Another Young Man,* Joyce was so taken with the music that he asked the young woman from the piano factory, who had just struggled through the demanding physical feat of pumping the pianola pedals in a consistent manner throughout the three rolls of the piece, to reload the second roll and replay a particular section of music. "Heard away from their context," Imbs writes, "these few bars lost none of their peculiar vitality. Mr. Joyce was highly satisfied. 'That's like Mozart,' he said" (57).

It was also during the period leading up to the first public performance of the *Ballet Mécanique* that Joyce and Antheil began to discuss collaborating on an opera based on the "Cyclops" episode of *Ulysses.* Why the two settled on "Cyclops" and not another episode is somewhat unclear. In fact, anyone familiar with Joyce's novel might be somewhat surprised they did not choose a more "musical" episode like "Sirens," or the "Aeolus" episode in which the setting of the newspaper office would provide an ideal industrial backdrop for the combination of Joyce's words and Antheil's mechanistic and "ultramodern" style.

Still, there is ample material in "Cyclops" to make it suitable for an operatic adaptation. The character of the Citizen, his mongrel Garryowen, and the mock-heroic battle between them and the unassuming Leopold Bloom, all the time paralleling Odysseus's encounter with Polyphemos, could easily be translated to the stage with dramatic and entertaining results. Although "Cyclops" is certainly not as fragmented as an episode like "Sirens," its multiple styles and layered parodies make it complex enough not to be incongruous with Antheil's avant-garde musical style. According to Hugh Ford, Joyce also considered the narrative of "Cyclops," "with its barroom fight and noisy pursuit into the street, [...] an ideal subject for Antheil's talents" (31). Of course, as one might expect given Antheil's penchant for publicity, news of this collaboration spread quickly throughout Paris. Al Laney reports that "there was much talk of this opera, which was expected, on the Left Bank, to be probably the greatest artistic achievement of the age" (167).

Despite all the public attention and the apparent enthusiasm, at least initially, of both Joyce and Antheil, the finished "Cyclops" opera never materialized. Written accounts of this failed collaboration, including those by Sylvia Beach, Richard Ellmann, and Hugh Ford, state that the opera never got off the ground. As Ellmann recounts, for instance, "the idea fascinated Joyce, but Antheil disappointed him by turning to other work" (558). There is evidence, however, to suggest that Antheil actually did do some work on the "Cyclops" opera. Perhaps the greatest proof of all that Antheil had begun setting that episode to music is to be found in the second issue of Ernest Walsh's *This Quarter,* which contained a special musical supplement dedicated to the works of Antheil. This section of the magazine contained the complete score for Antheil's *Airplane Sonata,* an excerpt from the "Sonata Sauvage," and, labeled "Extract (first pages)," three pages of score for "Mr. Bloom and the Cyclops," an "opera upon [the] 'Cyclops' episode in James Joyce's *Ulysses*" (Antheil, "Mr. Bloom," 22; see Figure 4–1).

Although three pages of score might seem like a significant excerpt, they represent only three measures of music and only the first sentence of Joyce's text; over a span of twenty-two beats, comprising three bars set in the time signatures of 4/4, 7/4, and 11/4 respectively,[2] the tenor part sings: "I was just passing the time of day with old Troy of the D.M.P. at the corner of Arbour hill there and be damned but a bloody sweep came along and he near drove his gear into my eye"

(Antheil, "Mr. Bloom," 22–24). There is, however, anecdotal evidence to suggest that Antheil did in fact write more of "Mr. Bloom and the Cyclops" than what was published in *This Quarter*. No further pages of score have ever been found for this opera, but in a 1925 letter to his brother Stanislaus, Joyce uses the past tense in referring to Antheil's work on "Cyclops": "Did George Antheil call on you? He has set *Cyclops* episode" (van der Weide, 91; *L*, III, 128). More persuasive is Bravig Imbs's account of having spent an evening with Antheil during which the composer played for him "a little aria [he] wrote for the 'Cyclops'" (25). As Imbs describes it, "the aria was noble and well proportioned, and I enjoyed it because I was able imaginatively to transpose George's voice into the beautiful soprano timbre for which the music was written" (27–28). That this aria was intended for "Cyclops" seems questionable, as anyone familiar with the episode in *Ulysses* will recall that there are no speaking female characters in this part of the book. There are a few female characters who appear in the grand parodies that frequently interrupt the more realistic diagesis, but it is unknown if Antheil intended the soprano voice to belong to either the true love of the revolutionary hero executed by H. Rumbold or to Miss Fir Conifer or another member of her wedding party. In either case—assuming, of course, that Imbs's story is credible—Antheil would have had to have worked far past the first sentence of the "Cyclops" episode to come across an opportunity to include such an aria. Given that he wrote in an article entitled "My Ballet Mécanique: What It Means" that his new work (one assumes Antheil is referring here to "Mr. Bloom and the Cyclops") would be "four hours long and without interruption or the break of a second's time," one would certainly expect an opera of that length to fully treat the non-diagetic scenes in the episode like that of the execution or the Conifer-Neaulan wedding.

Ultimately, the three pages of score in existence are of greater interest than any conjecture on whether any more of the "Cyclops" opera was actually composed. In fact, the "Mr. Bloom and the Cyclops" excerpt offers a definite sense of what the opera might have been like. The first thing that strikes one when examining the overall score is that the fragment is more a setting to music of Joyce's text than it is a collaboration; as noted earlier, the first sentence of the tenor part corresponds directly to the first sentence of the episode in Joyce's novel. When examined from a purely musical perspective, though, the fragment becomes far more interesting. As one can see from the orchestration of these initial measures, "Mr. Bloom and the Cyclops" contains many of the same elements of the *Ballet Mécanique* but also expands on them in interesting and significant ways. Despite the very obvious use of an unusual variety of mechanical percussion instruments like an auto siren, electric buzzers and pieces of steel all tuned to different pitches, and two different electric motors (one with a steel attachment and the other with a wood attachment), the sonic center of "Mr. Bloom and the Cyclops" remains the piano, albeit a mechanical one. Explaining this decision in a letter to Mrs. Bok in 1925, Antheil wrote: "I have, in two works, the *Ballet Mécanique,* and the *Cyclops,* used the piano as a BASIS of sonority, just as all of the composers preceding used the strings as the BASIS of sonority for their orchestras" (Whitesitt, 111). The original scores for both pieces call for sixteen mechanical pianos: when it came time to perform the *Ballet Mécanique,* however, the impossibility of synchronizing the pianos forced Antheil to reorchestrate the piano parts for that piece so that they could be performed with one mechanical piano and eight regular ones.

For Antheil, the value of the piano lay in its ability to be used more as an instrument of percussion than of melody. Composing for mechanical piano allowed Antheil to take this percussive quality of the piano to another level. Not only was the mechanical piano able to play complex musical figures at an almost superhuman speed, the instrument also was not limited by the number of notes a pianist could play simultaneously; as Imbs observes, the young woman who played the pianola for the private premiere of the *Ballet Mécanique* piano rolls found the performance to be extremely hard work because "sometimes half the keys went down at once" (55). There are no such passages in the "Cyclops" piece, but Antheil maintains the principles of the *Ballet Mécanique* and uses the piano almost entirely for percussive effect, combining booming chords so tightly clustered and discordant that they sound more like machines with rapid thirty-second note runs, so fast and mechanical that one can hardly distinguish the individual notes. The mechanical piano parts are even more difficult to make out as a result of the parallel structure of the part for eight xylophones, which often overlays the piano parts with even more densely clustered combinations of notes (such as the chord on the first beat of the first bar, comprised of eight notes covering a range of only an octave and a half). This is something of a departure from the *Ballet Mécanique,* which did include parts for xylophone, though they were relatively minor and much more independent of the piano parts.

The most significant expansion of the aesthetic behind the *Ballet Mécanique* in "Mr. Bloom and the Cyclops" comes with Antheil's idea of using an amplified gramophone "containing all of the ordinary orchestral instrument[s] registered upon gramaphone [sic] record" (Antheil, "Mr. Bloom," 22), as well as an electronically amplified chorus. Although the parts assigned to the gramophone and to the chorus in this score fragment are of little interest—the former is made up of a somewhat dissonant string part of repeating quarter-note triplets and a held note on the tuba, while the latter does not come in at all— what is especially innovative and intriguing is the use of amplification, which Antheil envisions as serving an artistic purpose and not—or at least in addition to—a technical one. In other words, by choosing to record the instruments of the orchestra on the gramophone and to have live singers singing through microphones, Antheil was using technology to affect the sound of the instruments rather than simply trying to ensure the audience could hear them. The audibility, too, would have been a consideration given the real potential that sixteen mechanical pianos playing simultaneously could easily overpower any unamplified acoustic instrument. Al Laney's description of the opera, while not entirely supported by the score printed in *This Quarter* or by what was technically feasible in the mid-1920s, offers one possible explanation for the aesthetic purpose of amplifying the voices: "This opera was to have been performed with invisible singers, who would sit down below the stage out of sight and sing into microphones attached to loud speakers on the stage" (167). Laney writes that unlike a traditional opera, where the singers are also the actors, in "Mr. Bloom and the Cyclops" "the action was to be given by a corps de ballet in pantomime" (167). Verifying Laney's comments is the fact that these same innovative ideas resurfaced in Antheil's 1930 opera *Flight,* in which he had the "characters sing from the orchestra pit as their actions are portrayed on stage by dancers" (Whitesitt, 130).

From a musical perspective, Laney's most interesting comments are that "the score was to be run off at top speed, with crescendos and diminuendos achieved only by switching pianos on and off" (167). Although there is nothing in the score or in any other writings about Antheil to verify what Laney says about the tempo and dynamics of the "Cyclops" opera, it is also important to note that there are in fact no tempo or dynamic markings on the score. Furthermore, the indication that the pianos, xylophones, and gramophone were all to be "controlled from switchboard" (Antheil, "Mr. Bloom," 22) suggests that Antheil envisioned controlling their sound and relative volumes himself. This idea, of course, is common practice today in any amplified musical performance where the sound is controlled by a "sound engineer," a term the Antheil of the mid-1920s might have been quite content to apply to himself. The idea that someone would ultimately "control" these sounds refines to some degree Antheil's vision of the *Ballet Mécanique,* which also had no dynamic markings; referring to this unusual aspect of the score, Antheil wrote in 1925 that "my Ballet Mécanique has absolutely no 'forte' or 'piano' moments. It is *merely played loud enough to be heard*" ("My Ballet Mécanique," 789).

Ultimately, the question of technology was the most significant factor in determining how, or if, Antheil would follow through with his grand scheme for the "Cyclops" opera. Regardless of how much (or how little) he wanted to continue work on "Mr. Bloom and the Cyclops," Antheil's experiences with the performance of the *Ballet Mécanique* revealed the impossibility of synchronizing twelve pianolas with one another, let alone with a prerecorded gramophone record.[3] Thus, although displaying a stunning vision of the possibilities of joining music and twentieth-century technology, the score for "Mr. Bloom and the Cyclops" represents not what the opera would have been, but what Antheil wished it could be. This is echoed entirely by the overblown rhetoric he uses to describe the "Cyclops" opera in a 1925 letter to Stanley Hart:

> The life of man. The destruction of music. Enormous phonographs with amplifiers. New musical machines. The *Sacre du Printemps* of the future which all composers to follow will have a hard time scrambling over. First complete reaction and then complete revolution—to everything including all my preceding works. (cited in Whitesitt, 110)

Needless to say, despite Antheil's fantastic and in some ways prophetic vision of what music could be, he found himself unable with "Cyclops" to achieve anything, either musically or technologically, that would surpass everything that had come before, including the *Ballet Mécanique.*

Given Antheil's propensity to comment on his own importance as a composer and on the revolutionary character of his work, it is both surprising and ironic that he mentions almost nothing about "Mr. Bloom and the Cyclops" in his own autobiography, *Bad Boy of Music,* except to say that Joyce "suggest[ed] writing an opera libretto for [him] to set to music" and that the two men talked often of the project (*Bad Boy*, 152). Furthermore, while the "Cyclops" opera would have obviously been "a more massive work embodying and intensifying the formal process of the 'Ballet'" (Whitesitt, 110), Antheil asserts in his book that the *Ballet Mécanique* represented an end point in his career:

> [*Ballet Mécanique*] closed a period of my work and life. For, after I had written it, I felt that now, finally, I had said everything I had to say in this strange, cold, dreamlike, ultraviolet-light medium. I could have written another "Ballet Mécanique," of course, but to have done so would have been for me repetitious, tedious. I always tend to write the same work over and over again, so to speak, until finally I get it as nearly perfect as I can, then I abandon it. (*Bad Boy*, 137)

Antheil's work on "Mr. Bloom and the Cyclops"—which was, for the most part, contemporaneous to the composing of the *Ballet Mécanique*—proves that he did not feel he had taken that style to its full potential and that he did therefore try to write another *Ballet Mécanique;* his comments perhaps also explain why he never even came close to completing what could have been the most important work of his career. In a way, it certainly was true that Antheil had written all he could in that style, but to suggest that this was because he had perfected it is disingenuous on Antheil's part. It is far more likely that Antheil realized he had left himself nowhere else to go; Antheil was not limited by his creative and musical ideas but by the inability of technology to realize them. Unfortunately for Antheil, his seemingly sudden turn to a more neoclassical style—the only direction in which he felt he could go—caused the public, the critics, and even his friends and supporters to conclude that Antheil had already said nearly all he had to say.

What interested me the most about the excerpt from "Mr. Bloom and the Cyclops" and what led me to create my own recording of the piece is that it clearly demonstrates the scope of Antheil's vision in such a way that we can no longer consider the *Ballet Mécanique* an end to his "ultramodern" period. We must rather see it as the beginning of a new path that Antheil did continue to follow for some time, before finding it, for various reasons, to be a dead end. As someone who composes music using synthesizers and digital samplers and then records it and plays it back via a computer-sequencing program, it was immediately evident to me that today's technology could easily overcome all the difficulties Antheil encountered with synchronizing the mechanical pianos and, in the case of "Mr. Bloom and the Cyclops," the prerecorded sounds of a regular orchestra. Antheil does seem to have given up a bit too easily in his attempts to conquer these technological obstacles, but he certainly foresaw their end years before anyone else. One of his most stunningly prophetic articles is entitled "Music Tomorrow" and was published in the January 1928 issue of *transition*. As well as anticipating a shift of emphasis in contemporary music from tonality to time—"Tonality in the future," he writes, "will become infinitely more subtle. Time, not tonality, will be considered the canvas of music" (Antheil, "Music Tomorrow," 125)—he precisely envisions the evolution of the musical "machine" (126):

> I believe that soon there will be electrical machines which can automatically reproduce every sound wave, and which will not only replace the old orchestra, but create every sound on earth the ear is capable of hearing. Until then we should preoccupy ourselves with mechanical instruments more and more. [...] [T]he greatest beauty will be that which comes out of the esthetic and possibilities of the instruments [...] and soon we shall be using machines. (126)

Although Antheil does not seem to anticipate the possibility of both electronic and traditional instruments coexisting as they do today, he does realize that someday works like "Mr. Bloom and the Cyclops" could be performed in the way he envisioned it.

As my recording of this short excerpt—it is only seventeen seconds in duration—demonstrates, there are nevertheless other difficulties inherent in creating a composition that cannot be heard by anyone, especially the composer. While "Mr. Bloom and the Cyclops" resembles the *Ballet Mécanique* in being centered around the piano part, Antheil's desire to make the former piece bigger and better than the latter seems also to move it away from much of what made the *Ballet Mécanique* so compelling. Not only does the xylophone part clutter the piano part, the violins from the gramophone part play a rhythm that seems to go against the parts of all the other instruments, and in the tenor line the same three notes are repeated to a continual rhythm of a dotted eighth note followed by a sixteenth note. Furthermore, while the *Ballet Mécanique* does contain a remarkable assortment of unusual percussion instruments, including an air siren and both steel and wooden airplane propellers, they are used relatively sparingly. During the mere twenty-two beats of the "Cyclops" excerpt, on the other hand, every instrument plays a considerable part, including the two electric motors that play held notes that last the duration of these three bars. Of course, given that we have only three bars of score to examine, it is impossible to guess whether this wall of sound would have continued for much longer in the piece or is just there for an initial dramatic effect.

Finally, comparing the cacophonous sound of the piece to the strangely cohesive chaos of the *Ballet Mécanique* also leads one to wonder if Antheil had truly thought this piece through, or if, to keep Joyce and Mrs. Bok happy, had quickly dashed together this brief excerpt that would give some idea of how he envisioned this opera. One can only speculate on whether Antheil would have altered the score after hearing it played, or whether it was precisely what he wanted. It is highly unlikely that these questions will ever be answered; the real value of resurrecting this piece of music is not in providing us with answers, but in permitting us, through hearing it for the first time, to ask questions of it we might otherwise not have considered.

For myself, as both a composer and an aspiring Joyce scholar, what is most striking about the relationship between Joyce and Antheil comes to light when one juxtaposes Joyce's success in stretching his medium to its limits in *Ulysses* and then far beyond those apparent boundaries in *Finnegans Wake* with Antheil's ultimate failure to do the same. Though both men were considered to be great artists in the mid-1920s, only Joyce's reputation as such stuck, and justifiably so. Joyce persevered with his "Work in Progress," a work that no one may ever fully comprehend, a work that challenges and subverts every preconceived notion about what literature is. Antheil, on the other hand, though having neither the established reputation nor the financial resources of Joyce, could never fully reconcile his position as an avant-garde artist with his goal of achieving both wealth and fame. In other words, Antheil became so obsessed with seeking public recognition and with the desire to explain his complex ideas to others—often using a less than modest approach—that he put himself in a position from which he could not take the time or make the effort to search for the difficult and complex answers to the problems that he himself raised in his writing and especially in his ideas on how to set the "Cyclops" episode. Naturally, Antheil's money woes were greater than Joyce's (who in the mid-1920s was at least earning some revenue from his works) and the composer did spend an inordinate amount of time trying to impress his conservative and disapproving patron Mrs. Mary Louise Bok, but it was still his own decision to sacrifice what could have been a great creative achievement in order to continue to pursue his "big break." Still, Antheil went on to have a reasonably successful career as a composer; yet by turning away from the "ultramodern" style of his earlier work, he became known far more for the circumstances surrounding the performances of the *Ballet Mécanique* than for any of his works themselves.

In my view, the continued neglect of Antheil's music is unjustified, for there is a great deal of his work, including "Mr. Bloom and the Cyclops," that remains interesting from a musical perspective. There is also much of value in several of his articles that not only envision new ways of conceptualizing music, but also anticipate many musical and technological developments that have occurred over the last seventy years. The sad and overwhelming irony of Antheil's early theories of music is that much of what he imagined then is now actually possible. As my recording of "Mr. Bloom and the Cyclops" demonstrates, the technological advances of synthesizers, digital sampling, audio signal processing, computer sequencers, and even true mechanical pianos (the Yamaha Disklavier) that can be easily synchronized and controlled via MIDI (Musical Instrument Digital Interface) means that were Antheil composing in the 1990s he could have achieved everything he dreamed of in the 1920s. He would still, however, have had to deal with many of the same problems he did in the 1920s, particularly in terms of how one negotiates between the desire for true artistic achievement and the need for commercial success. In this way, then, Antheil's life and the choices he made in the mid-1920s, especially in regards to his abandonment of "Mr. Bloom and the Cyclops," provide a strangely suitable parable for writers, composers, and scholars of today.

NOTES

1. I owe a great debt of gratitude to the International James Joyce Foundation for awarding me a graduate student travel scholarship to help me attend the Zurich Symposium. I would also not have been able to record the music without the technical and vocal assistance of Mr. Tim Mallandaine and the guidance of Mr. Maxwell Steer and of Mr. Charles Amirkhanian, musical executor of the Antheil estate.

2. Note that Antheil had pioneered the notion of incoherently fluctuating meters as a vehicle for text setting while helping Pound to notate *Le Testament* in 1923 (where there are consecutive bars with time signatures of 33/16, 21/8, and 36/32).

3. Virgil Thomson, of all people, was asked to help coordinate the multiple pianos.

WORKS CITED

Antheil, George. *Bad Boy of Music.* Garden City, N.Y.: Doubleday, Doran, 1945.

———. "Manifest der Musico-Mechanico." *De Stijl* 6, 8 (1924): 99–102.

———. "Mr. Bloom and the Cyclops." *This Quarter (Antheil Musical Supplement)* 1, 2 (1925): 22–24.

———. "Music Tomorrow." *transition* 10 (Jan. 1928): 123–26.

———. "My Ballet Mécanique." *De Stijl* 6, 12 (1925): 141–44.

Ellmann, Richard. *James Joyce.* Rev. ed. Oxford: Oxford University Press, 1982.

Ford, Hugh. *Four Lives in Paris.* San Francisco: North Point Press, 1987.

L'Herbier, Marcel. *La Tête qui Tourne.* Paris: Belfond, 1979.

Imbs, Bravig. *Confessions of Another Young Man.* New York: Henkle-Yewdale House, 1936.

Laney, Al. *Paris Herald: The Incredible Newspaper.* New York: D. Appleton-Century, 1947.

van der Weide, Jack. "James Joyce en George Antheil." *De steen der dwazen en de schone waarheid. Transartiestieke studies.* Eds. Hans Ester and Etty Mulder. Baarn: Ambo, 1996. 88–100.

Whitesitt, Linda. *The Life and Music of George Antheil.* Ann Arbor, Mich.: UMI Research Press, 1983.

Figure 4–1. George Antheil, "Mr. Bloom and the Cyclops," *This Quarter (Antheil Musical Supplement)* 1, 2 (1925), 22 (first page of score). Reproduced by permission of Charles Amirkhanian, Executor, Estate of George Antheil.

CHAPTER 5

Opus Posthumous: James Joyce, Gottfried Keller, Othmar Schoeck, and Samuel Barber
Sebastian D. G. Knowles

> That the dead do not stay buried is, in fact, a theme of Joyce from the beginning to the end of his work [...]. (Ellmann, 244)[1]

The bibliography of Samuel Barber's settings of Joyce has only recently been completed. Three previously unpublished settings of poems from *Chamber Music* appeared in a collection entitled *Ten Early Songs* in 1994,[2] bringing the total of settings by Samuel Barber of texts by Joyce to ten. The texts of these ten settings are reproduced, together with their dates of composition and publication, in an appendix at the conclusion of this essay. The posthumous pieces are pleasant examples of the art song, a genre that Barber would refine to its most elegant form, with an easy vocal range never going above a mezzo-soprano's F or below middle C, and the piano following the voice in chordal patterns all the way. The texts speak of lovers' trysts in the night ("Of That So Sweet Imprisonment"), in the music they make ("Strings in the Earth and Air"), and in a forest ("In the Dark Pinewood"). "Of That So Sweet Imprisonment" and "Strings in the Earth and Air" were written in 1935, when Barber was twenty-five at the American Academy in Rome; "In the Dark Pinewood" was written two years later in Austria, high up in the mountains in a cottage with Gian Carlo Menotti. They show Barber following in the musical footsteps of his uncle, Sidney Homer, who was himself a master of the art song.[3] The three songs have a blissful innocence about them, far from the suicides, live burials, and wreath-eating episodes that will be seen to distinguish the other songs.

Barber wrote three other song settings of poems from *Chamber Music* during this period, which were published together as Op. 10 in 1939: "Rain Has Fallen," "Sleep Now," and "I Hear an Army" have now entered the literature as standard pieces for the rising young vocalist. These are more complex pieces, both to play and to sing, tracing a new adventurousness in Barber's style. Where the three settings without opus numbers hold a single mood, reflective and undisturbed, the settings in Op. 10 each reach *appassionato* climaxes. The first climax, from "Rain Has Fallen," anticipates two of Joyce's siren songs, paralleling in its rhythm "Oh my Dolores" as trilled by Lydia Douce, the climax to "The Shade of the Palm,"[4] and paralleling in its text the final "*Come...! [...] To me!*" (*U,* 11.744–50) of "M'appari," sung by Simon Dedalus. The climax of "Sleep Now," in its text, takes us to "Sirens" again, via the aria "All is lost now" from *La Sonnambula* (*U,* 11.629). The third climax, from "I Hear an Army," is, like the other two but more obviously so, a moment out of the piece's natural rhythm, a lyrical elasticization of what is an otherwise forcefully rhythmic piece with a vibrant martial gallop; this is Barber's nod to Schubert's "Erlkönig," where a different horse's rhythm, also in the left hand, similarly stops for breath as the father discovers his dead son in his arms.[5]

In the three published poems Barber takes the art song to a more visceral level: the hoofirons that ring steelily in "I Hear an Army" are the heartbeats of the abandoned lover. The poem was set to music in 1936 while Barber was in Austria, two years before Hitler's incorporation of the country: the army is both a mobilizing war machine and an imaginary army of the heart. The heart, the last word of both "Rain Has Fallen" and "Sleep Now," is Barber's principal focus in Op. 10. The "unquiet heart" of "Sleep Now" continues the imagery of sleep found in "Of That So Sweet Imprisonment," in which "Sleep to dreamier sleep be wed, / Where soul with soul lies prisoned." And this imprisoned heart, beating in a perpetual sleep, may quop, as Bloom's does in "Lestrygonians" (*U,* 8.1169), less softly when we remember "In the Dark Pinewood," possibly the darkest of the six texts in its subject matter. There is an obvious pun on "wood" in "In the dark pinewood I would we lay," which conceals a second pun on "pine." The speaker pines to lie with his lover, yes, but pine is also the wood of choice when building a coffin. This further pun points obliquely to an issue that is central to all of Joyce's work, an issue that Barber continues in his later, much more experimental, and much more disturbing settings of Joyce. When Joyce writes "In the dark pinewood I would we lay" he is writing about being buried alive.

The heart of the three poems of Op. 10, thudding in the piano's left hand in "I Hear an Army," is a telltale heart. The subterranean presence of live burial beats throughout Joyce: from the third stroke of "The Sisters" to Finnegan's return from the dead, Joyce maintains a morbid fascination with the living dead. And nowhere is this clearer than in the final Joycean text that Barber chose to set to music, a translation of Gottfried Keller's "Da hab' ich gar die Rose aufgegessen":

> Now have I fed and eaten up the rose
> Which then she laid within my stiffcold hand.
> That I should ever feed upon a rose
> I never had believed in liveman's land.
>
> Only I wonder was it white or red
> The flower that in this dark my food has been.
> Give us, and if Thou give, thy daily bread,
> Deliver us from evil, Lord. Amen.[6]

How Barber came upon this translation is not clear. Jean Kreiling addresses the issue of the provenance of Barber's text for this song setting, and concludes that since Joyce's translation made its only public appearance in Gorman's *James Joyce,* Barber must have become attracted to the poem as a result of reading that biography.[7] Heyman, Barber's chief biographer, agrees, pointing out that the manuscript of Barber's setting indicates that the piece "was completed at Spoleto in March 1972" (489), at which time the text was available only in Gorman.

"Now Have I Fed and Eaten Up the Rose" (Op. 45, no. 1), was commissioned for Dietrich Fischer-Dieskau in 1972, and is the first of three songs to translated texts in Op. 45. The other two texts are "A Green Lowland of Pianos" to a translation by Czeslaw Milosz of the surrealist Harasymowicz, and "O Boundless, Boundless Evening," a translation by Christopher Middleton of Georg Heym. The use of translations is a deliberate anomaly in Barber, since of all the other songs in Barber's *oeuvre* only the *Hermit Songs* are also translations. The texts in Op. 45 are then themselves reincarnations of early texts, as the musical settings are further incarnations, at two removes, from Keller and Harasymowicz and Heym.[8] That the textual mediators in this transformative game are Joyce, Milosz, and Middleton speaks to Barber's conviction that nothing is lost in translation, either from language to language, or from the language of speech to the language of music.[9] Joyce translates Keller, and Barber translates Joyce. The poem itself retains the idea of transubstantiation in the final lines, turning, through the Lord's Prayer, the eating of the rose into an act of communion: "Give us, and if Thou give, thy daily bread, / Deliver us from evil, Lord, Amen!"[10] Joyce repeatedly uses the image of transubstantiation of Christ's body as a metaphor for the transformation of artistic representation of reality (the communion wafer in *Portrait,* the parody mass in the Martello tower), and Barber here follows his lead. The text is given the flowing line moving above and below the tonic that is familiar from the sung mass, a move that parallels the recitation for "Grasyaplaina dormimust echo!" in Barber's setting of "Nuvoletta."[11]

For Barber, then, "Now Have I Fed and Eaten Up the Rose" is an opportunity to transubstantiate, to reincarnate, to bring to life a poem about a man engaging in his own bizarre communion. But since Barber apparently found the translation in Gorman, it is unclear whether he was aware just how deep the communion was. Joyce's translation of Keller is the visible tip of an enormous hidden structure, the consequence of a long series of coincidences and connections, that includes a fifty-minute song cycle by another composer, and two separate versions by the Swiss poet Gottfried Keller of a cycle of poems on being buried alive. Barber has prised his song text out of a rich context that leads the curious researcher to the underground heart of Joyce's work.

In 1935 Barber studied at the American Academy in Rome and began his lifelong fascination with Joyce's texts as sources for his compositions; in that same year, Joyce heard Keller's poem set to music at a concert in Zurich, as part of a song cycle by the composer Othmar Schoeck. The cycle was called *Lebendig Begraben,* after the title of the second version of a group of poems by Gottfried Keller. *Lebendig Begraben,* or "Living Burial," is an unusual musical work in many ways. First, it is one of the very few sustained works for baritone and orchestra in twentieth-century music.[12] Second, it is the work of a Zurich native who has set the poems of another Zurich native, Gottfried Keller, to music, which helps to explain why it was performed in

Zurich in 1935. And third, it is a peculiar piece of music because the song cycle is about a man who has been buried alive. The poet has been accidentally placed underground and cries out from his coffin to be released. He rails against those aboveground who have consigned him to this unfortunate fate, one of whom he hears singing drunkenly through the cemetery, but his cries fall on inebriated ears. Understandably depressed, he begins to cry, and the wood shavings of the coffin become matted with the curls of his hair.[13] Finding nothing to eat, he turns to a rose he was buried with, which he eats, wondering, in the dark, if it was a white or a red one. That's why, in Joyce's translation, his hand is "stiffcold," and why he longs for "liveman's land." It's a grisly song cycle, anyway you look at it.

How Joyce came upon Keller's text is an interesting story, and has not yet been told correctly. On January 15, 1935, Joyce wrote to his son's family about hearing Schoeck's composition for the first time:

> Dear Giorgio and Helen: Please reply as soon as possible to Lucia's letter, forwarded yesterday by Dr (Mrs) Baynes. She left the sanatorium yesterday, we hope for good, and is living at Villa Elite (annexe of here) 25 Stockerstrasse, behind the Tonhalle with a nurse-companion. Be sure to do this, please and send her photographs and news.
>
> Helen, please go out and buy Cassells German-English, English-German Dictionary and sit down with Giorgio and study, first of all, the text of Gottfried Keller's poem sequence *Lebendig Begraben* which I forward under separate cover together with the piano score for bass voice by Othmar Schoeck, autographed by the composer. I heard this suite sung last night by the Bernese bass Fritz Loeffel (the leading bass in this country), bought the score just now and have rung up Prof. Fehr to ask O.S. to sign it for Giorgio. He is a youngish Zurich composer of about 42, principal works are lieder and two big operas *Penthesilea* (book by Kleist) *Don Ranudo* (comic). If I can judge by last night he stands head and shoulders over Stravinsky and Antheil as composer for orchestra and voice anyhow. I did not know Keller wrote this kind of gruesome-satiric semi-pious verse but the effect of it on an audience is tremendous. The singer got 8 or 10 calls. No voice but a bass could carry the text and music. He spares the singer by inserting 2 or 3 stretches of monotone recitative. The whole thing, without a break, lasts 50 minutes. Schoeck is a type rather like

> Beckett who gets up at 2:30 p.m. his wife says. But I hope to catch
> him before he falls asleep again. But he can write music all right.
>   Don't forget to write to Lucia. (*L,* I, 356)

According to Ellmann, this is the *second* time Joyce has heard the song
cycle; the first is said to have been in 1934, after a visit to the Zurich
eye doctor Alfred Vogt in April 1934: "Professor Vogt informed Joyce
that he still needed the two operations on his right eye and would gain
more sight by them. These two operations [...] might however be again
postponed until September [1934]. Joyce remained in Zurich a few
more days. Bernard Fehr, professor of English at the University of
Zurich, brought him to a concert where they heard Othmar Schoeck's
Lied-Zyklus *Lebendig-Begraben* [sic] (opus 40), a suite of fourteen
songs by Gottfried Keller for male voice and orchestra. Joyce was
amazed by them and later translated them" (669).
     There are two errors here. First, it cannot be true that Joyce heard
Lebendig Begraben before 1935, since in January 1935 Joyce responds
to the cycle as one who has heard it for the first time ("I did not know
Keller wrote this kind of gruesome-satiric semi-pious verse"). And
second, there is no evidence that Joyce translated any other poems by
Keller but "Now Have I Fed and Eaten Up the Rose." Only the one
poem is catalogued by Steven Lund in the Herbert Gorman Papers
(Lund, 68), and Derrick Puffett, Schoeck's principal English critic,
speaking of the missing translation of the other poems in the cycle, says
that "extensive enquiries, both in Switzerland and in America, have
found no trace of it (Frau Schoeck has no knowledge of such a thing)"
(235). Puffett, apparently citing a personal interview with Ellmann,
implies in 1981 that Ellmann subsequently retracted his earlier claim
for undiscovered translations: "Ellmann now thinks that what he saw
may have been Joyce's translation of Keller's eighth poem, reproduced
in the biography of Joyce by Herbert Gorman" (235n). When Ellmann
is wrong, there is always a ripple effect; Vogel's biography of Othmar
Schoeck repeats the first error: "Am 14. January 1935 horte Joyce den
Keller-Zyklus in Zurich zum zweiten Mal" (250). And the second error
has led Jean Kreiling to read the letter of January 15, 1935, backward:
"Joyce apparently obtained and intended to study all of Keller's
'Gedanken eines Lebendig-Begrabenen'; the request for the German
dictionary suggests that he contemplated substantial efforts in
translation" (352). The German dictionary was probably for Helen
Fleischman's benefit, not her father-in-law's: it is unlikely that a man

who was capable of translating the plays of Hauptmann at the age of nineteen would need a German dictionary to translate Keller at the age of fifty-two after living his adult life in Europe. The letter to Giorgio and Helen of January 15, 1935, does not, in fact, provide evidence that Joyce "contemplated substantial efforts in translation," and the issue of the missing texts, like the issue of the extra concert, can be put to rest.

Kreiling makes a further error in ascribing the text that Joyce translated not to the poet but, bizarrely, to the composer of *Lebendig Begraben*. In Kreiling's view, the eight lines that Keller wrote and Joyce translated are actually "Schoeck's version" (352) of Keller's original poem. The poem had, it is true, originally been much longer, and part of a cycle called *Gedanken eines Lebendig-Begrabenen*, which itself was longer, with nineteen poems instead of fourteen when it was first published in Keller's 1846 *Gedichte*. When it came time in 1888 to publish his *Gesammelten Gedichte*, Keller wanted the cycle removed, but changed his mind and reworked it into the shorter form, with the shorter title.[14] In the 1888 version Keller condensed the thirteenth poem, "Da hab' ich gar die Rose aufgegessen," from six stanzas to two, and placed it in the eighth position in the new cycle. These two versions of the poem Joyce was to translate have led Kreiling to the false impression that the new version was written by Schoeck: "In addition, Schoeck gave this briefer version of the poem a sense of closure by means of the prayer in the last two lines, which appear nowhere in Keller's cycle" (352). But Kreiling has the wrong Keller cycle, since Schoeck took the text verbatim from the 1888 version. As was the case with Ellmann, Kreiling's mistake has a ripple effect: Heyman has borrowed this misinformation from Kreiling (563), and speaks of "an English translation by James Joyce of an abbreviated version used for a song by composer Othmar Schoeck" (484). The version has been abbreviated from its first published form, but not by Schoeck: it is simply a later text. So when Kreiling writes, "Whether Barber knew how substantially Schoeck had altered the text cannot be determined" (354), it is important to recognize that it is not Schoeck but Keller himself who made the alterations, and thus that this speculation is needless.

That Keller once entertained the idea of deleting the song cycle from his *Collected Works* is entirely to his credit. The image of a man lying inside his coffin and forestalling his death by eating part of his funeral wreath is a kind of Everest in the grotesque mountain range of the nineteenth-century Gothic. One can take the reaction of one of Keller's critics, J. M. Lindsay, to be representative:

> The cycle of poems entitled *Lebendig begraben* is in poor taste, an unsavoury exercise in the macabre, which cannot possibly have appealed to many readers. The whole conception of the cycle reflects a primitive, childish fear of the poet, and several lines reach a level of tastelessness and sheer ugliness which can seldom have been surpassed. The drunken sacristan and his wife, with "Ihr Katzmiaulen und sein Mondsgebelle", walking over the unfortunate victim's grave, are an example of this kind of unsophisticated cruelty. Certainly in Heine and other romantic poets Keller might have found precedents for this disastrous exercise, but one cannot really plead anything in mitigation of this poem. (106)

The poem is better than that: the conceits are metaphysical in their grotesque inappropriateness and the unhappy selection of metaphor. Keller's extraordinary analogies—eternity is compared in poem I to a termite wandering happily through a wooden plank—match the perversities of Donne and Crashaw.

The macabre exercise may reflect a primitive, childish fear, but it is a fear shared by many, and found everywhere in Joyce. As Lindsay recognizes, the whole owes something to Heine's *Junge Leiden* (1817–21), where in the second poem of *Traumbilder,* the speaker meets a lovely maiden who washes his dying shroud, cuts down an oak for his coffin, and digs his grave, into which, in the final stanza, he plunges headlong:

> Und als ich in die Grube schaut,
> Ein kalter Schauer mich durchgraut;
> Und in die dunkle Grabesnacht
> Stürtz ich hinein—und bin erwacht. (Heine, 56)

> (And as I gazed into the pit,
> A cold shudder crept through me;
> And into the dark night of the grave
> I threw myself—and woke up.)[15]

In Keller, the speaker's vision of his own death is no dream; in a deleted poem, his position is exactly that of a nightmare from which he is unable to awake:

> Ich muß ein Weilchen wohl geschlafen haben,
> Denn wie aus Träumen schein' ich mir erwacht;
> Bin ich leibhaftig, wirklich denn begraben?
> Noch immer diese enge, schwarze Nacht? (*Gedanken*, 17)

> (I must have dozed off for a bit,
> Since from a dream I seem to have woken;
> Am I a living body, really then buried?
> Is it always to be this dark night?)

Reinforcing the idea of Keller's debt to Heine is the first line of Keller's poetry that Joyce translated, "Da hab' ich gar die Rose aufgegessen," which begins similarly to Heine's invocation to the ghosts in the last poem of *Traumbilder:* "Da hab ich viel blasse Leichen" (Heine, 68).

The perverse offshoot of graveyard poetry that gave rise to *Junge Leiden* and *Lebendig Begraben* can be traced back to Thomas Gray's "Elegy Written in a Country Churchyard" (1751), by way of Gottfried Bürger, who in 1773 revitalized the ballad form with the publication of "Lenore." In that poem, a soldier returns from the Seven Years War, comes to reclaim his bride, drives like mad to the cemetery, and turns into a skeleton:

> "Rapp'! Rapp'! Mich dünkt der Hahn schon ruft—
> Bald wird der Sand verrinnen—
> Rapp'! Rapp'! Ich wittre Morgenluft—
> Rapp'! Tummle dich von hinnen!—
> Vollbracht, vollbracht ist unser Lauf!
> Das Hochzeitsbette tut sich auf!
> Die Toten reiten schnelle!
> Wir sind, wir sind zur Stelle."— (Bürger, 187)

> ("Barb! Barb! methinks I hear the cock;
> The sand will soon be run:
> Barb! Barb! I smell the morning air;
> The race is well nigh done." [...]

"Hurrah! hurrah! well ride the dead;
The bride, the bride is come!
And soon we reach the bridal bed,
For, Helen, here's my home.") (Scott, 38)[16]

"Lenore" is, like "Erlkönig" and "I Hear an Army," a hoofiron poem,
with the sound of the horse ("Rapp'! Rapp'!") ringing throughout.
"Erlkönig" and "Lenore" were published within a decade of each other,
and the parallels between the two ghost rides are uncanny.[17] Then, in
1789, the novelist Jean Paul wrote a sketch of his own funeral called
"My Living Burial" that became the germ for *Siebenkäs* (11). In
Siebenkäs (1796), the idea of an afterlife is rejected by the dead Christ,
preparing the way for the nothingness that awaits those buried alive.[18]
Walter Muschg, the editor of Keller's *Ausgewählte Gedichte,* cites Jean
Paul in a useful catalogue of the romantic revival of the living burial
idea:

> Der Scheintod ist ein altes literarisches Motiv, seine grotesk-
> humoristische Behandlung bei Molière, Gryphius, Goldoni wurde
> durch Jean Pauls "Siebenkäs" erneuert [...]. Die Angst vor dem
> lebendig Begrabenwerden war eine ihrer Zeitkrankheiten, Nestroy
> [...] traf in seinem Testament umständliche Maßnahmen dagegen.
> Leben wie ein Toter war das Leiden Hölderlins, Mörikes, Platens,
> Leopardis, Mussets, Meyers, schon Goethe hatte es in "Des
> Epimenides Erwachen" dargestellt; vgl. auch Chamissos "Traum und
> Erwachen." (210–11)

> (The false death is an old literary theme: Jean Paul's "Siebenkäs"
> renewed awareness of the grotesquely humorous treatments of the
> theme by Molière, Gryphius, and Goldoni. The fear of being buried
> alive was suffered by all romantics; Nestroy took absurd precautions
> against it in his will. To live as a dead man was the fear of Hölderlin,
> Mörike, Platen, Leopardi, Musset, and Meyer; even Goethe spoke of
> it in "Des Epimenides Erwachen," and Chamisso in "Traum und
> Erwachen.")

Bürger's notion of the gravesite as a bridal bed leads to Schubert, where
in the twenty-first song of the *Winterreise* (1828) the cemetery is
presented as a "Wirthaus," an inn where the singer imagines a sweet
repose. The apogee of live burial arrived, of course, in Baltimore: in

1846, the same year that Keller published the first version of *Lebendig Begraben,* Edgar Allan Poe was burying Fortunato in "The Cask of Amontillado." Puffett points out that Poe's "The Premature Burial" appeared at the same time as Keller's first draft of the cycle, in 1844 (201).[19]

Through the fourteen poems of *Lebendig Begraben* Keller somehow sustains the gruesome conceit of a prematurely encoffined speaker alternating between frustrated attempts to escape, or at least to communicate with those above him in the present, and resigned elegies to a pastoral world that he can no longer revisit. Thus is neatly combined the alienation of the poet from the world he lives in, since the world is entirely envisioned in the mind while the body lies paralyzed, and the traditional nostalgia of the romantic poet for a lost natural world. But both the present alienation and the past emotion recollected in tranquillity are given a novel edge in the hapless condition of the speaker, for the tranquillity is now eternity, the pensiveness is now despair, and the couch upon which the poet lies is the bed of the grave. In Keller's cycle, the symbolic connection between the two worlds of present paralysis and past liberty is the pine tree. In poem XI, he imagines the sawn-up pine in which he is now incarcerated to be the mast of a ship sailing out to sea:

> Wie herrlich wär's, zerschnittner Tannenbaum,
> Du ragtest als ein schlanker Mast empor,
> Bewimpelt, in den blauen Himmelsraum,
> Vor einem sonnig heitern Hafentor! (XI)[20]

> (How splendid it would be, you sawn-up pine tree,
> If you were towering up, a slender mast,
> Your flags flying, in the blue heaven,
> Before a sunny and fair harbor!)

And in poem XII, the last pine tree he will ever see reminds him of his first visit to a nursery of baby pine trees, where the poet remembers tightening pine boughs around his forehead, gazing amorously at a kite, and then wearing a lizard as jewelry. In poem XIII, the pine tree is quite literally a symbol of freedom, as the "Freiheitsbaum" or Liberty Tree of a Swiss Rifle Festival. All these trees, reminders of a lost pastoral world, collapse into the present pine boards of his coffin:

> Damals war ich ein kleiner Pantheist
> Und ruhte selig in den jungen Bäumen;
> Doch nimmer ahnte mir zu jener Frist,
> Daß in den Stämmchen solche Bretter keimen! (XII)

> (I was in those days a little pantheist
> And lay blissfully in the young trees;
> Never would I have suspected at that time,
> That from those boughs would sprout these boards!)

We are in the "dark pinewood" of Joyce's earlier poem, but here the resonance with death is real.

Keller's poet, when he is not rhapsodizing over a lost past, sets his thoughts on the hope of escape. His first and last attempts are metaphysical: in poem II, he imagines having an idea, the force of which would be so powerful that it would release him, like a volcano, from his grave:

> Vielleicht, wer weiß, wüchs' er zu solcher Größe,
> Daß er, in Kraft sich wandelnd, ein Vulkan,
> Im Flammenausbruch dieses Grab erschlösse,
> Vorleuchtend mir auf neuer Lebensbahn! (II)

> (Perhaps, who knows, it would become so powerful,
> That it would transform itself into a volcano,
> Opening this grave in a burst of flames,
> Lighting me on to a new life's path!)

A second unconstructive fantasy is that, were he in a desert rather than a churchyard, a hyena might dig him up, which he could kill with his bare hands and spring "wie neugeboren" ("like one newborn") from his shroud (IV). Then he hears a drunken verger and his nagging wife argue over his head, but can't penetrate "her cat's cries and his howling to the moon" (V). Growing increasingly desperate, he first anticipates a water diviner picking up "the warm red stream" of his blood (VI), then a grave robber (IX), and finally a lover (X). But nothing is of any use: the divining rod won't respond to blood, there's nothing to steal in his grave, and he forgot to tell his girlfriend that he loved her. Finally, in one of the greatest escape acts of all time, abandoned by both time and space, he renounces his body and becomes pure thought:

Der letzte Hauch ein wallend' Meer von Leben,
Wo fliehend die Gedanken mir entschweben!
Fahr' hin, o Selbst! vergängliches Idol,
Wer du auch bist, leb' wohl du, fahre wohl! (XIV)

(My last breath is a rolling sea of life
On which my flying thoughts drift from me!
Farewell, O Self! You transient idol,
Whoever you may be, farewell to you, farewell!)

The epiphanies of Keller's poet are savagely undercut by his unfortunate position; his panegyrics to pine trees are brought literally down to earth by the pine boards of his coffin. In that oscillation between epiphany and grotesque parody, Keller clearly mirrors Joyce, as the ascent of Bloom/Elijah is undercut "at an angle of fortyfive degrees [...] like a shot off a shovel" (*U*, 12.1917–18), as the peroration to love in Barney Kiernan's pub is undercut by Jumbo the elephant (*U*, 12.1496), as Stephen's heroic cry, "*Nothung!*," is undercut by the rhyming "Pfwungg!" of the gasjet (*U*, 15.4241–47). Keller's poem is an antipastoral, a mock elegy that still retains all the standard elements of graveyard poetry: the celebration of nature, the longing for past life and love, the ascent into the empyrean and the separation of mind from body. But the poet isn't mourning a drowned shepherd or looking at gravestones in a country churchyard: he's seven feet under, mourning himself.[21] Keller's earlier sequence of 1846, *Gedanken eines Lebendig-Begrabenen*, is even more grotesque in its parody of the poet's position as chief recorder and chief victim, for the speaker is given, in one of the poems eliminated for the 1888 edition, a pencil to write his poems with. Keller's poet finds that he has been buried in his Sunday best, with a toothpick and a pencil in his vest pockets, leading to these magnificent and perfectly Joycean stanzas:

Sie haben mir, als sie der Tod belogen,
Wie's scheint, die Sonntagsweste angezogen:
In ihren Taschen fand ich einen alten
Zahnstocher und ein Bleistift aufbehalten.

Einst gab es Tage, wo man zum Geleite
Den Toten Schwert und Pfeile legt' zur Seite:—
Schmählich Jahrhundert du, das seinen Leichen

Zahnstocher nur und Bleistift weiß zu reichen! (*Gedanken,* 4)

(They have laid me out in my Sunday best,
As it appears, for my false death:
I have found my vest pockets to contain
An old toothpick and a pencil.

Once there was a time, when one lay beside
the dead a sword and spear:
Miserable century, that with your corpses
You distribute only toothpicks and pencils!)

Ulysses, in the same way, is an anti-epic, retaining in grotesque form all the grandeur and scope, in its celebration of the cemetery-cities of prewar Dublin and midwar Troy, of the Homeric source; substituting, like Keller, pencil and toothpick for sword and spear.

There are other thematic explanations for Joyce's deep connection with Keller that predate *Ulysses.* In *Lebendig Begraben* can be identified the three touchstones of *Dubliners:* paralysis, gnomon, and simony. Like the first story of *Dubliners,* Keller's cycle begins with a coffin: Flynn's paralysis becomes for the unfortunate speaker not a medical but a structural condition. Like the Reverend, the buried speaker was too scrupulous always, unable to declare his love and consequently abandoned: "Ich zauderte und hab' es nicht gewagt— / Die Krankheit kam und diese tolle Posse!" (X) ("I hesitated, and didn't dare to— / Then sickness came, and now this grotesque farce!"). There is no help for Keller's victim this time, it is the third stroke; and as gnomon is the sundial that proportions time, so Keller's buried speaker hears the clock strike twelve, and then, an interminable length of time later, the quarter hour:

Und wieder schlägt's—ein Viertel erst und Zwölfe!
Ein Viertelstündchen erst, daß Gott mir helfe,
Verging, seit ich mich wieder regen kann!
Ich träumte, daß schon mancher Tag verrann! (XIV)

(And again the clock sounds—a quarter past twelve!
A small quarter hour, God help me,
Has passed since I could move again!
I dreamed that already many days had gone.)

Finally, simony, in the association of the churchyard with money: as he lies there, grave robbers and gold diggers prowl the cemetery, looking for buried gold. The speaker curses his poverty, for no one will think to look for gold where he lies:

> Doch was für Kleinod sollt' er suchen hier?
> Er weiß zu gut, er findet nichts bei mir!
> Ein golden Ringlein nun erlöste mich,
> Jedoch umsonst ist nur der Tod für dich! (IX)

> (But what sort of jewels would he be searching for here?
> He knows too well, he won't find anything on me!
> A gold ring now would ransom me,
> But the only thing you can get for free is death!)

In *Lebendig Begraben* are buried the tools of *Portrait*'s artist: silence, exile, and cunning. In the grave no one can hear you scream: "Es hülfe nichts, wenn ich zu Tod mich riefe!" (V). And Keller's poet, like Dedalus, is an artist in exile, able from his unique position to comment on a society he is both a part of (because he can hear it from below) and apart from (seen in his efforts to reach the drunken verger and his wife). The desperate plan to attack the grave robbers or the water diviners who may come to disturb his grave demonstrates his cunning. Keller's poet also experiences an epiphany parallel to Stephen's: his embrace of the lizard in the pine nursery results in an outburst of profane joy:

> Ich hielt mich reglos und mit lindem Druck
> Fühlt' ich den leisen Puls am Halse schlagen;
> Das war der einzige und schönste Schmuck,
> Den ich in meinem Leben je getragen! (XII)

> (I held myself motionless and with a gentle pressure
> I felt the soft pulse beat against my neck;
> It was the only jewelry, and the most beautiful,
> That I've ever worn in my life!)

But the poem that Joyce chose to translate, after hearing its setting in Schoeck's song cycle in 1935, is the eighth:

Da hab' ich gar die Rose aufgegessen,
Die sie mir in die starre Hand gegeben!
Daß ich noch einmal würde Rosen essen,
Hätt' nimmer ich geglaubt in meinem Leben!

Ich möcht' nur wissen, ob es eine rote,
Ob eine weiße Rose das gewesen?
Gib täglich uns, o Herr! von deinem Brote,
Und wenn du willst, erlös' uns von dem Bösen! (VIII)

(Whereupon I even ate this rose,
That they[22] put in my rigid hand!
That I would ever eat a rose again,
Would I never have believed in my life!

I would like to know, whether it was a red one,
Or whether it was white?
Give us, O Lord, this day our daily bread,
And, if it is thy will, deliver us from evil!)

Eating up the rose makes one think of "Lotus-Eaters," and Bloom's thoughts on communion there: "Rum idea: eating bits of a corpse" (*U*, 5.352). This connects further to Stephen's ghoulish thoughts of his mother, who is both "Hyena" and "corpsechewer" (*U*, 15.4200, 4214): "eaten up," as Joyce correctly translated "aufgegessen," retains the suggestion of the ravenous appetite of an animal.[23] The color of the roses gives the connection its hook, since from Stephen's school days as a Yorkist to Molly's "shall I wear a red" (*U*, 18.1603) as she ends her soliloquy, the choice of white or red rose has always been an overdetermined symbol for Joyce. But the thematic connection of death and rebirth, of the transubstantiation of the dead, is the reason for Joyce's immediate connection to Keller. "Five fathoms out there" (*U*, 3.470), Stephen thinks of the dying man in "Proteus": Ariel never imagined a sea change this rich and strange.

For Joyce the experience of Keller via Schoeck was like an electric shock. Everywhere in Joyce characters are being raised from the dead, from "The Ballad of Joking Jesus" ("*tell Tom, Dick and Harry I rose from the dead*" [*U*, 1.597]) to Lazarus ("And he came fifth and lost the job" [*U*, 6.679]), and back to Michael Furey, who is reincarnated in "The Dead" as a spectral image from the past, to be reburied not in earth but in the snow that falls faintly over all the living and the dead. The return of Stephen's mother and the reawakening of Finnegan are only the first places to start in Joyce, for an eternity of being dead is Joyce's greatest preoccupation. The passing of a cemetery in "Eumaeus" recalls Ibsen's play *When We Dead Awaken* (*U,* 16.52), and later in the section the Italian curse *"Mortacci sui!"* (*U,* 16.318) raises again the rotting of the dead. There is a posthumous child in "Circe" (*U,* 15.1808) and a postmortem child in "Eumaeus" (*U,* 16.437). Dignam returns, ghouleaten, as a lugubrious beagle (*U,* 15.1204), and in the final pandemonium of "Circe" the earth trembles, a chasm opens, and *"The dead of Dublin from Prospect and Mount Jerome in white sheepskin overcoats and black goatfell cloaks arise and appear to many"* (*U,* 15.4671–73).

It is in "Hades" where the Plumtree vision of life in death is made most explicit, where all the funeral roses bloom. Here, in "Hades," is the thought that Paddy Dignam is buried alive: "And if he was alive all the time? Whew! By jingo, that would be awful" (*U,* 6.866). In "Hades," Dignam's corpse has life: the coffin "Got there before us, dead as he is" (*U,* 6.510). Bloom wonders, "Would he bleed if a nail say cut him in the knocking about" (*U,* 6.432–33) and remembers the practice of boring a hole into a coffin to let out the accumulated gas (*U,* 6.609–11).[24] He thinks of the nails and hair that "Grows all the same after" (*U,* 6.20), and the frantic search for one's body on the Last Day: "Then every fellow mousing around for his liver and his lights and the rest of his traps" (*U,* 6.679–80). Though Bloom maintains that "Once you are dead you are dead" (*U,* 6.677), his interest in resurrection is more than idle curiosity about a Catholic belief, for he does believe in the physical life of the body after death, in the need for death as a necessary condition for new life: "It's the blood sinking in the earth gives new life" (*U,* 6.771).

The fear of Dignam's premature burial recurs and expands in "Cyclops": "He's no more dead than you are" (*U,* 12.331), says Alf at Barney Kiernan's, and Joe Hynes's response, "They took the liberty of burying him this morning anyhow" (*U,* 12.332–33) inspires the following parodic interpolation:

> In the darkness spirit hands were felt to flutter and when prayer by tantras had been directed to the proper quarter a faint but increasing luminosity of ruby light became gradually visible, the apparition of the etheric double being particularly lifelike owing to

the discharge of jivic rays from the crown of the head and face. Communication was effected through the pituitary body and also by means of the orangefiery and scarlet rays emanating from the sacral region and solar plexus. Questioned by his earthname as to his whereabouts in the heavenworld he stated that he was now on the path of prálává or return but was still submitted to trial at the hands of certain bloodthirsty entities on the lower astral levels. In reply to a question as to his first sensations in the great divide beyond he stated that previously he had seen as in a glass darkly but those who had passed over had summit possibilities of atmic development opened up to them. Interrogated as to whether life there resembled our experience in the flesh he stated that he had heard from more favoured beings now in the spirit that their abodes were equipped with every modern home comfort such as táláfáná, álávátár, hátákáldá, wátáklását and that the highest adepts were steeped in waves of volupcy of the very purest nature. Having requested a quart of buttermilk this was brought and evidently afforded relief. Asked if he had any message for the living he exhorted all who were still at the wrong side of Máyá to acknowledge the true path for it was reported in devanic circles that Mars and Jupiter were out for mischief on the eastern angle where the ram has power. It was then queried whether there were any special desires on the part of the defunct and the reply was: *We greet you, friends of earth, who are still in the body. Mind C. K. doesn't pile it on.* It was ascertained that the reference was to Mr Cornelius Kelleher, manager of Messrs H. J. O'Neill's popular funeral establishment, a personal friend of the defunct, who had been responsible for the carrying out of the interment arrangements. Before departing he requested that it should be told to his dear son Patsy that the other boot which he had been looking for was at present under the commode in the return room and that the pair should be sent to Cullen's to be soled only as the heels were still good. He stated that this had greatly perturbed his peace of mind in the other region and earnestly requested that his desire should be made known. Assurances were given that the matter would be attended to and it was intimated that this had given satisfaction. (*U,* 12.338–73)

Dignam is on "the path of prálává or return": he does return in "Circe," together with Bloom's son and Stephen's mother (the "orangefiery rays" emanating from his solar plexus cast ahead to the "*orangeblossoms*" of May Goulding's wreath [*U,* 15.4158]). The "luminosity of ruby light" shining around his head and face prefigures the return of Rudy with his "ruby buttons" (*U,* 15.4965–66), who is also an "etheric double," as both Jew (reading right to left) and Catholic (with a lambkin in his pocket), as Rudy and Stephen, as phantom and presence, as specter and Sceptre. Dignam's communication is about the resoling of his boots; as the joke on "resoling" implies, the soul after death has a physical presence in Joyce. Dignam requests a quart of buttermilk, and the astral abodes of those more blessed than he have been equipped with "táláfáná," "álá.vátár," and "wátáklását": the spirit after death is still flesh. The "táláfáná," particularly, is reminiscent of the "telephone in the coffin" (U, 6.868–69) that Bloom wished Dignam's coffin had been equipped with to prevent death by premature burial.[25] H. P. Blavatsky, in whose spirit this interpolation was written, was known for her reappearances in the flesh after death (glimpsing "H.P.B.'s elemental" [*U,* 9.71] as Stephen delicately puts it), and there are many even outside "Circe" who reappear, such as the Commendatore, arriving for dinner in "Lestrygonians" (*U,* 8.1503), Yorick, by way of the grave diggers (*U,* 6.864), Reuben J. Dodd's resurrected son (*U,* 6.284), Rip van Winkle in the charade Bloom remembers in "Nausicaa" (*U,* 13.1113–14), and Parnell in "Eumaeus," whose death may have been faked and his coffin loaded full of rocks (*U,* 16.1304–5). Stephen's "perverted transcendentalism" (*U,* 14.1223–24) in "Oxen of the Sun" is devoted to raising the phantoms of the past; Joyce's retrospective arrangement has a similar agenda.[26]

"Love among the tombstones" (*U,* 6.758–59), thinks Bloom about the caretaker's wife, and in both Keller and Joyce the grave is a place of rebirth, even sexual rebirth. As the coffin band parallels the navel cord, and as Dixon leaves the hospice for the dying to work at the lying-in hospital, the life of a corpse is connected to procreation. In "Lenore," the soldier's grave is a "Hochzeitsbett"; in *Ulysses,* too, the bed is interchangeable with the grave: "Martin Cunningham (in bed), Jack Power (in bed), Simon Dedalus (in bed), Ned Lambert (in bed), Tom Kernan (in bed), Joe Hynes (in bed), John Henry Menton (in bed), Bernard Corrigan (in bed), Patsy Dignam (in bed), Paddy Dignam (in the grave)" (*U,* 17.1238–41). Keller predictably makes this pun:

Ja, hätt ich ein verlass'nes Liebchen nun,
Das vor dem Morgenrot zu klagen käme,
Auf meinem frischen Pfühle auszuruhn,
Und meinen Ruf mit süßem Grau'n vernähme! (X)

(Now, if only I had left behind a lover
Who would come to mourn me before sunrise,
And lie upon my fresh gravebed,
And, with tender horror, hear my cries!)

The "Pfühl" in Keller, on which his abandoned lover would have come to mourn, as before she might have come to his bed to make love if he had confessed his attentions, looks forward to the bed at 7 Eccles Street, which contains death in its crumbs of potted meat, crumbs advertised in the obituary column. Keller's poet, like Yeats's superhuman, is "death-in-life and life-in-death,"[27] he is buried but "neugeboren," in him are held the cycles of birth and death. To Stephen, the midwife throws her misbirth into the sea (*U,* 3.36); in "Oxen of the Sun" "we wail, batten, sport, clip, clasp, sunder, dwindle, die" (*U,* 14.394), a "retrogressive metamorphosis" (*U,* 14.390) from birth to death played out in both Joyce and Keller. "Therefore, everyman, look to that last end that is thy death and the dust that gripeth on every man that is born of woman for as he came naked forth from his mother's womb so naked shall he wend him at the last for to go as he came" (*U,* 14.107–10): these lines from "Oxen of the Sun" could be written in stone above the arch, "whose margin fades / For ever and for ever when I move,"[28] that stands over *Ulysses,* one foot in the bridal bed, one foot in the grave, one side in the womb, the other in the tomb.

Keller's poet is not only newborn, he has a new potency lying underground. The humidity in the coffin tells him that it's spring, and the ice is cracking: "Das Wetter muß seither gebrochen sein, / Denn feucht dringt es in diesen leichten Schrein" (VI) ("The weather must have broken since, / Damp is creeping into this flimsy shrine"). At the same time his spirit wakes: "Es dehnen sich die aufgetauten Glieder, / Und in der Brust schwillt junger Lebensmut!" (III) ("My thawing limbs stretch themselves, / And in my breast swells a new optimism!"). He compares his body to a growing seed: "Wie jeglich Samenkorn sich mächtig dehnt, / Der junge Halm an's warme Licht sich sehnt," (VI) ("As every grain of wheat expands tremendously, / And every stem years for the warm light"). In poem XIII he remembers a moment with another rose at a rifle festival, when a gypsy girl threw him a rose from her hair, at which "Erregt in Wasser eine Welle-flut" (XIII) ("a rousing wave disturbed the water"). The rousing of the water parallels the young poet's new lust for liberty, which begins to burgeon ("keimen") in his heart. This "erregen," or sexual arousal, of the dead is familiar in Joyce, as seen in the effect on the bugger's tool that's been hanged, and the phallic name of Plumtree, the company that advertises potted meat in the obituary column. In Zola's *La Mort d'Olivier Bécaille* (1879), where the title character finds himself taken for dead, encoffined, and forced to witness the seduction of his wife, the question of potency and premature burial is again linked: but for Zola, to be buried alive is to be made impotent. This also has implications for Bloom: like Bloom, Olivier Bécaille is at once cuckold and voyeur: "un homme l'avait ravie, avant même que je fusse dans la terre" (Zola, 817).[29]

The images of renewal and return, of sexuality in the face of death, reappear throughout Joyce's work as lines of defense, garlic held before a vampire. Death has a kind of life; the only way of defeating death is to live again. "Cyclops" is at the heart of this enterprise, and Bloom the man leading the charge: "As true as I'm drinking this porter if he was at his last gasp he'd try to downface you that dying was living" (*U,* 12.1362–63). What is the use of Homer but a form of transubstantiation? Who are the writers of "Oxen of the Sun" if not the ghosts of the past? What is the decision to place *Ulysses* in a prewar Dublin eighteen years earlier but a resurrection of the dead? All of *Ulysses* is an exhumation: of Irish politics and Irish music, of Homer and Shakespeare, of little Rudy and the beautiful May Goulding, of Bloom's youth, of the past. "There is a memory attached to it" (*U,* 15.3520) says Bloom of his potato, the temporary loss of which plunges him into chaos and nightmare: there is a memory attached to everything in Joyce, and it is for Bloom, for Joyce, and finally for the reader, to make these exhumations.

"*Mind C. K. doesn't pile it on*" (*U,* 12.362–63), says the spirit of Paddy Dignam, and both Keller—who is unlikely to bear any relation to the Kelleher of "*C.K.,*" save in the connection with the cellar—and Schoeck begin with this moment when the coffin is covered, piling on rocks, earth, and moldering bones over the body of the living poet:

Wie poltert es!—Abscheuliches Geroll
Von Schutt und Erde, modernden Gebeinen!
Ich kann nicht lachen und kann auch nicht weinen,
Doch nimmt's mich Wunder, wie das enden soll! (I)

(What a clatter! Repulsive rumbling
Of debris and earth and moldering bones!

I can neither laugh nor cry—
I'm just wondering how this will end!)

Schoeck's setting of *Lebendig Begraben* emphasizes this startling opening by piling it on himself, in the tympani. The burial music is cramped and constrictive, with triplets in the bass instruments breaking the meter of the second bar, perfectly mirroring the broken clods of earth on the baritone's coffin. A slightly more restrained burial motif is used by Barber in Op. 25, when Nuvoletta drowns. At the close Barber depicts her disappearance under water with a descending arpeggio, which itself mirrors the death of the miller in two thirty-second notes at the end of Schubert's "Der Müller und der Bach," the penultimate song in *Die Schöne Müllerin*. But both Barber and Schubert place death at the end; only Keller and Schoeck have the temerity to have the singer die before the members of the audience have settled into their seats.

Joyce, in comparing Schoeck to Stravinsky and Antheil in his letter to Giorgio and Helen, reveals his particular admiration for Schoeck's setting of Keller's words. Like Orff's setting of Hölderlin's translation of Sophocles's *Antigone,* or Britten's setting of Owen's "Strange Meeting" in the *War Requiem,* where in both cases each syllable of each word is directly accounted for in a sprung line that moves at the rhythm and tempo of the words themselves, Schoeck's setting of *Lebendig Begraben* is faithful to the intonations of Keller's poetry rather than to the dictates of his music. Further, Schoeck, like Joyce, displays in *Lebendig Begraben* what Puffett calls "a golden overflow of ideas" (238): the cycle is extraordinary in its sheer number of musical tropes, its multiple changes of mood, its episodic structure, its rhythmic virtuosity. Schoeck conceived of his work as a metamorphosis, a transmigration of the music: "The song is the poem in another shape. The poem is as it were the chrysalis, in which the miracle of metamorphosis takes place, and from which the butterfly, in the song, then escapes" (Puffett, 4). This metaphor, which is originally Schumann's, has been seen to be a sympathetic one for Joyce ("A seachange this" [*U,* 3.482]), and for Barber (*Reincarnations,* Op. 16), who are forever preoccupied with transubstantiation in their work, and who both chose to metamorphose the poem of Keller's that most clearly speaks of the transubstantiation, through communion, of the body and blood of Christ in the macabre transformation of "our daily bread" into a rose in a coffin.

There are subtler, more terrifying reasons for Joyce's affinity with Schoeck and Keller. At the end of *Lebendig Begraben,* Schoeck makes, following Keller, the same move that Joyce makes in all his work. *Lebendig Begraben* is a long unfolding, like the opening of a black rose: Schoeck moves over the long uninterrupted work from paralysis to freedom, to a free and open sailing released from any constrictions in "Schon seh' ich schimmernd fließen Zeit in Zeiten" (XIV) ("Already I see, shimmering, time becoming eternity"). *Dubliners* moves from a paralytic stroke to Gabriel Conroy's planned departure for the west of Ireland, Dedalus's labyrinth leads to his flying the nets of "nationality, language, religion" (*P,* 203), Bloom and Stephen's desolation as the cloud passes leads to "yes I will Yes" (*U,* 18.1608–9), and the fall of Eve and Adam is answered by Anna Livia's dying into the sea so that she can be reborn (*FW,* 627.34). The reemergence from the grave is a necessary condition of immortality: so it was for Christ, and for Anna Livia. The ecstasy of the dying speaker in Schoeck's cycle is instantly recognizable in the final pages of the *Wake.*

And there is another reason for Joyce's connection with Schoeck: both found that Keller's notion of live burial served as a focus for response to spiritual crisis. For Schoeck, the circumstances leading up to the composition of *Lebendig Begraben* in 1926 left him profoundly depressed: "The experience of the war, the banality of the postwar period, his confrontation with modern music, an unhappy love affair—all combined to produce in him a deep depression, coupled with almost obsessive feelings of loneliness and neglect" (Puffett, 204). Barber, too, may have shared this sense that Keller provided the appropriate outlet for spiritual crisis: at the time of his composition of "Now Have I Fed and Eaten Up the Rose" in 1972, Barber was agonizing over selling Capricorn, the house in which he and Menotti had lived for many years, and was highly emotional about the reality of burying that past life. According to Heyman, the texts of Op. 45 "are particularly portentous, considering the composer's anguished state of mind [...]. [H]aving 'eaten the rose' is a symbol of the depletion of the source of creative energy" (489). For Keller, the cycle was begun as the result of the spiritual crisis of another: the director of the Zurich hospital greatly feared a false death, and asked Keller, for a hundred bottles of tokay, to write a poem on this subject (Puffett, 201).[30]

But it is with Joyce that the timing of an interest in Keller is particularly telling. Coincidentally, a Zurich hospital played a role in Joyce's attraction to Keller: Joyce heard Schoeck after eye operations under Dr. Vogt in 1934. The effect on Joyce of Schoeck's cycle may have been intensified by the fears of his coming blindness, which, like the fear of being buried alive, is in all his work: "*Pull out his eyes / Apologise*" (*P*, 8); "I am getting on nicely in the dark" (*U*, 3.15); "Hee hee hee hee. He did not see" (*U*, 11.1283); "I'll be your aural eyeness" (*FW*, 623.18). The idea of visual paralysis is through Keller's cycle intensified, a "g.p.i." (*U*, 1.128) that moves from a general paralysis of the i (eye) to the general paralysis of the I (self). The farewell to the self at the end of Keller's cycle can then be seen, by a Joyce who is gradually becoming unable to see, as an escape from the nets of his coming blindness. And at the same time, there is a father's concern for his daughter, with which Joyce ends his letter to Giorgio and Helen: "But he can write music all right. / Don't forget to write to Lucia" (*L*, I, 356). By the time of the concert on January 14, 1935, his daughter's condition had worsened considerably, to such an extent that on the very day that Joyce first heard *Lebendig Begraben,* he had consigned her, against the wishes of her doctor, to a private pension with Eileen Schaurek as nurse-companion. It is not hard to understand the particular sympathy Joyce would have, later that same evening, with a text that speaks of a person prevented by physical circumstances from communicating with the outside world.

Then in the autumn of 1940, as Schoeck was writing on Joyce's behalf to arrange for his entry into Switzerland, Joyce heard the song cycle again on the radio.[31] His two hearings of *Lebendig Begraben,* in 1935 and 1940, act roughly as bookends for his writing of *Finnegans Wake,* a work whose title refers to a man, who, were it not for a bottle of whisky, would have been buried alive. Keller, as Kreiling points out, appears most prominently in Earwicker's dream of the debate of the four judges in Book I, Chapter 4: "Harik! Harik! Harik! The rose is white in the darik!" (*FW*, 96.1). It is in this chapter that Earwicker is placed in a "teak coffin" (*FW*, 76.11), sets to remembering his past, and waits for escape.[32] Schoeck also makes a characteristically protean appearance in the *Wake,* as Puffett has discovered (235), with vowels reversed in the tale of Treacle Tom: "Butting, charging, bracing, backing, springing, shrinking, swaying, darting, shooting, bucking and sprinkling their dossies sodouscheock with the twinx of their taylz" (*FW*, 524.22–24). Joyce took the cycle's appearance on the radio as a good omen for his Schoeck-sponsored Swiss passage, but it was more than that. Three months before he is to die, in the midst of a world war, the cycle is a passport to another world. A world, finally, where the artist is immortal.

For Schoeck, Keller's image of a man imprisoned in a coffin seven feet underground represented the artist trapped in a material, suffocating, and paralyzing universe. Keller often claimed that his talent was being stifled by public indifference (Puffett, 203), and the poem spoke to Schoeck's own situation, as a neglected composer, whose work itself was being buried alive. Schoeck complained that "every effusion by other contemporaries gets printed, but not even all my principal works": *Lebendig Begraben,* itself, has "hardly been played" (Puffett, 236). The underground thoughts of Keller's poet are condemned to be ignored from below—"Vielleicht sind dieses der Verdammung Qualen: / Geheim zu leuchten, ewiglich versenkt!" (II) ("Perhaps these are the torments of the damned, / Secretly to shine, eternally submerged!")—and from above, as the verger and his wife block out the screams beneath them: "Sie stopfen furchtsam ihre breiten Ohren / Vor jedem Ruf des Lebens aus der Tiefe" (V) ("They timidly stop their open ears / At any call of the living from the depths"). "Aus der Tiefe" is (particularly in Bach cantatas) the position of the sufferer calling to God, and can stand as a testament to any poet or writer whose work has been soundly ignored. Joyce was terrified of this. His famous jibe against the critics of *Ulysses* betrays a real fear of literary death: "I've put in so many enigmas and puzzles that it will keep the professors busy for centuries arguing over what I meant, and that's the only way of insuring one's immortality."[33] "Insuring one's immortality": Keller brought the expression to his greatest fear, of his work being shut up in a box with no one ever to let it out.[34] As Anna Livia says as she dies into the sea, "is there one who understands me?" (*FW,* 627.15).

Samuel Barber's settings of Joyce repeatedly evoke the dead; each one is in some way an Opus Posthumous. In "Now Have I Fed and Eaten Up the Rose," the man is buried alive. In "Nuvoletta," the woman drowns. And in "Solitary Hotel," the fourth poem of *Despite and Still* (Op. 41), Barber turns to "Ithaca" to write what appears to be a café piece based on Stephen's notional advertising campaign for stationery, but has a much darker purpose. This is the only setting Barber made from *Ulysses:* the others have been from *Chamber Music* (six of them), *Finnegans Wake* ("Nuvoletta" and the orchestral *Fadograph of a Yestern Scene*), and Joyce's translation of Keller. In Op. 41, no. 4, Barber has discovered Joyce once again. As he found

Keller in a translation in Gorman's biography, unearthing a text that had nowhere been reprinted, he now finds Joyce at his most cinematic, presenting a scene that works, like nothing else in *Ulysses,* as film:

> Solitary hotel in mountain pass. Autumn. Twilight. Fire lit. In dark corner young man seated. Young woman enters. Restless. Solitary. She sits. She goes to window. She stands. She sits. Twilight. She thinks. On solitary hotel paper she writes. She thinks. She writes. She sighs. Wheels and hoofs. She hurries out. He comes from his dark corner. He seizes solitary paper. He holds it towards fire. Twilight. He reads. Solitary.
>
> What?
>
> In sloping, upright and backhands: Queen's Hotel, Queen's Hotel, Queen's Hotel. Queen's Ho ... (*U,* 17.612–20)

The project as ideated by Stephen is far superior, both in conception and execution, to Bloom's showcart "in which two smartly dressed girls were to be seated engaged in writing" (*U,* 17.609–10). The scene is vibrant, condensed, shaping to a fine pitch the plodding suspense that Bloom's ox-drawn cart is intended to provide. "Everyone dying to know what she's writing" (*U,* 8.134–35), says Bloom in "Lestrygonians," and Barber plays with this suspense, setting the piece in a jazzy tango for a voice who abruptly breaks the frame to ask, supported by a thud from the piano, "What?"

And here the mood shifts, as it must, for as Stephen gives the answer, Bloom is sent back to the past, and to the death of his father. The music dies in a whisper, but Barber doesn't explain, as Joyce does, why his gay jaunty rhythm suddenly goes grave. Buried beneath "Solitary Hotel" is the ghost of Joyce's answer; for in "Queen's Hotel" Bloom is given a coincidental exhumation of the place where his father took his own life. The act of inscribing "Queen's Hotel" on the notepaper is both a re-creation of the act of writing and an evocation of a father: in that, it mirrors the word inscribed on the desk in *Portrait* (*P,* 89). Stephen sees the word "*Foetus*" as his father is looking for his initials, and Bloom is similarly presented with the phrase as an accidental reminder of the richly communicative power of language. "Queen's Ho ..." (*U,* 17.620) is a collapse, a surprise ending revealing an unexpected corpse. The last seven bars of "Solitary Hotel" can be taken to represent this breakdown, in the rumbling subterranean bass, in the jagged play of the 3/2 rhythm between singer and accompanist, and in the broken space that follows "Ho ...," that mirrors the broken fragments of the suicide note Bloom tries to recollect later in "Ithaca": "my dear son ... always ... of me ... *das Herz ... Gott ... dein ...*" (*U,* 17.1885–86).[35] The spectral image of Bloom's father hangs like a veronica over the café piece. Bringing back the dead is Joyce's obsession, and by breathing new life into Joyce's texts, Samuel Barber, over the course of a long engagement with the themes and images of Joyce, does the same.

Barber, Keller, Schoeck, and Joyce are all connected by a silver cord. The phrase is Keller's, from "Jugendgedanken," where he speaks of a "Silbersaite," a cord that, once struck (as one would strike the string of a piano or a harp), resounded through his life:

> Ich will spiegeln mich in jenen Tagen,
> Die wie Linden wipfelwehn entflohn,
> Wo die Silbersaite, angeschlagen,
> Klar, doch bebend, gab den ersten Ton,
>
> (I want to see my mirrored image in those days
> Which fled like the flutterings of the tops of lindens,
> When the silver cord, struck,
> Clear, yet quivering, gave its first note,)[36]

In a letter to Frank Budgen written on Joyce's behalf by Lucia, Joyce suggests that Budgen use this quatrain as the motto for his book (*L,* III, 284). The passage continues: "Der mein Leben lang, / Erst heut noch, widerklang" ("which, my whole life long, / And still today, resounded"). The "Silbersaite" that sounds through Joyce's life, from the first note to the last, is the infinite string of repetition and return. It is the navel cord and the coffin band. It is the silver thread that connects the three Zurich dwellers, Keller, Schoeck, and Joyce, to a fourth, Frank Budgen. It is the musical chord that sounds throughout Joyce's writings, for music, in Joyce, is the tone struck his "whole life long." There is a silver cord that binds a text to its translation, whether the translation be into music (as Schoeck translated Keller), or into a new language (as Joyce, hearing Schoeck's musical translation, then translated Keller) or into music again (as Barber, coming upon Joyce's translation of Keller in Gorman's biography, then translated Joyce).

Joyce and Barber, Keller and Schoeck: writer and composer are
connected one to the other, two notes sounding "Klar, doch bebend"
together, as words resonate with music, death resonates with life.

NOTES

    1. Cited in Kreiling, 354.

    2. These ten early songs also appeared as part of an excellent recording of
all of Barber's songs, *Secrets of the Old* (titled after Barber's setting of the
Yeats poem), with Cheryl Studer, soprano, Thomas Hampson, baritone, and
John Browning, piano. Deutsche Grammophon 4358672.

    3. Homer, too, was fond of striking the Celtic note, and set the poems of
Yeats and Stephens to music. His *Seventeen Songs* include "Robartes Bids His
Beloved Be at Peace" and "The Fiddler of Dooney." Barber's penchant for
Joyce may, however, have come not from his distinguished composer uncle but
from his family's cook, Annie Sullivan Noble, who had "an unlimited
repertoire of Irish songs" (Heyman, 21), and who provided the libretto, when
Barber was the Mozartean age of ten, to an opera entitled "The Rose Tree."
Yeats, coincidentally, published a poem with the same title a year later, in
Michael Robartes and the Dancer (1921). The last name of Barber's uncle is
also a coincidence.

    4. Though, as mentioned in this volume's introduction, Lydia gets it
wrong, singing "*O, Idolores*" instead of "Oh my Dolores" (*U*, 11.226), for
reasons discussed in Knowles, "That Form Endearing: A Performance of Siren
Songs," 214.

    5. Barber's horse, heard in the left hand of measures 57–59 of Op. 10 no.
3, has three notes to a beat, like Schubert's famous triplets, but the quarter-note-
and-two-eighths rhythm staggers the pace.

    6. James Joyce, translation of Gottfried Keller, *Lebendig Begraben,* VIII
(1888). The original is located, according to Jean Kreiling, in "Notes for
Illustrations," in the Herbert Gorman Papers in the Harley K. Croessmann
Collection of James Joyce, Morris Library, Southern Illinois University at
Carbondale, 2–3. Joyce's translation was first printed in Gorman, 345. Aside
from minor changes in punctuation, Barber's song text makes one lexical
alteration: "this dark" in line six becomes "the darkness" (see appendix).

    7. "Barber's choice of an obscure text found in translation in a biography
may be considered especially unusual, but it does not surprise anyone familiar
with the composer's reading habits and his special fascination with Joyce"
(Kreiling, 354).

8. Reincarnation is a theme Joyce shares with Barber, whose choral settings of three poems by James Stephens are called *Reincarnations* (Op. 16), in which Mary Hynes and Anthony O'Daly are brought to life (though "O'Daly is dead") in Barber's music.

9. Barber will often play upon this theme, writing three musical "Essays" for Orchestra (Op. 12, Op. 17, Op. 47), and an unpublished series of three essays for piano, written when he was sixteen (Heyman, 39).

10. "Our daily bread" is from the Lord's Prayer, rather than communion, but the connection between the two in *Ulysses* is clear, from the morning loaf and the opening mass in "Telemachus" to the rock-hard buns of "Eumaeus." The buried victim's eating of the rose is as much a parody of the communion as Mulligan's mockery with the shaving bowl.

11. The text of "Nuvoletta" is interesting in its parallels with Keller here: in the musty earth, the singer hears an echo of sounds above ("dormimust echo") and turns for small comfort to the Catholic mass. Barber's "Nuvoletta" is a fascinating work in its own right, with quotations from Wagner (a *Tristan* chord at "Tristis Tristior Tristissimus"), and an extended cadenza on "*O! O! O! Par la pluie*" before Nuvoletta drowns. In its audacity, playfulness, and complexity, "Nuvoletta" acts as a perfect mirror to *Finnegans Wake*.

12. Curiously, Samuel Barber wrote another of them, a setting of "Dover Beach" (Op. 3).

13. Compare Stephen's wood shavings at the end of "Circe" and the beginning of "Eumaeus" (*U*, 15.4891, 16.2), which Bloom wipes with a "soapsuddy handkerchief after it had done yeoman service in the shaving line" (*U*, 16.19–20), providing a link back to the shaving lather at the opening of "Telemachus," and a hint that Telemachus's beard is growing, itself an indication that Penelope is now free to accept a suitor.

14. Kauffman's edition of Keller's *Gedichte* prints both the 1846 and 1888 versions. In a note on the two texts, Kauffman details Keller's process of revision (1150). To compress nineteen poems into fourteen, Keller omitted three poems (nos. 4, 5, 17), collapsed two poems (nos. 11-12) into one, and collapsed the two final poems (nos. 18-19) into one. It is not hard to see why the three deleted poems were left out: one is about the speaker finding a pencil to write with in his vest pocket, one wishes that the coffin lid had a mirror, and the third has the immortal line: "Die Luft ist heiß und dumpf in diesem Sarg" (no. 17) ("The air is hot and dank in this coffin"). Each of the other poems were considerably revised, and particularly the thirteenth poem, "Da hab' ich gar die Rose aufgegessen," which became poem VIII. For the original version of the poem that Joyce translated, see Kreiling, who also provides a translation of that version.

A chart of the genesis of *Lebendig Begraben* follows, with the original first lines of each poem:

Gedanken eines Lebendig-Begrabenen (1846)		*Lebendig Begraben* (1888)
Poem #	First Line	Poem #
1	"Ei wie das kracht!—Abscheuliches Geroll"	I
2	"Da lieg' ich nun, ohnmächtiger Geselle"	II
3	"Ha! was its das? Die Sehnen zucken wieder"	III
4	"Sie haben mir, als sie der Tod belogen"	Deleted
5	"In's Innre jedes Sarges sollte man"	Deleted
6	"Horch! Stimmen und Geschrei, doch kaum zu hören"	IV
7	"Läg ich, wo es Hyänen gibt, im Sand"	V
8	"Als endlich sie, nach langem, schwankem Lauf"	VI
9	"Tief im Gehirne brennt mich diese Stille!"	VII
10	"Zwölf hat's geschlagen—warum denn Mittag?"	IX
11	"O, ich mag rufen, schreien, wie ich will"	X
12	"Wenn einsam Sie vielleicht und ungeliebt"	X
13	"Da hab' ich gar die Rose aufgegessen"	VIII
14	"Viel besser wär's, zerschnittner Tannenbaum"	XI
15	"Der erste Tannenbaum, den ich gesehn"	XII
16	"Der schönste Tannenbaum, den ich gesehn"	XIII
17	"Ich muß ein Weilchen wohl geschlafen haben"	Deleted
18	"Ich bin befreit, mein Weh hat sich gewendet"	XIV
19	"O teure Luft! Mit jedem Odemzug"	XIV

15. All translations are mine unless otherwise indicated. I should like to acknowledge here the tremendous help provided by Ray Ockenden, Professor of German at Wadham College, Oxford, who provided valuable encouragement at the start of this project, read the translation as it was first drafted, and guided me past some truly embarrassing pitfalls, such as the conviction that "Lenz" was not an old-fashioned word for "spring" but a town in the Alps ("thus I, citizen of Lenz..."). Any infelicities in the translated text of *Lebendig Begraben* are either mine or faithful reproductions of Keller's.

16. Walter Scott's very loose translation is one of three English versions of the poem that appeared in 1796. See Jonathan Wordsworth's introduction to Scott's translation for the impact of "Lenore" on European Romanticism. Scott himself is a standard-bearer of the nineteenth-century Live Burial Brigade: Clare Simmons has written of the legendary practice of immuring pregnant nuns in niches and its relevance for *Marmion,* and for Gothic law and

architecture in the romantic period generally. Compare also the end of Part I of Tennyson's *Maud* (1855):

> My heart would hear her and beat,
>   Were it earth in an earthy bed;
> My dust would hear her and beat,
>   Had I lain for a century dead;
> Would start and tremble under her feet,
>   And blossom in purple and red. (Tennyson, 280)

(Arthur Somervell has set these lines to music as part of his *Maud* song cycle.)

17. In Lenore's speech to Wilhelm in stanza 15, for instance, different lines from the "Erlkönig" can be heard in every line:

"Lenore"	"Erlkönig"
Ach, Wilhelm, erst herein geschwind!	Dem Vater grauset's, er reitet geschwind,
Den Hagedorn durchsaust der Wind	In dürren Blättern säuselt der Wind.
Herein, in meinen Armen	In seinen Armem das Kind war tot.
Herzliebster, zu erwarmen!	Er faßt ihn sicher, er hält ihn warm.
(Bürger, 181)	(Goethe, 303–4)

Goethe spoke enthusiastically of Bürger's poem on its publication in 1773 and wrote the "Erlkönig" nine years later, so it can be assumed that with lines this similar he is acknowledging a debt. "Lenore" is the subject of Joachim Raff's Symphony no. 5, and of a tone poem by Henri Duparc.

18. In *Siebenkäs,* the hero disguises his death by burying an empty coffin (as Parnell's death is disguised, according to partisans in "Eumaeus" [*U,* 16.1304]), and the Dead Christ has a ghastly nightmare of visiting an open cemetery where only the children sleep. He walks through the shadows of centuries before the watchful eyes of two basilisks, and encounters a dead man who awakes, and opens his eyelids to reveal open sockets. His hands and arms fall off, and the dead all cry "Christ! Is there no God?" to which he answers: "There is none" (Paul, 181). This is the "First Flowerpiece" of *Siebenkäs:* given the dead flower in Keller and the orangeblossoms that surround Stephen's mother in "Circe" (*U,* 15.4158), it is easy to trace this nightmare's line through Keller to Joyce.

19. After Keller and Poe the line can be traced forward to Hardy's "Art Thou Digging at My Grave," which doubly twists the knife on the romantic idea of live burial, in having the gravebed visitant being the buried speaker's dog, and then in having the dog, rather than paying his respects to his master, be digging for a bone. Hardy is drawing on a separate well of folk materials for

his grisly subject, for ballads frequently refer to the theme of live burial. In "The Ballad of the Unquiet Grave," the female victim asks "who sits weeping on my grave," and apologizes for her bad breath: "My breath smells earthy strong" (Housman, 89). "The Mistletoe Bough," a ballad recited by a German in Mr. Britling's drawing room in *Mr. Britling Sees It Through,* tells of "how a beautiful girl hid away in a chest during a Christmas game of hide-and-seek, and how she was found, a dried vestige, years afterwards" (Wells, 131).

In ballads the speaker rarely escapes: it is the literary hero who is prone to miraculous recoveries from accidental interment. The hero, to prove himself, must go down among the dead and return to the living. Several heroes of particular importance for *Ulysses* take the downward path of Dante and Aeneas. Sindbad the Sailor, who appears at the end of "Ithaca" searching for daylight, is in his Fourth Voyage buried alive with his dead wife, in a cave with other spouses of dead people, where he survives by eating the food charitably left with the incarcerated living, finally making his way, through the defeat of a corpse-chewing monster, into the sunlight (*Arabian Nights' Entertainments,* 157–64). Ronald Bush has established the eleventh book of the *Odyssey,* where Odysseus descends among the dead, to be invaluable for the modernist enterprise (Bush, 129–34), and it is in the Nekyia where Odysseus, like Stephen in "Circe," meets his dead mother, and where Achilles lives forever, racing along fields of asphodel at the news of the glory of his son, paralleling Bloom's astonishment at the scholarly and sartorial success of Rudy at the close of "Circe." The King of Glory, too, has his own descent into hell: Bloom is at various points Sindbad, Odysseus, and Christ.

20. All Roman numerals, except those prefixed by *CM,* refer to poems within Keller's 1888 song cycle *Lebendig Begraben.*

21. The Swiss are more careful than the English, burying their corpses one foot deeper: "Und lassen mich hier sieben Fuß tief liegen" (I) ("And left me here to lie seven feet deep").

22. Joyce has romanticized this funeral wreath, choosing to interpret the "sie" of the second line as feminine third-person singular. But the pronoun is more likely to be plural, especially since the speaker particularly regrets not having left a lover behind (X).

23. This animal-like "eating up" is even more pronounced in Joyce's mistyping of the first line in the typescript of "aufgegessen" as "aufgefressen," which is precisely what animals do. Gorman faithfully reproduces this typographical error in his biography (345). For other differences between Joyce's typescript and Keller's poem, see Kreiling, 356.

24. This is very much in the style of Vardaman, though Vardaman's gimlet is for letting the air in rather than the gas out. Addie's speech after her death

makes one see her as buried alive: Faulkner provides the same death's eye view as Keller does with his interred narrator. Other modernist texts with this theme are *The Waste Land,* with a sprouting corpse in "The Burial of the Dead," Kafka's *Metamorphosis,* and *Sarah of the Sahara,* that most peculiar novel of the 1920s, with its chapter on being "Buried Alive." In Abel Gance's film, *J'Accuse,* the soldiers from a forgotten war return, like the soldier in Bürger's poem, from their graves to visit the living. And in *The Magic Mountain,* Hans Castorp is in some sense buried alive at the Berghof—an X-ray provides him a glimpse into his own grave—which perhaps explains his fascination with Radames and Aïda's final duet:

> You had only to picture coolly and calmly what was actually happening here. Two people were being buried alive; their lungs full of the gases of the crypt, cramped with hunger, they would perish together, or even worse, one after the other; and then decay would do its unspeakable work on their bodies, until two skeletons lay there under those vaults, each indifferent and insensitive to whether it lay there alone or with another set of bones. (Mann, 636)

Opera has always been fond of the return from the grave: John Gordon marvelously demonstrates elsewhere in this volume that the return of May Goulding is modeled after the return of Laura in *La Gioconda.* Judith Harrington has also called my attention to the dead nuns in Meyerbeer's *Robert le Diable,* who come back to haunt the living as temptresses. Derrick Puffett, in his overview of the theme, cites Scott and Eichendorff's "Der Schatzgräber," set to music by Schumann in 1840 (203).

25. This telephone in the coffin is itself reminiscent of a story told of Mary Baker Eddy, who was said to have been so confident of her resurrection that she maintained a telephone line from her coffin to the guard at the Mount Auburn Cemetery gate. Robert Peel dispels the rumor, explaining that a telephone line was temporarily laid down for the benefit of a twenty-four-hour guard, who kept watch over Eddy's unburied coffin during the construction of the great vault in 1910. Nevertheless, as Peel says, "the legend still persists that 'the Christian Scientists have a telephone in Mrs. Eddy's tomb'" (514).

26. The reference to Blavatsky in "Scylla and Charybdis" establishes the Theosophical Society framework for the Literary Revival that is presented in that chapter, for AE, Eglinton, and especially Yeats belong to both groups. Blavatsky, incidentally, makes a neat connection between the end of "Lestrygonians" and the beginning of "Scylla." The final word of "Lestrygonians" is "Safe!," as Bloom slides into the museum unseen by Boylan (*U,* 8.1193). This is Bloom's thought, of course, but as with "Usurper," which

was Stephen's thought at the end of "Telemachus" (*U,* 1.743), the narrative implications are equally interesting, since the narrator is in "Telemachus" being usurped by Stephen, and resents it, and since the narrator in calling Bloom "Safe!" acts as baseball umpire. This raises the ghost of another member of the Order of the Golden Dawn, Abner Doubleday. Doubleday, whose father's name was Ulysses, was born in Cooperstown, New York, and was a distinguished general in the Civil War. He is best known, not for being the vice president of the Theosophical Society, but for being the putative inventor of baseball. (See Blavatsky, 459–61, for more biographical information on Doubleday.) "Safe!" thus takes *Ulysses* through Doubleday from Cooperstown to Blavatsky, and from Bloom in "Lestrygonians" to Stephen in "Scylla."

27. "Byzantium," in Yeats, 248.

28. "Ulysses," in Tennyson, 89. The untraveled world gleams for Tennyson's Ulysses through a similar arch.

29. In the much more brutal original version of Zola's story, published in *La Voltaire,* Bécaille's wife is raped before his eyes, by the man she then marries: says Zola's editor Ripoll, "il s'agit explicitement d'un viol commis auprès du mari impuissant" (Zola, 1561). Bécaille is also interesting for his confrontation, while buried alive, with the "néant," the Nothingness after death against which Joyce is fighting a rear-guard action all his life: "Seul, le néant m'avait terrifié, depuis mon enfance" (Zola, 807). See also Balzac's *Le Colonel Chabert,* Antonin Mulé's *L'Histoire de Ma Mort,* and Léo Lespès's *Entre Quatre Planches; Souvenirs d'un Déterré* for other French takes on the live burial theme.

30. Keller's editor Walter Muschg places little credence in the tokay story, and suggests that Keller is playing a joke on his biographer: "der Dichter kann mit ihr nur die Biographen gefoppt haben" (Muschg, 210).

31. There's some confusion on the chronology of this. Ellmann dates the radio broadcast before September 13, 1940 (Ellmann, 736), but in a letter dated November 1940 Joyce says that he listened to it only a few days ago: "J'ai écrit un petit mot à Schoeck lui disant que j'ai entendu l'autre soir son oeuvre *Lebendig Begraben* à la radio" (*L,* I, 424). Schoeck's letter on Joyce's behalf came after the rejection of Joyce's first application for visas on September 30, and the November letter suggests that the radio broadcast must have as well.

32. HCE's coffin is "Pughglasspanelfitted" (*FW,* 76.11), which parallels, though there is no evidence that Joyce had any knowledge that it did so, an idea in an eliminated poem from Keller's original *Gedanken eines Lebendig-Begrabenen:* "In's Innre jedes Sarges sollte man / Hell von Metall 'nen Spiegel schlagen an" (*Gedanken,* 5) ("They should have put inside this coffin / A bright metal mirror"). More likely references to Keller in the *Wake* include "in my

graben fields [...] pineshrouded" (*FW*, 545.34–46.1), with its suggestion of pine boards in the grave, and "to fress up the rinnerung and to ate by hart" (*FW*, 300.15–16), which has the hint of Joyce's mistyped "aufgefressen" for Keller's "aufgegessen."

33. Cited in Ellmann, 521, from a 1956 interview with Jacques Benoîst-Méchin.

34. Stoppard's Rosencrantz puts this deplorable situation most succinctly:

> ROS: Because you'd be helpless wouldn't you? Stuffed in a box like that, I mean you'd be in there for ever. Even taking into account the fact that you're dead, it isn't a pleasant thought. *Especially* if you're dead, really ... *ask* yourself, if I asked you straight off—I'm going to stuff you in this box now, would you rather be alive or dead? Naturally, you'd prefer to be alive. Life in a box is better than no life at all. I expect. You'd have a chance at least. You could lie there thinking—well, at least I'm not dead! In a minute someone's going to bang on the lid and tell me to come out. (*Banging the floor with his fists*.) "Hey you, whatsyername! Come out of there!"
>
> GUIL (*jumps up savagely*): You don't have to flog it to death! (71)

35. Note that Barber uses the 1961 edition, which has one less iteration of the phrase "Queen's Hotel" than the 1984 text.

36. Citation and translation by Ellmann, in *L*, III, 284.

WORKS CITED

Arabian Nights' Entertainments. Ed. Robert Mack. Oxford: Oxford University Press, 1995.

Barber, Samuel. *Fadograpn of a Yestern Scene*. Op. 44. For Orchestra. New York: Schirmer, 1972.

———. "I Hear an Army." Op. 10, no. 3. *Collected Songs for High Voice*. New York: Schirmer, 1955. 19–25.

———. "In the Dark Pinewood." *Ten Early Songs*. Ed. Paul Wittke. New York: Schirmer, 1994. 29–30.

———. "Now Have I Fed and Eaten Up the Rose." Op. 45, no. 1. *Three Songs for Voice and Piano*. New York: Schirmer, 1974. 3–5.

———. "Nuvoletta." Op. 25. *Collected Songs for High Voice*. New York: Schirmer, 1955. 49–57.

———. "Of That So Sweet Imprisonment." *Ten Early Songs*. Ed. Paul Wittke. New York: Schirmer, 1994. 20–22.

————. "Rain Has Fallen." Op. 10, no. 1. *Collected Songs for High Voice.* New York: Schirmer, 1955. 10–14.

————. *Secrets of the Old. The Songs: Complete.* Cheryl Studer, soprano, Thomas Hampson, baritone, John Browning, piano. CD. Deutsche Grammophon 4358672.

————. "Sleep Now." Op. 10, no. 2. *Collected Songs for High Voice.* New York: Schirmer, 1955. 15–18.

————. "Solitary Hotel." Op. 41, no. 1. *Despite and Still.* Song Cycle for Voice and Piano. New York: Schirmer, 1969. 14–18.

————. "Strings in the Earth and Air." *Ten Early Songs.* Ed. Paul Wittke. New York: Schirmer, 1994. 23–24.

Blavatsky, H. P. *Collected Writings 1874–1878.* Vol. I. Wheaton, Ill.: Theosophical Press, 1966.

Bürger, Gottfried. "Lenore." *Sämtliche Werke.* Eds. Günter and Hiltrud Häntzschel. Munich: Carl Hanser Verlag, 1987. 178–88.

Bush, Ronald. *The Genesis of Ezra Pound's Cantos.* Paperback ed. Princeton, N.J.: Princeton University Press, 1989.

Eliot, T. S. *The Waste Land and Other Poems.* New York: Harcourt Brace Jovanovich, 1962.

Ellmann, Richard. *James Joyce.* Rev. ed. Oxford: Oxford University Press, 1982.

Faulkner, William. *As I Lay Dying.* New York: Vintage, 1985.

Goethe, Johann Wolfgang. "Erlkönig." *Gedichte 1759–1799.* Ed. Karl Eibl. Vol. I. *Sämtliche Werke.* Frankfurt: Deutscher Klassiker Verlag, 1987. 303–4.

Gorman, Herbert. *James Joyce.* New York: Farrar & Rinehart, 1939.

Heine, Heinrich. *Junge Leiden. Gedichte.* Ed. Werner Vordtriede. Vol. I. *Sämtliche Werke.* Munich: Winkler-Verlag, 1969. 53–100.

Heyman, Barbara. *Samuel Barber: The Composer and His Music.* Oxford: Oxford University Press, 1992.

Housman, John, ed. *British Popular Ballads.* New York: Barnes & Noble, 1952.

Joyce, James. *Ulysses.* New York: Random House, 1961.

Keller, Gottfried. *Ausgewählte Gedichte.* Ed. Walter Muschg. Bern: Francke Verlag, 1956.

————. *Gedanken eines Lebendig-Begrabenen* (1846). *Gedichte.* Ed. Kai Kauffman. Vol. I. *Sämtliche Werke.* Frankfurt: Deutscher Klassiker Verlag, 1995. 100–15.

————. *Lebendig Begraben* (1888). *Gedichte.* Ed. Kai Kauffman. Vol. I. *Sämtliche Werke.* Frankfurt: Deutscher Klassiker Verlag, 1995. 474–85.

Knowles, Sebastian D. G. "That Form Endearing: A Performance of Siren Songs; or, 'I was only vamping, man.'" *Joyce in the Hibernian Metropolis: Essays.* Eds. Morris Beja and David Norris. Columbus: Ohio State University Press, 1996. 213–36.

Kreiling, Jean. "A Note on James Joyce, Gottfried Keller, and Music." *James Joyce Quarterly* 25, 3 (1988): 349–56.

Lindsay, J. M. *Gottfried Keller: Life and Works.* London: Oswald Wolff, 1968.

Lund, Steven. *James Joyce: Letters, Manuscripts, and Photographs at Southern Illinois University.* Troy, N.Y.: Whitston, 1983.

Mann, Thomas. *The Magic Mountain.* Trans. John Woods. New York: Vintage, 1996.

Mulé, Antonin. *L'Histoire de Ma Mort.* Paris: Poulet, 1862.

Paul, Jean. *Jean Paul: A Reader.* Ed. Timothy Casey. Baltimore, Md.: Johns Hopkins Press, 1992.

Peel, Robert. *Mary Baker Eddy: The Years of Authority.* New York: Holt, Rinehart and Winston, 1977.

Poe, Edgar Allan. "The Cask of Amontillado." *The Complete Edgar Allan Poe Tales.* New York: Avenel Books, 1981. 542–46.

———. "The Premature Burial." *The Complete Edgar Allan Poe Tales.* New York: Avenel Books, 1981. 432–41.

Puffett, Derrick. *The Song Cycles of Othmar Schoeck.* Publikationen der Schwiezerischen Musikforschenden Gesellschaft. Serie II. Vol. 32. Bern: Haupt, 1982.

Schoeck, Othmar. *Lebendig Begraben.* Dietrich Fischer-Dieskau, baritone. Fritz Rieger, conductor. Radio-Symphonie-Orchester Berlin. CD. Claves 50–8610.

———. *Lebendig Begraben. Vierzehn Gesänge nach der gleichnamigen Gedichtfolge von Gottfried Keller.* Op. 40. Ed. Karl Krebs. Wiesbaden: Breitkopf & Härtel, 1956.

Schubert, Franz. "Erlkönig." Deutsch 328. Text Johann Wolfgang Goethe. *Gesänge.* Frankfurt: Peters, n. d. 170–75.

———. "Der Müller und der Bach." *Die Schöne Müllerin.* Deutsch 795. Text Wilhelm Müller. Frankfurt: Peters, 1976. 49–51.

———. *Winterreise.* Deutsch 911. Text Wilhelm Müller. Frankfurt: Peters, 1975.

Scott, Walter. *The Chase and William and Helen. 1796. Two Ballads from the German of Gottfried Augustus Bürger.* Ed. Jonathan Wordsworth. Oxford: Woodstock Books, 1989.

Simmons, Clare. "Gothic Architecture and Gothic Law: National Critique in Romantic-Era Narratives of Immuring." Unpublished.

Stoppard, Tom. *Rosencrantz and Guildenstern Are Dead*. New York: Grove, 1967.

Tennyson, Alfred, Baron. *Poems and Plays*. Oxford: Oxford University Press, 1975.

Traprock, Walter E. *Sarah of the Sahara*. New York: Putnam, 1923.

Vogel, Werner. *Othmar Schoeck*. Zurich: Atlantis, 1976.

Wells, H. G. *Mr. Britling Sees It Through*. New York: Macmillan, 1916.

Yeats, W. B. *The Collected Poems of W. B. Yeats*. Ed. Richard Finneran. New York: Macmillan, 1989.

Zola, Emile. "La Mort d'Olivier Bécaille." *Contes et Nouvelles*. Ed. Roger Ripoll. Paris: Gallimard, 1976. 802–30.

APPENDIX

Barber's Musical Settings of Texts by James Joyce

	Opus No.	Text	Composition	Publication
1.	Op. 10, no. 1	"Rain Has Fallen"	1935	1939
2.	Op. 10, no. 2	"Sleep Now"	1935	1939
3.	Op. 10, no. 3	"I Hear an Army"	1936	1939
4.	Op. 25	"Nuvoletta"	1947	1952
5.	Op. 41, no. 4	"Solitary Hotel"	1968	1969
6.	Op. 44	*Fadograph of a Yestern Scene*	1971	1972
7.	Op. 45, no. 1	"Now Have I Fed and Eaten Up the Rose"	1972	1974
8.	Op. Posth.	"Of That So Sweet Imprisonment"	1935	1994
9.	Op. Posth.	"Strings in the Earth and Air"	1935	1994
10.	Op. Posth.	"In the Dark Pinewood"	1937	1994

Texts set by Samuel Barber. Omissions of Joyce's text are indicated in square brackets. Where Barber's version differs from Joyce's text, Barber's text is first given in angled (< >) brackets, followed by Joyce's text in square ([ ]) brackets.

1. "Rain Has Fallen" (*CM*, XXXII)

Rain has fallen all the day.
    O come among the laden trees:
The leaves lie thick upon the way
    Of memories.

Staying a little by the way
    Of memories shall we depart.
Come, my beloved, where I may
    Speak to your heart.

2. "Sleep Now" (*CM*, XXXIV)

Sleep now, O sleep now,
    O you unquiet heart!

A voice crying 'Sleep now'
    Is heard in my heart.

The voice of the winter
    Is heard at the door.
O sleep for the winter
    Is crying 'Sleep no more!'

My kiss will give peace now
    And quiet to your heart—
Sleep on in peace now,
    O you unquiet heart!

3. "I Hear an Army" (*CM*, XXXVI)

I hear an army charging upon the land
    And the thunder of horses plunging, foam about their knees.
Arrogant, in black armour, behind them stand,
    Disdaining the reins, with fluttering whips, the charioteers.

They cry unto the night their battlename:
    I moan in sleep when I hear afar their whirling laughter.
They cleave the gloom of dreams, a blinding flame,
    Clanging, clanging upon the heart as upon an anvil.

They come shaking in triumph their long, green hair:
    They come out of the sea and run shouting by the shore.
My heart, have you no wisdom thus to despair?
    My love, my love, my love, why have you left me alone?

4. "Nuvoletta" (*FW*, 157.8–159.10)

Nuvoletta in her light dress, spunn of sisteen shimmers, was looking
down on them, leaning over the bannistars and listening all she
childishly could. [...] She was alone. All her nubied companions were
asleeping with the squirrels. [...] She tried all the winsome wonsome
ways her four winds had taught her. She tossed her
sfumastelliacinous hair like *la princesse de la Petite Bretagne* and she
rounded her mignons arms like Mrs Cornwallis-West and she smiled
over herself like the [beauty of the] image of the pose of the daughter
of the [queen of the] Emperour of Irelande and she sighed after

herself as were she born to bride with Tristis Tristior Tristissimus.
But, sweet madonine, she might fair as well have carried her daisy's
worth to Florida. [...] Oh, how it was duusk<.>[!] From Vallee
Maraia to Grasyaplaina dormimust echo! Ah dew! Ah dew! It was so
duusk that the tears of night began to fall, first by ones and twos, then
by threes and fours, at last by fives and sixes of sevens, for the tired
ones were wecking, as we weep now with them. *O! O! O! Par la
pluie*<.>[!] [...] Then Nuvoletta reflected for the last time in her little
long life and she made up all her myriads of drifting minds in one.
She cancelled all her engauzements. She climbed over the bannistars;
she gave a childy cloudy cry: *Nuée! Nuée!* A light dress fluttered. She
was gone.

5. "Solitary Hotel" (*Ulysses* [1961 edition], 684)

Solitary hotel in mountain pass. Autumn. Twilight. Fire lit. In
dark corner young man seated. Young woman enters. Restless.
Solitary. She sits. She goes to window. She stands. She sits. Twilight.
She thinks. On solitary hotel paper she writes. She thinks. She writes.
She sighs. Wheels and hoofs. She hurries out. He comes from his
dark corner. He seizes solitary paper. He holds it towards fire.
Twilight. He reads. Solitary.

What?
In sloping, upright and backhands: Queen's hotel, Queen's hotel,
Queen's <ho>[Ho] ...

6. *Fadograph of a Yestern Scene* (*FW*, 7.15)

[No Text]

7. "Now Have I Fed and Eaten Up the Rose" (Translation of poem VIII of Gottfried Keller's 1888 version of *Lebendig Begraben*)

Now have I fed and eaten up the rose
Which then she laid within my stiffcold hand.
That I should ever feed upon a rose
I never had believed in liveman's land.

Only I wonder was it white or red
The flower that in <the darkness>[this dark] my food has been.

Give us, and if Thou give, thy daily bread,
Deliver us from evil, Lord, Amen.

8. "Of That So Sweet Imprisonment" (*CM,* XXII)

Of that so sweet imprisonment
    My soul, dearest, is fain—
Soft arms that woo me to relent
    And woo me to detain.
Ah, could they ever hold me there,
    Gladly were I [a] prisoner!

Dearest, through interwoven arms
    By love made tremulous,
That night allures me where alarms
    Nowise may trouble us;
But sleep to dreamier sleep be wed
    Where soul with soul lies prisoned.

9. "Strings in the Earth and Air" (*CM,* I)

Strings in the earth and air
    Make music sweet;
Strings by the river where
    The willows meet.

There's music along the river
    For Love wanders there,
Pale flowers on his mantle,
    Dark leaves on his hair.

All softly playing,
    With head to the music bent,
And fingers straying
    Upon an instrument.

10. "In the Dark Pinewood" (*CM,* XX)

In the dark pinewood
    I would we lay
In deep cool <shadows>[shadow]

At noon of day.

How sweet to lie there,
   Sweet to kiss.
Where the great pine forest
   Enaisled is!

Thy kiss descending
   Sweeter were
With a soft tumult
   Of thy hair.

O, unto the pinewood
   At noon of day
Come with me now,
   Sweet love, away.

Section 3: Contemporary Music and Joyce

CHAPTER 6

The Euphonium Cagehaused in Either Notation: John Cage and *Finnegans Wake*

Scott W. Klein

[...] those whapping oldsteirs, with sycamode euphonium in either notation in our altogether cagehaused duckyheim [...] (*FW*, 533.17–18)

In this passage from *Finnegans Wake* Joyce's neologism "duckyheim" puns on Ibsen, the Norwegian *Et dukkehjem, A Doll's House*. This is appropriate, not only because Ibsen was a significant literary and political presence for the young Joyce, but because Ibsen's play came to stand for a kind of avant-garde liberation from entrenched nineteenth-century ideals. Yet in quirkily Wakean fashion the "oldsteirs" invoked (both the "oldsters," and perhaps the "old stairs" by which new and higher things may be reached) are impossibly juxtaposed against "cagehaused," which seems usefully to allude to the names of John Cage and Karlheinz Stockhausen, post-World War II liberators of music from entrenched nineteenth-century ideals. The occurrence is purely fortuitous, and depends upon the suspension of both chronology and context, a willingness to read the allusion to a woman's breaking free of a repressive "cagehouse" as a found allusion to a liberational theory of music. To do so is to use *Finnegans Wake* as a kind of *sortes virgilianae,* to pick random phrases and read in them augurs of a future clearly outside the author's intentions. That one is tempted to do so, however—to find meanings where meanings cannot possibly have been intended—exemplifies the kind of discovery through unforeseen juxtapositions found in the compositions of John Cage, whose work, particularly from the late 1970s until his death in 1992, drew heavily upon the *Wake*.

Cage's use of Joyce is a striking and unusual case within a much larger phenomenon. Joyce exerted an enduring influence on younger composers, particularly Americans, of almost impossibly different aesthetic presuppositions.[1] But Cage is unique among American composers for confronting Joyce's final work for both musical and linguistic ends, setting passages from *Finnegans Wake* as songs, discovering in Joyce a mode of multilevel punning for the titles of late works, and constructing raucous music "circuses" that drew explicitly and implicitly upon the model of the *Wake*. Moreover, Cage's use of Joyce extended beyond purely musical inspiration into experimentation with prose composition. Among composers, Cage was unusually interested in writing. He produced a series of what he called "writings through" *Finnegans Wake,* which he based upon an idiosyncratic method of composition called the "mesostic," creating new poetic texts upon "keywords" found throughout Joyce's text. In turn, in his Wakean sound-collage *Roaratorio* (1979), Cage blended his verbal expropriations from the *Wake* with a collage of geographically appropriate sounds to produce the most thoroughly Joycean work of music yet written.

Why this attraction to Joyce's work, when Cage's own work depended so notoriously upon attempting programmatically to exclude the composer's personality from his works? Joyce's influence on Cage was a matter of two notations (or, as the *Wake* would have it, "either notation"): two manners of "composition." Cage's musical and typographical work resonate philosophically with Joyce's, and both come together in Cage's masterpiece *Roaratorio,* which investigates the relationship among voice, text, and musical composition. Cage, no less than Joyce, provides through those juxtapositions a complex meditation on the relationship between the author—or composer—and his aesthetic productions.

Cage's career began as Joyce's was drawing to a close. His earliest surviving works date from 1932, and demonstrate simultaneously a literary bent and an attempt to develop new strategies of composition within the relatively nascent doctrine of serialism. In his autobiographical essay "A Composer's Confessions" (1948), Cage admits that his earliest inspirations were the unlikely literary pair of Aeschylus and Gertrude Stein (*Writer,* 29), and his earliest artistic interests crossed wide generic lines. While a young man in Paris he attended closely to painting as well as musical composition, and upon returning to the United States he began composition lessons with the composer Arnold Schoenberg. A lack of interest in harmony, however, caused him to leave behind his earliest experiments with atonal chromaticism (such as the 1933 *Sonata for Clarinet*) and to begin composing for percussion ensemble. Subsequent works for the prepared piano, an invention in which the traditional timbres of the piano are altered by the insertion of objects among the strings, began with the dance piece *Bacchanale* in 1940, and culminated in what many critics consider to be Cage's most enduring early composition, the *Sonatas and Interludes* of 1948.

Cage became dissatisfied by the lack of consistency among different performers' preparations for his piano works, and his subsequent recognition that the composer could never truly determine the conditions of his performance of his music, led to his most radical aesthetic gestures: in 1951 he accepted chance techniques in the composing and interpretation of his scores, and the use of silence and noise as significant components of his work. As Cage wrote to Pierre Boulez in 1950, composition was "throwing sound into silence" (cited in Pritchett, 74). Beginning with *Music of Changes* for piano (1951), Cage began to use the Chinese book of prophecy the I Ching to establish the parameters and often the most minute details of his scores. Shortly thereafter, in 1952, Cage produced his most notorious score, *4'33"*, during which a pianist sits in absolute silence at the keyboard for the titular duration, an act of compositional audacity still unmatched in the twentieth century.

These near-simultaneous turns to chance and silence were related. Not merely gestures toward novelty, they were Cage's attempt to put into action ideas about the relation between the author and his work, and the listener and the world, that he had gleaned from studies of Zen as well as from the artwork of Marcel Duchamp and the music of Erik Satie. Cage wished to redefine the relation between creativity and sound. Silence and chance release composition from intentionality, and thereby from the taste of the composer. When Marcel Duchamp invented the "Ready-Made," he was attempting to move beyond taste in art, to extinguish "personality" in art in ways that resonated with other roughly contemporaneous modernist theories, especially of literary art.[2] In one of his notorious musical indications in the piano piece *Le Fils des Etoiles,* Erik Satie wrote "ignore your own presence." Cage as epigone sought to do precisely that. In his first book, *Silence* (1961), he states, "Personality is a flimsy thing on which to build an art" (*Silence*, 90). Turning to the I Ching (and later computer programs that produced similar chance instructions), Cage attempted to eliminate authorial control from the immediate processes of composition. Sounds would come of their own volition. The rest of Cage's career was a set of variations on this idea.[3] Within all of his pieces, however, silence figures: not silence as the pure absence of sound, but silence that allows other chance or random environmental sounds to enter and alter the audible landscape. Cage never intended *4'33"*, however notorious it became, to provide a duration of uncomposed dadaist time, but rather to make an audience aware of the many sounds around them that they usually ignore. The formality of the concert setting leads to a heightened awareness of "ready-made" sounds: chance occurrences that may be as justly considered "art" as those sounds knowingly composed.

Cage's fascination with Joyce may thus seem surprising. Despite the capitalized "SILENCE" in *Finnegans Wake* interrupting the question "What is the ti..?" (*FW*, 501.5–6), there is little overtly Cagean about Joyce's written works. Yet *Finnegans Wake* became a compelling presence throughout Cage's career, so much so that in a late interview he claimed Joyce as his principal inspiration (*For the Birds*, 181). That interest was slow to make its way to the center of his work. As late as 1960–61 Cage's own list of his most influential books did not include Joyce's works.[4] And until the end of his career Cage was interested only in the overtly avant-garde experimentation of late Joyce. Cage was consistently compelled by the idea of innovation; his teacher Schoenberg had called him "an inventor of genius" rather than a "composer" (cited in Hines, 93). Late in his career Cage himself freely admitted that his frequent changes of techniques were intended to shake up traditional apprehensions of what music is, saying in an interview with Calvin Tompkins, "whenever I've found that what I'm doing has become pleasing, even to one person, I have redoubled my efforts to find the next step" (Tompkins, 107). His initial interest in Joyce, then, lay in the unremitting inventiveness of Joyce's language, and Cage discovered *Finnegans Wake* as passages from "Work in Progress" began to appear in *transition* in the late 1920s.

From his earliest work of the 1940s Cage drew titles and verbal materials in his compositions from the *Wake*. In 1942 he composed *The Wonderful Widow of Eighteen Springs,* a setting of a passage adapted from *FW* 556 for soprano, accompanied by a pianist who strikes the lid of a closed piano with knuckles or fingers. In 1942 another short piece for prepared piano bears the Wakean name *In the Name of the Holocaust* (derived from *FW,* 419.9–10).

Explicit use of the *Wake* in Cage's compositions then diminished for several decades, although Joyce's influence may be found in the titles of other works of the period, such as *Root of an Unfocus* (1944) and the dances for Merce Cunningham, *Tossed As It Is Untroubled* (1943) and *The Unavailable Memory of* (1944). The *Wake* remained present, however, in many of Cage's writings.[5] His compositions, moreover, continued to show oblique Wakean effects. The score of *Variations VI* (1966), for instance, calls for the performer to drop a series of sigla and lines on a sheet; the resulting combination of intersecting lines and the spatial orientation of the sigla (up, down, pointing right or left) lead to a sonic interpretation of the performer's choosing. The sigla—triangles, domes, horizontal lines bisected by smaller vertical lines—and their transformations as they rotate around their axes bear uncanny notational resemblance to the sigla of the *Wake.*[6]

In 1969 Cage's interest revived in using Joyce as source material for his musical work, and then it is present without cease until Cage's death in 1992. In that earlier year Marshall McLuhan suggested that Cage fulfill a commission from the Koussevitsky Foundation with a work based upon the thunderwords of the *Wake,* to be called *Ten Thunderclaps,* planned for amplified chorus and string orchestra.[7] Cage never produced this work—a sojourn at the University of Illinois led to involvement with other large projects—but the stimulus took hold. In the *Song Books* (1970) several pieces have Joycean lineage.[8] In the mid-1970s Elliot Anderson, the editor of *TriQuarterly,* asked Cage to write something for a special issue dedicated to the *Wake,* and thereafter, Cage reported, he was "stuck in the *Wake*" and "couldn't get out" (*Empty Words,* 135). The *Wake* became, in Cage's words, a productive cage for Cage, an expanding limit for his imagination: he wrote, "I have gone to Joyce as to a jail" (*X,* 54). *Roaratorio* followed in 1979, and *Muoyce* (a title combining the words "music" and "Joyce"), a taped and manipulated reading of "Writing for the Fifth Time through *Finnegans Wake*" dates from 1983. In 1984 Cage composed a "sequel" to *The Wonderful Widow of Eighteen Springs* called *Nowth upon Nacht* (derived from *FW,* 556.23), and he was also commissioned to present a work for the Los Angeles Olympics. The resulting tape collage of international folksongs was called *HMCIEX* (or Joyce's "HCE," the letters interspersed with the word "mix"). A late piano piece *ASLSP* (1985) is named from the end of *Finnegans Wake* (Junkerman and Perloff, 269). A series of five stage works bears the Wakean title *Europeras* (1987–91), while at his death Cage was working on two Joycean projects. A written work to be called *Muoyce II* was based on a "writing through" of *Ulysses,* and Cage planned a ninety-minute ballet for Merce Cunningham to be called *Ocean.* This last work was based upon a hint from Joseph Campbell that after *Finnegans Wake* Joyce wished to write a novel about the sea. As a work that would have, in a sense, gone "beyond" the *Wake,* the ballet was to have nineteen sections, extrapolated from the fact that *Finnegans Wake* had seventeen sections and *Ulysses* eighteen (McKinley, 6).[9]

For much of Cage's career, then, the *Wake* was a source for the occasional phrase, a model for punning titling, a mellifluous lode of textual matter. Cage was indeed not a close reader of Joyce, but rather a browser. Nor was he a conventional Joycean in the literary sense. As a young man Cage had read *A Portrait of the Artist as a Young Man* and reported that he was "not enthusiastic," and claimed in 1983 that "I don't understand any" of *Dubliners* or *Ulysses* (X, 54).[10] *The Wonderful Widow of Eighteen Springs* resulted, he noted, from "*impressions* received from the text from *Finnegans Wake*" (*Writer,* 8; emphasis added) rather than careful analysis or even a full reading. Yet ultimately Cage felt that the lack of understanding he felt about Joyce's earlier works became a virtue for his apprehension of the *Wake.*[11] Cage preferred observation to analysis, favoring, for instance, the biographical and geographical censuses of Adaline Glasheen and Louis Mink over other critical works about *Finnegans Wake,* writing, "I prefer [the commentaries on *FW*] that pay attention but stop short of explanation" (*X,* 53). This preference for description over analysis was related to Cage's growing interest in Zen Buddhism. In *Silence,* Cage describes discussing Joyce with the Japanese scholar Daisetz Teitaro Suzuki. When Suzuki ends a subsequent metaphysical discussion, he explains, "That's why I love philosophy: no one wins" (*Silence,* 40). The same may be said for Cage's appropriations from Joyce before the 1970s. Cage's excerpts from Joyce's text place the question of interpretation in abeyance. The *Wake* simply is what it is, and Cage uses it without the annoyance of resolving competing explanations into a single interpretive approach.

Yet the Zen turn against interpretation provides a too easy, and perhaps disingenuous, explanation for Cage's resurgent interest in Joyce in the late 1960s. There were other biographical confluences. Cage, like Joyce, had considered becoming a cleric before college and discovered his vocation as an artist thereafter (Pritchett, 9–10); Cage may have sensed a kinship in Joyce's assumption of art as a form of displaced spirituality. He may also have seen parallels in Joyce's role as innovator and tutor to younger artists in his own New York coterie. The composer Morton Feldman, a longtime associate of Cage, explicitly compared Cage's cultivation of artistic friends to Joyce's relationship with Samuel Beckett.[12] The 1960s was also a time of aesthetic rethinking for Cage. His striving for innovation may have left him feeling misunderstood as Joyce did when drafts of "Work in Progress" appeared. Cage complained in 1966 that his recent greater recognition had inhibited his ability to do new things, noting that "what [people] want is not anything new from you but rather what you have done before" (cited in Pritchett, 144).[13] At the same time, intellectuals in Cage's social group, such as Marshall McLuhan and Norman O. Brown, were becoming devoted to Joyce and his radical potential, and brought *Finnegans Wake* once more to the forefront of Cage's intellectual world.[14]

These spiritual and biographical factors converged as well upon Cage's embrace of political radicalism in the late 1960s and early 1970s, when he became interested in benign forms of anarchy and socialism, including, like Joyce before him, the ideas of the American Benjamin Tucker (Kostelanetz, *John Cage,* 7).[15] His performance pieces of the 1960s, as well as some of the neodadaism of his work in the 1970s, stemmed from social and musical utopianism: first, from the belief that music is an action, and second, that action could produce political effects, change the "global mind" (Pritchett, 146). That music is action is already implicit in the instructions in the score for *Variations VI* (1966), where Cage writes of the scattered patterns of the sigla "let the notations refer to what is to be done, not to what is heard or to be heard."

And what was "to be done," in Cage's larger social sense, was the destruction of aesthetic and political hierarchies. Cage's early attempts to introduce both silence and noise into music becomes in his ideas of the 1960s a political agenda. Just as Theodor Adorno had argued that Schoenberg's system of composition using all twelve notes of the chromatic scale was a metaphor of political liberation—the tonal hierarchies of the diatonic scale replaced by the ultimately "democratic" twelve-tone row—so did Cage's attempts to free ideas of what music could be suggest an ultimately pan-democratic politics. And Cage found this sense of democratic polity hand in hand with avant-garde innovation in *Finnegans Wake.*

This is particularly apparent in Cage's career-long recurrent citations of Joyce's Wakean initials HCE, to stand for "Here Comes Everybody."[16] In *Finnegans Wake* HCE is the father, the universal dreaming mind. For Cage the initials signal the political presence of total democracy, a welcoming of all peoples and aesthetic effects to the circus of the world, what the *Wake* calls a "funforall" (*FW*, 458.22). Cage's work for the 1984 Olympics, *HMCIEX*, thus contains both a Joycean and a political message. If the world has become a global village—and later in "Overpopulation and Art" Cage writes explicitly "the world hAs become / a siNgle minD" (Junkerman and Perloff, 37)—then all nations are welcome to the feast of music, and all sounds are welcome together in human experience. Vincent Sherry has argued that in modernism, music—*melos*—became the art of democracy and populism, as opposed to the elitism represented by the visual arts (Sherry, passim). Cage, recognizing the *Wake*'s confluence of linguistic and musical effects and its democratizing of the global mind, was able to make similar claims in the late 1970s. "We live," Cage said in an interview with Kostalanetz, "in a very deep sense, in the time of *Finnegans Wake*" (Brent and Gena, 146).

In the 1970s, then, Cage found the ideal aesthetic precursor in *Finnegans Wake*. Indeed, many of the *Wake*'s specific features find echoes in Cage's writings: his interests in holding aesthetic opposites together and in cyclicality, his nonsurrealist interest in the work done by the sleeping mind, and a consistent distrust of the separation of the categories of space and time within art.[17] But the final step toward the composition of *Roaratorio* was a blending of these aesthetic and political ideas with Cage's newfound interest in language per se. Although Cage had always been a copious essayist and lecturer, in the 1960s and 1970s he became interested in creating prose works, first his series of *Diaries,* then works based on the writings of Thoreau, and finally a series based upon *Finnegans Wake*. The two sets of works on Thoreau and *Finnegans Wake* were benignly parasitic on previous texts, as a new way of breaking down hierarchies between past and present art.

Cage's writerly impetus derived from his compositional ideas of the period. In 1969, because of copyright problems with the original score of Satie's *Socrate,* Cage composed *Cheap Imitation,* a work for a dance for Merce Cunningham that followed the outlines of Satie's original work while altering its intervals. The new work was thus derived from Satie's, but was independent from it. The work was and was not Satie's, and—as the jocular title insists—was and was not Cage's. Within a few years Cage began composing other works that drew upon previously composed materials, such as *Apartment House 1776,* a commission for the American bicentennial that uses pastiche and the superimposition of previously existing early American songs. In this work, and in *Quartets I–VIII,* also of 1976, Cage used previous compositions with some of their notes removed. The "gaps" in the musical argument, along with randomly derived juxtapositions of material, produce new music from previously existing compositions.

Cage's late and intensive preoccupation with *Finnegans Wake* also began in 1976. The idea of making new texts from old through imitation and the introduction of gaps into original material provided Cage with one aesthetic rationale behind his series of "Writings Through *Finnegans Wake*."[18] The other was Cage's desire to break down the last remaining hierarchy that he saw functioning in Joyce's language. Although fascinated by Joyce's innovations, Cage was dissatisfied with Joyce's conventional grammar. He notes disapprovingly in his *Diaries:* "Finnegans Wake *employs syntax. / Though Joyce's subjects, verbs and / objects are generally unconventional, / their relationships are the ordinary / ones*" (*M,* 102–3). Harking to Norman O. Brown's assertion that "syntax is the arrangement of the army," and Thoreau's assertion that "when he heard a sentence he heard feet marching," Cage set out to create a nonsyntactical language out of fragments of *Finnegans Wake* (*Empty Words,* 133), a demilitarized version of Joyce's global language.

Yet the "Writings Through *Finnegans Wake*" are not entirely unstructured. While largely free of traditional syntax, they are composed according to a poetic form of Cage's own invention, the "mesostic." Like an acrostic, in which the first letters of a series of lines of poetry read down spell a name or hidden title, each mesostic arrays phrases as poetic lines around a keyword to be found in the lines' middle, which Cage capitalizes for visibility. Cage's earliest mesostics were occasional pieces, gifts to friends, and were usually keyed around the recipient's name and composed of words chosen freely by the author. A thematic mesostic keyed to Joyce's first name, for example, looks like this:

> **J**oyce
> **A**
> **M**usic
> h**E**
> i**S** is music

(from "James Joyce, Marcel Duchamp, Erik Satie: An Alphabet" [*X*, 61])

The language used, in other words, reflects an aspect of the subject of the keyword, and although some of the words chosen begin with a letter of the key name, not all do. The name, which would be inaudible if the mesostic were spoken and scarcely recognizable if the keyword were not capitalized, provides an implicit thematic subject between the words, which in this case are neatly syntactical and communicate a simple thematic idea.

The "Writings Through" present a considerable series of nonsyntactic mesostics. The first series of *Wake* mesostics, in response to the *TriQuarterly* commission, was "7 out of 23" (1977). For this brief work Cage used samples of text from pages 366–82 of *Finnegans Wake*, and built a series of mesostics around the name "James Joyce" using phrases, taken in order from the text, in which the necessary next letter for the keyed name appeared:

> **J**oh joseph's
> be**A**uty
> **M**outh, sing mim.
> look at lokman! whatb**E**tween
> the cupgirl**S** and the platterboys.
>
> **J**uke
> d**O**ne it.
> in his perr**Y** boat
> the old thalasso**C**rats
> of invisibl**E** empores,

(*Writer,* 127)

On the page, then, Joyce's deracinated phrases hang as though in the air in groups of five. Largely divorced from syntax or context the name "James Joyce" acts as the only link holding together "stanzas."

In the "Writings Through" Cage treats words as he treats music. They are valued for their intrinsic qualities rather than for their use within larger narrative structures, and their linking together through keywords revels in the arbitrariness of the design. The mesostics, Cage wrote, are musical: with their keywords they are like "counterpoint in music with a cantus firmus" (*Empty Words,* 135). At times at great length—the first "Writing Through" is so long that it was issued as a separate book by the *James Joyce Quarterly*—the "Writings Through" go painstakingly through the *Wake,* excerpting needed phrases and reorganizing them into Cage's idiosyncratic blend of text and poetry. "Made" rather than written, they are literally "compositions," works put together rather than created. Not unlike Duchamp's "Ready-Mades," the "Writings Through" present themselves as works without meaning, declaring that their value derives solely from the force of the Cage's assertion that they are intrinsically valuable.

Cage's political, philosophical, and aesthetic use of Joyce's work within his own reaches its apex in the work *Roaratorio: An Irish Circus on* Finnegans Wake (1979), which combines the "Writing for the Second Time Through *Finnegans Wake*" (1977) with a collage of sounds suggested by Joyce's work. Commissioned by Klaus Schöning of West German Radio, *Roaratorio* takes to its logical extreme Cage's fascination with juxtaposition of sounds, Joyce, and the musical possibilities of words. Schöning suggested that Cage compose a "soundtrack" to accompany a reading of his "Writing for the Second Time," and the result drew upon his desire to treat language, as had some of the Italian Futurists and the artist Kurt Schwitters, simply as sounds capable of musical expression as well as upon his experience with producing sound collage pieces.[19] *Roaratorio*—which takes its name from *Finnegans Wake (FW,* 41.28)—juxtaposes Cage's hour-long reading of his second "Writing Through" with a panoply of other sounds, including the music of six Celtic musicians playing a variety of traditional melodies, and sixty-two tracks of environmental sounds recorded at as many of the geographical locations mentioned in the *Wake,* in Ireland and throughout the world, as Cage could manage through his own travels and the help of radio stations and universities in many countries. The resulting version of *Roaratorio* created at the Institut de Recherche et de Coordination Acoustique / Musique

(IRCAM) in Paris, and broadcast widely in Europe and America, draws upon over a thousand sounds recorded at over a thousand places, which were determined by using Louis Mink's *A Finnegans Wake Gazetteer*.[20] The environmental sounds are mixed according to chance operations, according to Cage's schema, against the Celtic musicians and Cage's speaking voice, and are placed within the hour-long work in proportion to the place within the *Wake* where the cited location appears.

Like *Finnegans Wake, Roaratorio* is fundamentally a conceptual work. As decades of Wakean exegeses stand witness, one needs to understand Joyce's subjects and processes before one can make inroads into analysis of the *Wake*. Similarly, understanding Cage's working assumptions about the aesthetics and construction of *Roaratorio*—the composition of the spoken mesostics, and the relationship among geographical allusion, text, and sound—is necessary before one can make "sense" of Cage's sonic tapestry. The result, however, flouts analysis: it is a vast panorama consisting of Cage's recitation of his version of Joyce's text against a constantly shifting collage of sounds that are identifiable as partly Joycean and partly universal. Cage's voice varies in prominence throughout the work, and his reading of the text moves from straightforward recitation to a form of improvisatory *Sprechstimme*, a half-singing of Joyce's disjunct words. The human voice, in other words, becomes merely a nonsyntactic sound amid many other nonsyntactic sounds, sometimes the most prominent, at other times merely part of the larger sonic fabric.

At times that fabric is unremittingly dense. Cage's voice is heard alone only for perhaps two minutes of the hour-long piece, and the barrages of noise—carefully orchestrated in waves of overwhelming sonic collage alternating with more lightly scored sections—suggests that Cage was guided by the phrase from the seventh Wakean mesostic of the work, "and all thE uproor / aufroofS" (*Empty Words*, 138). Particular kinds of sounds thematically relevant to the *Wake*, however, establish their thematic importance through repetition. Water, church bells, babies crying and children laughing, seagulls, thunder, snippets of voices, all work their way through the sonic tapestry frequently, underlining the *Wake*'s emphasis on the waters of the Liffey, the encompassing presence of the Church, the cycles of life and the games of children, and the density of voices jostling and melding in Joyce's fictive Ireland.[21] Yet if Ireland, through the mediation of Joyce, is for Cage both the source of chance and a productive chaos, throughout

Roaratorio the sounds of not only Irish history but of multinational experience intrude. Occasionally a snippet of an old recording of opera appears like a long-deceased singer from Joyce's "The Dead," while fragments of gamelan music weave in and out of duets for bodhran, blending Celtic music with world musics. Fragments of a jazz band, military fanfares, choirs, and classical music for strings (even a snippet of piano music by Debussy) suggest *Roaratorio*'s attempt to capture not only Joyce's sonic world, but also in Joycean fashion, to act as a kind of democratizing agent for music. The title is both secular and religious—an "oratorio," or sacred work for accompanied voice, plus the "roar" of the crowded world—and *Roaratorio* says "Here Comes Everybody" not only to environmental sounds but to the history and universal experience of music.

Within this fabric of sounds, Cage's use of the speaking and chanting voice, the soloist of the "roaratorio," suggests the tradition of bardic poetry, at times blending with the actual Celtic singing in the collage, and reminding one of the origins of the epic in the author's voice.[22] But, as such, the voice functions in paradoxical relation to many of Cage's earlier aesthetic presuppositions. While the mechanisms of his compositional technique were developed originally to suppress the personality of the author—the randomly discovered connection of disjunct materials replacing carefully compositional authority—Cage's voice instead acts as an oddly reassuring thematic presence, restoring continuity and personality within the fragmented sonic landscape. Such is the larger paradox of *Roaratorio*. It denies, as does all of Cage's work, the ultimate authority of the composer, but also reinstalls the composer within his work through his speaking voice. The impersonality of chance operations is philosophically at odds with the vocal presence of their creator, even as that presence blends into the sonic materials of the overall composition.

But the use of the human voice as the primary component of the composition, swirled about by the sounds of many other voices, may itself be understood as a canny homage to *Finnegans Wake*. Like Joyce's work, *Roaratorio* presents the human voice submerged within a world of which it is simultaneously a part and apart: both texts are, in some sense, about blindness. The narrator or narrators of *Finnegans Wake,* asleep and dreaming, are voices amid the histories of family, nation, and world. HCE is both everyman and comic singularity amid an estranging world. Analogously, Cage's voice both is and is not part of the sonic collage of *Roaratorio,* for it is mixed in separate tracks of the tape, at the same time as it thematically links otherwise disjunct sounds. *Roaratorio* juxtaposes selfhood against environment as does the *Wake*. But where Joyce implies multiplicity within that juncture of voice and world by superimposing meanings through punning and multilingual language, Cage uses sonic collage, within his own aesthetic, to the same ends.

Cage's structuring of *Roaratorio* around mesostics keyed to the name of Joyce suggests a further aesthetic complementarity. Both the *Wake* and *Roaratorio* hold up to question the relationship between the forms of communication offered by typography and by sound. *Finnegans Wake* is first and foremost a written text, but it gives over many of its punning meanings only when read aloud. Cage's mesostics, on the other hand, are structured around keywords that are inaudible when heard aloud—as they are in *Roaratorio*—but which instantly reveal their structure when seen on the page. Both *Finnegans Wake* and *Roaratorio* try, in Joyce's language, to "singsigns to soundsense" (*FW,* 138.7). And while Cage imitates other Wakean features—his insistence on sounds from the geographical locations mentioned in the *Wake,* for example, is directly analogous to Joyce's punning on the names of rivers in "Anna Livia Plurabelle"—the combination of voice with text, sound, and geography, produces in *Roaratorio,* as in *Finnegans Wake,* an innovative work that captures both the language and the sense of place of Ireland, vocalizes them, and places them within the larger world. Joyce's words and Cage's manipulations of sound both capture Ireland in miniature, and install it within the places of the earth. The solitary human voice appears within the hubbub of a multinational humanity.[23]

Further, Cage's use of his own voice and of mesostics keyed to the name of Joyce throughout *Roaratorio* suggest an additional philosophical point of connection between Cage's and Joyce's aesthetics of impersonality. In *A Portrait of the Artist as a Young Man* Joyce's Stephen Dedalus imagines the perfect artist as godlike, sublimated above and beyond his work and indifferent to it. Later, in his lecture on Shakespeare in "Scylla and Charybdis" a more mature, yet more conflicted, Stephen attempts to grapple with the issue of the relationship between self and art. Joyce's work as a whole shows the struggle between the act of attempted self-erasure—the stylistic multiplicity of *Ulysses,* the dream language of the *Wake*—and the declaration of the centrality of selfhood to art, through the veiled autobiography of much of his fiction. Cage's "Writings Through" may be seen as an interrogation in the postmodern vein of the same relationships between the author and his text. Where Stephen in *Ulysses* finds traces of authorship in the verbal texture of an author's works, Cage reclaims the name of the author within Joyce's own text, albeit through the chance operations of random occurrences.

Cage claimed for himself an aesthetic based upon the impersonal atomization of traditional artistic building blocks—letters, words, noise, musical notes—or taking over previously existing musical "narratives" and leaving "holes" in them; his work *4'33"* may be taken as emblematic of the most profound act of authorial disappearance possible. Yet even as the Joycean or Cagean artist withdraws himself from his work—through style for Joyce, through chance for Cage—by using his own voice in his work and by finding Joyce's name everywhere in *Finnegans Wake,* Cage reinstalls the author—both of the subject text and of the new work—everywhere within the aesthetic artifact. As in Stephen's lecture on Shakespeare, where the playwright has "hidden his own name [...]. He has revealed it in the sonnets where there is Will in overplus" (*U,* 9.921–24), Cage finds the name of Joyce in overplus throughout the *Wake,* and makes it musically his own. The author both is and is not within his work: as the voice, and in the letters of the text, that give it being.

To note the points of philosophic connection between Cage and Joyce is not finally to argue for their philosophic unity. Cage indeed has said that although his work was inspired by Joyce he would never call his work "Joycean" (*For the Birds,* 181). Cage's claims for the absence of depth in his written works,[24] at least, align him more with the surrealists or Beckett than with Beckett's Irish mentor, and despite the story of Joyce allowing Beckett to include the chance phrase "come in" in the text of the *Wake,* the apocryphal nature of which is well known, there are no signs that chance played any part of Joyce's aesthetic. Yet in his writings Cage would frequently cite a story from Irish folklore in which a hero, with the help of a magical horse, finds his way through an unknown land by casting a ball before him; abandoning himself to chance, the hero passes safely through his trials (cited in Pritchett, 77). The "Writings Through *Finnegans Wake*" and *Roaratorio* may be seen as Cage's Irish journey, the claiming of an unknown territory one cast at a time. By divorcing Joyce's word from his intentions, Joyce's language become Cage's new work. By dismembering Joyce's text, Cage also "remembers" it through music. In the light of *Roaratorio* "writing through" becomes a doubled term. It means both the act of starting at the beginning and concluding at the end, and the act of creative ventriloquism involved in any such artistic appropriation. In his notes for *Etudes Boreales* (1978), Cage wrote, "In the writings of Erik Satie, somewhere, I don't know just where, I read that music notation is nothing but points and lines" (*Writer,* 105). In *Roaratorio* and his Joycean writings Cage takes apart *Finnegans Wake* and reproduces it as points and lines in the doubled notation of text and sound. Disconnected, resonant, both written and spoken, Cage's Joyce is authorial yet free from authority, and reinstalled into the randomness, and the chance shapeliness, of the world.

NOTES

1. Compare, say, the neoromantic aesthetics of the Joycean song settings of Samuel Barber with the atonality of similar settings by the young David Del Tredici, or the effusive *Wake*-titled orchestral works of Stephen Albert with the formal logic of Elliott Carter, whose first two string quartets draw inspiration from the *Wake:* the first quartet explicitly, in its cyclical logic, the second, less openly, in the idea of separate musical narratives coexisting simultaneously within a larger discursive framework.

2. Ironically, given the desire for an escape from personality, Duchamp's profile was used by Cage to make a piece for trombone: the drawing was turned 90 degrees, and the trombone player asked to vary the pitch of the instrument accordingly, in a continuous glissando.

3. Some of Cage's subsequent works depend largely on the musicians' interpretation of chance-derived but traditional notations (for instance, the *Freeman Etudes* [1978–90]); some depend upon the musicians' interpretation of chance-derived nontraditional notation (for instance, the *Concert for Piano and Orchestra* [1958]); some depend upon the musicians creating chance operations of their own in order to develop their own "scores" for performances (as in the *Variations*); others depend upon fixed performance materials that overlap in unpredictable ways according to the performers' understanding of where given musical materials fit within preordained systems of time brackets (as in the series of late "number pieces" [1987–92]).

4. The list does include Gertrude Stein, Luigi Russolo, and a number of works of Eastern and Western philosophy ("List No. 2," Kostelanetz, *John Cage,* 138).

5. In a letter to *Musical America* in 1951 defending the musical reputation of Erik Satie, Cage slightly misquotes "riverrun" as "past riverrun" from the first page of the *Wake* (repr. in Kostelanetz, *John Cage,* 93). In 1958

an antimanifesto he prepared for the program notes for his *Concert for Piano and Orchestra* contains extensive collaged citations from the better-known sections of the *Wake:* "Shem," "unhemmed at it is uneven" (*FW*, 104.3), "hoppy on akkant of his joyicity" (*FW*, 414.22–23), "Tell me, tell me, tell me, elm!" (*FW*, 216.3) (repr. in Kostelanetz, *John Cage*, 131).

    6. See the score to *Variations VI*. For a detailed discussion of the sigla in the *Wake*, see Roland McHugh.

    7. McLuhan's suggestion came from his son Eric, who was then working on a book about the thunderwords. Eric McLuhan's book has since appeared as *The Role of Thunder in* Finnegans Wake.

    8. "Solo 12" uses as part of the glossolalia of its text several of the same Wakean phrases as in the 1958 antimanifesto, while the text of "Solo 84" contains a "Vocalise [that] is a mix of letters and syllables from the last sixty-four lines of *Finnegans Wake* (James Joyce)" (*Song Books*, II, 284; the Indo-European roots that provide the text of "Solo 40" may also suggest a linkage to the *Wake*).

    9. *Ocean* was completed according to Cage's schema by Cage's longtime associates, the composers Andrew Culver and David Tudor, and was posthumously premiered in 1996.

    10. Shortly before he died, however, Cage told Joan Retallack that he was "going through *Ulysses*" with the help of Clive Hart and David Hayman's *James Joyce's* Ulysses, and singles out an essay by Hugh Kenner, "Circe," for special praise (*Musicage*, 132, 158–59).

    11. In the introduction to his lecture "James Joyce, Marcel Duchamp, Erik Satie: An Alphabet" (1980), Cage notes that he links the three figures together for their uninterpretability, for the fact that they "resisted the march of understanding and so are as fresh now as when they first were made" (*X*, 53).

    12. "H.C.E.: 'Here Comes Everybody,'" in Brent and Gena, 68. This comparison is made all the more cogent by Feldman's own later collaborations and production of works dedicated to Beckett, such as the music for *Words and Music* (1961, 1987) and the late orchestral piece *For Samuel Beckett* (1987).

    13. Cage and Morton Feldman, "Radio Happening II," recorded at WBAI, New York, July 1966.

    14. Cage once cited McLuhan's article "The Agenbite of Outwit" (1963), which takes its title from the phrase "Agenbite of inwit" in *Ulysses* (*U*, 1.481), as McLuhan's most important work (*For the Birds*, 225). Norman O. Brown's text *Closing Time* (1973), a text collage of *Finnegans Wake* and Vico, cites Cage on its opening page.

15. Stirner and Tucker come up in conversation with Kostelanetz; Pritchett makes a similar comparison between Cage's social ideas and Tucker's ideas of "associative combination" (Pritchett, 193).

16. In the "Juilliard Lecture" in 1952 he writes "H.C.E. Each one of us is thinking his / own thoughts, his own experience and each experience is different and / each experience is changing and while we are thinking, but / since we don't, it is free and so are we" (*A Year from Monday,* 109). In the "Lecture on Something" (printed 1959), the idea of freedom and multiplicity in unity is similarly tied to the *Wake:* Cage writes "everything's different but in going in it all becomes the same / H.C.E." (*Silence,* 129). In his lecture from the early 1990s, "Overpopulation and Art," Cage harks to the idea of universal connection through technologies with the same Joycean initials: "aRe you / in Touch hce" (Junkerman and Perloff, 16).

17. Cage says, for instance, that "opposites have to be seen as nonopposites" (Kostelanetz, *John Cage,* 9) and notes that his intention in his 1958 *Concert for Piano and Orchestra* is "to hold together extreme disparities" (Kostelanetz, *John Cage,* 130). In "Listening to Music" (1937) he asserts, "And the natural flow of sounds which music is reassures us of order just as the sequence of the seasons and the regular alternation of night and day do" (*Writer,* 19), while his attraction to the idea of sleep-producing work is seen in several places in his writing. He was fond of an anecdote about how his inventor father would do his best work while asleep; in an appreciation of Robert Rauschenberg, he asks, "Does his head have a bed in it?" (*Silence,* 98). As for space and time, a major component of the arguments between Shem and Shaun in the *Wake,* Cage wrote, "the distinctions made [...] between the space and the time arts are at present an oversimplification" (*A Year from Monday,* 31).

18. For thorough discussions of Cage's writings, see Pritchett (175–80), and the essay "Talking about 'Writings Through *Finnegans Wake,'*" by Richard Kostelanetz (Brent and Gena, 142–50).

19. For a full description of the conditions that produced *Roaratorio* and its place within the tradition of German radio drama (*Hörspiel*), see Richard Kostelanetz, "John Cage as a *Hörspielmacher,*" in Kostelanetz, *Writings,* 213–21.

20. The version of *Roaratorio* executed by Cage is only one of many possible versions of the work, and the work is itself only one execution of a more general work called _____, ___ _____ *Circus on* _____ (1979), a set of instructions for producing a sound collage from any book. The first space is to be filled with the title of the composition, the second by an article, the third by an adjective, and the last by the title of the subject book.

These instructions are reprinted in the booklet accompanying the Mode release of *Roaratorio,* 59–61.

21. For a list of the primary sounds used in the work, see *Roaratorio,* booklet, 71.

22. Cage has suggested that a work similar to *Roaratorio* could be produced from Homer's *Iliad.* The parallel between works that are epic in both language and geography—as well as the sequence Homer, Joyce, Cage—signals Cage's bardic intent ("Laughtears: Conversation about *Roaratorio*" [1979], in *Roaratorio,* booklet, 42).

23. A similar effect is achieved by Stockhausen's *Hymnen* (1966), an electroacoustical work also composed for West German Radio, with which Cage would have been well familiar. Stockhausen's work consists of a torrential collage of national anthems, but at the end the din gives way to the sound of the composer's solitary breathing.

24. See for instance *45' for a Speaker* (1954): "I / have nothing to say and I am saying it / and that is poetry" (*Silence,* 183).

WORKS CITED

Brent, Jonathan and Peter Gena, eds. *A John Cage Reader: In Celebration of His 70th Birthday.* New York: Peters, 1982.

Brown, Norman O. *Closing Time.* New York: Random House, 1973.

Cage, John. *Empty Words: Writings '73–'78.* Middletown, Conn.: Wesleyan University Press, 1979.

———. *For the Birds: In Conversation with Daniel Charles.* Boston: Marion Boyars, 1981.

———. *John Cage: Writer.* Selected and introduced by Richard Kostelanetz. New York: Limelight Editions, 1993.

———. *M: Writings '67–'72.* Middletown, Conn.: Wesleyan University Press, 1973.

———. *Musicage: Cage Muses on Words, Art, and Music.* With Joan Retallack. Hanover, N.H.: Wesleyan University Press, 1996.

———. *Roaratorio: An Irish Circus on* Finnegans Wake. New York: Mode Records 28/9, 1992.

———. *Silence.* Middletown, Conn.: Wesleyan University Press, 1961.

———. *Song Books (Solos for Voice 3–92).* New York: Henmar Press, 1970.

———. *Variations VI.* New York: Henmar Press, [1966].

———. *Writing Through* Finnegans Wake. University of Tulsa Monograph Series, 16. Tulsa, Okla.: University of Tulsa, [1978].

————. *X: Writings '79–'82*. Middletown, Conn.: Wesleyan University Press, 1983.

————. *A Year From Monday: New Lectures and Writings*. Middletown, Conn.: Wesleyan University Press, 1967.

Hart, Clive and David Hayman, eds. *James Joyce's* Ulysses. Berkeley: University of California Press, 1974.

Hines, Thomas S. "'Then Not Yet "Cage"': The Los Angeles Years 1912–1938." Eds. Charles Junkerman and Marjorie Perloff. *John Cage: Composed in America*. Chicago: University of Chicago Press, 1994. 65–99.

Junkerman, Charles and Marjorie Perloff, eds. *John Cage: Composed in America*. Chicago: University of Chicago Press, 1994.

Kostelanetz, Richard. *Writings about John Cage*. Ann Arbor: University of Michigan Press, 1993.

Kostelanetz, Richard, ed. *John Cage*. New York, Washington: Praeger Publishers, 1970.

McHugh, Roland. *The Sigla of* Finnegans Wake. Austin: University of Texas Press, 1976.

McKinley, Jesse. "Cunningham, Cage and a Circle of Completion." *New York Times*, July 28, 1996.

McLuhan, Eric. *The Role of Thunder in* Finnegans Wake. Toronto: University of Toronto Press, 1997.

Pritchett, James. *The Music of John Cage*. Cambridge: Cambridge University Press, 1993.

Sherry, Vincent. *Ezra Pound, Wyndham Lewis, and Radical Modernism*. Oxford: Oxford University Press, 1993.

Tompkins, Calvin. *The Bride and the Bachelors, Five Masters of the Avant Garde*. New York: Penguin Books, 1976.

CHAPTER 7

Davies, Berio, and *Ulysses*
Murat Eyuboglu

In 1970, Mauricio Kagel published *Ludwig van,* a work that consists exclusively of juxtapositions of many Beethoven works. Kagel called *Ludwig van* a "meta-collage";[1] explicit in his description of the work and its content was a cluster of different and contradictory attitudes toward history: a homage to Beethoven's oeuvre paradoxically imbued by an ironic inversion of the autonomy of its individual *opera,* a need to recount and reemplot history, an impulse to displace and diminish the artist's own authorial voice, and a simultaneous reliance on and an antagonism toward models of the past. Nor was Kagel alone in his preoccupations. During the late sixties, Berio, Cage, Crumb, Davies, Foss, Stockhausen, and Zimmermann all showed consuming interest in parody, pastiche, palimpsest, paraphrase, auto-quotation, allusion: in short, in techniques that can be subsumed under the more general rubric of meta-music. It is my contention that the period in question presents a compositional moment that is highly assonant with Joycean techniques of representation. Focusing primarily on Peter Maxwell Davies's *Missa Super L'Homme Armé* and Luciano Berio's *Sinfonia,* both from 1968, I propose to study the terms and the historical implications of this assonance.

Before turning to Berio's and Davies's works, however, it might be illuminating to make a brief digression to Joyce's musical contemporaries, not simply in order to marvel at the mysterious operations of *Zeitgeist,* but rather to trace patterns of compositional thinking (both musical and literary) that will, as we shall see, reemerge in the late sixties. Adorno, in his *Mahler: A Musical Physiognomy,* observed that "the unity of the years throws an unsteady bridge" (145) between Marcel Proust and Gustav Mahler. Another unsteady bridge may be said to bestride the oeuvres of Mahler and Joyce, however great a difference of tone and character might seem to divide the works of the two artists. A fundamental convergence of the languages of Mahler and Joyce occurs in the representation of experiences as a complex simultaneity of multiple narrative strands. In addition to encountering the protagonists' experiences that are manifold themselves, the reader of *Ulysses* is entangled in a playful network of textual referentiality studded over the principal Homeric palimpsest. Similarly, for the listener of Mahler's symphonies, entering into an interpretive interplay within the presence of multiple layers of meaning is a fundamental component of the act of listening. On the one hand, this simultaneity is due to Mahler's richly interwoven polyphonic writing, which, according to a telling anecdote recorded by Natalie Bauer-Lechner, the composer derived from his childhood experiences of listening to several organ grinders and military bands playing all at once on fairgrounds (cited in Mitchell, 342). On the other hand, an interpretive polyphony is suggested by different and not always reconcilable programs operating within the same work. Mahler's Symphony no. 1 is a case in point. While the overall design of the work reemplots the composer's earlier song cycle *Lieder eines fahrenden Gesellen,* and thus "narrates" the protagonist's epic journey, disparate musical, literary, and pictorial references complicate the interpretation of the work according to the *Gesellen* cycle alone. Set against this epic plot, the more localized references, such as those to Beethoven's Symphony no. 9 (the *creatio ex nihilo* opening), to popular tunes such as "Frère Jacques" (presented as a sardonic funeral march depicting Moritz von Schwind's woodcut "The Hunter's Procession"), and to other works such as Jean Paul's novel *Titan,*[2] create the same kind of tension that exists between the Homeric background and the referential proliferation that takes place in the foreground of *Ulysses.*

Another composer whose oeuvre resonates closely with Joyce's (as well as with Mahler's) is Charles Ives.[3] Ives's works, spanning from 1888 to 1918, combine similar procedures with a considerably more extended use of the quotation technique and other experiments in micro- and polytonality. His Symphony no. 4 (1909–16), for instance, featuring fifty-seven musical quotations so far identified,[4] denies a unified and harmonious perspective from which to view the work, as if to depict realistically the bewildering and irreconcilable forces that act upon an individual's psyche. Considering the nature of the works of Mahler and Ives, the correspondence of the revival of their music in the sixties to an intense interest in quotation, parody, and meta-music manifested in the works of the above-mentioned composers is hardly a coincidence.

The two pieces I would now like to discuss in greater detail are in different manners both richly informed by their composers' reading of Joyce. In his introduction to the score of *Missa Super L'Homme Armé* Peter Maxwell Davies articulates the Joycean connection when he writes that "the eventual treatment [of the work] stems from the chapter in the *Ulysses* of Joyce corresponding to the Cyclops chapter in Homer" (ii). In order to investigate the nature and significance of the Joycean parallel, however, we need to start by tracing the many different layers of the work's conception and the parodized historical references operating therein.

At every level of its compositional process Maxwell Davies's *Missa Super L'Homme Armé* engages a historical antecedent, and thus creates a hall-of-mirrors effect in which techniques, styles, and genres of the past parade before our ears. The work that most fully underlies the conception of the *Missa* is Arnold Schoenberg's theatrical *Pierrot Lunaire* from 1912. The instrumental ensemble for which Davies's *Missa* is written, called the Pierrot Players, was not only named after Schoenberg's work, but it reproduced the instrumental combination of its model, with the addition of a percussionist. Maxwell Davies and his friends Harrison Birtwistle, Alan Hacker, and Stephen Pruslin were interested in both the ensemble combination and in the theatrical aspects of *Pierrot Lunaire:* staging of Schoenberg's work, in other words, was among the foremost objectives of the Pierrot Players.[5] Schoenberg's employment of *Sprechgesang* (speech-song) to evoke, in Pierre Boulez's words, a *cabaret noir* that flirts with bad taste (335), its ensemble that integrates rather than features the piano in a configuration of timbres that vary throughout the piece, and its use of learned baroque or Renaissance styles to parodic ends, are influences that permeate Davies's *Missa*.

On a historically remote, yet programmatically available level, the *Missa* parodies the Parody Mass. The Parody Mass, a genre that flourished in the sixteenth century and was baptized *Missa Parodia* by Jakob Paix in 1587 (Grout and Palisca, 227), entails the compositional practice of borrowing the entire polyphonic texture of a secular song or motet and subjecting it to various transformations in the form of a mass. The word "parody" in Parody Mass does not imply an ironic inversion or satire, but rather testifies to the free circulation of musical material, unencumbered by notions of originality and ownership. Davies's *Missa,* on the other hand, ironizes the notion of completion, which is essential to the sixteenth-century genre, when the narrator of the piece madly foxtrots off the stage to the accompaniment of an out-of-tune honky-tonk piano, which itself gets cut off in midstream.

Although no staging is required for the *Missa,* its speaker, who recites an abbreviated and reordered version of the Last Supper from Luke 22, appears in costume. In his stage directions Davies writes that "the speaker should be dressed as a nun if taken by a man, or as a monk if by a woman" (i–ii). While the biblical themes of betrayal and communion are being spelled out by the speaker, the instrumental sections present a plethora of readily recognizable musical styles: the work opens with a statement of a section from an anonymous fifteenth-century mass based on the popular tune *L'homme armé.* The theme of the borrowed mass is later cast in the foxtrot style, tremendously popular in the 1920s and 1930s. A section in the style of a hymn is accompanied by the speaker's words: "And he [Judas] promised, and sought opportunity to betray him unto them in the absence of the multitude."[6] The section that follows in baroque style bears the score indication: "like a bad gamba; sharp on higher notes, scratchy and swoopy" (Davies, 23). Later, the foxtrot idea is once again taken up and this time cast in *Tempo di quickstep.* It is in this parodic revisiting of at times unrelated styles, against a narration ending with hysterically reiterated charges of betrayal—"but behold, the hand of him that betrayeth me is with me on the table" (Davies, ix)—that Davies establishes the parallel with "Cyclops." He continues his introduction as follows:

> The eventual treatment stems from the chapter in the *Ulysses* of Joyce corresponding to the Cyclops chapter in Homer. In the Joyce, a conversation in a tavern is interrupted by insertions which seize upon a small, passing idea in the main narrative, and amplify this, often out of all proportion, in a style which bears no relationship to the style of the germinal idea which sparked off the insertion. (ii)

"Cyclops" captures the distracted and haphazard nature of a "confab" at Barney Kiernan's bar where a fanatic Irish nationalist, the "Citizen," fulminates with increasing vociferousness against Bloom on account of the protagonist's perceived Jewishness. A unique feature of the chapter is the asides that Joyce inserts into the narrative. At times directly, at others remotely triggered by themes from the main narrative, these asides reproduce nineteenth-century styles of writing such as medical, legalese, journalistic, epic-revivalist, religious, and political prose. We could call these asides examples of pastiche had Joyce simply reproduced their style, emphasizing primarily the similarity between the original style and his simulation of it. Most of the asides, however, are ironized through parody and thus expose a difference from, rather than a similarity to, the original. Although there is a definite centrifugal tendency in Joyce's writing, an illusion of uncontrolled proliferation (an effect replicated, as we shall see, in Berio's *Sinfonia*), the thematic patterns of the asides in "Cyclops" are fairly perceptible: an account of the first-person narrator's activities as a "Collector of bad and doubtful debts" (*U,* 12.24–25) is followed by a pastiche of legalese language; a conversation about a hanged man's erection is followed by a parody of a medical journal style where the phenomenon of postmortem erection is given "scientific" explanation (*U,* 12.468–78). Most of the Irish revivalist asides parody a nationalism that cherishes the glamorous past of a serene homeland. The grotesque figure of the Citizen, parodying Homer's brutish Cyclops, is (in)directly teased through these asides. In addition to the historical sense conveyed through the asides, as Dominic Manganiello's *Joyce's Politics* demonstrates, an intricate historical background dealing with the debates among Arthur Griffith, Francis Skeffington, and others, concerning Home Rule, *Sinn Féin,* and nationhood in general, can be traced within the chapter.[7]

How deeply and at what levels does "Cyclops" inform Davies's *Missa?* Davies cites only the centrifugal and refractory narrative structure of the chapter, without, however, engaging in the centripetal and historical thematicization of its model. While Davies's parodic evocation of Renaissance, baroque, and foxtrot styles simulates a certain sense of history, this evocation stops short of establishing a historically specific referentiality. If it is unfair to expect of a musical work to reproduce the intricacies of Joycean prose, we may then ask, at what other levels does Davies's work enter into a dialogue with *Ulysses?*

A reading of the "Circe" chapter, although not mentioned by Davies, reveals significant correspondences between *Ulysses* and the *Missa.* Although Stephen's chanting of "*the* introit *for paschal time*" (*U,* 15.74) at the beginning of "Circe" sets the tone for the mass, it is actually the Black Mass presided over by the cross-dressed Father

Malachi O'Flynn toward the end of the chapter that seems to have
served as the model for Davies's *Missa:*

> ([...] *Father Malachi O'Flynn in a lace petticoat and reversed
> chasuble, his two left feet back to the front, celebrates camp mass.
> The Reverend Mr Hugh C Haines Love M. A. in a plain cassock and
> mortarboard, his head and collar back to the front, holds over the
> celebrant's head an open umbrella.*)

FATHER MALACHI O'FLYNN

Introibo ad altare diaboli.

THE REVEREND MR HAINES LOVE

To the devil which hath made glad my young days.[8]

FATHER MALACHI O'FLYNN

(*takes from the chalice and elevates a blooddripping host*) *Corpus
meum.*

THE REVEREND MR HAINES LOVE

(*raises high behind the celebrant's petticoat, revealing his grey bare
hairy buttocks between which a carrot is stuck*) My body.

THE VOICE OF ALL THE DAMNED

Htengier Tnetopinmo Dog Drol eht rof, Aiulella!

> (*From on high the voice of Adonai calls.*)

ADONAI

Dooooooooooog!

THE VOICE OF ALL THE BLESSED

Alleluia, for the Lord God Omnipotent reigneth!

> (*From on high the voice of Adonai calls.*)

ADONAI

Goooooooooood! (*U,* 15.4693–716)

This passage, echoing Buck Mulligan's mock-mass at the opening of *Ulysses,* presents the church and theater in satirical contiguity. Cheryl Herr, in her *Joyce's Anatomy of Culture,* richly documents the traditions of parodic sermonizing and transvestism in the music halls of Ireland (136–88, 222–55). In fact, it is the theatricality and the popular cultural aspects shared by the music hall and the church that lead Joyce and Davies to create images where stage acts and religious ceremonies appear in conflation. A communion service led by a cross-dressed priest appears in both "Circe" and the *Missa.* Another intriguing correspondence is the use of the gramophone that in "Circe" blares "The Holy City" of Stephen Adams. Although the music of "The Holy City" does not appear in Davies's work, the distortion effect— "Whorusalaminyourhighhohhhh ..."—that occurs in "Circe" when *"the disc rasps gratingly against the needle"* (*U,* 15.2211–12), causing the three whores to cover their ears, is replicated in the *Missa* (Davies, 33). These further correspondences with "Circe" explain to a limited extent the origin of the theatrical elements in the *Missa.* The intricate context that *Ulysses* provides for the themes of transvestism, the mass, and the music hall, however, are absent in the *Missa.* Once again, the theatricality of the *Missa* is void of the historical context of its model in *Ulysses.*

Evocation of a sense of history has largely to do with the referential nature of the artistic material. Identifying the references and allusions in *Ulysses,* as well as articulating the ways in which Joyce tropes and emplots his preexisting material, are interpretive acts crucial to understanding the historical content of Joyce's work. In this respect, Davies's *Missa* poses a problem in that it parodies preexisting styles, rather than preexisting works. Parody in the *Missa,* in other words, occurs through a detour into pastiche. This ironized pastiche, while defining a satirical stance toward the styles it represents, does not anchor us in a specific historical reality or a compositional history.

Luciano Berio's *Sinfonia* does precisely that: it provides us with a "history of music" (Berio, *Interviews,* 107) worthy of *Ulysses* in the profuseness of its allusions. Commissioned by the New York Philharmonic during Berio's years of residence on the East Coast of America, and written partially in Sicily, *Sinfonia* was also composed in 1968, against a political background of student uprisings and Martin Luther King's assassination, and an artistic background where the extreme compositional practices of integral serialism and chance operations appeared to be the Scylla and Charybdis of musical composition. In an interview with Rossana Dalmonte in 1981, Berio described the third movement as follows:

> This third part of *Sinfonia* has a skeleton which is the scherzo from Mahler's *Second Symphony*—a skeleton that often re-emerges fully fleshed out, then disappears, then comes back again.... But it's never alone: it's accompanied throughout by the "history of music."
> (*Interviews*, 107)

Much like the palimpsest effect that Joyce creates through his treatment of Homer's *Odyssey,* Berio embeds a dizzying number of simultaneous and successive quotations from music history into Mahler's Scherzo, and thus creates a disorienting and seemingly chaotic musical surface. As is characteristic of the parody technique, however, the semantic content emerges out of the various tensions between the host work and the target works. Berio borrows the topos of Mahler's Scherzo as a "satire upon mankind"[9] and greatly elaborates its theme: the *Wunderhorn* poem on which Mahler's movement is based depicts, in a comically pictorial setting, Saint Anthony's sermon to the fish. The fish listen to the sermon attentively like "rational creatures" but remain unaffected by the saint's words: the closing stanza of the poem tells us that in the end "the pike remain thieves [...] the crabs go backwards [...] the carps gorge a lot [...] the sermon had pleased" (Porter, 52), but it is forgotten. To this forgetting Berio responds by a large number of recollections. How do we come to terms with the parodic manipulations of the past and comment on the "sense of history" thus evoked in Berio's work?

The first problem that should give us pause, in this respect, is in which terms, if at all, this vertiginous movement represents a "history of music." I propose to approach this question through Hayden White's meditations on the poetics of historiography in his *Metahistory*. White defines a historical work as "a verbal structure in the form of a narrative prose discourse that purports to be a model, or icon, of the past structures and processes in the interest of *explaining what they were by representing* them" (2; emphasis in the original). In drastically simplified terms, it is the central thesis of *Metahistory* that in their renditions of reality, history and fiction are both subject to the same models of emplotment, such as tragedy, comedy, and satire, and both exploit the rhetorical tropes that establish, at precritical levels, relationships of cause-and-effect, and agent-and-act. In other words, "the difference between 'history' and 'fiction' resides in the fact that the historian 'finds' his stories whereas the fiction writer 'invents' his" (White, 6). For several reasons, the categories articulated by White may appear incongruous with the language of music criticism: fiction and nonfiction are not meaningful categories in music, and even if musical forms can be said to emplot conflicts and reconciliations, the essential difference between literal and figural language that allows the rhetorical devices of metaphor, metonymy, and synecdoche to operate is an ambiguous one in music.

When a fragment of music appears as a quotation, however, recontextualized in a new environment, it is deprived of the immediacy with which we would have understood it in its original context. I do not mean to suggest here that musical experience is an immediate one, only shattered by parody and decontextualization. The difference between the *mediacy* and *im*mediacy of various musical experiences is a difference of degree. While the rhetoric and the impact of a certain kind of repertoire might depend on an *immediacy effect*—in which case mediation is not absent but only transparent to the listener—parodic compositions self-consciously cultivate a *mediation effect*. It is through the distance between the *mediacy* and the *i m*mediacy of musical experience that the works and quotations that are parodied (depending, as we shall see, on how they are used) acquire a meta-musical quality, a quality that by virtue of its reflexiveness as well as its self-reflexiveness allows the composer a rhetorical space for tropological and meta-tropological maneuvers. It is not my intention to provide a thorough analysis of *Sinfonia*'s third movement, but to show the tropological means by which the work is able to make a comment on history and thus become a historical work.

If the "history of music" that accompanies Mahler's Scherzo is a conspicuously incomplete one, it is not because the music library in Sicily to which Berio had access while writing *Sinfonia* had a poor collection. The refractory layout of the third movement is, in fact, highly thematicized, its principal focus being a water theme derived from Mahler's aquatic evocation of Saint Anthony's sermon to the fish. Other water references are sprinkled throughout Berio's score: Schoenberg's *Opus 16,* including the *Farben* movement (with its subtitle "Summer Morning by a Lake"), Debussy's *La Mer,* the drowning scene from Act III of Berg's *Wozzeck,* and the second movement of Beethoven's Symphony no. 6, "Scene by the Brook," are all represented through quotations.[10]

Let us now attempt a tropological reading of some of these quotations. The citation from Beethoven's Symphony no. 6 is a six-note arching motif, quoted at its original pitch level and B-flat clarinet instrumentation (Berio, *Sinfonia,* X+3; Figure 7–1).[11] The first operation is a synecdochic one in which the part stands for the whole; in other words, the short clarinet motif from the second movement of the symphony stands for the work in its entirety. The reason for citing the Pastoral Symphony is its celebration of nature (on a brook) and the reconciliation of nature and culture implicit therein: nature is neither a self-evident given nor a lost and irretrievable phenomenon; rather, it is one that can be enjoyed and represented in a symphony. In Berio's score, this quotation is accompanied by the line "It is late now, he shall never hear again the lowing cattle, the rush of the stream" from Beckett's *Unnamable.* This juxtaposition negates the ethos of the musical citation, inverts its implicit content as a celebration of nature by overlaying upon it a pessimistic statement of "no longer."

Wozzeck citations in *Sinfonia* are handled quite differently. Quoting the music of Wozzeck's drowning from Act III of the opera, Berio presents the water scene as a site of disenchantment, guilt, murder, and suicide. In the accompanying text the alto makes a trivializing remark regarding Wozzeck's murder of Marie: "Just a small murder," she says, while the basses take up the lines of the Captain and the Doctor (Berio, *Sinfonia,* S–T+4). In a metonymic relationship the topoi of *Wozzeck* and the third movement of *Sinfonia* appear in contiguity. Of the overall satirical Mahlerian plot of Saint Anthony's fruitless preaching to the fish, the tragic pessimism of Wozzeck becomes an exemplum.

Another piece that is represented with a large number of quotes is Ravel's *La Valse.*[12] Much like *Sinfonia,* the rhetoric of *La Valse* depends on quotation, obliteration, and distortion. The waltz is not the substance but rather the topos of *La Valse* where the Viennese dance form stands at the same meta-musical remove to the host work, as do the quotations in *Sinfonia. La Valse* also shares the satirical-historical emplotment of *Sinfonia* in its depiction of—in Ravel's words—"the glow of the chandeliers" at an "Imperial Court about 1855" (Larner, 174) through the perspective of Vienna's dilapidated glamour in the immediate aftermath of the Great War. *La Valse* then is a historically anterior model to *Sinfonia* and in the language of rhetorical tropes, the two works stand in a metaphorical relationship to each other on account of the similarity they display.

Though this tropological analysis could be extended indefinitely, I don't believe that all the quotations in the third movement of *Sinfonia* can be explained with the same degree of specificity. Berio's close study of Joyce is nevertheless highly detectable in *Sinfonia:* both *Ulysses* and the third movement of *Sinfonia* rely on preexisting models that they "explode"—to use Berio's term (*Interviews,* 107)—through an overabundance of historical references. In both works the dizzying surface gives rise to consistent patterns, which at the same time, shot through with parody, irony, and satire, defies reductionist attempts at explanation. History in Joyce and Berio appears as a phenomenon that can be referred to and grasped, but an emplotment that grants it a teleological form is denied. Davies's *Missa,* on the other hand, presents a more synchronic view of history on account of its self-conscious avoidance of a historically specific referentiality. Both Davies and Berio, however, borrow the satirical ethos of *Ulysses,* cultivating a manner of excess that perpetually risks overwhelming its own historical commentary.

Another glimpse at the homologies evoked earlier between Joyce and his musical contemporaries on the one hand, and their successors in the late sixties on the other, might bring these relationships into sharper focus. To generalize, we can maintain that by the turn of the century and during the two decades that followed, the objectifying and coherent point of view of the bourgeois individual was replaced by the simultaneous presence of multiple perspectives in literature, painting, and music alike: the multipersonal representation of consciousness in the works of Joyce and Woolf, the attempts to dissolve the unifying gaze of the painter in Cézanne and the ensuing cubism, and the heterogeneity of musical material in Ives and Mahler are symptoms of a condition in which the subject's consciousness is depicted as both fractured and composite. The return to the musical languages of decentered subjectivity in the late sixties when, as Boulez once put it, "contemporary music had finished its ascetic period and was turning increasingly towards the luxuriant" (296), suggestively coincided with the emergence of a plurality of new voices in the social realm, represented by decolonized populations, the rise of feminism, civil rights, and antiwar movements. It was in this historical moment that Joyce was reread by composers as a model of parodic palimpsest, and an open text that emplots an ironic teleology.

It might be argued that the major musical works from the late sixties and early seventies display a manifest tendency to progressively obliterate an inherent parodic duplicity, a duplicity in which the target work both *represents itself* and *is represented* by the host work. Stockhausen's *Telemusik* (1966), Cage's *HPSCHD* (1969), and Rochberg's Third String Quartet (1972), each in different ways, introduce an element of doubt into the very possibility of a dialogue with other works and styles. The unironized reproduction of Mahlerian, Brahmsian, and Bartokian styles in Rochberg's quartet, for instance, pretends to undercut the parodic and tropological remove between past and present and thus claims the possibility of an authentic regestation of historical styles. Even if the notion of history that emerges from such works is one in which the pastness of styles is subsumed in a perpetual present and consequently stripped of its historicity, we need not conclude that the tensions we have seen operating in Joyce and Berio no longer inform current works of art and their audiences. Obfuscation of history is itself a trope paradoxically predicated on our awareness of historical time. It is not despite but rather because of the changing image of Joyce that Davies and Berio were motivated to turn to his work in order to respond to the artistic demands of their own era through the refractory looking glass of *Ulysses*.

NOTES

1. Mauricio Kagel, interviewed by Karl Faust. See the record jacket insert to Mauricio Kagel, *Ludwig van,* Deutsche Grammophon 14931.

2. For the song-symphony relationship in general, as well as the connection between the *Gesellen* cycle and Symphony no. 1 in particular, see Mitchell, 25–44. For the programmatic complexity of Symphony no. 1, see Mitchell, 149–60 and 195–240.

3. A compelling comparison of Ives and Mahler is found in Morgan.

4. For an inventory of quotations in Ives's works, see Henderson.

5. The history of Pierrot Players is recounted in Seabrook, 100–7.

6. This citation appears in Latin in Davies, 22. The English translation is provided in Davies, ix.

7. See especially "The National Scene: Ourselves, oursouls alone" in Manganiello, 115–47.

8. This line is an inversion of Stephen's earlier line, "*ad deam qui leatificat iuventutem meam*" (*U,* 15.122–23), which is itself a perversion of the Latin mass, substituting "*deam*" (i.e., Georgina Johnson) for "*Deum*."

9. Mahler's own words, cited in Bauer-Lechner, 33.

10. For an inventory of musical quotations in *Sinfonia,* see Osmond-Smith, 57–71.

11. Letters represent rehearsal letters; numbers indicate the number of measures to be counted from the preceding rehearsal letter.

12. Berio, *Sinfonia,* C+20 (Bsn., C.Bsn.), C+22 (Ten.), D+12 (Fl.), N+13 (Fl.).

WORKS CITED

Adorno, Theodor. *Mahler: A Musical Physiognomy.* Trans. Edmund Jephcott. Chicago: University of Chicago Press, 1992.

Bauer-Lechner, Natalie. *Recollections of Gustav Mahler.* Trans. Dika Newlin. Cambridge: Cambridge University Press, 1980.

Berio, Luciano. *Luciano Berio: Two Interviews.* Interviewed by Rossana Dalmonte and Bálint András Varga. New York and London: Marion Boyars, 1985.

————. *Sinfonia for Eight Voices and Orchestra.* London: Universal Edition, 1969.

Boulez, Pierre. *Orientations.* Trans. Martin Cooper. Cambridge, Mass.: Harvard University Press, 1986.

Davies, Peter Maxwell. *Missa Super L'Homme Armé.* London: Boosey & Hawkes, n.d.

Grout, Donald J. and Claude V. Palisca. *A History of Western Music.* New York: Norton, 1988.

Henderson, Clayton W. *The Charles Ives Tunebook.* Warren: Harmonie Park Press, 1990.

Herr, Cheryl. *Joyce's Anatomy of Culture.* Urbana and Chicago: University of Illinois Press, 1986.

Kagel, Mauricio. *Ludwig van.* Deutsche Grammophon, 14931.

Larner, Gerald. *Maurice Ravel.* London: Phaidon, 1996.

Manganiello, Dominic. *Joyce's Politics.* London: Routledge & Kegan Paul, 1980.

Mitchell, Donald. *Gustav Mahler Volume II: Wunderhorn Years.* Berkeley and Los Angeles: University of California Press, 1995.

Morgan, Robert P. "Ives and Mahler: Mutual Responses at the End of an Era." *19th-Century Music* 2 (1978): 72–81.

Osmond-Smith, David. *Playing on Words: A Guide to Luciano Berio's Sinfonia.* London: Royal Music Association, 1985.

Porter, Cecelia H., trans. Liner notes. Gustav Mahler, *Lieder eines fahrenden Gesellen* and *Des Knaben Wunderhorn*. Sony SK 44935.

Seabrook, Mike. *Max: The Life and Music of Peter Maxwell Davies*. London: Victor Gollancz, 1994.

White, Hayden. *Metahistory*. Baltimore, Md.: Johns Hopkins University Press, 1973.

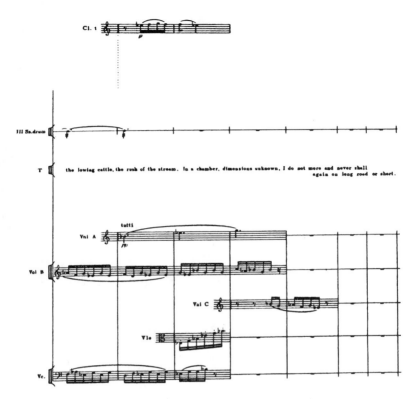

Figure 7–1. Luciano Berio, *Sinfonia for Eight Voices and Orchestra,* 3 measures after X (section of score). ©1972 by Universal Edition (London) Ltd., London. All Rights Reserved. Reprinted by permission of European American Music Distributors Corporation, sole U.S. and Canadian agent for Universal Edition (London) Ltd., London.

PART II
Gold: Text

Section 1: *Dubliners* and *A Portrait of the Artist as a Young Man*

CHAPTER 8

Noise, Music, Voice, *Dubliners*

Allan Hepburn

The singing voice, like the speaking voice, masks and betrays the unconscious through combinations of pitch and word. Why sing if not to communicate supplementary information that words alone cannot convey? In *Dubliners,* numerous characters sing folk ballads or operatic arias that belie concealed motives, unacknowledged pasts, personal unhappiness, or covert threats. The voice is the place where hysterical passion erupts, as Freud, bending his ear to patients who talked their way to cure, understood. Joyce links music to memory and the unconscious to reveal latent antagonisms between auditors and performers. Music, particularly in "Araby," "A Painful Case," "A Mother," and "The Dead," tells stories without words; the modern voice sings with a memory of its own in a process of signification that ultimately refutes language. The cycle of stories in *Dubliners* evolves from noise and melody ("Araby"), to song and performance ("A Mother"), to opera and silence ("The Dead"). Psychologically indeterminate in the minds of various Dubliners, music generally is the sign of intersubjective turmoil. Where speech fails them, they fill in silences and misunderstandings with vocal music. As a social rite, singing enacts identity, not straightforwardly, but in a medium that revels in ambiguity. In these stories, not hearing music accurately, not listening for encrypted clues, leads to wrongheaded actions. Joyce's Dubliners perform when they can no longer speak directly about their frustrations or passions. By a contradiction in the act of performance, singing also broadcasts personal feeling forcefully and directly. People sing to put their bodies and desires into circulation, sometimes with the consequence that the performer is sacrificed for giving voice to desire.

Joyce's understanding of music, especially when he was writing the stories in the *Dubliners* cycle between 1904 and 1907, is more indebted to the conventions of Dublin's music halls, pantomimes, and repertory of nineteenth-century opera than to harmonic experiments happening in France, Austria, and Germany during this period (Herr, 96–188). Although he attended a performance of Richard Strauss's *Salome* in Trieste in 1909, the opera inspired an essay on Oscar Wilde, whose play provided Strauss with his libretto, rather than speculations on the musical qualities or innovations Strauss made in the opera (*CW*, 201n). His references to opera in *Dubliners* and *Ulysses* dwell on narrative works from the grand tradition: Mozart's *Don Giovanni* (1787), Vincenzo Bellini's *La Sonnambula* (1831) and *I Puritani* (1835), Gaetano Donizetti's *Lucia di Lammermoor* (1835), and Michael William Balfe's *The Bohemian Girl* (1843), among others. Although knowledgeable about Richard Wagner's *Gesamtkunstwerke* and his transformations of the Tristan and Isolde legend, Joyce rarely mentions music written after Wagner by composers such as Janacek, Strauss, Wolf, and Mahler (T. Martin, *Joyce and Wagner*). Puccini's *Tosca* (1900), Debussy's *Pelléas et Mélisande* (1902), or Janacek's *Jenufa* (1903) escape Joyce's notice because they had not entered the repertory, and because diffusion of opera was strictly through theater or parlor performance, not mechanical reproduction. Even in promoting John Sullivan, the renowned Irish tenor, in the 1932 essay "From a Banned Writer to a Banned Singer," Joyce's references to operatic repertory hew closely to nineteenth-century favorites: Wagner's *Tannhäuser,* Meyerbeer's *Les Huguenots,* Saint-Saëns's *Samson et Dalila,* and Rossini's *Guillaume Tell* (*CW*, 258–68). In short, his ideas of voice did not derive from contemporary sources. However, he uses the voice as a marker of identity and nostalgia, deception and class, in a way that is characteristically modern. As in Alban Berg's opera *Lulu,* which allies speech and song in clangorous fashion, or instrumental music such as Schoenberg's *Verklärte Nacht,* which implies a narrative subtext to a wordless score, Joyce's use of music is modern in its emphasis on the psychological dimensions of musical performance, its insinuation of narrative where none is overt, and its registering of the body as expressive presence.

Music also figures in *Dubliners* as a substitute for theories of language or as a surplus of meaning that lies beyond language. Certainly the mysterious origins of language as complex image and

rhythmic speech are manifest in the poems that Stephen Dedalus writes
about the *"fallen seraphim"* (*P,* 223) in *A Portrait of the Artist as a
Young Man* and about pale vampires in *Ulysses* (*U,* 3.397, 7.524). Like
language, music enters the body through the ear and may, as theorist
Giambattista Vico hypothesizes, precede language as a means of
communication. Joyce's indebtedness to Vico for a gestural and
imitative theory of language is well known. Samuel Beckett, with
Joyce's encouragement, identifies Vico as a guiding theorist for
language games and paronomasia in *Finnegans Wake.* Following Vico,
Beckett identifies the roots of words in "pre-lingual symbol[s]" and
"gesture" (Beckett, 11). In his theory of human terror when faced with
omnipotent nature, Vico speculates that a clap of thunder institutes
structures of kinship and language (Norris, 56). Thunder causes a
shrinking away from preternatural voices and a banding together of
frightened people who then imitate unearthly sounds. The threshold of
speech, for Vico and for Joyce, is terror. The gestural origins of
language that Vico proposes—the combination of movement and
sound, of terror and babbling—are significant for Joyce's fiction in the
way he manipulates characters' silences and unspoken motives. Music,
similarly, may return listeners and performers to "pre-lingual" states of
emotion, where spontaneous response is both awed and cowed.[1]

In *Dubliners,* auditors wrongly infer meanings from songs. This
technique of inference permits listeners to identify with Irish culture
without examining its underlying ideological meanings. A surprising
number of songs are alluded to in *Dubliners* without being fully
transcribed. In the case of "I Dreamt That I Dwelt in Marble Halls"
from *The Bohemian Girl,* the popular tune that Maria sings in "Clay,"
the song appears only partially. Auditors, nevertheless, supply missing
verses. Everyone seems to have attended a performance of *The
Bohemian Girl,* and everyone recognizes its principal tunes. The
allusive presentation of songs creates an aural ambiance that demands
supplementary knowledge on the part of auditors and readers.
Allusions, like stage whispers, beg for attention; they point to nodes of
difficulty and deception on the part of characters. For instance,
"Arrayed for the Bridal" establishes a virginal, youthful identity for
Aunt Julia in "The Dead" that is at odds with her age. Folk songs like
"The Lass of Aughrim" in "The Dead" or "Silent, O Moyle" in "Two
Gallants" refer to songs only by title, yet to most Dublin inhabitants,
they are accessible as a code. Music defines and sustains the characters

as a national group, even if the meaning of any piece of music is associative and individual. The repertory performed during the concerts in "A Mother" is not specified, with the exception of "Killarney," a sentimental ballad by Balfe poorly executed by Madam Glynn, but it is clear that operatic airs are intermingled, revue style, with Irish songs and a theatrical recitation (*D*, 147). The dissemination of operatic "numbers" concentrates, it seems, on changeling plots, as in *The Bohemian Girl,* or folk songs that embody resurgent Irish nationalism. Operatic hits and folk songs enact nostalgic or sentimental myths about lost homelands, failed romance, abduction, or political conquest. These are the myths that Dubliners sing to shape their cultural identity.

Such assumptions about the meaning of music and sound are duplicitous because sound itself does not necessarily have meaning. In *Dubliners,* environments are acoustic without being verbal: the air is full of British accents, creaking floors, wailing children, restaurant hubbub, train rumbles, screams, murmurs, speeches, sermons, concerts, even "noisy dresses" (*D*, 72). Characters bridge discord with musical interludes or noises. Sometimes they vocalize alone as a defense against demands that impinge on them. Singing to oneself may also give the illusion of having an audience where there is none. The singer splits into two identities: one that sings, one that listens. "Is pure songfulness a consolation or a lie?" Lawrence Kramer wonders (76). Never "absolute" or "unironic," music can deceive either listeners or performers.

"Araby" dramatizes the emergence of the boy who narrates the story from undifferentiated sound to articulation of meaning through sound. On the day he goes to the bazaar, the boy, unaccompanied, sings in the "high cold empty gloomy rooms" of his aunt and uncle's house to liberate himself from the competing demands of romance and family (*D*, 33). He sings to cheer his own solitude, to encourage himself, to sort out conflicting emotions for which he has no words, or to conquer unnameable fears. Singing in those silent spaces confirms his identity to himself only, since no one witnesses this performance and he invokes no audience, unless, perhaps, he conjures up bogeymen and spirits that please and frighten him and that he hopes to quell by singing. He is, after all, prone to romantic excess and fantasy. Though he does not specify what he hopes to be liberated from, singing expresses his romantic delusion. Music ambiguously promises a realm of freedom or liberation beyond the constraints of school and love that hem him in. A nephew taken in by an aunt and uncle, the boy already stands somewhat outside the bonds of family. The movement of the story toward increasing isolation, concluding with the boy's self-understanding as a spurned "creature driven and derided by vanity" (*D*, 35), is prefigured by his remoteness from family, friends, and meaningful language. Music and noise disguise his liminal status, and his identification with noisy environments allows him to avoid the pressing questions of his identity.

The boy loves words without knowing their full connotations. Allowing his soul to luxuriate in silence, he repeats the syllables of the word "Araby" to himself. The word "called to me through the silence," he says, and "cast an Eastern enchantment over me" (*D*, 32). The boy practices being in love by speaking aloud words that have no real object or point of address. He even repeats rote gestures of romance: "I pressed the palms of my hands together until they trembled, murmuring: *O love! O love!* many times" (*D*, 31). Although he may be addressing Mangan's sister *in absentia,* he also conjures up the abstraction of love as a phenomenon he hopes to inhabit by talking his way into feeling. When Mangan's sister, whom he covertly watches, does speak to him, he is too confused to give coherent answers to her questions. Agitated, he compares his body to "a harp" (*D*, 31); his metaphor recalls the "Aeolian harp" adopted by Shelley and Coleridge as a trope that covers romantic sensitivity and responsiveness (in "A Defense of Poetry" and "The Eolian Harp," respectively). As a "harp," the boy is predisposed to be played upon, like a recipient object that expresses sounds without words when a player touches it. Becoming a wordless instrument of music itself, the source and body of sound, he conceives of himself as something passive, inexpressible, expectant. The metaphor of the harp indicates that only a musician, or something beyond himself, could make him live fully; it also betrays music in the boy's imagination as the representation of a fate he doesn't control. Without stating whether his song has any words, the boy implies that he sings, like Tristan calling for the absent Isolde in Wagner's opera, for the sake of trying out the appropriate attitudes of romantic affection.

Like an aria performed in an opera without listeners, the song he sings to himself, pitted against the faint cries of his companions playing in the street, perpetuates his delusion about the abstract emotionality of music. As Carolyn Abbate points out in her discussion of the conflict between libretto and score in Wagner's operas, "music can lie" (19).[2]

Whereas the acoustic atmosphere of "Araby" relies on an undifferentiated luxuriation in cries, songs, foreign accents, and epiphanic snippets of conversation and questions, all of which the boy takes pleasure in for the sake of sound itself, he comes to learn that sounds bear meaning when he overhears the conversation between British buyers and a teasing saleswoman at the Araby bazaar. Buying, selling, flirting, and fibbing all depend on words, not to announce passionate love, but to betray the dismal, commercial reality that underlies passion. Singing while his companions shout outside, the boy lives at the edge between music and language. Walking through the marketplace with his aunt, he hears "bargaining women," "curses of labourers," "shrill litanies of shop-boys," and "the nasal chanting of street-singers" (*D*, 31). He lists these noises without understanding that this barrage of sounds signifies economic activity, animosity, and politics. At the bazaar, however, the sounds of chinking silver and English accents assume the meanings of betrayal and commerce. He interprets the sound of the woman's voice by its timbre: "The tone of her voice was not encouraging," he remarks somewhat plaintively (*D*, 35).

The boy's singing, which is given no explanation in "Araby," may be justified by the psychological importance of music and noise in the *Dubliners* stories. Joyce's use of sound in these stories always suggests a psychological importance that the characters themselves cannot articulate. Linked to "Araby" in its treatment of sound, "A Painful Case" traces an opposite arc from language and music into silence. Although both stories end with the isolation of the principal male character, the boy at the end of "Araby" intuits that sounds deceive him, whereas Mr. Duffy in the later story exempts himself from sound in order to remain in self-imposed isolation. In both stories, music figures a misunderstanding between a male and a female character. As a rewriting of both *Anna Karenina* (Emily Sinico's death by train recalls Anna's suicide), as well as *Madame Bovary* (Emily's romantic illusions, like Emma's, concentrate on visits to the opera and grandiose expectations of amorous affection), "A Painful Case" spells doom for Mrs. Sinico.[3] Music is the sign of her frustrated hopes. Mr. Duffy meets Mrs. Sinico and her daughter at an evening concert. An unswerving Nietzschean in his devotion to music, Mr. Duffy spends his evening "before his landlady's piano or roaming about the outskirts of the city. His liking for Mozart's music brought him sometimes to an opera or a concert: these were the only dissipations of his life" (*D,* 109). To label concertgoing a dissipation precludes a satisfactory outcome to his meetings with Mrs. Sinico, since his rigid, egotistical superiority forbids him from yielding to any more serious dissipation. Listening to and encouraging Mr. Duffy's talk, Mrs. Sinico assumes, by contrast, that conversation creates attachment. They meet in her cottage and, when the light fades, they sit in the enfolding dark: "the music that still vibrated in their ears united them" and "emotionalised his mental life" (*D,* 111). Music mediates attachment, brought about through mutual listening.

Listening creates bonds of fondness and fidelity, or so Mrs. Sinico thinks. However, Mr. Duffy associates music and listening strictly with the past. He attempts to translate Mrs. Sinico into a "memory" (*D,* 109) when they first meet at the concert; fostering his own sense of being an *Ubermensch,* he denies all sensation and bodily pleasure by treating music and human attachment as things lost in another time than the present. When he reads about Mrs. Sinico's death in the newspapers, he realizes that "she had become a memory" (*D,* 116). He recalls her physical presence with distaste. Insufficiently expunged from his thoughts, she shrinks further into oblivion: "He began to doubt the reality of what memory told him" (*D,* 117). Memory speaks, but for the repressive Mr. Duffy, it speaks with a forked tongue that he feels obliged to silence.

Duffy treats music as an Apollonian abstraction removed from the body, whereas Emily Sinico treats music as an opportunity for conversation and communion, if not physical touch. Duffy roams the outskirts of the city to catch sight of lovers embracing among bushes, like those "human figures" engaged in "venal and furtive" (*D,* 117) love whom he looks down upon as they lie in the shadows of the park walls. He identifies Mrs. Sinico's tentative affection with music, and blots it out when he learns of her death. As the train reiterates the "syllables of her name," he pauses to listen until he no longer feels "her voice touch his ear" (*D,* 117). Perfect silence envelopes him. The absence of any name or sound leaves Duffy in perverse psychological safety, detached from human company and any possibility of love. In a story chiefly concerned with a love affair that never reaches beyond words into actions, an affair that stops short because of a presumptuous gesture (Mrs. Sinico passionately seizing Mr. Duffy's hand), music stands as a cipher for the unspoken allegiances between the two that

Mr. Duffy disavows at a crucial juncture because he considers music a dissipation that he must repulse. For Mrs. Sinico music leads to physical contact. For Mr. Duffy all acoustic systems break down at the moment of physical contact. Gesture instigates terror in Duffy's mind. Music thus counterbalances the actions of the story, not as a condition for art to aspire to as the fulfillment of human passion, but, paradoxically, as the negation of that passion. The rhythmic clacking of the train and the voice in Mr. Duffy's ear bring him to a final repudiation of sound in "A Painful Case." When he no longer hears anything, the story breaks off, having, in effect, killed the organ of sense that might have opened up human contact.

Contemporary musicology emphasizes the socializing force of sound and music as a cultural (sometimes nationalist) phenomenon. Jacques Attali argues in *Noise: The Political Economy of Music* that "All music, any organization of sounds is then a tool for the creation or consolidation of a community, of a totality. It is what links a power center to its subjects, and thus, more generally, it is an attribute of power in all of its forms" (6). Noise stupefies through repetition, as does music that does not attract attention to itself, such as Muzak, soundtrack, white noise. Attali claims that music provides ritual sacrifice when it is expedient to consolidate a group; thus noise arises as a communal, if irrational, attribute of power. Because music is mathematical and reasonable—as Bloom says in *Ulysses,* "Numbers it is. All music when you come to think" (*U,* 11.830)—and as the reflection of good taste and *mesure,* it imposes a tyranny of numerical logic and social harmony. Attali suggests that any opposition to that logic and order, any introduction of dissonant "noise," is repressed. The inherent primitivism of music disappears into power formations that forbid noise as a viable challenge to the status quo.

By the same token, making noise is an atavistic trait. David Appelbaum claims that "Sung voice is the barbarism of voice, voice's savage rites" (92). The refusal to hear rupture or violence in music, to hear instead only orderly progression of beguiling harmony and pretty melody, stifles the disruptive potential of music and the singing voice. The conception of "classical" music as orderly and sophisticated deprives it of any consequence in the political or social sphere and converts it instead to a badge of class. Repetition of hits, from the *Eroica* to "Strawberry Fields," enforces their banality. The noise of repetition "no longer constructs differences" among auditors, performers, or kinds of music (Attali, 45). In an analysis of the class bias in Western diatonic music, Richard Leppert states that sonorities identified as "music" have been, since the Renaissance, isolated and differentiated from "noise." The discrimination between "folk" and "art" music, defined by amateur and professional status of musicians, as well as the degree of technique required for its execution, has stratified listeners into self-proclaimed "classicists," folk music enthusiasts, or rockers (Leppert, 43–44).[4] Noise, according to Attali and Leppert, consolidates power and class identification when, in truth, harmonious sound resides in the predispositions of the ear to hear in a certain way.

This political challenge in musicology changes the way we consider musical performance in *Dubliners.* The attention paid to performances—Maria's in "Clay" or the concert in "A Mother"—suggests that listeners are attuned to aspects of performance beyond words. When Eveline goes to *The Bohemian Girl,* "she felt elated as she sat in an unaccustomed part of the theatre" (*D,* 39). Where she sits affects her sense of social prestige. Furthermore, operatic performances disseminate nationalism through allegories of political enslavement followed by conversion to the enemy or, in a variation of that plot, allegories of kidnapped aristocrats who commingle with and come to love the peasant classes (as happens in such nineteenth-century operas known to Joyce as *The Bohemian Girl, La Fille du Régiment, Aïda, Lakmé,* or *Il Trovatore*). Yet these songs lose their political valence when casually performed at home. They have no direct influence on lives, however widely they are spread through Dublin culture. Attali's point, that music subsumes violence and enacts ritual sacrifice, is processed into banality by the plots of operas that nullify sacrifice or opposition and prove that love conquers all. The plot of an opera like *La Fille du Régiment* or *The Bohemian Girl* demonstrates that aristocrats and peasants happily fraternize and that true love soars across class lines. Yet the class markers in *Dubliners* do not budge. Mrs. Kearney in "A Mother" insists on seaside holidays with her respectable family, and her animosity toward the *Eire Abu* music society derives partly from her sense of superiority: convent-educated, tasteful, tactful. Similarly, Mr. Duffy despises workmen for being too timorous and equally despises the "obtuse middle class" for relinquishing their morality (*D,* 111). Although he likes listening to Mozart (a composer who wrote more than one opera on the subject of amorous *contretemps*), Mr. Duffy translates none of the operatic precedents for behavior into his own life. Just as Maria fails to perceive the irony of singing a lovelorn song about aristocratic birth, Mr. Duffy does not perceive the irony of listening to Mozart and failing at love because neither character takes music seriously enough as a system of meaningful gestures, sounds, and actions. Performance, particularly of opera, requires death or sacrifice.

Although Joyce uses musical allusion ironically, he also exposes gender biases and sacrificial impulses in Dublin society through his allusive technique. The stories in *Dubliners* about performers and performances—"The Boarding House," "A Mother," and "A Painful Case"—generally represent the symbolic sacrifice of women. This is especially true for those who perform music, the majority of whom are women in Joyce's fiction. Attali's claim that music exacts punishment and embodies ritual violence is borne out by the fates of female performers in *Dubliners*. Men perform, often improvisationally, sometimes hesitantly, whereas women, like Kathleen Kearney or Miss Healy (and Molly Bloom in *Ulysses*), perform professionally, in exchange for fees. When called upon for an opinion about the backstage kerfuffle over money in "A Mother," the noncommittal baritone does not defend Mrs. Kearney, for, by a double standard that unites fair treatment of men with the baritone's complacency, "He had been paid his money and wished to be at peace with men" (*D,* 147). He has been paid, but Kathleen Kearney has not. The unfair treatment of the accompanist is explicable only by invoking a logic that she will be ladylike and not complain. The Dublin ethos of being "at peace with men" excludes the possibility of being at peace with women because they are invisible in business relations, despite their appearance on the stage as performers. Exclusion of Kathleen amounts to sacrifice through the symbolic substitution of music, which, the committee implies, ought to breed harmony, not discord. The sacrifice of women is double: both Kathleen and her mother are dismissed by the inept men who run the business side of the amateur concert after competent Mrs. Kearney has established the program. Although it is unfair, as Jane Miller rightly points out, to scrutinize Mrs. Kearney "as a 'type' of 'Woman,' rather than as a Dubliner in a public situation" (408), all the men treat her thus. Defeated by men who make up business rules as they go along—such as paying the baritone but not paying Kathleen— Mrs. Kearney is judged and dismissed as a woman who abides by contracts and agreements. Ironically, "the supremacy of art as well as the proper behavior of women are hypocritically invoked as being more important than crass considerations of money" (Miller, 415). The passions incited by business misdeeds siphon into music, which becomes the excuse for crushing Mrs. Kearney. Men discount the economic component of music, but only as a ruse to silence and eliminate women from the scene of music making.

Noise, punishment, and music converge in "A Mother" as an accompaniment to Mrs. Kearney's anguish. The vaudevillian performance given by various *artistes* is crossed by currents of nationalism (Irish against English), money (Mrs. Kearney against the Committee), fame (the tenor and the contralto against Madam Glynn), and class (the bumptious bass, Mr. Duggan, who wipes his nose on his sleeve, against the nervous, fastidious tenor, Mr. Bell). The green-room maneuvering of Mrs. Kearney to make the music committee adhere to the four-concert contract they promised her daughter unfolds to a susurrus of audience noise that mounts to a *fortissimo* racket: "From the hall came sounds of encouragement, clapping and stamping of feet" (*D,* 146). Noise demands requital. The "clamour," punctuated with derisive whistles, does not die away until music sounds. Despite half payment for playing the piano, Kathleen Kearney is sacrificed, not to the crowd, but to the petty politics of musical committees and nationalism. Although she fulfills her end of the contract, she loses all future hope of success as a musician; her musical career "was ended in Dublin after that" (*D,* 147). The logic of sacrifice in *Dubliners,* based as much on operatic precedents as on the Joycean predilection for betrayal, determines that even if Kathleen does not appear in public as a performer, she will lose face. In fact, Mr. Holohan and other members of the committee force her into a position of losing her reputation as a condition of her class and her mother's arrogance.

Music, inherited by Kathleen from her mother who learned "French and music" in a "high-class convent" (*D,* 136), intermingles with conversation and noise in "A Mother" as an identification of class. Mrs. Kearney's desire to mock Holohan takes the form of an imagined imitation of his accent: "And who is the *Cometty,* pray?" (*D,* 141). Although she preserves a "ladylike" (*D,* 141) silence on the first crossing of lances with Holohan, she loses control of her speech when "haughty," and lapses into sputtering, mocking slang: "I'm a great fellow fol-the-diddle-I-do" (*D,* 149). This lapse in standards of voice— not upholding speech patterns of class—causes Holohan to reproach her with a slight on her gender and her class standing: "I thought you were a lady" (*D*, 149). Voice betrays the first symptoms of breakdown in Mrs. Kearney. The sacrifice of two women, Kathleen and her mother, fulfills the operatic intertext of the story. Breaking class boundaries, from "high-class" (*D*, 136) to music-hall, might work in *The Bohemian Girl* or Vincent Wallace's 1845 opera *Maritana* (from which the bass sings a solo during the concert), but these expectations of transformation get forestalled in "A Mother." Opera, and music in general, intervenes ironically in the lives of these characters. Prone to communicate through ambiguous codes of music and performance, these Dubliners nevertheless embody immovable social roles. Music may ennoble operatic characters, but it has no permanent, transformative power on the lives of ordinary people. It displaces, and replaces, what cannot be spoken in polite conversation.

In another union of money and music, "The Boarding House" presents an operatic circumstance that ends in the sacrifice of a daughter and her suitor. A retelling of *La Bohème*, the story revolves around Mrs. Mooney's manipulation of her daughter Polly, who vamps at the parlor piano with music-hall artists and, as Mimì does from Rodolfo in Puccini's opera, solicits a light for her candle from a male boarder when "hers had been blown out by a gust" (*D*, 67). A minor performer, Polly nevertheless sacrifices her "honour" (*D*, 65) to win a steadfast husband. In this sense, the sacrifice reconfigures typical opera plots that require the ruin or death of women who show the slightest indications of deviating from purity (*Norma, Manon Lescaut, La Bohème*).[5] Heroines in these operas can marry Roman warriors, aristocrats, or kings. Class lines can be crossed in opera plots, but not by women in paralytic Dublin. Even as women break through lines of gender and class and enter the public domain to perform or to conduct business, they must learn to manipulate men, as Mrs. Mooney does, to preempt maltreatment or punishment.

Men do not suffer the same fate as Polly or Kathleen. Those men who perform music, like the male *artistes* in "A Mother," as well as Bartell D'Arcy and Michael Furey in "The Dead" (not to mention Simon Dedalus in "Sirens"), are not directly represented. Masculinity is not seen when it performs. Male performers sing off-stage in connecting rooms or behind walls. Joyce's sense of the acoustic relies on a suppression of the visual in favor of sound, and a suppression of the male in preference for the female. Simon Dedalus belts out

"M'appari," an aria from *Martha,* in a room adjoining the restaurant in
the Ormond Hotel. In "The Dead," D'Arcy sings in a separate,
unviewable space on another floor of the Morkans' apartment;
furthermore, he pleads illness and refuses to carry his performance
through to completion. Michael Furey serenades Gretta many years
prior to the action of the novella and waits for her in darkness at the
bottom of the garden. Only through Gretta's story of Michael, not
through immediate presentation of his actions, do we know that he
loses his life for his heroic nocturnal visit.

Singing from other rooms prevents men from suffering the
vicissitudes of performance: namely, being spurned as women are.
"The Dead" alters this pattern of the operatic undoing of women insofar
as Gretta remains impervious to Gabriel's desires and falls asleep,
leaving him to sort through his own desire "to overmaster her" and "to
be master of her strange mood" (*D,* 217). Gretta's silence defeats him
and spares her from Gabriel's desire to assume supremacy in their
marriage. Although he tries to wear her down with irony, Gabriel fails
to repudiate, chastise, or injure Gretta. Charged with "distant music"
(*D,* 210), he nevertheless has no entry into the meaning that a particular
ballad bears for his wife. At the party, he strains to hear the sounds that
enrapture Gretta, but "he could hear little save the noise of laughter and
dispute on the front steps, a few chords struck on the piano and a few
notes of a man's voice singing" (*D,* 209). While Gretta listens to
D'Arcy singing at the Morkans', Gabriel treats her as an intermediary
to unheard music, as his only access to something that he cannot hear
with his own ears. Not a symptom of Gabriel's desire, Gretta, by falling
asleep, resists the typical fate of the operatic heroine, who dies in order
to allow the hero to reach insight by himself. The novella also reverses
the trajectory of the previous *Dubliners* stories about female performers
by refusing to display a woman's humiliation for the sake of satisfying
the male appetite for sacrifice.

Notwithstanding Attali's insistence on the ritual violence in music,
which takes its toll on women in opera plots, there is a difference
between war cries and arias in terms of rhythm, pitch, volume, and
verbal articulation. Although opera often approaches the state of
sonority for pure acoustic effect—the tally-hos of Valkyries, the dying
gasps of Scarpia, or the sobs of Rodolfo—such breakdowns merely
prove that the hitching together of word and music is inevitably a tug-
of-war, a perpetual battle between meaning and sheer sound. Michel

Poizat traces the history of sung words as a struggle for predominance between words and music: "on the one hand, fusion or confusion of music and speech, and on the other hand, music's antagonism toward, challenge to, and even destruction of the spoken word" (51). In the acoustic milieus of "The Dead," a *charabia* of sound lies just outside hearing.

If music presses toward a point of convergence between word and sung note, then opera struggles to unmake itself by pitting language and music in hostile relation to each other. Put otherwise, in Joyce's presentation of words and music, especially in *Ulysses,* the moments when sound becomes speech and speech becomes music are moments worth philosophical and aesthetic contemplation. *Ulysses* reworks *Dubliners'* trajectory of noise—sound—music—silence by establishing again the relationship between a female performer and musical tidbits. After all, *Ulysses* is a novel about a soprano, her husband, and her impresario. The chief event of Molly Bloom's day is a rehearsal for her upcoming tour of provincial towns, where she intends to sing Zerlina's part in the duet "Là ci darem la mano" from *Don Giovanni.* In performance, Molly does not always remember her words, especially in foreign languages; Leopold wonders if she pronounces *"voglio"* correctly (*U,* 4.328). The first preverbal monosyllable she utters while lying in bed in "Calypso" defies comprehension: "Mn" (*U,* 4.57). Molly's vocalizing begins in an animalistic grunt: not speech, just sound. Yawn, sigh, response, grunt, moan: Molly's "mn" buzzes between noise and word. Its meaning is ambiguous, though her husband takes it to mean "no." In a recapitulation of the Viconian theory that mimicry is the origin of language, Leopold talks to the cat in the same episode in a mock-animal voice: "Afraid of the chookchooks. I never saw such a stupid pussens as the pussens" (*U,* 4.30–31). Repetitive and imitative of cat-talk, the moment is operatic, in Poizat's sense of the term, insofar as it treats sound as an effect converging on sense and nonsense, imitation and articulation. Joyce's modernity expresses itself in this fascination with the mysteries of the voice as an instrument embodying human identity.

In a 1928 essay on "Voice in Opera," Alban Berg claims that "an art form that uses the human voice should not deprive itself of any of its numerous possibilities," including bel canto, *Sprechstimme,* and coloratura (113). Berg goes on to say that "these diverse possibilities prove to what degree opera is predestined, more than any other musical genre, to put itself at the service of the human voice, to protect its rights" (115). As the composer of *Wozzeck* and *Lulu,* Berg pushes the human voice to strained limits of intelligibility by intermingling *Sprechstimme* and arias with nonmusical shrieks, groans, and yelps. Opera, or, more generally, art, serves the human voice, not vice versa. Berg intimates, without specifying how this would come about, that the human voice may lose its primacy in the modern period, perhaps to sentimental love songs, popular radio tunes, or Broadway musicals. These forms limit the range of the human voice by not drawing on its full expressiveness. The voice therefore becomes the servant of the music, whereas Berg wants music to serve the voice. Nonverbal cries (as when, in Act I of *Lulu,* the protagonist, both siren and femme fatale, discovers the corpse of one of her husbands) convey despair and horror that lie beyond the powers of speech and music. As Berg claims, only by exaggerating the latent possibilities of the human voice can significance be communicated; modernity forbids the full articulation of horror and resorts instead to gaps, silences, and noise to suggest the realm of despair or anguish that language can never adequately conjure up. This is the gnomic technique of *Dubliners,* which promotes silences as moments of revelation. In a muted case, Gabriel Conroy does not understand his wife or her past as she stands on the stair in "The Dead"; as if he were painting the tableau, he labels his miscomprehension *"Distant Music"* (*D,* 210). Literally, he does not hear Bartell D'Arcy; figuratively, the "distant music" (*D ,* 210) bespeaks his misunderstanding of his wife's grief for lost love. Gabriel is cut off from feelings of loss and grief that lie beyond hearing.

Opera dwells on the border between meaning and sound. The meaning of the sung word is not always intelligible, not only because of imprecise enunciation or lack of projection, but also because meaning is conveyed through timbre, pitch, and the idiosyncracies of a singer's voice. Roland Barthes calls this the "grain of the voice," the singularity of any voice as an instrument of signification. The voice has meaning "independently of what it says" that implies "a certain erotic relationship between the voice and the listener" (*Grain,* 183, 184). What lies within, behind, beside, or around a voice imparts itself to the astute listener. Joyce habitually marks his characters with adverbial or adjectival tags to describe the "grain" of each voice, and, synecdochically, character itself. In "Grace" for instance, Kernan speaks first with a "grunting noise" (*D,* 150), then with a characteristic

omission of letters because he has bitten off the tip of his tongue: "I'
'ery 'uch o'liged to you, sir" (*D*, 152). Lenehan speaks "dubiously" (*D*,
52) or exclaims "boldly" (*D*, 54) in "Two Gallants"; his pal Corley
speaks "amiably" (*D*, 54). Lenehan has a voice "winnowed of vigour"
because he talks until "His tongue was tired" in a pub (*D*, 50). Their
voices register signs of class difference and masculinity. Although
Lenehan has a ready trove of "stories, limericks and riddles" (*D*, 50),
the focus of the narrative in "Two Gallants" is Corley's ability to
persuade, through suave speech, a serving girl to give him money.

In *Ulysses,* also, characters have grained voices that can signify
foreignness (Haines) or sophistication ("the quaker librarian" who purrs
[*U*, 9.1]) or torment (Stephen). Buck Mulligan speaks "sternly,"
"briskly," and "frankly" at the start of the "Telemachus" episode (*U*,
1.19, 28, 51). He intones, chants, sighs, and squawks in a perpetual
parody of sounds. His voice is a compendium of received ideas and
snatches of trivia, blended together in a voice best characterized as
parodic and modern. Buck's jingoistic jive suggests that all utterances
are performances. Modernity takes up residence on the tongue as a
collocation of bon mots, witticisms, advertising slogans, and speeches
that are not personal property. Speech may never be sincere or
"individual." Human identity is a collocation of other voices. Voice, in
this regard, is the sign of inauthenticity, as when a performer sings a
role with scripted words that denote passion, a broken heart, or rapture
that he or she imitates without believing. Performers succeed best when
they fully embody the roles they sing, when they behave least as
themselves.

Such performative denotations of sound bypass the question of
meaning in music, which Plato raises, Kant critiques, Rousseau
pursues, and contemporary musicologists have reconsidered. Kant
likens the arrangement of sensations (harmony and melody) to "the
form of a language" that expresses an "unspeakable wealth of thought
[*unnennbaren Gedankenfülle*]" (cited in Kivy, 254).[6] In his *Essay on
the Origins of Language,* Rousseau resorts to music to describe
meaning in language and implicitly elevates music beyond words.
However, as Carolyn Abbate argues, "since music possesses a meaning
that is notoriously indefinable," it may enable analysis of the
antagonism between words and music if "the *trope* of music as a
language" is resisted (18). The universe that music summons appeals to
the ear, like language; unlike language, music does not designate

objects in the world. It "falls entirely within the province of the sensations," Claude Lévi-Strauss claims, and therefore "the universe to which it refers cannot be represented" (105, 163). Abbate writes that "*Language,* as a bearer of subjective impressions, capitulates before *music* as a force of objectification and hence greater power of expression" (149). Jacques Attali weighs in with the opinion that "music cannot be equated with a language [...]. It has neither meaning nor finality" (25). The configuration of sound and meaning changes when words are added to music. Meaning becomes delimited. As Bloom notes in *Ulysses* as he listens to strummed piano chords, "Might be what you like, till you hear the words" (*U,* 11.838–39).

Words are not music. However, the antagonism between words and music cannot be resolved, especially since the two entwine in Western sacred and secular music. Confusion about sound and meaning is compounded by an identification of instrumental with vocal music. Felix Mendelssohn's popular compendia of "*Lieder ohne Worte*" for piano solo, for instance, defy language and kidnap human voice for the keyboard: no longer reliant on the voice, the "lieder" are sung on the piano "without words," as an act of vocalizing with the fingers. The piano replicates the human voice as a "song" but supplements that voice with something—the unutterable, the unconscious—that words cannot convey. Songs *without* words denote loss; they recollect sound that precedes sense. Like the boy who does not understand the meaning of the word "Araby" yet luxuriates in its vowels and consonants, the singer of a song without words fetches into consciousness the remote pre-Oedipal experience of sound without words, words without sense. Mendelssohn claims that the meaning of music is too precise for language to capture (Kramer, xi). Music communicates *in excess* of a language; it imparts more than can be taken in or deciphered.

Instead of likening music to language, it might be more apt to think of music as the expression of the body and its desires. Except for Roland Barthes, most musicologists have avoided the bodily aspects of singing. An originary point, bodies emit voices. David Appelbaum argues that "sung voice is incapable of clarifying its position in the war of opposites" between demands of the flesh, the spirit, and the intellect (88). As a mediator, singing effaces neither the body, nor instincts, nor passions, nor reason, nor cognition; it remains the gesture of emotion, unlike speech, which flattens, regularizes, grammaticizes, and declaims. Singing obviates identity (any number of singers can perform the same song) and expands it (no two singers sing alike). Singing announces secret wishes and desires that cannot be spoken in straightforward speech, and these wishes arise from the flesh. Music, especially sung words, embellishes and reinvigorates prosody with emotion that Plato thought harmful to the republic because it effeminizes the body and stupefies the intellect. Or, conversely, martial music stirs the flesh to aggressive action. Singing communicates viscerally, not rationally. Sung language then, as in Aunt Julia's performance of "Arrayed for the Bridal" in "The Dead," taps a source of nonrational, physical memory that the body itself belies and reason cannot interrupt.

In an expansion of his definition of "the grain of the voice," Roland Barthes argues that the voice is an apparition, the ghostly point where the material converts into the immaterial: "The singing voice, that very specific space in which a tongue encounters a voice and permits those who know how to listen to it to hear what we can call its 'grain'—the singing voice is not the breath but indeed that materiality of the body emerging from the throat, a site where the phonic metal hardens and takes shape" (*Responsibility,* 255). What Gabriel Conroy hears in his aunt's aria is a premonition of her death. The "grain" of her voice, the idiosyncratic and nonlinguistic indices of her material body, betray her mortality to "those who know how to listen," like Gabriel. The difference between sung and spoken voices needs to be extended to the difference between voice and tonal quality. Barthes distinguishes "voice" from "language": "we rarely listen to a voice *en soi,* in itself, we listen to what it says" (*Grain,* 183). As when the Saturday afternoon opera quiz from the Met requires contestants to identify the voice of Schwarzkopf, Callas, von Otter, or other divas after a few bars of played music, the voice gives itself away not in the repetition of a vocal line, but in the peculiarities and indefinable aspects that are particular to each singer. The "grain of the voice" is surplus meaning that announces itself apart from words and their tyranny of logic and syntax. A misunderstood "absent object" (*Grain,* 183) according to Barthes, the voice is immaterial yet issues from the body; not the body per se, it depends on and emerges from the body. Instead of thinking about the voice as a metaphysical problem, Barthes offers a definition rooted in the physical. Music is corporeal, not linguistic.

Taking the grainy physicality of the voice as a point of departure, Wayne Koestenbaum relates aural experience to visceral pleasure and bodily behavior: "I started listening to opera because the convulsive vibrato of a trained voice embarrassed me" (154). For Koestenbaum the operatic singing voice exceeds definition. It tells "a story about the body" and "the story of sexuality" as the voice journeys from hiddenness into the world (155).[7] Michel Poizat in *The Angel's Cry* argues that the pushing of vocal limits to the highest registers for tenors and sopranos over the history of operatic composition forces the voice toward the pure cry, the shriek, where words are no longer articulate, where notes are pure melisma, where sounds are yelps of death and destruction, like Lakmé vocalizing in Délibes's opera to attract the attention of the British officer Frederic until she faints with fright, or like Lulu's shriek at the end of Berg's opera to signal her death at the hands of Jack the Ripper. The ecstatic cry is, for Poizat, the *jouissance* of opera that, beyond the pleasure principle, cancels the body itself in ecstatic death. At these moments, language and music defy each other yet come together in pure sound that causes the body to quiver with unnameable, unspeakable pleasure.

The physicality of the voice applies to those stories in *Dubliners* where bodies sing in order to remember. "The Dead," in particular, links music to memory. Mr. Browne recalls days of operatic glory when "one night an Italian tenor had sung five encores to *Let Me Like a Soldier Fall,* introducing a high C every time" (*D,* 199). Browne does not remember the name of the tenor, but he remembers numbers: five encores, five high Cs. The height of glory is recalled as vocal accomplishment. Memory is rooted in the body: the spine-shivering ecstatic Cs are remembered as unparalleled frissons for the auditor. Although deconstructive criticism has attempted to dislodge voice as presence and subjectivity as univocal, and postmodernists have attempted to demonstrate that innovations in technology and advertising decenter the subject, singing and the recollection of singing in Joyce's stories demonstrate that characters sing to incite subjective memory.

Like the phrases of the Vinteuil sonata in Marcel Proust's *Remembrance of Things Past,* the evocation of events through sound in Joyce's fiction suggests that the hearing body remembers, and recaptures, lost youth and lost time. Proust records the defamiliarizing effects that modern culture had on the human voice when Marcel speaks with his grandmother on the telephone. The newfangled device allows him to hear, for the first time, elements of pathos and sweetness in his grandmother's voice that had always before been hidden from

him by her physical presence: "for always until then, every time that
my grandmother had talked to me, I had been accustomed to follow
what she said on the open score of her face, in which the eyes figured
so largely; but her voice itself I was hearing this afternoon for the first
time" (Proust, *Remembrance,* II, 135). Face and gesture have prevented
Marcel from hearing the fragility, sweetness, and tenderness in the
tones of her voice: "having it alone beside me, seen without the mask of
her face, I noticed in it for the first time the sorrows that had cracked it
in the course of a lifetime" (Proust, *Remembrance,* II, 136). Distance,
paradoxically, permits intimacy and sympathetic rapport. Proust's
narrative makes physical presence illusory and a repetition of an
anticipated permanent separation from the object of affection. The
telephone renders the beloved voice closer, more touching than
physical presence can do. Marcel demotes the physical to
representations; his grandmother's face is a musical "score" ("la
partition ouverte") and a "mask" ("le masque du visage"), not a
physical amalgam of wrinkles and flesh (Proust, *Le Côté,* I, 127). The
voice usurps the body and makes the modern writer reconsider the
illusoriness of physical presence as a projection of genuine intimacy or
authentic identity. Technology transfigures intimacy by allowing the
voice to enter directly into the ear of the attentive auditor. The human
voice has more eloquence, not less, than was previously suspected.
Proust's discovery of hidden qualities in his grandmother's voice might
be taken as a prototype for modern conceptions of the voice, hiding and
bespeaking aspects of identity.

In "The Dead," dinner conversation centers on the great opera
singers of the past. Before dinner, Aunt Julia sings "Arrayed for the
Bridal" from Bellini's *I Puritani,* with an effect similar to the one that
Marcel's grandmother has on him: "Her voice, strong and clear in tone,
attacked with great spirit the runs which embellish the air and though
she sang very rapidly she did not miss even the smallest of the grace
notes. To follow the voice, without looking at the singer's face, was to
feel and share the excitement of swift and secure flight" (*D,* 193). The
irony of Aunt Julia preparing for a nuptial ceremony is palpable, as is
the irony of a Catholic singing an aria from an opera about Puritans in
the English Civil War. The song permits Julia to adopt a role that she
otherwise can never execute (bride-to-be), and performance returns her,
by bodily memory, to a younger version of herself that defies death. To
hear her "without looking at the singer's face" induces security and

excitement. The song defies the body, not, as in Proust, to the detriment of the elderly woman who is cracked by age, but by returning the singer to a more secure and capable version of herself. Singing rejuvenates her, though this rejuvenation comes about by not looking at her face, which tells an altogether different story.

Everyone compliments Aunt Julia on the "clear and fresh" (*D*, 193) qualities in her singing. This freshness contradicts the "grey" and "flaccid" appearance she otherwise gives off, "the appearance of a woman who did not know where she was or where she was going" (*D*, 179). Whereas she appears to sing freshly and clearly to Mr. Browne's ears, Gabriel hears her performance as a swan song whose meaning runs counter to the linguistic content of "Arrayed for the Bridal." Not only are words and music at odds with Julia's physical body, Julia's singing voice is at odds with itself, conveying a counter-gesture of mortality despite her fresh, clear performance. Gabriel makes death the center of her performance, not vitality or youth. Thinking about Julia's probable death, he recalls "that haggard look upon her face for a moment when she was singing *Arrayed for the Bridal*" (*D*, 222). Gabriel was looking at her face during the performance when looking away would have allowed him to hear the voice in and of itself, detached from Julia's dying body. In this novella that contrasts different kinds of performance—piano recital, church chorus, operatic turn, after-dinner speech, dance songs, impromptu ballad, family story—Aunt Julia's singing raises the problem of immortality in performance. Her voice masks her age, her decrepitude, and her impending death. Her body betrays her. Singing, she splits between the woman who surely will die and the woman who sings out of her body as a younger, unactualized self.

Voices in *Dubliners* disclose more than they understand. Aunt Julia's voice betrays the discrepancy between her youthfulness and her certain death. Like Orpheus calling for Eurydice in the underworld, Julia's voice deceives her, for it promises to usurp death. Singing cannot accomplish such a feat of deathlessness because it tells the story of the body. Nevertheless, what lies outside language and time discloses itself in the medium of music. The voice of desire and remembrance, antagonism and consolation, music expresses what the characters in *Dubliners* never directly speak.

NOTES

1. Wagner notes, in his centennial essay on Beethoven, that all music consists of varying degrees of weakening of the scream: "[Music's] sounding message to our ear is of the selfsame nature as the cry sent forth to it from the depths of our own inner heart" (70–71).

2. Abbate argues throughout *Unsung Voices* that libretti, notations in scores, leitmotifs, and other devices establish internal divisions within music. Using the diegetical theories of Mikhail Bakhtin, Abbate undoes the naive assumption that music necessarily represents unified subjects or transcendental wholeness: "textual manipulations of narration in various forms" and oscillations "between action and narration, between music unheard and heard" (144) create intertextual and extramusical tensions.

3. Emma Bovary goes to the opera to hear Donizetti's *Lucia di Lammermoor* in *Madame Bovary:* "when [Edgar and Lucia] uttered the final farewell, Emma gave a sharp cry that mingled with the vibrations of the last chords" (Flaubert, 162).

4. Theodor Adorno instigated a sociological analysis of music in various critical works, the implications of which are only now being examined. See Peter Martin, *Sounds and Society: Themes in the Sociology of Music:* "particular patterns of culture—in this case the rules according to which music is normally organised—are both consistent with and ultimately derived from fundamental characteristics of the society as a whole" (76). See also Janet Wolff, "The Ideology of Autonomous Art": "it is often argued that music somehow does transcend the social and the contingent in ways which literature, film and representational painting do not [...]. [T]he non-representational character of music is no explanation for its exemption from sociological analysis" (10).

5. For a reading of gender in opera plots that informs this discussion of women as sacrificial victims in *Dubliners,* see Clément, *Opera, or the Undoing of Women.*

6. For an interpretation of Kant's musical aesthetics, which ultimately demote music to an after-dinner diversion, far inferior to thought or language, see Kivy, 250–64.

7. Koestenbaum has inspired a host of opera lovers to proclaim their adoration of divas or their identification with Valkyrie-voiced performers. Two works about bodies and opera openly acknowledge indebtedness to Koestenbaum. See Sam Abel, *Opera in the Flesh,* and Leonardi and Pope, *The Diva's Mouth.*

WORKS CITED

Abbate, Carolyn. *Unsung Voices: Opera and Musical Narrative in the Nineteenth Century.* Princeton, N.J.: Princeton University Press, 1991.

Abel, Sam. *Opera in the Flesh: Sexuality in Operatic Performance.* New York: HarperCollins, 1996.

Appelbaum, David. *Voice.* Albany: State University of New York Press, 1990.

Attali, Jacques. *Noise: The Political Economy of Music.* Trans. Brian Massumi. Foreword by Fredric Jameson. Afterword by Susan McClary. Minneapolis: University of Minnesota Press, 1985

Barthes, Roland. *The Grain of the Voice: Interviews 1962–1980.* Trans. Linda Coverdale. Berkeley and Los Angeles: University of California Press, 1991.

———. *The Responsibility of Forms.* Trans. Richard Howard. New York: Hill & Wang, 1985.

Beckett, Samuel, et al. *Our Exagmination Round His Factification for Incamination of Work in Progress.* New York: New Directions, 1972.

Berg, Alban. *Ecrits.* Ed. Dominique Jameux. Trans. Henri Pousseur, Gisela Tillier, Dennis Collins. Paris: Christian Bourgois, 1985.

Clément, Catherine. *Opera, or the Undoing of Women.* Trans. Betsy Wing. Minneapolis: University of Minnesota Press, 1988.

Flaubert, Gustave. *Madame Bovary.* Trans. Paul De Man. New York: Norton, 1965.

Herr, Cheryl. *Joyce's Anatomy of Culture.* Urbana and Chicago: University of Illinois Press, 1986.

Kivy, Peter. *The Fine Art of Repetition: Essays in the Philosophy of Music.* Cambridge: Cambridge University Press, 1993.

Koestenbaum, Wayne. *The Queen's Throat: Opera, Homosexuality, and the Mystery of Desire.* New York: Vintage, 1993.

Kramer, Lawrence. *Music as Cultural Practice, 1800–1900.* Berkeley: University of California Press, 1990.

Leonardi, Susan J. and Rebecca A. Pope. *The Diva's Mouth: Body, Voice, Prima Donna Politics.* New Brunswick, N.J.: Rutgers University Press, 1996.

Leppert, Richard. *The Sight of Sound: Music, Representation, and the History of the Body.* Berkeley: University of California Press, 1993.

Leppert, Richard and Susan McClary, eds. *Music and Society: The Politics of Composition, Performance and Reception.* Cambridge: Cambridge University Press, 1987.

Lévi-Strauss, Claude. *Look, Listen, Read.* Trans. Brian C. J. Singer. New York: HarperCollins, 1997.

Martin, Peter J. *Sounds and Society: Themes in the Sociology of Music.* Manchester, U.K.: Manchester University Press, 1995.

Martin, Timothy. *Joyce and Wagner.* Cambridge: Cambridge University Press, 1991.

Miller, Jane E. "'O, she's a nice lady!': A Rereading of 'A Mother.'" *James Joyce Quarterly* 28, 2 (1991): 407–26.

Norris, Margot. *The Decentered Universe of* Finnegans Wake. Baltimore, Md.: Johns Hopkins University Press, 1976.

Poizat, Michel. *The Angel's Cry: Beyond the Pleasure Principle in Opera.* Trans. Arthur Denner. Ithaca, N.Y.: Cornell University Press, 1992.

Proust, Marcel. *Le Côté de Guermantes I.* Ed. Thierry Laget. Paris: Folio, 1988.
———. *Remembrance of Things Past.* Trans. C. K. Scott Moncrieff and Terence Kilmartin. New York: Random House, 1981.

Wagner, Richard. "Beethoven." *Richard Wagner's Prose Works.* Vol. V. Trans. William Ashton Ellis. London: Kegan Paul, 1896. 57–126.

Wolff, Janet. "The Ideology of Autonomous Art." *Music and Society: The Politics of Composition, Performance and Reception.* Eds. Richard Leppert and Susan McClary. Cambridge: Cambridge University Press, 1987. 1–12.

CHAPTER 9

The Distant Music of the Spheres

Thomas Jackson Rice

Perhaps when a man considers the arts, he may fancy that mankind need number only for minor purposes—though the part it plays even in them is considerable. But could he see the divine and the mortal in the world process—a vision from which he will learn both the fear of God and the true nature of number—even so 'tis not any man and every man who will recognize the full power number will bestow on us if we are conversant with the whole field of it—why, for example, all musical effects manifestly depend upon the numeration of motions and tones—or will take the chief point of all, that 'tis the source of all good things, but, as we should be well aware, of none of the ill things which may perhaps befall us. No, unregulated, disorderly, ungainly, unrhythmical, tuneless movement, and all else that partakes of evil, is destitute of all number, and of this a man who means to die happy must be convinced. (Plato, 977e–978b)

Toward the end of his evening at the "Misses Morkan's annual dance" (*D*, 175) Gabriel Conroy, standing in the darkness at the foot of a staircase, gazes upward at "A woman," his wife Gretta, "standing near the top of the first flight, in the shadow also" (*D*, 209). Gretta, he quickly realizes, is "listening to something," something he cannot hear: "Gabriel was surprised at her stillness and strained his ear to listen also. But he could hear little save the noise of laughter and dispute on the front steps, a few chords struck on the piano and a few notes of a man's voice singing" (*D*, 209). Gabriel remains standing "still [...], trying to catch the air that the voice was singing and gazing up at his wife" (*D*, 210). Gabriel compensates for his failure "to catch the air" by weaving in another kind of air a fantasy of his wife and this scene composing something like a late-nineteenth-century genre painting: "If he were a painter he would paint her in th[is] attitude. [...] *Distant Music* he would call the picture if he were a painter" (*D*, 210). More like the literary critic he is than the aspiring painter he is not, Gabriel attempts to *read* this scene: he sees his wife "as if she were a symbol of something." He asks himself the quintessential question of literary criticism: "what is a woman standing on the stairs in a shadow, listening to distant music, a symbol of[?]" (*D*, 210).

Other critics have followed Gabriel's lead, and there is no shortage of directions we could take for reading this passage in "The Dead": tracing Gabriel's egoistic projection of his own desires upon his wife, or seeing here a foreshadowing of Gretta's unknowable otherness to Gabriel, or connecting Gretta's physical distance from Bartell D'Arcy's rendition of "The Lass of Aughrim" to her temporal distance from Michael Furey's singing of the same song (*D*, 218), or perhaps juxtaposing the relation of Gabriel to Gretta here to that of the young boy in "Araby," who gazes similarly upward toward Mangan's sister, from the shadows, earlier in the collection (*D*, 30). Rather than pursuing any of these leads, however, I would like to take a different direction in looking at this often-discussed moment in *Dubliners* and trace not only the interesting conjunctions among the literary, pictorial, and musical arts working in this intensely visual scene, but also argue that these conjunctions emerge from a mathematical substratum in this story and in Joyce's early aesthetic that he continues to explore and interrogate through *A Portrait of the Artist as a Young Man, Ulysses,* and *Finnegans Wake.*

Gabriel, we know, is fond of himself and fond of his coinages, so he resurrects his "distant music" phrase a few minutes after this staircase scene, and four pages later in the story, as he recalls a love letter he had written to Gretta: "Like distant music these words that he had written years before were borne towards him from the past" (*D*, 214). However, more than another sign of Gabriel's egoism is involved in Joyce's repetition of the term "distant music" here; words are not just the stuff of a particular kind of musical art, as in vocal music: words themselves *constitute* music for Gabriel, metaphorically perhaps, and for Joyce, both literarily and literally.

I have long wondered, and well before my students ever asked me this, why does anyone read "The Dead"? It is a very peculiar story, an apparently pointless narrative slice of Dublin life until the readers discover its true direction only in the final few pages. What keeps these readers reading? What sustains the readers' involvement in the story while they await its point? My best answer to this question is that Joyce's stylistic virtuosity, his extraordinarily skillful stimulus of visual and auditory responses through language—and one is tempted to add tactile, olfactory, and gustatory responses as well—gives "The Dead" a quality of felt life that belies its title. We experience something of Joyce's synaesthetic technique in the staircase scene, when he evokes Gabriel's auditory sensation of music faintly heard by rendering this intensely visual moment through words, words that are themselves distantly musical, through onomatopoeias like "noise," through alliterations like "_s_tood _s_till," "_s_inging," "_s_he," "_s_ymbol," and "_s_omething," and especially through pervasive assonance like "g_a_zing" and "gr_a_ce," or once more "symb_o_l" and "s_o_mething" (*D*, 209–10; emphasis added here and throughout). We find even better examples of this synaesthetic method that Mary Reynolds, arguing the influence of Dante's similar "linguistic virtuosity" on "Sirens," describes as "the close 'fit' of acoustic and semantic properties [...] in Joyce's prose" (94), in those wonderful two paragraphs that immediately precede Gabriel's after-dinner speech in "The Dead."

In the first of these paragraphs, Joyce exploits a variety of auditory devices—alliteration, assonance, consonance, onomatopoeia, phonetic intensives ("nudge," "unsettlings," "pushed"), even punctuation ("A pause followed," followed by a *comma*)—to make his visual description *audible:*

> The raisins _a_nd _a_lmonds _a_nd figs _a_nd _a_pples and _o_ranges and ch_o_colates and _s_weets were now pa_ss_ed abou_t_ the _t_able and Aunt Julia invited all the gue_s_ts to have either port or _s_herry. At _f_irst Mr B_a_rtell D'_A_rcy re_f_used to take either but _o_ne of his _n_eighbours nudg_ed_ him and whispered s_o_mething to him upon which he _a_llowed his gl_a_ss to be fi_ll_ed. Gr_a_dually _as_ the _l_ast gla_ss_es were being fi_ll_ed the conver_s_ation cea_s_ed. A pause followed, br_o_ken _o_nly by the n_oi_se of the w_i_ne and by unsettlings of chairs. The _M_isses _M_orkan, all three, looked d_o_wn _at_ the _t_ablecl_o_th. Some_o_ne cough_ed_ _o_nce or _t_wice and then a few _gent_lemen pa_tt_ed the _t_able gent_l_y as a _s_ignal for _s_ilence. The _s_ilence came and G_a_briel push_ed_ b_a_ck his ch_a_ir _a_nd _s_tood up. (*D*, 201)

One might say that in this marvelous paragraph, bracketed by the parallel sequences in space (the cornucopia of fruits and sweets) and in time (Gabriel's rising), the "noise of the wine" is the least audible sound present, even if the filling of D'Arcy's glass *is* "allowed." Within a "rectangular" block of text, framed like a painting by unbroken parallel "lines"—unpunctuated sequences in space and in time—the reader experiences the distantly musical, auditory dimension of a represented, visual real, "the ineluctable modality of the audible" contained within the "Ineluctable modality of the visible" (*U*, 3.13, 1).

And the next paragraph continues to exploit these same auditory techniques: with the "patting" growing louder "in encouragement," Gabriel leaning "his ten trembling fingers on the tablecloth," and "skirts sweeping against the drawing-room door" (*D*, 202), as Joyce emphasizes the sensory access for character and reader alike to what he calls, in *Finnegans Wake,* the "morphomelosophopancreate[d]" world (*FW*, 88.9).

But in what sense can I claim that Joyce's verbal music in "The Dead," his conjunction of the literary, the pictorial, and the musical arts in the narration of such intensely visual scenes as Gretta on the staircase or Gabriel rising to speak, emerges from a mathematical substratum? For an answer to this question we must turn to *A Portrait of the Artist as a Young Man,* where Joyce, no less fond of a coinage than Gabriel, resurrects once again the phrase "distant music."[1] At the beginning of chapter three, just before the announcement of the religious retreat, Stephen Dedalus sits in his classroom at Belvedere College solving an algebraic equation. As he works his way through his mathematics assignment, expanding and canceling out terms and exponents, or "indices" as exponents were then called, Stephen transforms the solution of a mathematical problem into a vision of a Beardsleyesque fin-de-siècle design, accompanied by the silent music of, perhaps, Richard Strauss's *Salome,* and strangely invoking astronomical images:

> The equation of the page of his scribbler began to spread out a widening tail, eyed and starred like a peacock's; and, when the eyes and stars of its indices had been eliminated, began slowly to fold itself together again. The indices appearing and disappearing were eyes opening and closing; the eyes opening and closing were stars being born and being quenched. The vast cycle of starry life bore his

weary mind outward to its verge and inward to its centre, a <u>distant music</u> accompanying him outward and inward. (*P,* 102–3)

While the repetition of the key phrase "distant music" ties this passage interestingly to "The Dead," what actually ties the paragraph's curious concatenation of images together is Joyce's embedded allusion to the classical quadrivium, his union through Stephen of arithmetic (algebra), geometry (design), astronomy (stars), and the curious fourth partner of these three, music. Of course, what both Joyce and the Boethian quadrivium acknowledge is the traditional recognition, as old as the school of Pythagoras, of the intimate welding of music, mathematics, and the heavens.

"Legend-veiled Pythagoras" (Kline, *Culture,* 40), the inventor of the gnomon (James, 29–30), recognized that both music and nature share a common language: mathematics.[2] The later Pythagorean school expanded this discovery into a cosmology that supported the union of mathematics, music, and astronomy of the medieval quadrivium, and that survived in the idea "that music was the sound of mathematics, no less" (Barrow, *Artful,* 199), long after the new Copernican cosmology of the Renaissance finally silenced the fabled Pythagorean music of the spheres in the sciences, or "untuned" the sky as John Dryden and John Hollander put it, by the beginning of the nineteenth century.[3] Pythagoras's discovery of the mathematical language of music not only has survived, but still flourishes because we can as readily demonstrate the numerical ratios that account for musical tones on any stringed instrument today, as Pythagoras is reputed to have done on the day of his miraculous discovery of the octave, one morning in the sixth century B.C., after hearing the harmonious sound of hammers ringing on the anvils of his neighborhood blacksmith (Levenson, 21–22). (This was the original "harmonious blacksmith," I presume.) More than this, by the early nineteenth century the French mathematician Joseph Fourier could demonstrate through Newtonian physics that "all sounds, vocal and instrumental, simple and complex, are completely describable in mathematical terms" (Kline, *Culture,* 287). To my knowledge, however, only Plato, in his *Epinomis,* dared to assert that mathematics is also the language of language, at least until the early-twentieth-century surge of interest in logical systems, seen in Russell, Whitehead, and Wittgenstein, and more recently in the linguistic theories of Noam Chomsky.[4] What I want to suggest is that Stephen

Dedalus, as well as the early James Joyce, invokes something resembling the Pythagorean astronomical concept of the celestial, unheard, distant music of the spheres as the goal toward which all literature aspires, and if, in Pater's formulation, *"All art constantly aspires towards the condition of music"* (111), the language of these arts is, as it is for music itself, ultimately mathematical.

Or better yet, invoking Plato's *Epinomis,* Joyce might argue that, could they "see the divine and the mortal in the world process," humankind would recognize that "the part [number] plays [...] in [the arts] is considerable" (977e).[5] In other words, Joyce aspires toward the harmonious Pythagorean ideal of oneness, the Monad (James, 77), by seeking a union of mathematics—as in the quadrivium of arithmetic, geometry, astronomy, and music—with language, the trivium of grammar, dialectic, and rhetoric. This oneness derived from seven would be the harmonious union experienced by the guardians and musicians of the spheres, the angels, in the Christian adaptations of "Pythagoras's vision of the musical cosmos" (68), which Jamie James (53–75) traces from the conclusions of Plato's *Republic* ("The Myth of Er") and Cicero's *De republica* ("Scipio's Dream"), through Clement of Alexandria's *Exhortation to the Greeks* and Saint Augustine's *De musica,* to Boethius's *De institutione musica,* which "remained a standard text for the teaching of music theory at Oxford until 1856" (75). Or as Joyce himself echoes this idea in his precocious undergraduate essay "The Study of Languages": "as mathematics and the Sciences of Numbers partake of the nature of that beauty which is omnipresent, which is expressed, almost noiselessly [as a "distant music"?], in the order and symmetry of Mathematics, as in the charms of literature; so does Literature in turn share in the neatness and regularity of Mathematics" (*CW,* 26).

This ideal Monad imbedded in Stephen's mathematics class in chapter three of *Portrait* also lurks within Joyce's later description of Stephen's awakening on the morning he composes his villanelle, a waking touched by the distant music of another Gabriel, "Gabriel the seraph" (*P,* 217):

> Towards dawn he awoke. O what sweet music! [...] He lay still, as if his soul lay amid cool waters, conscious of faint sweet music [...] A spirit filled him, pure as the purest water, sweet as dew, moving as music. But how faintly it was inbreathed, how

passionlessly, as if the seraphim themselves were breathing upon him! (*P*, 217)

Elsewhere I have discussed the quadrivial images drawn from geometry, astronomy, arithmetic, and music, that work within this villanelle scene, as geometrical "rays of rhyme" and the image of the "ellipsoidal ball" (*P*, 218) of the earth inspire the numbers of Stephen's song, for his *trivial* language exercise in grammar, dialectic, and rhetoric (Rice, 74–77). Yet this quadrivial imagery represents only part of the story, four-sevenths to be exact, of the harmonious union of the four modes of mathematics and three elements of language within the Monad of the distant music of the spheres, the "faint sweet music" breathed upon Stephen by "the seraphim." In other words, the Joyce of *Dubliners* and *Portrait* exploits both the language of mathematics and the language of literature as equivalent vehicles for encoding, for representing the "visible world," "beauty," "realit[y]" (*SH*, 80). As Stephen claims in *Stephen Hero*: the artist "alone is capable of absorbing in himself the life that surrounds him and of flinging it abroad again amid <u>planetary music</u>" (*SH*, 80).

We might be tempted, like Madden in *Stephen Hero* (81), to regard Stephen's or Joyce's formulation as some sort of woolly mysticism, some vestige of late-nineteenth-century romanticism. As Stephen tells Madden, however, "there's nothing mystical" (*SH*, 81) in his ideas that the literary work aspires to the "planetary music" of the spheres and that critics, like the astronomers of old, "When the poetic phenomenon is signalled in the heavens [...] verify their calculations in accordance with it" (*SH*, 80). These ideas are inherently classical, located in the unbroken tradition from Pythagoras, through Plato, Boethius, and the Renaissance *Musici*—Stephen's preferred music, by the way—and well into the eighteenth century, and they correspond directly to Stephen's distinction, moments earlier, between the classical and the romantic tempers. Unlike the "spiritual anarchy" of the romantic or mystic tempers,

The classical temper on the other hand, ever mindful of limitations, chooses rather to bend upon [...] present things and so to work upon them and fashion them that the quick intelligence may go beyond them to their meaning which is still unuttered. (*SH*, 78)

This striving for the unuttered, the unutterable, the ineffable, which of course resides in Stephen's later conception of the epiphany, that moment when the mind apprehends the inarticulable yet "eternal [image] of beauty" (*SH,* 213), is the straining to grasp the inaudible distant music of the spheres, or better yet, to attune oneself, one's own "instrument," to this music. Through the limited medium of language—comprising grammar, dialectic, and rhetoric—the artist strives after either or both the structural and verbal *articulations* of "universal beauty," as Stephen says in *Portrait* (*P,* 211), spatially or geometrically defining the "esthetic image" (*P,* 212), temporally or musically apprehending "the rhythm of its structure" (*P,* 212) (Aquinas's *consonantia,* after Hucbald's tenth-century *The Principles of Harmony,* possesses both musical and intellectual connotations [James, 80–81]), to approach the astral union of Thomistic-Platonic-Pythagorean *claritas:* "the supreme quality of beauty being a light from some other world, the idea of which the matter is but the shadow, the reality of which it is but the symbol" (*P,* 213). And this symbol, this material form given to the idea, may of course equally be an object, a word, a musical note, a number, a geometrical figure, an algebraic equation, or a mathematical *symbol,* any one of which may be a concrete element of the universal of the Monad, a whole always greater than the sum of its parts.

In suggesting that the apprehension of beauty involves not just a straining to grasp the inaudible distant music of the spheres, but also an attempt to attune oneself, one's own "instrument," to this music, I am referring to the Pythagorean trinity of the musical orders, formalized by Boethius as a hierarchy descending from the *musica mundana* (the music of the spheres proper), to the *musica humana* (the similarly inaudible music generated by living organisms), and down to the *musica instrumentalis* (the lowest order, the audible sounds produced by the voice or the musical instrument) (James, 74). When the young boy in "Araby," in his "confused adoration" of Mangan's sister, claims that his "body was like a harp and her words and gestures were like fingers running upon the wires" (*D,* 31), Joyce alludes to the classical concept of the *musica humana,* while his boy seems merely to be voicing a romantic cliché for the sensitive, responsive self. The distinction between Joyce and the boy is the difference between a classically based conception of the vital "relationship between [the self] and the cosmos" (James, 182), a harmonic relation inherent in the hierarchical orders of music in the Pythagorean system, and a romantically inspired reduction of the self to the inferior condition of the instrument, a reduction that, with its consequent focus on the impact of nature upon the autonomous individual of bourgeois liberalism, erases the classical emphasis on the integration of the individual into the cosmic harmony.[6] (Compare the integration of the individual within a cosmic order in *Die Zauberflöte* with the triumph of the individual against the constraints of an oppressive, imposed order in *Fidelio.*) The "great emotional outpouring that overwhelmed the expressive arts in the nineteenth century," Jamie James writes, "brought about the virtual exile of the great theme of cosmic harmony" (184); the "focus on the human in the [music of the] Romantic age," evident both in the new "concentration on the performer and composer as personality, and in the scope of the music itself," is consistent with generalized cultural shifts in "scale and emphasis [...] from the cosmic to the human" (192) seen not only in music and literature (compare Pope's universalizing impulse in his "Essay on Man" with Wordsworth's autobiographical account of the "Growth of a Poet's Mind" in his *Prelude*), but in the development of early-nineteenth-century science, mathematics, philosophy, and political and economic theories.

When the boy compares his body to a harp in "Araby," Joyce, I would argue, both reflects the classical conception of the *musica humana* and treats with irony the romantic reduction of the *musica humana* to the *musica instrumentalis;* this reduction, moreover, involves the characteristically romantic anthropomorphic transformation of a cosmic "reality" in the harmonious Pythagorean system into a metaphor for the self, or simile to be exact, a mere literary "instrument." Joyce is exploiting and scrutinizing the romantic sensibility from the vantage of the classical temper. In other words, Joyce writes *Dubliners,* or at least "Araby," from the vantage of Stephen Dedalus's aesthetic.

Accordingly, in *A Portrait of the Artist as a Young Man* Stephen pursues the harmonious ideal of the Monad "in the real world," one among the many "unsubstantial image[s] which his soul so constantly beheld" (*P,* 65); Joyce, however, now simultaneously exploits and distances himself from this obsolete idea of the distant music of the spheres in *Portrait,* maintaining his often-noted equivocal relationship to both Stephen and Stephen's ideals. The Pythagorean union of language, music, and mathematics, then, fully disintegrates as Joyce moves into *Ulysses* and *Finnegans Wake*. What most interests me in the moves Joyce makes in his use of music, and particularly in his evolving sense of the relations among language, music, and mathematics, is that rather than reenacting the historical sequence, he simply o'erleaps the cultural transition from classic to romantic, shifting from the classical temper of his early work, to equivocation in *Portrait,* and then to the modernist, indeed postmodernist, viewpoint embodied most memorably in Leopold Bloom's reflection on music in "Sirens":

> Numbers it is. All music when you come to think. Two multiplied by two divided by half is twice one. Vibrations: chords those are. One plus two plus six is seven. Do anything you like with figures juggling. Always find out this equal to that. Symmetry under a cemetery wall. [...] Musemathematics. And you think you're listening to the etherial. But suppose you said it like: Martha, seven times nine minus x is thirtyfive thousand. Fall quite flat. It's on account of the sounds it is. (*U,* 11.830–37)

Initially, in this passage, it appears that Bloom merely rehearses the ancient conviction that mathematics is the language of music, but on a closer examination this impression rapidly dissolves, much as it does for Bloom at the end of this paragraph (he ends by refuting his opening premise, asserting that music is not all or only "Numbers"). Likewise, a moment's reflection will tell us that Bloom's calculations are all haywire here: "Two multiplied by two divided by half" is not "twice one," but eight; "One plus two plus six" is not "seven," it's nine. But is Bloom deliberately miscalculating? His errors could very well be intentional, according with the skepticism of his next remarks about mathematics, followed by his similarly skeptical response to the games of language: "Do anything you like with figures juggling. Always find out this equal to that. Symmetry under a cemetery wall." I would argue that Bloom's skeptical awareness of the games played by mathematics, language, and music, despite some incoherence, dimly reflects the turn-of-the-century recognition that all representational systems—mathematical, cosmological, linguistic, and musical—and, by extension, all cultural systems—scientific, religious, political, and economic—are simply "axiomatic" systems, logical and coherent in their own right perhaps, but essentially unrelated, part of no Pythagorean hierarchy, and ultimately distinct from any existential reality they may be supposed to represent.[7] A similar recognition, as I argue in *Joyce, Chaos, and Complexity,* explains why Joyce o'erleapt the cultural transition from classic to romantic in his literary development, as he shifts from the classical temper of his early work to the modernist, indeed postmodernist, viewpoints of *Ulysses* and *Finnegans Wake.*

In the sundering of these systems of representation in *Ulysses,* Joyce sustains his interest in the music of language, in "Sirens," for example, but at the expense of some of the referential value of language (a direction *Finnegans Wake* further pursues). And like Bloom, Joyce now seems to discount mathematics, literally dis-*counting* the mathematical language of music within the Pythagorean tradition, to attend to that other language of music: its words, the lyrics of the song, which become a constant source for play or allusion, as in the L-O-S-S acrostic of "Love's Old Sweet Song" in *Ulysses* (compare *U,* 5.157–60) and the title of *Finnegans Wake,* to cite only two examples.[8] Mathematics now, rather than the language of music or the language of language, becomes for Joyce largely either a resource for metaphor, as in the geometrical patterns of "Ithaca" and the "Night Lessons" chapter of the *Wake,* for instance, which establish an alternate language for ciphering and deciphering, or an end in itself in the number, as in his use of numerology, for instance, which intensifies through *Ulysses* and the *Wake.*[9] Mathematics, music, language—and now, increasingly, *languages*—thus become separate but equal axiomatic systems of representation in Joyce's last two books. Once unified by the common language of mathematics, these systems Joyce now reduces to numbers in another sense: they become mere "counters" in the game of representation.

As modernist works, *Ulysses* and *Finnegans Wake* reflect Joyce's recognition that all language systems—including mathematics, music, and language itself—are imperfect human constructions; as postmodernist works, *Ulysses* and *Finnegans Wake* reflect Joyce's realization that all these referential systems are, as human constructions, arbitrary and equivalent. Yet, does not this second recognition return Joyce, in a way, to Pythagoras's position, much as his intensified interest in numerology—an important feature of Pythagorean mysticism (Kline, *Culture,* 77–78)—brings him closer to the ancient Greeks? Rather than seeing Joyce's realization that all referential systems are arbitrary and equivalent as a thoroughgoing skepticism, I would argue that Joyce implies the possibility, once again, that these *disjecta membra* may, at another level, compose a complex harmony, a union yet unheard but sought by the readers of the *Wake,* like the harmony of the legendary "lost chord" (*U,* 11.407), which, as a word representing both musical and mathematical concepts, implies the very union sought. If so, Joyce finds himself in the company of others, like Arnold Schoenberg, Paul Hindemith, and Karlheinz Stockhausen, all of whom have sought in our own century the ideal of a cosmic harmony, a creative reintegration emerging out of disintegration, a music of the spheres (James, 214–30, 238–41).

Rather than a representation of entropic disintegration, *Finnegans Wake,* as I argue in *Joyce, Chaos, and Complexity,* provides a model of the anti-entropic, self-organized complex system that will progressively evolve toward an emergent order through its readership (Rice, 112–40). This cosmic harmony may seem far beyond our grasp, yet lest we fall to the skepticism of the heretical schoolboy of chapter two in *Portrait,* let us remember that as much in the Pythagorean tradition as in orthodox Catholicism, our search will be flawed not by the "[im]*possibility of ever approaching nearer*" this harmony, but by the "[im]*possibility of ever reaching*" the distant music of the spheres (*P,* 79).

NOTES

1. The likelihood that Joyce had Gabriel's "distant music" phrase in mind when he drafted the opening of chapter three of *Portrait* increases when we realize that he completed writing "The Dead" in September 1907, immediately before turning his attention to his revision of *Stephen Hero;* he had completed the third chapter by April 7, 1908 (Ellmann, 264). Gabler argues convincingly that the relations between Joyce's composition of "The Dead" and the early chapters of *Portrait* are considerably more complex than Ellmann suggests, and that "Chapters I–III [...] [are], in the form in which we possess them, five or more years removed in time from *Dubliners,* and the consummation of its art in 'The Dead'" (Gabler, 37). It seems clear, nonetheless, from Gabler's study of the novel's chronology of composition, that Joyce's subsequent revisions were concentrated on the latter portions of the third chapter, rather than its opening, where the "distant music" phrase reappears (26–33).

2. In the words of Galileo, "we cannot understand" that "great book which ever lies before our eyes, I mean the universe, [...] if we do not first learn

the language [...] in which it is written. The book is written in the mathematical language" (cited in Barrow, *World,* 238). For a recent discussion of the "language of mathematics" and the "intrinsically mathematical aspects" of "natural phenomena," see Barrow, *World,* 238–92.

3. Hollander's working assumption is that the music of the spheres ceased to function as a belief and had become, at best, only a poetic conception, by the beginning of the eighteenth century; however, to accept this assumption we would have to ignore both distinguished scientific speculations about the musical nature of the cosmos (e.g., Newton) and important, representative artistic attempts to embody this idealization (Mozart's *Die Zauberflöte*) through the eighteenth century. See James's chapter, "Newton and *The Magic Flute,*" 159–79.

4. Joyce himself seems to anticipate this development in his schoolboy essay, "The Study of Languages": "Now the study of languages is based on a mathematical foundation, and sure of its footing, and in consequence both in style and syntax there is always present a carefulness, a carefulness bred of the first implantings of precision" (*CW,* 27). Also see Barrow, *Artful,* 207–9.

5. For useful overviews of the impact of Pythagorean ideas on Plato and of the influence of Platonism on the development of Western mathematics, see Barrow, *Pi,* 251–76.

6. Hollander discusses the "long history" of the images of the "World-Lyre, or the stringed instrument of the human soul," from the classical era through the Renaissance (44), and observes the survival of "the very notion of heart-strings," still current today (49).

7. For valuable discussions of the development of mathematical formalism, the work of David Hilbert, and the axiomatic movement at the turn of the century, see Kline, *Certainty,* 245–64; for an account of Henri Poincaré's popularization of these developments through his "conventionalist" philosophy in "such works as *Science and Hypothesis* (1902)," see Passmore, 326–27 and passim.

8. There is a large literature on the musical elements and allusions in Joyce's work (to which this present volume of essays contributes): see, particularly, Bauerle, ed.; Bauerle and Hodgart; Bowen, "Libretto"; Bowen, *Musical Allusions*; and Hodgart and Worthington.

9. For excellent studies of the mathematics of *Ulysses* and *Finnegans Wake,* see McCarthy and Solomon, respectively; Atherton considers the fact that "Numbers have a magical, not an arithmetical significance" one of the "main axioms of the *Wake*" (53, 52).

WORKS CITED

Atherton, James S. *The Books at the Wake: A Study of Literary Allusions in James Joyce's* Finnegans Wake. New York: Viking, 1960.

Barrow, John D. *The Artful Universe*. Oxford: Clarendon, 1995.

———. *Pi in the Sky: Counting, Thinking, and Being*. Oxford: Clarendon, 1992.

———. *The World Within the World*. Oxford: Oxford University Press, 1988.

Bauerle, Ruth, ed. *Picking Up Airs: Hearing the Music in Joyce's Text*. Urbana: University of Illinois Press, 1993.

Bauerle, Ruth and Hodgart, Matthew. *Joyce's Grand Operoar: Opera in* Finnegans Wake. Urbana: University of Illinois Press, 1997.

Bowen, Zack. "Libretto for Bloomusalem in Song: The Music of Joyce's *Ulysses.*" *New Light on Joyce from the Dublin Symposium*. Ed. Fritz Senn. Bloomington: Indiana University Press, 1972. 149–66.

———. *Musical Allusions in the Works of James Joyce: Early Poetry Through* Ulysses. Albany: State University of New York Press, 1974.

Ellmann, Richard. *James Joyce*. Rev. ed. Oxford: Oxford University Press, 1982.

Gabler, Hans Walter. "The Seven Lost Years of *A Portrait of the Artist as a Young Man.*" *Approaches to Joyce's* Portrait. Eds. Thomas F. Staley and Bernard Benstock. Pittsburgh: University of Pittsburgh Press, 1976. 25–60.

Hodgart, Matthew and Mabel Worthington. *Song in the Works of James Joyce*. New York: Columbia University Press, 1959.

Hollander, John. *The Untuning of the Sky: Ideas of Music in English Poetry, 1500–1700*. Princeton, N.J.: Princeton University Press, 1961.

James, Jamie. *The Music of the Spheres: Music, Science, and the Natural Order of the Universe*. New York: Grove Press, 1993.

Kline, Morris. *Mathematics in Western Culture*. Oxford: Oxford University Press, 1953.

———. *Mathematics: The Loss of Certainty*. Oxford: Oxford University Press, 1980.

Levenson, Thomas. *Measure for Measure: A Musical History of Science*. New York: Simon & Schuster, 1994.

McCarthy, Patrick A. "Joyce's Unreliable Catechist: Mathematics and the Narration of 'Ithaca.'" *ELH* 51 (1984): 605–18.

Passmore, John. *A Hundred Years of Philosophy*. 2nd ed. Harmondsworth, U.K.: Penguin, 1966.

Pater, Walter. "The School of Giorgione." *The Renaissance.* New York: Modern Library, 1919. 107–27.

Plato. *Epinomis.* Trans. A. E. Taylor. *Plato: The Collected Dialogues.* Eds. Edith Hamilton and Huntington Cairns. Princeton, N.J.: Princeton University Press, 1961. 1517–33.

Reynolds, Mary T. *Joyce and Dante: The Shaping Imagination.* Princeton, N.J.: Princeton University Press, 1981.

Rice, Thomas Jackson. *Joyce, Chaos, and Complexity.* Urbana: University of Illinois Press, 1997.

Solomon, Margaret C. *Eternal Geomater: The Sexual Universe of* Finnegans Wake. Carbondale: Southern Illinois University Press, 1969.

Section 2: *Ulysses*

CHAPTER 10

Bronze by Gold by Bloom: Echo, the Invocatory Drive, and the 'Aurteur' in "Sirens"

Susan Mooney

Amoroso ma non troppo. (*U,* 11.541)

I have sought, but I seek it vainly,
That one lost chord divine
Which came from the soul of an organ
And enter'd into mine. (Proctor and Sullivan, "The Lost Chord")

Sound is contained within time and space in ways different from the visual. From the point of view of traditional phenomenology, the visual is predominantly a spatial form and the acoustic temporal. Nevertheless, sound happens inside space, and our perception of sound depends on positions and barriers, walls and doors, empty spaces and vibrating instruments, discord and simultaneity. The relay and echo of sound depends on space across which sound waves flow and ebb. In Joyce's "Sirens," this complicated interplay of acoustic emissions, repetitions, and resonances accounts for an hour spent at and around the Ormond Hotel; this interplay also attempts to withhold and repeat experience and memory in the characters' mental lives.

The narrating or narrated subject can be thought of as an "aurteur," the creative (often unconscious) organizer or mediator of acoustic fragments (instances or memories of voices, music, noise, sounds).[1] Within the aurteur's arrangement of this episode is an aurally inclined protagonist, Bloom. His own silent musings inside and around the

Ormond Hotel reflect the aurteur's impulse to arrange, locate, classify, repeat, examine. While sounds, songs, and chatter go on all around him, the usually garrulous voice of Bloom is marked by its interiority and silence.

In this essay, I will not be trying to rekindle a debate about the fugue-like structure of "Sirens." I feel that Jean-Michel Rabaté and others have amply demonstrated that we need not depend so heavily on this musical approach: classical rhetoric, for example, can easily and more precisely identify the verbal acrobatics in this episode than can musicology.[2] There is, however, another definition of "fugue" that interests me as a psychiatric term: a fugue is a period during which a person suffers from a loss of memory, often begins a new life, and, upon recovery, remembers nothing of the amnesiac phase.[3] From the point of view of psychoanalysis, there is a fugue-like experience that we all go through in early childhood development—a series of painful renunciations of womb, breast, and so on—until we abandon these props to prop ourselves up, in turn, on the cash register of the symbolic. While this rebirth of the subject into language pays off in invaluable ways, the memory of the pre-mirror, pre-Oedipal stage remains only in traces in the unconscious.

Acoustic dynamics not only includes hearing and interpreting the collage of sonority in the world, but also involves the listener's mental life. Thus the aural implies mediation between exteriority and interiority in a way that reflects, but also differs from, that of the visual.[4] The aural aspects of the "Sirens" episode accentuate memory, desire, anticipation, and waiting in various ways.

> Pat is a waiter hard of his hearing. Pat is a waiter who waits while you wait. Hee hee hee hee. He waits while you wait. Hee hee. A waiter is he. Hee hee hee hee. He waits while you wait. While you wait if you wait he will wait while you wait. Hee hee hee hee. Hoh. Wait while you wait. (*U*, 11.915–19)

This passage comes at the moment when Bloom has calculated that Boylan has arrived to see Molly; Bloom hopes that the singers will sing some more to take his mind off the unseen scene of adultery. The laughter hinges on the masculine "he"; it is unclear whether these thoughts belong to the observant, wily aurteur or to Bloom. The intended tone of this laughter (and of this often repeated and reworked pun) is uncertain, too: hysterical, gleeful, cynical, childish, devilish, hollow? Bloom's restless attention then turns from Pat the waiter to another waiter: Lydia Douce and her acoustic inclinations. He overhears snippets of her talk, and spies on her actions. I will return to Lydia in a moment. Wait while I. Hee.

The Ormond Hotel, the setting of "Sirens," is a compartmentalized place of rooms, divided by doorways, the bar (or the "reef" [*U*, 11.109]), the mirror, the crossblind across the window. The name "Ormond" reminds us of the French, *"hors monde," "hors du monde"*: out of the world, out of the ordinary, the ordinary reunited outside its original context in the world. "Ormond" also suggests "or" ("gold") and "aural"/"oral" (the heard and spoken); the name is suggestive of a "Golden Ear World" and an "Or World" (an Other World).[5] The scene at the Ormond Hotel revolves around waiting and anticipation. Miss Douce and Miss Kennedy wait for the afternoon clientele and then wait on them. Some of the men are waiting for the result of the horse race. Over his sloe gin at the bar, Blazes Boylan waits for his rendezvous with Molly. Sequestered in the dining room where he can hear and partially see, Bloom waits for his wife's infidelity to take place. The waiting is endured by listening and looking, two activities that are often contiguous in the folds of Joyce's language.

The waiting game—the deferred action—is incorporated into the acoustic language of the episode: narration that revolves and returns to earlier motifs, phrases, key words. The echoic transformation and repetition of sounds and voices mark the beginning of each new little happening within the episode, as well as the prolongation, reverberation, and recall of action and thought. The ear of the text filters and sifts through snatches of sound, fragments of conversation; at times the metaphoric metals of bronze and gold, the "aural," seem to conduct and relay sonority. Douce's and Kennedy's hair is closely aligned with "hearing" and the "ear" and spatialization—"Where bronze from anear? Where gold from afar? Where hoofs?" (*U*, 11.59):

> Miss Kennedy sauntered sadly from bright light, twining a loose hair behind an ear. Sauntering sadly, gold no more, she twisted twined a hair. Sadly she twined in sauntering gold hair behind a curving ear. (*U*, 11.81–83)

This Odyssean language of many twists and turns represents a pleasurable/unpleasurable drive to hear, to linger over the reverberating elements of sound and the act of hearing. Deferred action is captured in language by representing noises before revealing the sources of noise (such as the tapping stick of the blind stripling who returns to the Ormond); what seems to be prioritized is a kind of synecdochic *démontage* of phenomenology, the obsessive, hyperconscious scanning of the hysterically omniscient narrator.[6] We hear it before it happens, before we see it; the parts imply the whole, the whole that is never wholly represented and often becomes confused or associated with another alternative source (*"trompe l'oreille"*).[7] The leisurely, languid pace of the episode quickens toward its end, as Bloom makes his move to leave strategically before the end of a song (and as the stripling gets closer to his destination); during this short period of time, the aurteur frenetically repeats, rearranges, collapses already familiar parts of the text: "said before" (*U*, 11.519, 569, 761).

In "Sirens," sounds are often emblematic or synecdochic of a person's action. Boylan's comings and goings are communicated acoustically: the creaking shoes, the "Jingle a tinkle jaunted" (*U*, 11.456), the rap "on a door, one tapped with a knock, did he knock Paul de Kock, with a loud proud knocker, with a cock carracarracarra cock. Cockcock" (*U*, 11.986–88). The tapping stick of the blind piano tuner becomes increasingly persistent as he approaches the Ormond Hotel to retrieve his forgotten tuning fork. His unseeing arrival is blind to the bar scene, and the too late newcomer (come again) has missed the predominantly acoustic episode for which he would presumably have been the most capable listener; in a way, the stripling acts as a sign for the return of the acoustic repressed, a return that is repressed yet again by his late arrival in the episode.[8]

Some psychoanalytic notions about the acoustic may help us to consider some aspects of the "Sirens" text. The activity of hearing (indeed, the capacity to hear) begins in infant development well before vision reorganizes (and perhaps even comes to dominate) our perception of the world and our place in it. Even before entering the world, the subject has been listening in the womb (what we could call one's "hysterical audition"). What I will call, after Silverman, the acoustic mirror stage—the pre-Oedipal stage of mirroring oneself in the mother's voice—is a reflexive period of the infant's gradual mastery of receiving and producing sounds, a mastery negotiated with the mother (and others). The subject's psychic development during this period has later consequences for sexual differentiation, sexual relations, and entry into the symbolic register of language.

The subject's primary narcissism emerges during this pre-Oedipal stage. It has been recognized that primary narcissism is involved with the initial organization of the drives (or in neo-Freudian terms, the initial scaffolding of the id). Sound and hearing play important roles for the subject during this stage. By reexamining the story of Narcissus, we can notice and reevaluate the role of the mountain nymph Echo in that myth. She falls in love with the beautiful youth and wastes away until only her voice remains.

This little romantic tragedy dramatizes the cleavage (*Spaltung*) in the infant's relationship with his mother, and problematizes the fantasy of the maternal voice as a source of language and love. In *The Acoustic Mirror,* Kaja Silverman lists various theorists' assessments of the maternal voice: it can be thought of as a "sonorous envelope" that "surrounds, sustains, and cherishes the child"; or as a "mobile receptacle" that absorbs the infant's "anaclitic facilitations"; or as a "bath of sounds," or quite simply, "music." The maternal voice can be given a much more sinister inflection; within Michel Chion's account, "that voice not only envelops but entraps the newborn infant" (Silverman, 72).

This voice also functions to introduce the infant to separation, identity, entry into that same language where there will necessarily be a gaping lack. Lack is always already inscribed in the mother's and the child's voices. For example, the voice can be heard without the simultaneity of vision of the voice's source. In this early stage, the infant often perceives space and presence through listening, listening in particular for the whereabouts of the mother; this early development of hearing and making himself heard through his cries relates to the early organization of the infant's drives; these drives later become bound in secondary developments.

Lacan has pointed out that, among all the drives (scopic, oral, etc.), *only* the invocatory drive, the drive to make oneself heard, does not return to the subject. In his account, the subject's other drives reach out to an object of desire, loop around it, and return to the subject; with the invocatory drive, this is not the case. According to Lacan, the drive to make oneself heard reaches out to the *objet petit a* and keeps on going ("Libido," 195).[9] It seems to me that this argument does not take into account that this invocatory drive is destined for at least two possible, imperfect receivers—the subject and the other—and thus seems to stretch out toward two aims. Echo is the acoustic counterpart to Narcissus; the early development of the invocatory drive and the aural orifice precedes and then is partially overcome by the subject's increasing interest in the scopic and other drives. The hearing of oneself, the equivalent of seeing oneself in a mirror, occurs long before one apprehends one's imaginary wholeness in the mirror. We hear our mother, we hear ourselves: we make noise, we call out to her, often seemingly in vain, with our incoherent cries. On the one hand, our babble and first words are mirrored back to us by our mother, on the other, they are forever lost and must be repeated to be experienced again. Before we achieve articulate speech, our sounds relay the drive of the body to make itself heard.[10] The fragmented ugliness of our own sonority, in contrast to the beauty and masterfulness of the mother's voice, makes a lasting impression on us. No one actually likes the sound of one's own voice; that repulsion comes to be censored as the subject must rely on that voice to enter into language. The desire to hear a particularly pleasing voice might hark back to our early auditory days, our bathing in that sonorous envelope of the maternal voice: why indeed do tenors score highly with women, we might ponder with Bloom?

Let us now return again to "Sirens." In a strange way, the shell that Lydia Douce has brought back from her seaside holiday, the shell that adorns the gilt (guilty) mirror, operates as an aural mirror—it reflects the sound of one's own ear:

> Douce now. Douce Lydia. Bronze and rose.
> She had a gorgeous time, simply gorgeous, time. And look at the lovely shell she brought.
> To the end of the bar to him she bore lightly the spiked and winding seahorn that he, George Lidwell, solicitor, might hear.
> —Listen! she bade him.
> Under Tom Kernan's ginhot words the accompanist wove music slow. Authentic fact. How Walter Bapty lost his voice. Well, sir, the husband took him by the throat. *Scoundrel,* said he, *you'll sing no more lovesongs.* He did, faith, sir Tom. Bob Cowley wove. Tenors get wom. Cowley lay back.

Ah, now he heard, she holding it to his ear. Hear! He heard. Wonderful. She held it to her own. And through the sifted light pale gold in contrast glided. To hear.

Tap.

Bloom through the bardoor saw a shell held at their ears. He heard more faintly that that they heard, each for herself alone, then each for other, hearing the plash of waves, loudly, a silent roar.

Bronze by a weary gold, anear, afar, they listened. (*U,* 11.920–37)

In this passage, the slippage of the aural trope shifts us from the flirtation between Lydia and Lidwell, sidetracks to the song's theme of prohibition of adultery, introduces the first tap of the returning stripling, and returns us to the initial sadness and solitude established by Mina Kennedy's sauntering: Mina, Lydia, and Bloom are twisted and twined into this particular realignment as kindred melancholy listeners. Of course, it has already been well noted by other scholars how Bloom is inserted into various passages in this episode regardless of whether he belongs there or not. His name is prominent among several wandering, echoic, associative sounds that lap and ebb against the ear of the text: "Seabloom, greaseabloom" (*U,* 11.1284).[11]

Bloom listens to Richie Goulding wax lyrical about the night he heard Joe Maas, a lyrical tenor, sing *La Sonnambula:*

Never would Richie forget that night. As long as he lived: never. In the gods of the old Royal with little Peake. And when the first note.

Speech paused on Richie's lips.

Coming out with a whopper now. Rhapsodies about damn all. Believes his own lies. Does really. Wonderful liar. But want a good memory.

—Which air is that? asked Leopold Bloom.

—*All is lost now.*

Richie cocked his lips apout. A low incipient note sweet banshee murmured: all. A thrush. A throstle. His breath, birdsweet, good teeth he's proud of, fluted with plaintive woe. Is lost. Rich sound. Two notes in one there. Blackbird I heard in the hawthorn valley. Taking my motives he twined and turned them. All most too new call is lost in all. Echo. How sweet the answer. How is that done? All lost now. Mournful he whistled. Fall, surrender, lost.

Bloom bent leopold ear, turning a fringe of doyley down under the vase. Order. Yes, I remember. Lovely air. In sleep she went to him. Innocence in the moon. Brave. Don't know their danger. Still hold her back. Call name. Touch water. Jingle jaunty. Too late. She longed to go. That's why. Woman. As easy stop the sea. Yes: all is lost. (*U*, 11.623–41)[12]

All is lost now. "Tutto è sciolto." The aria from *La Sonnambula* is about a young woman who unwittingly sleepwalks into a compromising situation to the despair of her tenor fiancé. The Italian *tutto è sciolto* could be construed (particularly in Bloomian Italian) as "all is hearing" (*tutto è ascolto*). "Sciolto" can mean lost, but also loose. The sea of feminine desire cannot be held back, according to Bloom. "Call name" implies calling her name would wake her up, returning her to her proper position, as well as suggesting the call name "Molly" for "Marion." Her fiancé recoils from doing this, from calling her name, from going to her. "She longed to go." "Too late." By intentionally postponing his action, he allows for the adultery to take place. The aria is about temporary despair; the supposed adulteress in *La Sonnambula* maintains her innocence.[13] Of course, Molly does not have recourse to this claim.

The tactile toying with substitute cords—a strand of hair, a triple of piano keys, the garter strap, the elastic bands, the doyley's fringe, the image of the two tiny silky vocal cords—accompanies the complicated procedure of listening, the incorporation of the other's invocatory drive through one's own always already open ear:

Taking my motives he twined and turned them. All most too new call is lost in all. Echo. How sweet the answer. How is that done? All lost now. Mournful he whistled. Fall, surrender, lost. (*U*, 11.633–36)

The confusion of subjectivity is announced in the first sentence of this passage: is Bloom here a split subject, reincorporating his motives, the circularity of the drive perceived as someone else's? Or does someone else (Boylan, Bellini, the fiancé, or the aurteur) twist and turn the motives for him? Or is that other "he" Bloom yet again?

In the second line, the words are overextended into multiple meanings when read aloud. Even when we silently read this passage, our sense of syntactic logic struggles with the overabundance of senses in what is actually written: "All most too new call is lost in all." Bloom calls this "Echo." The circularity of the sentence emphasizes wholeness, doubleness, or a multitude, as well as a singular miasmic negativity. The suggestion of completeness ("all") and majority ("most") disintegrates into a singular almost making a double, "almost two." This play on words aptly describes the mystery of the love relationship, whether between infant and parent or between lovers, and inevitably between the subject and its ego ideal: the impossibility of two being "all" or "one," the cleavage that joins the two and the too (also). The "too new call is lost" introduces more nuances into this impossible but desired relationship: the call is "too new" and yet despite its excessive novelty, it is already lost, accompanying the fading of the subject. In an alternative reading, the "too" understood as numerical "two" obliges the "new" to become the verb "knew" (past tense)—now "almost two knew" breaks away from "call is lost"—and indeed that new call will be lost to the two who almost knew it. But it's too late, because the "call is lost in all": that is, this too new call is already lost in the all discussed at the outset. The "call" is lost in everyone, but also in the "all" of wholeness or completeness. The call is an excessive fragment of the desire for plenitude, and it is also an echo of that irretrievable new or once known new call, the sound of the mother's voice, the unbearable ugliness of the infant subject's voice before mastery, the too late or also known call of the other. This is what Bloom seems to identify as "Echo," both the physical phenomenon and the psychical one. "Echo. How sweet the answer. How is that done?" (*U*, 11.634–35).

The *techne* and psychical expression of Echo are exemplified in the musical performances during this episode. The sound of the tuning fork left by the tuner (who had played so exquisitely earlier in the day to the audience of Lydia) is the first sound from the saloon, sounded by Simon Dedalus who, as yet alone, goes to check out the piano:

> From the saloon a call came, long in dying. That was a tuningfork the tuner had that he forgot that he now struck. A call again. That he now poised that it now throbbed. You hear? It

throbbed, pure, purer, softly and softlier, its buzzing prongs. Longer
in dying call. (*U*, 11.312–15)

Later, Bob Cowley and Ben Dollard join Simon in playing and singing.
Voices travel in and out of song, voices veiled in love-song words so
that love turns into Echo, the voice of love. "Love that is singing" (*U*,
11.681) could also mean the act of singing stands for love and sex.
Obviously Simon Dedalus's and Ben Dollard's singing can be seen as
sublimation. But Bloom muses over more aspects of music making as
he listens to Dedalus sing:

> Through the hush of air a voice sang to them, low, not rain, not
> leaves in murmur, like no voice of strings or reeds or
> whatdoyoucallthem dulcimers touching their still ears with words,
> still hearts of their each his remembered lives. Good, good to hear:
> sorrow from them each seemed to from both depart when first they
> heard. When first they saw, lost Richie Poldy, mercy of beauty, heard
> from a person wouldn't expect it in the least, her first merciful
> lovesoft oftloved word. (*U*, 11.674–80)

Simon's beautiful voice prompts Bloom to decide that "Tenors get
women by the score" (*U*, 11.686).[14] Simon and Ben's voices
demonstrate a kind of lack at the core of masculinity.[15] Bloom's
memories of activities encircling music making—such as Molly
listening in the concert hall while her goods are on display or Bloom
turning the pages while Molly sang a song called "Waiting" (*U*,
11.730)—are erotically charged. After Simon has finished singing
"M'appari," Bloom reflects: "The human voice, two tiny silky cords,
wonderful, more than all others. That voice [Si's sigh] was a
lamentation. Calmer now. It's in the silence after you feel you hear.
Vibrations. Now silent air" (*U*, 11.791–94). Simon's voice was also
silent when he first starting playing earlier on in this episode before his
companions arrive: "A voiceless song sang from within, singing" (*U*,
11.321). Simon's voice is also analyzed as a valuable, but neglected,
natural treasure; if he had taken better care of himself and his voice, he
could have made "oceans of money" (*U*, 11.696).

It would seem that the conjunction of this use of language with the
themes of waiting, listening, and adultery provides us with a tangential
impression of acoustic reflection. Under the musicological

interpretation of "Sirens," the narrator has been taken to be a musical conductor or composer. I have preferred to think of him as an acoustic auteur—or aurteur—who twists the strands of an hour spent waiting around the ear of the reader/listener. This aurteur arranges not only sonority into a vibrating, reverberating narrative of memory and desire, but also incorporates and spatializes the lively activity of listening and the drive to make oneself heard. Part of his strategy is to detach the hearing from the heard, to play on associations from anear and from afar, and to layer aural impressions over visual fragments. Little pieces of the real—sounds and objects—are draped in language, and then that language is woven and rewoven and then worried away between one's ceaselessly seeking fingers, twisted and twined through one's cocked, shell-like, waiting ear (the unclosable orifice).

NOTES

1. The term "aurteur," the aural auteur, has been derived from two streams of thought: in film criticism, the auteur is the sort of director who leaves his special imprint on his work; in literary theory, the authorized text or reader can be thought of as the result of a kind of creative transference between author and work, writer and reader. Of course, in their schema of "Sirens," Gilbert and Linati agree that the organ is the Ear.

2. For an array of illuminating, nonmusicological approaches to "Sirens," see the essays by Derek Attridge, Maud Ellmann, Daniel Ferrer, André Topia, Jean-Michel Rabaté, and Robert Young in the section "Sirens Without Music" of *James Joyce: The Centennial Symposium*. Although not denying that music is a seminal element in "Sirens" and elsewhere in Joyce, I am taking my cue from Bloom or the aurteur: "Words? Music? No: it's what's behind. Bloom looped, unlooped, noded, disnoded" (*U*, 11.703–4). In this way I attempt to node and disnode, to analyze, the acoustic devices of this particular text.

3. I do not wish to suggest that this particular definition of "fugue" would have been available to Joyce, though it is worth noting that Auden uses the word in the sense of an amnesiac state in 1930: "the prey to fugues" (Auden, 47). "Fugue" derives from the Latin "fuga," or "flight," and the many variables of "flight" would have been suggestive for Joyce. Bloom behaves like a fugitive (elusive, evasive, struggling with and against memory).

4. Let us not forget that the labyrinthine (both membranous and bony) structure of the ear (external, middle, internal) further complicates mediation between the *Umwelt* and the *Innenwelt*. The ear's functions go beyond the

calling of an orifice. The internal ear determines both hearing and balance (balance, in turn, determining our sense of our ontological presence in the world and our vision of it); the middle ear consists of the tympanic membrane and the air-filled chamber through which sound waves are ushered in; the external ear (the auricle and canal) gathers sound vibrations. The often disorienting juxtapositions of the seen and the heard in "Sirens," as well as the intervention of the aurteur ("Greasy I knows" [*U*, 11.176–77]), reveal our dependence on the ear to provide us with a sense of equilibrium. Even the proximity of the internal ear to the sinuses complicates our sense of the acoustic (the nose knows or "Greasy I knows"); Roland Barthes speaks of the odor of his spoken words that lingers in his perceptual memory in a far more pervasive way than do his written words:

> As soon as one has finished speaking, there begins the dizzying turn of the image: one exalts or regrets what one has said, the way in which one said it, one *imagines oneself* (turns oneself over in image); speech is subject to remanence, it *smells*.
>
> Writing has no smell: produced (having accomplished its process of production), it *falls*, not like a bellows deflating but like a meteorite disappearing; it will *travel* far from my body, yet without being something detached and narcissistically retained like speech; its disappearance holds no disappointment; it passes, traverses, and that's all. (204)

The fascinating paradox at hand in this examination of "Sirens" and the acoustic is that Joyce's writing conveys the plenitude and fragmentation of aurality, sonority, and speech: as with the function of all signifiers, signifiers of sound signify other signifiers, but remember, too, that the subject drapes himself in the effects of the signifier. (This is where Lacan's lovely dress-up trope, *se parer*, fits in so nicely with separation and lack when it comes to trying to describe the subject's infringement on the hems of the Real, the Imaginary, and the Symbolic. See Lacan, "Alienation," 214.)

5.   There is a further hint of the song sung by Bluebeard's stifled wives in Dukas's *Ariane et Barbe-Bleue:* "Cinq filles d'Orlamonde."

6.   The tactile scanning of the blind youth as he spans the space between him and the Ormond echoes the impervious, uncanny beating out of time by an unseen metronome.

7.   My pun is intended to tie in the golden-ear motif along with the deceitful conceit of the *trompeuse* or siren into a knotty tangle of signification.

Mina Kennedy and Lydia Douce, for example, are more disappointed by men than the ruin of them; gold and bronze listen far more than they make themselves heard. Except in private, when their laughter and talk are intended only for each other, and the hilarious object of scorn is the old fogey in Boyd's, the antithesis of the dream fiancé:

>—O greasy eyes! Imagine being married to a man like that! she cried. With his bit of beard!
>   Douce gave full vent to a splendid yell, a full yell of full woman, delight, joy, indignation.
>—Married to the greasy nose! she yelled.
>   Shrill, with deep laughter, after, gold after bronze, they urged each each to peal after peal, ringing in changes, bronzegold, goldbronze, shrilldeep, to laughter after laughter. And then laughed more. Greasy I knows. (*U,* 11.169–77)

8. Repressed, too, is the association we could have made between the stripling's stick and Stephen's ashplant. If it had been Stephen headed for the Ormond, then the deferred moment of the son's encounter with the father would have ceased to be perpetual.

9. This argument is troubled by Lacan's own account of the unconscious: "The unconscious is the sum of the effects of speech on a subject, at the level at which the subject constitutes himself out of the effects of the signifier" ("Presence," 126). Transference is at the center of the ◊ relation between the subject and the other: recall, memory, and repetition are not just elements of the analytic experience, but are also fundamentals of infant development vis à vis the (m)other's voice: I will cry out for "ju, ju, ju" and she will hear and, I hope, bring "juice." Lacan started the seminar "Presence of the Analyst" by quoting a truism inscribed on his matchbox: "'the art of listening is almost as important as that of saying the right thing.' This apportions our tasks" ("Presence," 123).

Restraining my wish "if only he could have heard himself," I will simply point out that, whereas the truism might hold true for the seminar lecturer talking about transference, the opposite of the truism can be the only answer for the practicing analyst, especially at the point at which the analysand collides into the wall of repetition, resistance, and silence.

All of this is not to say that Lacan is not able to discuss the analytic situation in meaningful ways. His earlier work in the 1950s on technique is rich evidence of that; for example, in "The Wolf! The Wolf!" and "On Narcissism," he discusses not only the imaginary, resistance, and the core of speech, but also the notion of "full speech":

> Full speech is speech which aims at, which forms, the truth such as it becomes established in the recognition of one person by another. Full speech is speech which performs. One of the subjects finds himself, afterwards, other than he was before. That is why this dimension cannot be evaded in the analytic experience.
>
> We cannot think of the analytic experience as a game, a lure, an intrigue based on an illusion, a suggestion. Its stake is full speech. ("On Narcissism," 107–8)

This view hardly squares with Lacan's account of the one-way invocatory drive later on in "From Love to the Libido" (195, 200); it could very well be that the analyst's position, his role as the Ear, is the cause for this (mis)perception.

10. See *Voice,* David Appelbaum's work on nonverbal, as well as verbal, human sonority (the cough, the laugh, etc.). Appelbaum owes much to Jacques Derrida's *Of Grammatology* and *Speech and Phenomena: And Other Essays on Husserl's Theory of Signs,* and seems to establish new ways of relating philosophy to phenomenology. For Appelbaum, "Voice of any pitch or timbre is an echo of the page, having the same substantiality of Echo in the myth. [...] Presumably, Echo cannot cough" (12). I would counter that Echo—voice and voice alone—is not the embodiment of voice; indeed, she is even bereft of ears with which to hear her own repetitive, fading call. I also have to disagree with his first point: voice can hardly be an echo of the page (semiotic linguistics and psychoanalysis, Silverman and Barthes back me up on this).

11. Waiting, mourning, and deferred desire can result in alienation, which is somewhat how the fugitive Bloom appears as pure signifier in the *vel* of someone else's alienation (Simon's, for example, as he stands at the bar, "staring hard at a headless sardine. Under the sandwichbell lay on a bier of bread one last, one lonely, last sardine of summer. Bloom alone" [*U,* 11.1219–21]). In general, the "Or World" of the Ormond seems to serve as the site of the symbolic "or" or the logic of the *vel.* For a discussion of the *vel* of alienation, see Lacan, "The Subject and the Other: Alienation."

12. Note that the tropes "thrush" and "throstle" are first compared by Bloom to Molly's voice in "Hades" (*U,* 6.240).

13. Strictly speaking, an unmarried woman cannot commit adultery, but the engagement provides enough of a suggestion. Moreover, the psychic subplot works off of the possibility that the man's room toward which she is

sleepwalking is her father's. Adultery, incest, and the primal scene are all suggestively entwined in this fantasy. Even Milly, the Blooms' daughter, becomes spun into the acoustic web of associations. Bloom's thoughts betray the association between the two women, and his continual postponement of action permits a kind of tangled, deferred, unrealizable desire.

14. See Bloom's contemplation of the scopic magnetism of men's fancy military dress in "Lotus-Eaters": "There he is: royal Dublin fusiliers. Redcoats. Too showy. That must be why the women go after them. Uniform" (*U,* 5.68–69). The showiness of the tenor's voice, its proximity to the female pitch, its alluring, invocatory exhibitionism (making oneself heard), can indeed be considered the counterpart to scopic exhibitionism (making oneself seen). Exhibitionism (an exaggeration of the partial drives) along with narcissism, historically slide over from the male domain to the female starting around the end of the eighteenth century. Following J. C. Flügel's argument in *The Psychology of Clothes,* Silverman writes about the Great Masculine Renunciation: "identification of woman with narcissism and exhibitionism is the result of a series of defensive activities calculated to shield the male subject from himself. [Flügel] suggests that the male subject protects himself from specularity which defines him in part by converting it into its opposite, scopophilia, and in part by projecting it onto woman" (26).

15. The tenor and the baritone, heard from the other room, disembodied (but nonauthorial) male voices on display, present us with a scenario curiously familiar in the eroticism of scopophilia/exhibitionism, narcissism, and identification. It would seem that the "aurteur" is not only an acoustic auteur, but also an acoustic equivalent of the voyeur.

While listening to the men sing, Bloom finds something to fault in women's voices: "Like tearing silk. Tongue when she talks like the clapper of a bellows. They can't manage men's intervals. Gap in their voices too. Fill me. I'm warm, dark, open. Molly in *quis est homo:* Mercadante. My ear against the wall to hear" (*U,* 11.972–76).

Bloom's remarks reflect just as much on male inadequacy as on the perceived gap in women's voices. "Gap" is close enough to "gasp," the erotic sound of Molly catching her breath in Bloom's recurring fantasy about hearing aurteuristically the "act" of adultery. His slide into the first-person form positions him suddenly as female, a sudden act of identification that demands to be reciprocated by his simultaneous presence on the other side of the door. Note, too, that he remembers Molly singing "Who is the man" in Rossini's *Stabat Mater,* another twist in this complicated series of associations about lack, sexual identity, desire. *Quis est homo:* Bloom or Boylan? "Mercadante" could allude to the Italian "mercante" ("merchant"): Boylan or Bloom in the production of Molly? Erotic economy hinges here on monetary economy just as Bloom's "menagerer" (*U,* 15.325) does.

WORKS CITED

Appelbaum, David. *Voice.* Albany: State University of New York Press, 1990.

Auden, W. H. *The English Auden.* Ed. Edward Mendelson. London: Faber & Faber, 1977.

Barthes, Roland. "Writers, Intellectuals, Teachers." *Image, Music, Text.* Ed. and trans. Stephen Heath. London: Flamingo, 1984. 190–215.

Beja, Morris and Maurice Harmon, Phillip Herring, David Norris, eds. *James Joyce: The Centennial Symposium.* Urbana and Chicago: University of Illinois Press, 1986.

Derrida, Jacques. *Speech and Phenomena: And Other Essays on Husserl's Theory of Signs.* Trans. David B. Allison. Evanston, Ill.: Northwestern University Press, 1973.

Flügel, J. C. *The Psychology of Clothes.* London: Hogarth Press, 1930.

Lacan, Jacques. "From Love to the Libido." *The Four Fundamental Concepts of Psycho-analysis.* Ed. Jacques-Alain Miller. Trans. Alan Sheridan. London: Penguin, 1977. 187–200.

———. "On Narcissism." *The Seminar of Jacques Lacan, Book I: Freud's Papers on Technique, 1953–1954.* Ed. Jacques-Alain Miller. Trans. John Forrester. New York: Norton, 1991. 107–17.

———. "Presence of the Analyst." *The Four Fundamental Concepts of Psycho-analysis.* Ed. Jacques-Alain Miller. Trans. Alan Sheridan. London: Penguin, 1977. 123–35.

———. "The Subject and the Other: Alienation." *The Four Fundamental Concepts of Psycho-analysis.* Ed. Jacques-Alain Miller. Trans. Alan Sheridan. London: Penguin, 1977. 203–15.

———. "The Wolf! The Wolf!" *The Seminar of Jacques Lacan, Book I: Freud's Papers on Technique, 1953–1954.* Ed. Jacques-Alain Miller. Trans. John Forrester. New York: Norton, 1991. 89–106.

Silverman, Kaja. *The Acoustic Mirror: The Female Voice in Psychoanalysis and Cinema.* Bloomington and Indianapolis: Indiana University Press, 1988.

CHAPTER 11

Strange Words, Strange Music: The Verbal Music of "Sirens"
Andreas Fischer

Words? Music? No: it's what's behind. (*U*, 11.703)

There's music everywhere. (*U*, 11.964)

Among the many codes human beings have at their disposal for expressing themselves and for communicating with each other, language and vocal music share a number of common traits. In their primary, basic form they are produced orally, transmitted by sound waves and received through the ear, but both can also be represented by a written code, in which the primary acoustic signals are converted into secondary graphic ones, written or printed on paper. Both words and music are subject to the laws of time: speech sounds and musical notes as acoustic signs can only be produced and received one after the other, in a linear sequence, which is represented in the written code by signs that are written and read (conventionally) from left to right and from top to bottom. However, this is where the similarities end, and a number of differences come to mind, the following four being the most obvious ones.

1. The suprasegmental features of stress and intonation excepted, language is exclusively sequential or syntagmatic, the paradigmatic axis only offering options from which a speaker has to select, either choosing one item at the expense of another or placing two or more items in a particular sequence.[1] Thus we must say *John and Mary* (or *Mary and John*) *came to see me,* although *John and Mary* do not semantically represent a sequence. Two speakers could, of course,

articulate the words *John* and *Mary* at the same time, but the resulting acoustic signal would be judged as unintelligible rather than as a meaningful combination of the two names. In writing one could, in principle, resort to a representation like

> *John*
> ——— *came to see me*
> *Mary*

but even then our convention of reading from left to right and from top to bottom would make us read the above as *John* [*and*] *Mary* and not, say, as *Mary* [*and*] *John*. Music, as we have seen, is also essentially sequential, but in contrast to language it may employ what I want to call co-sequentiality. Two speakers cannot (or should not) speak simultaneously, but two singers can easily sing together in homophony (singing the same melody together as chords), or in polyphony or counterpoint (singing different melodies). Musical notation easily represents this co-sequentiality with two or more staves written or printed above each other. Language, then, is essentially monophonous, while music may be monophonous, homophonous, or polyphonous.

If we call sequentiality a form of *nacheinander* and co-sequentiality a form of *nebeneinander,* we realize that the case of language versus music is a side issue of the aesthetic problems discussed by Lessing in his *Laokoon* (Chapter XVI and passim), where he claims "that poetry has to do with *Handlungen* (actions), i.e. objects existing one after the other (*nacheinander* or *aufeinander*) in time. In painting and sculpture, objects are *Körper* (bodies), presented one beside the other (*nebeneinander*) in space" (cited in Senn, "Esthetic Theories," 134).[2]

2. In (1) above I mentioned intonation as one of the suprasegmental features of language, but variation of pitch (or intonation) is clearly of less importance than the segmental phonemes and their sequence. In English, for example, intonation may be used over and above syntax to mark grammatical structure (such as clause and sentence boundaries or sentence types) or to communicate personal attitude (such as irony or annoyance). In music, by contrast, variation of pitch is a central feature, for what is melody if not a sequence of sounds of varying pitch (together with rhythm, discussed below)? In accordance with this difference in importance, written language has hardly any means of

indicating intonation except punctuation,[3] whereas in musical notation the lines of a stave serve this purpose well.[4]

3. Language has rhythm, but like intonation it is a marginal feature that is employed, for example, for added emphasis or for aesthetic purposes in literary language, especially poetry. With music, on the other hand, rhythm (and a regular beat that underlies rhythmic variation) is an essential constituent. The conventions and possibilities of the two written codes may again serve as an indicator of the relative importance of meter or beat and rhythm: in music, meter (to use this word now) is indicated by the time signature at the beginning of a piece and by the vertical bar lines indicating measures, while rhythm is marked primarily by the different values given to individual notes. In written prose rhythm can only be imperfectly hinted at through repetitions, syntactic arrangements, and punctuation.[5] Even poetry, rhythmical language par excellence, is conventionally written without metrical notation (though measure is an unmistakable aspect of metric verse), and the reader has to make do with line breaks as the only overt indicators of meter (and hence, rhythm).

4. Finally, and most important, language or rather the linguistic sign is the arbitrary and conventional combination of a form (a signifier) with meaning (the signified).[6] A permissible combination of phonemes in a particular language may or may not have meaning (/ sɪt / has a conventional meaning in modern English, whereas / tɪs /, with a hard "s," though permissible, does not), but a combination of musical sounds, even a well-known one, does not: nearly everyone is familiar with the beginning of Beethoven's Symphony no. 5, but it is nevertheless not associated with a specific, conventional meaning.

Human beings normally use language and music separately and for different purposes. However, there are a number of ways in which the two may come together and interact. "Prosaic" cases like, for example, music criticism (language dealing with music) apart, there seem to be three "artistic" forms of interaction, namely words and music going hand in hand, music representing words, and words representing music.

Words and music may accompany each other as lyric and song or, in opera, as libretto and aria. Although the two codes are nominally equal in this case, in practice music is usually felt to be the dominant partner. A song cycle like *Winterreise* evokes the name of Schubert before that of Wilhelm Müller, and *Die Zauberflöte* is Mozart's before it is Schikaneder's. However, this inequality may well be due to the historical fact that composers often chose poems or libretti written by people who are nowadays felt to be minor writers, Richard Strauss and Hofmannsthal providing the exception that proves the rule.

Music attempts to take over the functions of language in what may be called program (versus absolute) music, when it wants to tell a story or to conjure up a poetic or dramatic scene. However, Liszt, the inventor of the form, still relied on language when he defined program music as "any preface in intelligible language added to a piece of instrumental music, by means of which the composer intends to guard the listener against a wrong poetical interpretation, and to direct his attention to the poetical idea of the whole or to a particular part of it" (cited in Scholes, 834). Even later tone poems based on literature, but without such a preface, like Richard Strauss's *Till Eulenspiegels lustige Streiche,* do not manage to tell the story on their own, but rely on the listener's familiarity with it. For music to tell a story in the strict sense of the word it needs words to precede, accompany, or follow it, and on its own it can only produce certain acoustic effects that form part of a story or scene (such as the cannons in Tchaikovsky's *1812 Overture* or the shepherds' flutes in Beethoven's Symphony no. 6). Program music thus remains music and does not escape from its limitations or break its norms.[7]

If music cannot become language, can language become music? This question and its implications will be the main concern of this essay, its title indicating that in an attempt to become music language will break some of its conventions, will disrupt some of its norms, will—in short—become strange. Poetry as the form of language that is most akin to music is an obvious candidate for study, but here I would like to concentrate on an experiment in prose, namely "Sirens." To begin with I will discuss a number of devices used by Joyce in his attempt to turn language into music. Although these devices may strike the reader as highly original, some of them are not confined to "Sirens" and may be encountered singly or in combination in other literary works as well. In conclusion I will look at the overall effect produced by the musical devices in "Sirens." It is my contention that in their totality they form a whole that transcends the sum of its parts and that the strangeness of this whole is both novel and significant in ways not appreciated so far.

The connection of "Sirens" with music is obvious and fully explicit. In the famous schema reprinted by Stuart Gilbert the "scene" of the episode is given as "The Concert Room [of the Ormond Hotel]," the "organ" is the "Ear," the "art" is "Music," and the "technic" "*Fuga per canonem*" (38).[8] This last, explicit reference to a well-defined musical form, namely "a fugue with invariable congruent repetitions of theme" (Bowen, "Libretto," 156), has given rise to a lively debate concerning the musical form of "Sirens." The result appears to be that it is neither a *fuga per canonem* nor any other explicit musical form and that its most musiclike part is the introduction, a kind of overture that introduces "themes," that is, words and fragments of sentences that will recur in their proper context later in the episode.[9]

Two examples from the very beginning of the episode will suffice:

Bronze by gold heard the hoofirons, steelyringing. (*U,* 11.1)[10]

is taken up by

> Bronze by gold, miss Douce's head by miss Kennedy's head, over the crossblind of the Ormond bar heard the viceregal hoofs go by, ringing steel. (*U,* 11.64–65)

while

Imperthnthn thnthnthn. (*U,* 11.2)

is later contextualized as

> A haughty bronze replied:
> —I'll complain to Mrs de Massey on you if I hear any more of your impertinent insolence.
> —Imperthnthn thnthnthn, bootssnout sniffed rudely, as he retreated as she threatened as he had come. (*U,* 11.97–101)

How can one characterize the musical quality of this overture?

Like pure music the "themes" sounded in the overture have no intelligible meaning. Or rather, they appear to be practically meaningless at first, but gain meaning when they recur later on in the episode in their proper context. A first, "meaningless" sounding of a theme thus points forward (cataphorically or proleptically) to a second, "meaningful" one.[11]

The overture is, further, characterized by various kinds of lexical and nonlexical onomatopoeia. The first kind is exemplified here by the word "steelyringing," whose four light (or front) vowels may be taken to represent the sound of horseshoes on cobblestones. The second line at first looks like nonlexical onomatopoeia (a rendering of pure sound), but in its later context it turns out to be half-lexical, that is a "rudely sniffed" version of "impertinent insolence." It is often pointed out that an onomatopoetic word is rarely, if ever, a direct, fully iconic representation of pure sound, and that its interpretation, like that of ordinary words, depends on conventional associations between form and meaning.[12] This is borne out by these two examples: the noise of hoofs can also be represented, in English, by the verb "clop," and the difference between "steelyringing" and "clop" shows that conventionalized meaning and context ("hoofirons," "steelyringing") are at least as important here as purely phonological associations. Furthermore, following the equine context of the first line, "Imperthnthnthn thnthnthn" could easily be taken for the snorting of horses (an association, by the way, which was strengthened by the fact that in older editions of *Ulysses* it erroneously followed "steelyringing" without a line break!)[13] and it is only in the context of lines 97–101 that it is explained as the "rude sniffing" of boots. If, in the following, onomatopoeia is quoted as an exception to the arbitrariness of the linguistic sign, then for these reasons it will always be understood as a partial exception only.

It is worth mentioning, finally, that the two examples of onomatopoeia just discussed represent noises rather than music. This is true by and large for the whole of "Sirens" and for onomatopoeia in general, since noises are more easily imitated by speech sounds (especially consonants) than "pure" music. This does not invalidate my argument here, however, since the music of "Sirens" explicitly encompasses the whole (or nearly the whole) universe of sounds:

> Sea, wind, leaves, thunder, waters, cows lowing, the cattlemarket, cocks, hens don't crow, snakes hissss. There's music everywhere. Ruttledge's door: ee creaking. No, that's noise. (*U*, 11.963–65)

It is thus only fitting that the episode that begins with a half-musical overture should end in the same fashion with the polyphony of Robert

Emmet's last words in Bloom's interior monologue (and associated by him with Mercadante's oratorio [Bowen, *Allusions,* 210]), the noise of a passing tram, and Bloom's breaking wind:

> Bloom viewed a gallant pictured hero in Lionel Marks's window. Robert Emmet's last words. Seven last words. Of Meyerbeer that is. [...]
> Seabloom, greaseabloom viewed last words. Softly. *When my country takes her place among.*
> Prrprr.
> Must be the bur.
> Fff! Oo. Rrpr.
> *Nations of the earth.* No-one behind. She's passed. *Then and not till then.* Tram kran kran kran. Good oppor. Coming. Krandlkrankran. I'm sure it's the burgund. Yes. One, two. *Let my epitaph be.* Kraaaaaa. *Written. I have.*
> Pprrpffrrppffff.
> *Done.* (*U,* 11.1274–94)

Explicitly "musical" music is, of course, also present in "Sirens," but less in the form of onomatopoeia than through songs and arias (that is, music accompanied by words!) that are woven into the fabric of the episode in a multitude of ways, be it as leitmotifs that introduce a character ("When the Bloom Is on the Rye," [*U,* 11.390, 1126]), be it as a topic of conversation (for instance, "Tutto è sciolto" [*U,* 11.610] from Bellini's *Sonnambula*), or be it as songs that are actually sung in the Ormond (notably "M'appari" from Flotow's *Martha* and "The Croppy Boy") (see Bowen, *Allusions,* 174). Bowen has counted no less than "one hundred fifty-eight references to forty-seven songs" (*Allusions,* 53) in the whole episode, and they play a major role in giving depth to the seemingly trivial events of the plot and in connecting "Sirens" with other parts of *Ulysses.*[14] My concern is not with these songs, however, but with other, more narrowly linguistic ways of rendering music in "Sirens," and for this purpose I would like to go back to the four features distinguishing music from language that I briefly discussed at the beginning, namely (1) polyphony, (2) melody, (3) rhythm, and (4) absence of referential meaning.[15]

  1. Language is sequential, a *nacheinander,* whereas music combines *nacheinander* with *nebeneinander* (what I have called the co-

sequential or polyphonic aspect of music). How can Joyce indicate this *nebeneinander,* short of using deviant typography (which is a means not used in *Ulysses*)?[16] The technique he resorts to is to cut up the various parallel continua of sound (the "themes") into short fragments and to splice them together as one continuum. A classical example is to be found in the following passage at the end of Simon Dedalus's rendition of "M'appari," where his audience's appreciative shouts and their clapping happen together as two parallel continua of sound (a. and b. are my reconstruction of the technique, c. is the text as found in *Ulysses*):

a.   —Bravo! Good man, Simon. Encore! Sound as a bell. Bravo, Simon!
    —Clapclap. Clappyclapclap. Clapclipclap clap. Clapclopclap.

b.   —Bravo!   Good man, Simon.   Encore!
    —   Clapclap.   Clappyclapclap.

c.   —Bravo! Clapclap. Good man, Simon. Clappyclapclap. Encore! Clapclipclap clap. Sound as a bell. Bravo, Simon! Clapclopclap. Encore, enclap, said, cried, clapped all, Ben Dollard, Lydia Douce, George Lidwell, Pat, Mina Kennedy, two gentlemen with two tankards, Cowley, first gent with tank and bronze miss Douce and gold miss Mina. (*U,* 11.756–60)

In passing we note that Joyce carries this experiment of *nebeneinander* one step further into word formation, with the neologism "enclap" incorporating the *en-* of the word *encore,* the onomatopoetic sound of *clap* plus (in this combination) the repetition of the clapping.

In a second example the clock striking four provides one sound-continuum ("Clock whirred," "Clock clacked," "Clock clacked," "A clack," "O'clock"), the noisy activities of the two barmaids and of Blazes Boylan the other:

Clock whirred. Miss Kennedy passed their way (flower, wonder who gave), bearing away teatray. Clock clacked.
    Miss Douce took Boylan's coin, struck boldly the cashregister. It clanged. Clock clacked. Fair one of Egypt teased and sorted in the till

and hummed and handed coins in change. Look to the west. <u>A clack</u>.
For me.
—What time is that? asked Blazes Boylan. Four?
   <u>O'clock</u>. (*U*, 11.380–86)

Such cutting and splicing is not limited to brief passages of text and
time, as shown by the following example, which extends across the
whole of the latter part of the episode. The sound in question is the
tapping noise made by the blind piano tuner's cane as he makes his way
back to the Ormond Hotel to retrieve the tuning fork forgotten earlier
(compare *U*, 11.275–82, 313–16). It begins lightly (and presumably far
away) as a single "Tap" (*U*, 11.933), but gradually increases and
culminates in an intense "Tap. Tap. Tap. Tap. Tap. Tap. Tap. Tap" (*U*,
11.1223) before subsiding to a low "Tap. A youth entered a lonely
Ormond hall" (*U*, 11.1273) and "Tip. An unseeing stripling stood in the
door" (*U*, 11.1281).[17] In its monotony the tapping of the piano tuner's
cane functions as a kind of "pedalpoint" (Burgess, *Here Comes,* 141),
or metronome, within the music of the whole episode. It signals one
continuum of sound (and action), which is paralleled in the whole
episode by a number of others that together amount to polyphony from
the musical point of view and to "genuine counterpoint of action"
(Burgess, *Here Comes,* 138) from the point of view of narrative
technique.

In doing so, does Joyce break any linguistic conventions? I would
maintain that he does, if we take into account the communicative
function of language, for Joyce's cutting and splicing results in severely
weakened textual cohesion within the episode. Intermittent occurrences
of the isolated word "Tap," for example, which are not explained by
their immediate context, remain erratic blocks of language, unless the
reader pieces them together as parts of one continuum of sound and
action and connects them with what he already knows about the piano
tuner and his forgotten tuning fork. It is mainly the reader, then, who
creates the coherence of the episode, and he is helped little
(considerably less than usual) by its textual cohesion.

2. Music differs from spoken language (and also from most noises)
by its full exploitation of variation of pitch as melody.[18] The only way
for language to represent melody onomatopoetically is through vowel
quality, but the limited vowel repertoire of English (as of human
language in general) does not offer many possibilities. In "Sirens" there

are only a few attempts to render actual music in this way, but the representation of certain noises draws on the same resource. Here is an onomatopoetic rendering of music, namely of Bob Cowley's improvising on the piano:

> But wait. But hear. Chords dark. Lugugugubrious. Low. In a cave of the dark middle earth. Embedded ore. Lumpmusic. (*U*, 11.1005–6)

And here are some noises:[19]

> O, look we are so! Chamber music. Could make a kind of pun on that. It is a kind of music I often thought when she. Acoustics that is. Tinkling. Empty vessels make most noise. Because the acoustics, the resonance changes according as the weight of the water is equal to the law of falling water. Like those rhapsodies of Liszt's, Hungarian, gipsyeyed. Pearls. Drops. Rain. <u>Diddleiddle addleaddle ooddleooddle</u>. <u>Hissss</u>. Now. Maybe now. Before. (*U*, 11.979–85)

> —True men like you men.
> —Ay, ay, Ben.
> —Will lift your glass with us.
>   They lifted.
>   <u>Tschink</u>. <u>Tschunk</u>. (*U*, 11.1276–80)

The resource exploited in each of these examples is the difference between the "light" front vowel /ɪ/ and the "dark" back vowels, with /æ/ taking a middle and thus neutral position. The auditory similarity between "pure" sounds and their representation in speech is further strengthened by their similar method of production, since the oral cavity as a resonance chamber iconically represents the clapping hands, the chamber pot, and the glasses respectively. This kind of onomatopoeia may be called auditory iconicity,[20] and Joyce employs it with great dexterity. However, because of the limited number of vowels, not to mention vowel graphemes (as compared with the far greater number of musical notes), it can never be more than a marginal phenomenon, and like all onomatopoeia it relies for its effect not just on its (imperfect) mimesis of sound, but also on context, on literary and lexical associations and even on visual patterns. In lines 756–60 the fully lexicalized "clap" is the reference point for the more directly onomatopoetic "clip" and "clop," in lines 979–85 "ooddleooddle" conjures up both *pool* and *puddle*, while the repetition of *oo* and *dd*, like that of *sss* in "Hissss," works visually as well as onomatopoetically, in lines 1276–80 "Tschink" (*Chink*) is a literary reference to "the patriotic boozy thirty-two counties song" (Bowen, *Allusions*, 209), and so on.

It is obvious that onomatopoeia, especially of the nonlexical kind, is a form of deviation. A word like "clap" is fully lexicalized and as such a conventional lexical item of English. A word like "ooddleooddle," however, is not and can only be interpreted onomatopoetically and in relation to its context.

3. Rhythmical patterns would appear to be obvious devices that need no special exemplification. The only exclusive means ordinary written prose has to indicate rhythm is punctuation (spatial configurations and capitalization as well as more unusual typography excluded), and Joyce makes full use of it by deviating from standard practice through underpunctuation and overpunctuation. Compare:

> Miss Douce halfstood to see her skin askance in the barmirror gildedlettered where hock and claret glasses shimmered and in their midst a shell. (*U*, 11.118–20)

with:

> Will? You? I. Want. You. To. (*U*, 11.1096)

In the first example the uninterrupted sequence of words may be seen as another attempt to catch the *nebeneinander* of all the things visible to Miss Douce at a glance in the barmirror: her skin, the gilded letters on the mirror, hock and claret glasses, and the shell. In the second example we have an extreme case of the breathless, staccato-like rhythm of interior monologue.

The extreme musical rhythmicality of Joyce's prose is most evident in those passages where he attempts to represent pure music. He makes use of a dazzling array of devices such as onomatopoeia, repetitions, and punctuation, which in their totality escape the fetters of syntactic organization and meaning and approach the quality of pure music. The following is a selection from Bloom's interior monologue while he follows Bob Cowley first improvising and then playing the minuet from *Don Giovanni* on the piano:

> Bloom mur: best references. But Henry wrote: it will excite me. You know how. In haste. Henry. Greek ee. Better add postscript. What is he <u>playing now</u>? <u>Improvising</u>. <u>Intermezzo</u>. P. S. <u>The rum tum tum</u>. How will you pun? You punish me? Crooked skirt swinging, whack by. Tell me I want to. Know. O. Course if I didn't I wouldn't ask. <u>La la la ree</u>. <u>Trails off there sad in minor. Why minor sad</u>? Sign H. They like sad tail at end. P. P. S. <u>La la la ree</u>. I feel so sad today. <u>La ree</u>. So lonely. <u>Dee</u>. (*U*, 11.888–94)

> <u>Bob Cowley's twinkling fingers in the treble played again</u>. The landlord has the prior. A little time. Long John. Big Ben. <u>Lightly he played a light bright tinkling measure</u> for tripping ladies, arch and smiling, and for their gallants, gentlemen friends. <u>One: one, one, one, one, one: two, one, three, four</u>. (*U*, 11.958–62)

> <u>Minuet of *Don Giovanni* he's playing now</u>. Court dresses of all descriptions in castle chambers dancing. Misery. Peasants outside. Green starving faces eating dockleaves. Nice that is. <u>Look: look, look, look, look, look: you look at us</u>. (*U*, 11.965–68)

In these examples language may be said to mimic actual (though wordless) music, but the text of "Sirens" is musical in a playfully rhythmical way even where there is no such iconic connection. This is especially evident in the passages of third-person narration dealing with Pat the waiter of the Ormond restaurant. The following is again a selection:

> Bloom signed to Pat, bald Pat is a waiter hard of hearing, to set ajar the door of the bar. The door of the bar. So. That will do. Pat, waiter, waited, waiting to hear, for he was hard of hear by the door. (*U*, 11.669–72)

> Bald Pat at a sign drew nigh. A pen and ink. He went. A pad. He went. A pad to blot. He heard, deaf Pat. (*U*, 11.822–23)

> Bald deaf Pat brought quite flat pad ink. Pat set with ink pen quite flat pad. Pat took plate dish knife fork. Pat went. (*U,* 11.847–48)

> Bald Pat who is bothered mitred the napkins. Pat is a waiter hard of his hearing. Pat is a waiter who waits while you wait. Hee hee hee hee. He waits while you wait. Hee hee. A waiter is he. Hee hee hee hee. He waits while you wait. While you wait if you wait he will wait while you wait. Hee hee hee hee. Hoh. Wait while you wait. (*U,* 11.915–19)

Pat is practically deaf and is not quoted as actually saying anything (let alone singing!) in the episode. Nevertheless Joyce gives him an ingenious verbal "soundtrack" all on his own, which, like real music, is much easier to read (aloud!) than to describe in detail. Very occasionally Joyce's "musical tricks" (Burgess, *Here Comes,* 139) convey meaning,[21] but mostly they simply produce verbal music.[22]

4. Can one generalize from this list of norm-breaking, music-making devices found in "Sirens"? Is there any significance to the strangeness we encounter in the episode? I think there is, and I believe that the key to it is to be found in a book published only six years before *Ulysses*.

In his *Cours de Linguistique Générale,* posthumously published in 1916, Ferdinand de Saussure defines the linguistic sign as the arbitrary and conventional linking of a signified with a signifier, of meaning with form (or vice versa). This linking is arbitrary, because there is no natural connection between a meaning and the form through which it is expressed. At the same time it is conventional, that is, institutionalized by a society (which is also a linguistic community) that defines itself and its values through a shared and reasonably stable system of such signs. (In this connection it is important to see how Saussure again and again stresses the inherent stability and regularity of the synchronic system and the—to him almost annoying—irregularity of diachronic changes!) Seen from this point of view convention is not just an aspect, but the very essence of the linguistic sign. Linguistic signs and the systems constituted by such signs *are* convention.

By way of conclusion I will now claim that "Sirens" shakes the very foundations of this position, but not in the way as it appears at first sight. Onomatopoeia (and for the sake of simplicity I will now call all music-making devices in "Sirens" by this name) is an exception not to the conventionality of the linguistic sign, but to its arbitrariness. The word *cuckoo,* for instance, is not an arbitrary sequence of sounds that somehow has become linked to the call of the bird in question, but it represents the very sound itself (or at least an approximation to it governed by the phonological and phonotactic rules of English). Truly onomatopoetic devices (and for the moment we assume that they are possible) would thus be nonarbitrary, or natural, and would not need the sanction of convention for their existence. If a linguistic community had no options in assigning forms to meanings, if that connection were given by nature, then there would be no need to make it legitimate and stable through convention. Onomatopoetic signs, in this view, are "better" than conventional signs, because they are natural and absolutely (rather than just relatively) stable. A text like "Sirens," in which onomatopoeia reigns supreme, thus conjures up a natural and stable world in which meanings are naturally linked with forms, in which signified and signifier are so near to each other as to be almost one. "Sirens" is not about music, "Sirens" directly represents music.[23]

And yet this is all wrong, for there is another aspect of onomatopoeia in "Sirens" that tells a completely different story. Onomatopoetic devices, first of all, are foregrounded in the episode through their much higher than normal frequency and through their unconventional originality. Second, the link between many of these devices and the sounds they supposedly represent is really a very tenuous one, the best example (from the ones quoted here) being the waiter Pat who makes music linguistically although on the level of plot he makes no music at all. The essence of Joycean onomatopoeia in "Sirens" is thus not that it *represents* music iconically, but that it *makes* music linguistically and all by itself. Joycean onomatopoeia is not the natural union of meaning and form, of signified and signifier, but quite on the contrary it is the signifier freeing itself from the link with the signified and taking off all on its own. "Sirens" is thus a step toward absolute form, toward abstraction, but it obviously just loosens rather than severs its ties with meaning: as part of the narrative of *Ulysses* it continues and elaborates the story of Leopold Bloom and the other protagonists, but language, the means by which the story is told, emancipates itself and draws attention to itself as pure form. "Sirens" could thus be compared to a cubist painting, which still has a recognizable subject but which gives equal emphasis to the forms that the subject is composed of, to "the cylinder, and the sphere and the cone," to quote Cézanne's famous remark (cited in Gardner, 783). Like cubist art, "Sirens" thus calls into question or even breaks with the representational conventions of naturalistic and realistic fiction and points the way toward modernism. It is of course not the only modernist episode in an otherwise conventional *Ulysses,* as indeed each episode breaks with one or several such representational conventions. However, the formal, material side of language is sound, and by concentrating on sound, by not only writing strange words but by making these strange words make strange music, Joyce places himself in the very center of the modernist revolution not only of literature, but of the language of literature.[24]

NOTES

This essay was first published in *On Strangeness,* ed. Margaret Bridges (Tübingen: Gunter Narr Verlag, 1990), 39–55, the fifth volume of *SPELL* (Swiss Papers in English Language and Literature), general editor Max Nänny. Reprinted by permission of Gunter Narr, Gunter Narr Verlag, Tübingen.

1. According to Saussure, this "caractère linéaire du signifiant" (103) is the second of the two basic characteristics ("deux caractères primordiaux," 100) of the linguistic sign, the other being "l'arbitraire du signe" (100–102, 180–84).

2. Senn discusses in his "Esthetic Theories" Joyce's preoccupation with the problems of *nacheinander* and *nebeneinander* and his indebtedness to Lessing.

3. "[W]e may assume that written prose has an implicit, 'unspoken' intonation, of which punctuation marks are written indicators. This certainly seems to be what many writers on prose style have in mind when they discuss the 'rhythm of prose'" (Leech and Short, 215). See also Leech, 103–4.

4. Crystal (169–73) neatly summarizes linguistic functions of intonation as well as similarities and differences between speech and music.

5. See note 3.

6. This is the first of the two basic characteristics of the linguistic sign according to Saussure: see note 1.

7. In avant-garde music, of course, one finds combinations of words and music that transcend traditional genres like opera or program music.

8. On Joyce's schemas for *Ulysses,* see Ellmann, xviff., 187ff.

9. The debate is summarized in Bowen, *Allusions,* 51–53; for a musical interpretation of the introduction together with an interesting discussion of the problems involved see Lees.

10. All underlinings are the author's throughout.

11. Gilbert perceptively notes that these fragmentary phrases "are like the overtures of some operas and operettas, in which fragments of the leading themes and refrains are introduced to prepare the hearer's mood and also to give him, when these truncated themes are completed and developed in their proper place, that sense of familiarity that, strangely enough, enhances for many hearers their enjoyment of a new tune" (213).

12. For an informed discussion of onomatopoeia in "Sirens" and a detailed analysis of its last lines (1284–94, quoted below), see Attridge.

13. See, for instance, the 1968 Penguin edition (*Ulysses* [1968 edition], 254).

14. For a full documentation see Hodgart and Worthington (68–72), Bowen, "Bronzegold Sirensong," and Bowen, *Allusions,* 160–211.

15. This is not by any means a complete list. From "the hundreds of musical forms verbally reproduced in the course of this episode" (223), Gilbert mentions a few at the end of his "Sirens" chapter (221–25).

16. In her early article on "The Language of James Joyce" (which deals mainly with *Finnegans Wake,* however), Margaret Schlauch already comments on Joyce's revolutionary attempts to approximate "the values of polyphonic music in literary discourse" (483). In his essay on "Narrative Dissimulation" Senn discusses this aspect of Joyce's narrative technique in detail and with many examples.

17. The onomatopoetic effects here are quite subtle: the increasing number of taps presumably represents increasing proximity and loudness, while the contrast between earlier "Tap" and final "Tip" may indicate a different surface (the street outside versus the floor of the Ormond hotel).

18. Crystal (173) also points out that musical pitch is absolute while pitch in language is relative.

19. See also lines 756–60, quoted above.

20. I use this term to distinguish it from what I call articulatory iconicity, where it is the position of the articulatory organs rather than the resulting sound that is taken to be represented iconically. Examples of the latter would be *this* versus *that* (proximity versus distance of tongue and palate) or *little* versus *large* (narrow versus wide opening between tongue and palate).

21. The repetition of the phrase "the door of the bar" in lines 669–70 thus may indicate Bloom's insistent signaling to Pat to open the door. The twice eight monosyllables of "Bald deaf Pat brought quite flat pad ink. Pat set with ink pen quite flat pad" (*U,* 11.847–48), on the other hand, probably represent

the "scales up and down" of line 842. The second of these examples was brought to my attention by Fritz Senn.

22. David Crystal points out to me that deaf people often speak in an extremely clipped way. Pat's "soundtrack" may thus be partly iconic after all.

23. Beckett makes a similar claim for *Finnegans Wake:* "His writing is not *about* something; *it is that something itself*" (Beckett, 14).

24. I am grateful to Daniel Ammann, Udo Fries, and Hans-Jürg Suter (in addition to David Crystal and Fritz Senn) for comments on the original version of this paper.

WORKS CITED

Attridge, Derek. "Literature as Imitation: Jakobson, Joyce, and the Art of Onomatopoeia." *Peculiar Language: Literature as Difference from the Renaissance to James Joyce*. London: Methuen, 1988. 127–57.

Beckett, Samuel. "Dante ... Bruno . Vico .. Joyce." *An Exagmination of James Joyce*. Repr. of 1939 ed. New York: Haskell, 1974. 1–22.

Bowen, Zack. "The Bronzegold Sirensong: A Musical Analysis of the Sirens Episode in Joyce's *Ulysses*." *Literary Monographs* 1 (1967): 245–98.

———. "Libretto for Bloomusalem in Song: The Music of Joyce's *Ulysses*." *New Light on Joyce from the Dublin Symposium*. Ed. Fritz Senn. Bloomington: Indiana University Press, 1972. 149–66.

———. *Musical Allusions in the Works of James Joyce: Early Poetry through Ulysses*. Albany: State University of New York Press, 1974.

Burgess, Anthony. *Here Comes Everybody: An Introduction to James Joyce for the Ordinary Reader*. London: Faber & Faber, 1965.

———. *Joysprick: An Introduction to the Language of James Joyce*. London: André Deutsch Limited, 1973.

Crystal, David. *The Cambridge Encyclopedia of Language*. Cambridge: Cambridge University Press, 1987.

Ellmann, Richard. *Ulysses on the Liffey*. London: Faber & Faber, 1972.

Gardner, Helen. *Renaissance and Modern Art. Art through the Ages*. Vol. 2. 7th ed., rev. Horst de la Croix and Richard G. Tansey. San Diego: Harcourt Brace Jovanovich, 1980.

Gilbert, Stuart. *James Joyce's* Ulysses: *A Study*. Rev. ed. 1952. Harmondsworth, U.K.: Penguin, 1963.

Hodgart, Matthew and Mabel Worthington. *Song in the Works of James Joyce*. New York: Columbia University Press, 1959.

Joyce, James. *Ulysses*. With *"Ulysses:* A Short History" by Richard Ellmann. Harmondsworth, U.K.: Penguin, 1968.

Leech, Geoffrey N. *A Linguistic Guide to English Poetry*. English Language Series 4. London: Longman, 1969.

Leech, Geoffrey N. and Michael H. Short. *Style in Fiction: A Linguistic Introduction to English Fictional Prose*. English Language Series 13. New York: Longman, 1981.

Lees, Heath. "The Introduction to 'Sirens' and the *Fuga per Canonem.*" *James Joyce Quarterly* 22 (1984): 39–54.

Saussure, Ferdinand de. *Cours de Linguistique Générale*. Ed. Tullio de Mauro. Paris: Payot, 1982.

Schlauch, Margaret. "The Language of James Joyce." *Science and Society* 3 (1939): 482–97.

Scholes, Percy A. *The Oxford Companion to Music*. 10th ed., rev. John Owen Ward. London: Oxford University Press, 1970.

Senn, Fritz. "Esthetic Theories." *James Joyce Quarterly* 2 (1965): 134–36.

————. "The Narrative Dissimulation of Time." *Myriadminded Man: Jottings on Joyce*. Eds. Rosa Maria Bosinelli, Paola Pugliatti, and Romana Zacchi. Testi e Discorsi 5. Bologna: Cooperativa Libraria Universitaria Editrice Bologna, 1986. 145–65.

CHAPTER 12

Mining the Ore of "Sirens": An Investigation of Structural Components

Margaret Rogers

The sirens' seductive sounds echo down through the ages, enchanting, sometimes destroying those who succumb to their enigmatic songs. The sirens have been described variously as beings half-bird, half-woman, as temptresses luring unsuspecting seafarers onto the rocks of destruction and, in antiquity, as the initial notes of the musical modes from which were derived the structural harmonies of the music of the spheres. In James Joyce's *Ulysses,* two of these modes are incorporated in the names of the barmaids of the Ormond bar: Miss Lydia Douce and Miss Mina Kennedy. Lydia indicates Lydian mode and Mina, minor or Aeolian mode.

In a conversation with Georges Borach, Joyce stated that he wrote the "Sirens" episode of *Ulysses* "with the technical resources of music. It is a fugue with all musical notations" (cited in Ellmann, 459). In a letter to his benefactress, Harriet Weaver, he wrote, "They are all the eight parts of a *fuga per canonem*" (*SL,* 242). He added that it took five months for him to complete the episode after which he never wanted to hear another note of music. These statements have given rise to endless conjecture and many theories have been proposed about what he meant and what he did. Obviously, for Joyce, text was music: "Words? Music? No: it's what's behind" (*U,* 11.703). I believe Joyce used a variety of devices to encipher his music in "Sirens" including encoded notes based on a Renaissance model, which in turn was based on ancient Pythagorean concepts of music. The writer who can do anything with words can even write music with them.

Technically, writing music in text without using musical notes is a challenge. It demands a code of some sort and a code demands a key. And for Joyce, in addition to the practical consideration of writing music in words, there was the lure of the cryptic. Hugh B. Staples, in his article "Joyce and Cryptology: Some Speculations," explains this lure:

> A corollary to the idea of literature as epiphany is the idea of literature as secret, and the art of James Joyce is both arcane and radiant. The visions of *Dubliners* are the more moving because they are unshared, and the epigraph *"Et ignotas animum dimittit in artes"* [Dispatch the spirits into unknown art] both summarizes the principal theme of the *Portrait* and points toward an important element in the remaining works of the canon. Language itself, whether liturgical Latin or gipsy argot, Joyce very early came to regard as a part of a mystery; a means of communication, but also a way of concealing secret knowledge from all but the few. [...] One must consider first of all what motive Joyce would have had for adding the tricky, laborious business of encipherment to a text [*FW*] already sufficiently complex in structure and detail. [...] But a more intriguing possibility is that he wished to provide in this arcane fashion a fuller and clearer exposition of the meaning. (167)[1]

What follows here are some of the ideas I have explored of Joyce's methods and models for encoding music in the "Sirens" episode.

DECODING THE FUGUE IN "SIRENS"

A fugue is a polyphonic musical composition of one or more themes repeated or imitated by successive voices sounding against each other, creating a single harmonic texture in a continuous interweaving of voices. A canon is a contrapuntal musical composition in which the melody is imitated by successive voices, or, in its original meaning, a musical form guided by the text at the discretion of the composer. What is required to write a fugue? Fundamentally, the composer needs notes, the letters of music that in turn outline scales, chords, intervals, and melodic motifs.

When Joyce declared that he was writing "Sirens" as a fugue, he was playing a difficult game because he had to find a method of giving musical clues to his hidden fugue without actually writing out the music in the text. The fugue had to be contained in the text itself. At the beginning of "Sirens" there are sixty-three lines of expository material from which the themes of the chapter are developed.[2] It is these sixty-three lines that outline the fugue "with the technical resources of music [...] with all musical notations." In "Sirens" the musical notations are the letters that designate musical notes: *a, b, c, d, e, f,* and *g.* It is these letters that contain the musical information Joyce encoded. For example, letter *a* is also musical note *a.* What better way to encode music in written language? Line 1, for instance, "Bronze by gold heard the hoofirons steelyringing," contains the following letter-notes: *Bebgdeadefeegg.*

Figure 12–1 shows the letter-notes, line by line, of lines 1–12 of "Sirens." The letter-notes reveal musical keys, chordal outlines, melodic motifs, structural patterns, and musical hints. In Figure 12–1, the line of text is printed above a musical staff. The musical letter-notes are written chronologically as they appear in the text, on the line or space of the musical staff employed in a work of music: the lines are *egbdf,* the spaces *face.* The triad chords written on the right of the staff are those suggested by the linear notes on the staff to the left.

Every musical scale contains a structural triad of three notes composed of the first, third, and fifth degrees of the scale. The structural triad for the C-major scale is *ceg,* for A minor (the relative minor scale of C major), *ace,* for G major, *gbd,* and for its relative minor, E minor, *egb.* Notes of the composition are analyzed for chordal outline; for example, a string of consecutive notes such as *gabedc* outlines a melodic fragment, but also contains chordal outlines *egb* and *ace.* Two methods will be used to determine the musical keys Joyce used in "Sirens," the first based on a line-by-line analysis of the melodic material and the triad chords it contains, the second on clues contained within the words of the text.

Four triad chords appear repeatedly and predominate throughout the opening. They are (in order of frequency) *ace,* present in forty-seven lines, *egb,* in forty lines, *dfa,* in twenty-nine lines, and *gbd,* in twenty-six. If these chords are tonic triads, that is, triads with their first note based on the first degree of the scale (*g* in *gbd,* first note of G-major scale), they would outline the musical keys of A minor, E minor,

D minor, and G major. The repeated use of these chords suggests not only the keys but the musical form Joyce intended and provides a clue to the meticulous nature of his encipherment.

Information relating to the keys provided by chordal outlines is reinforced by subtle clues in words of text in other ways. A recurring example is the suffix "ing," which can be read not only as the present participle but as "in g" or "in the key of g." G major is one of the four keys outlined by a predominant triad. The opening text fairly rings with "ing," which appears in twenty-three lines of text, often more than once per line. The first example is in the first line: "steelyr<u>inging</u>." In

> Jingle jingle jaunted jingling.
> Coin rang. Coin clacked. (*U*, 11.15–16)

not only is "in *g*" found, four times, but other keys as well: in *e*, in *e*, in *a*, in *e*, in *d*, in *C*, in *a*, in *C*, in *c*, in *a*, in *c*, in *e*, and in *d!* A further example of encoding "key" information with "in" occurs in "*Naminedamine*. Preacher is he" (*U*, 11.42). "*Naminedamine*" reveals in *e*, in *d*, in *a*, in *e*. The last ten letters of "Preacher is he" might be anagrammatized to read "Each is here." So the key is in the key.

More is embedded in the ore of "Sirens." Lowercase letter-notes are those in the *k e y* of the music. Capital letters may indicate accidentals (sharps and flats), in turn signifying modes and harmonic patterns connected with individual characters. For example, the capital Bs of "Blew. Blue bloom" (*U*, 11.6) are B flats, lowering the pitch of B natural by a half-step, and creating a diminished fifth enharmonic augmented fourth, or tritone, given a key of E. This mournful interval is particularly appropriate for Bloom's diminished mood.

From the typescript of June 1919 through the placards and page proofs, the opening sixty-three lines of "Sirens" stand essentially uncorrected, pointing to the fact that the introductory section of "Sirens" is a fairly rigid model. Joyce, the singer and student of music, friend of Otto Luening, neighbor of Jarnach, and observer of Busoni, certainly had access to and knew the basic music theory that his letter-note musical manuscript suggests. The theory may be basic, but the concept and implementation are pure genius. And there are musical precedents for such a process.

THE *SOGGETTO CAVATO* IN "SIRENS"

The sixteenth-century musical precedent for the encoding process used by Joyce is, I believe, *soggetto cavato.* The term was coined in 1558, by G. Zarlino in *Istitutioni Harmoniche,* to denote the special class of thematic subjects for polyphonic compositions that were derived from a phrase associated with them by matching the vowels with the traditional Guidonian solmization syllables *ut re mi fa sol la.* The full term used by Zarlino is "soggetto cavato dalle parole": a subject "carved out of words" (Randel, 758).[3] One of the best-known examples of *soggetto cavato* is the sixteenth-century mass by the Netherlands composer Josquin Des Prez, "Hercules dux Ferrariæ," the vowels of which (*e u e u e a i e*)[4] yield the subject *re ut re ut re fa mi re,* whose musical realization based on the key of C is (in modern notes) *dcdcdfed:*[5]

H	e	rc	u	l	e	s	d	u	x	F	e	rr	a	r	i	æ
	e		*u*		*e*			*u*			*e*		*a*		*i*	*e*
	re		*ut*		*re*			*ut*			*re*		*fa*		*mi*	*re*
	D		C		D			C			D		F		E	D

An early example of the same principle is implied in a method recommended in the eleventh century by the groundbreaking musical theorist Guido D'Arezzo in his *Micrologus,* or "Little Discourse," in a chapter entitled "Quod ad cantum redigitur omne quod dicitur" ("How anything spoken can be turned into music") (Randel, 846). Guido, who was responsible for devising the solmization system, the musical staff, and the Guidonian hand (Grout, 53–55),[6] assigns the vowels *aeiou* to five successive notes (pentachord) of the scale *cdefg,* so that the text "Sante Johannes meritorum tuorum" receives through the syllables, *aeoaeeiouuou,* the melody *cdfcddefggfg.* Both Josquin and Guido employ a form of the hexachord, while Joyce's addition of the letter-note *b* allowed his scale to become a modern seven-note scale.

Did Joyce know of the process and the musical works embodying the principle? He had access to the information about *soggetto cavato,* for it was described in *Grove's Musical Dictionary* as early as 1899 in an article about Josquin des Prez (41). He was familiar with other composers of the period, referring to the sixteenth-century composer Sweelinck in *Giacomo Joyce:* "I hear his variations for the clavichord on an old air" (*GJ,* 16). Was Joyce familiar with Josquin's mass? The corollaries are tantalizing but could also be made with many other composers of polyphonic music. But it is interesting to mention a few: Josquin's mass is fugal in style with choruses scored for soprano, alto, tenor, and bass with duets and trios. Joyce scored in a similar fashion with ensembles. Josquin used no accidentals, as was the practice of the time. Joyce used keys with no accidentals or a minimum of them, like G and F major.[7] Both used a variety of modes. Josquin's mass is in a retrograde pattern; Joyce delighted in palindromes.

All conjecture, but did Joyce give a hint in *Finnegans Wake,* where we read "and harmonise your abecedeed responses?" (*FW,* 140.13–14)? Casaubon warns of the dangers of loose connections in Eco's *Foucault's Pendulum* (274–75). Yet speaking of connections, does anyone hear "Joyce can" in "Josquin"?

THE INELUCTABLE MUSICAL MODALITIES OF "SIRENS"

Ineluctable: not to be avoided, changed, resisted. That which is inevitable. The definition of the word describes a predetermined outcome; a system constructed in such a manner that a predictable conclusion can be assumed, relied upon. The modes, or their companions, scales, are the underlying structures of music, and contain this quality of inevitability. A major scale always sounds like a major scale. The tonalities and modalities of traditional Western music are not random. They are musical laws, as carefully constructed as the properties of elements, and because of their construction, their emotional impact on the listener is predictable. Composers manipulate the psychology and the effect of music, coloring their works with different modes for different moods. Joyce understood this concept and used it in the "Sirens" episode.

A musical mode is an arrangement of the eight diatonic notes of a scale (the eighth note being the octave of the scale), according to one of the several fixed schemes of intervals. The traditional modes are Ionian, Dorian, Phrygian, Lydian, Mixolydian, Aeolian, and Locrian.[8] An ascending scale from middle C to the next C played entirely on the white keys yields a scale in the Ionian mode. If you were to play the scale beginning on D (still only on the white notes), you would have played a scale in the Dorian mode. Beginning with E is Phrygian, F, Lydian, G, Mixolydian, A, Aeolian, and B, Locrian. The difference in the modes is in the occurrence of the half-steps between E and F and B and C. The "character" of each mode is related to the occurrence in the scale of these two half-steps. This is an ineluctable law of the harmonics of Western music and has a bearing on Joyce's "Sirens." Each mode has a different musical personality, whether stable or unsettling, each has a separate color. They are comparable to the Eleusinian mysteries, part of myth and magic. Socrates tells us that the Mixolydian mode is dirgelike and ought to be done away with, for it is useless "even to women!" (cited in James, 57). The Ionian and certain Lydian modes, on the other hand, are relaxing and convivial; because of their softening influence he would prohibit youths from singing or hearing them. That leaves the Dorian and Phrygian modes, which he allows: the former because it emboldens warriors and the latter because it has potent persuasive powers. The major Ionian mode is always cheerful and the minor Aeolian, sad. It is no accident that Lydia, the Lydian mode, is ever so convivial and Miss Mina, the Aeolian mode, is wistful.

At this point I would like to dig a little deeper into the ore of the past. "Low in dark middle earth. Embedded ore" (*U,* 11.42). Legend has it that Pythagoras of Samos was listening to a blacksmith striking hammers of different weights and, in the difference of the sounds he heard, discovered the arithmetical relationships between the harmonic intervals, the perfect fourth, perfect fifth, and perfect octave of music. This was not only the beginning of music theory and much of science; it also gave rise to the idea of the "music of the spheres" that Pythagoras claimed he could hear. These musical consonances were the underlying principle of an ordered cosmos. Pythagoras taught the interrelatedness of all human knowledge and believed that musical numbers guide soul and cosmos alike. Music *was* number and the cosmos *was* music.

> Numbers it is. All music when you come to think. Two multiplied by two divided by half is twice one. Vibrations: chords those are. One plus two plus six is seven. Do anything you like with figures juggling. Always find out this equal to that. [...] Musemathematics. And you think you're listening to the etherial. (*U,* 11.830–35)

Not only was there harmony in the cosmos, the ancients believed that the ethical task of music consisted in bringing the music of man into accord with its cosmic prototype.

More particularly, Joyce may have taken the idea of his sirens' song from Plato's "Myth of Er":

> The spindle of Necessity, Er tells us, was made of adamant, while the whorl was made "partly of adamant and partly of other substances." The cosmic whorl is described as a set of nested bowls the top surfaces of which create a series of rings. "For there were in all eight whorls, set one within another, with their rims showing above as circles and making up the continuous surface of a single whorl round the shaft, which pierces right through the center of the eighth." The eight circles of the whorl, beginning with the outermost and moving toward the spindle, are: the ring of fixed stars, which is spangled; the moon; the sun, which is brightest; Aphrodite (Venus), Hermes (Mercury); Ares (Mars), "somewhat ruddy"; Zeus (Jupiter), which is whitest; and Kronos (Saturn), similar to Hermes and somewhat yellower than the others.
>
> On each of the rings there stood a Siren, and as the celestial whorl revolved, the Sirens sang, each one a different note "so that all the eight made up the concords of a single scale." (Plato, *Republic,* cited in James, 56)

Plato's eight sirens made up the concords of a single scale.[9] In Joyce, there are all "the eight parts of a *fuga per canonem.*"

Perhaps it would be best to consider some of the underlying elements in the "Myth of Er" before exploring its possible relationship to the "Sirens" of *Ulysses.* In his book *The Music of the Spheres,* Jamie James quotes F. M. Cornford's theory that the myth may be based on the Greek Orphic tradition: the ur-Er, as it were (55–56). In addition to the tale of the spinning whorls and singing sirens, Er, who was a soldier slain in battle, was permitted to return from the afterlife to tell humanity what awaits us on the other side of death. Similarly, Orpheus sang his love, Eurydice, back to life. Thus, the story of Orpheus "unites two key elements of Er's story, and indeed of the Pythagorean concept of the harmonious universe: the power of music and the renewal of life" (James, 55–56). This concept reverberates in the "Sirens" episode. It is *music* with its healing powers that restores the cuckolded Bloom to life and helps him deal with his loss and hurt. Love's Old Sweet Song: L-O-S-S (Staples, 167).[10]

In "Sirens" the syllables *er* and *re* or some form thereof (*ear, or, ar, air, ray*) appear in thirty-two of the opening sixty-three lines. Both are present in line 1. In lines 4–16, *re* predominates. A change is indicated in lines 17–18: "Avowal. *Sonnez.* I could. Rebound of garter. Not leave thee. Smack. *Lacloche!* Thigh smack. Avowal. Warm. Sweetheart, goodbye!" (emphasis added). *Er* rebounds. *Er* or its variants *ar* and *or* hold sway until line 42 where *re* reappears. "Low in dark middle earth. Embedded ore" (*U*, 11.42) is a definite pivot point in the musical narrative. "Embedded ore" contains *do* and *re*, the initial syllables of the solfeggio system of identifying scale notes, and twice mentions "ore," which for the purpose of this analysis contains *or* (*er*) and *re*. In line 49, *re* reappears. After line 55, both are present.

What is the significance of *re* and *er*? What is their function? *Re* is the second syllable of the solfeggio system: *do re me fa sol la ti do.* Here *er* refers to *ear,* the organ of "Sirens" but most likely also the Er of the myth that contains the tale of the sirens of antiquity singing the initial notes of the modes, which are also scales. Because of the pattern created by their appearance and because both are related to scales, we can assume that these scales are related to the structure of Joyce's enciphered musical masterpiece. It is interesting to observe that the changes signified by the occurrence of *re* and *er* correspond to changes in structure indicated by chordal outlines of the letter-note theory presented earlier. Based on changes of the appearance of predominant keys, the sixty-three lines are divided into four sections creating an A, A[1], B, A musical form. Lines 1–21 revolve around E minor and A minor, A minor predominates in lines 22–29, D minor and A minor in lines 30–52, then E minor and A minor return in lines 53–63. Here we have two entirely different indicators of structural change. Though not exact, the shifts occur at about the same point.

The use of color is a third indicator of structural change. Bronze, gold, blue, and rose occur in profusion through line 14, then except for the appearance of black in line 39 are absent until line 48 where they once again are featured. The midsection is more concerned with sound. It throbs, chirrups, breaks, jingles, gnashes, smacks, warbles, roars, and hisses in a cacophony of sound. The change of feeling in the lines in text where it occurs is similar to that of the two previously mentioned techniques indicating change in structure. This change elicits a vision of a photograph and its negative: the first part bright and clear, perhaps because of the high spirits of the characters, but the second part dark and dense, full of self-conscious angst reflecting blue Bloom's blue mood.

To summarize, I believe Joyce enciphered music in "Sirens" by using letters that correspond with the signifiers for musical notes, *abcdefg*. His method of encoding notes in text was previously employed by Renaissance composers, most notably Josquin Des Prez who successfully used the technique of *soggetto cavato,* or carved subject, in his mass "Hercules dux Ferrariæ." Ancient musical modes are an element in "Sirens," and Joyce's sirens may be based on those in Plato's "Myth of Er." Changes in structural patterns are indicated and supported by an analysis of change in musical keys, in occurrence of *er* and *re,* and in words relating to color and sound.

Joyce said to Frank Budgen, "I have the words already. What I am seeking is the perfect order of words in the sentence. There is an order in every way appropriate. I think I have it" (Budgen, 20). Is more embedded in the ore of "Sirens"? Probably. So if on a lazy summer afternoon when the hours hang heavy, some adventurous soul would like to write out all the capital letters in the opening sixty-three lines of text and solve them as an acrostic, we might find even more treasures in the embedded ore.

NOTES

Parts of this essay have appeared before in Margaret Rogers, "Decoding the Fugue in 'Sirens,'" *James Joyce Literary Supplement* 4, 1 (1990). Reprinted by permission of Zack Bowen, *James Joyce Literary Supplement.*

1. My thanks to Ruth Bauerle for directing my attention to Staples's article.

2. For the purpose of the argument here, the sixty-third line, "Begin!," will be included as part of the expository material, though it could be technically said to stand apart from it.

3. "Cavato" literally means "extracted," or "wormed out."

4. Understanding *æ* as a digraph for *e* in this musical scheme.

5. See also Reese, 236–37, for a description of "Hercules dux Ferrariæ" and the process of *soggetto cavato.*

6. The Guidonian hand worked as follows: pupils were taught to sing intervals as the teacher pointed with the index finger of his right hand to the

different joints of his open left hand; each one of the joints stood for one of the twenty notes of the Guidonian hexachord system, a combination of six notes of the scale, beginning on C or G.

7. The keys Joyce seems to have preferred, according to the letter-note theory, are E minor, A minor, D minor, and G major. E minor is the relative minor of G major, which contains only one accidental, F sharp. A minor is the relative minor of C major, which contains no accidentals. D minor is the relative minor of F major, which contains only one accidental, B flat.

8. A second mass of Josquin's, entitled "Missa L'Homme Armé," employs a cantus firmus presented in a modal series of Ionian, Dorian, Phrygian, Lydian, Mixolydian, and Aeolian scales. Peter Maxwell Davies borrows Josquin's title for his *Missa Super L'Homme Armé,* discussed by Murat Eyoboglu in chapter 7.

9. Plato's sirens seem to have an extra note in their scale unless *do,* the first note, is sung twice. Both the solfeggio scale and the letter-note scale include seven notes.

10. See Thomas Jackson Rice earlier in this volume for more on this acronym, and on the mathematics of music.

WORKS CITED

Apel, Willi, ed. *The Harvard Dictionary of Music.* Cambridge, Mass.: Belknap Press, 1969.

Budgen, Frank. *James Joyce and the Making of* Ulysses. Bloomington: Indiana University Press, 1960.

Eco, Umberto. *Foucault's Pendulum.* Trans. William Weaver. New York: Harcourt Brace Jovanovich, 1989.

Ellmann, Richard. *James Joyce.* Rev. ed. Oxford: Oxford University Press, 1982.

Grout, Donald J. *A History of Western Music.* New York: Norton, 1960.

Grove, George. *A Dictionary of Music and Musicians.* London: Macmillan, 1899.

Guido D'Arezzo. *Micrologus. Hucbald, Guido, and John on Music: Three Medieval Treatises.* Trans. Warren Babb. Ed. and introd. Claude Palisca. New Haven, Conn.: Yale University Press, 1978. 57–83.

James, Jamie. *The Music of the Spheres: Music, Science, and the Natural Order of the Universe.* New York: Grove Press, 1993.

Plato. "The Myth of Er." *Collected Dialogues*. Eds. Edith Hamilton and Huntington Cairns. Princeton, N.J.: Princeton University Press, 1961. 834–44.

————. *Republic*. Ed. F. M. Cornford. Oxford: Oxford University Press, 1980.

Randel, Don, ed. *The New Harvard Dictionary of Music*. Cambridge, Mass.: Belknap Press, 1986.

Reese, Gustave. *Music in the Renaissance*. New York: Norton, 1959.

Rogers, Margaret. "Decoding the Fugue in 'Sirens.'" *James Joyce Literary Supplement* 4, 1 (1990): 15.

Staples, Hugh B. "Joyce and Cryptology: Some Speculations." *James Joyce Quarterly* 2 (1965): 167–73.

Zarlino, Gioseffo. *Istitutioni Harmoniche: A Facsimile of the 1558 Venice Edition*. New York: Broude Bros., 1965.

Figure 12–1. The Letter Notes of the First Twelve Lines of "Sirens"

CHAPTER 13

"Circe," *La Gioconda,* and the Opera House of the Mind

John Gordon

Richard Ellmann tells this story of how John Joyce came to be reconciled to his son's elopement with Nora:

> He took James for a walk into the country, and stopped with him at a village inn for a drink. There was a piano in the corner; John Joyce sat down at it and without comment began to sing. "Did you recognize that?" he asked James, who replied, "Yes, of course, it's the aria sung by Alfredo's father in *Traviata.*" John Joyce said nothing more, but his son knew that peace had been made. (Ellmann, 276–77)

Ellmann notes that in the opera this aria comes when the formerly implacable father relents and asks forgiveness for having spurned his son's beloved. This essay will give an account of a similar occurrence in "Circe," a sequence in which one passage from an opera conjures up a real-life reenactment of the larger narrative from which that passage comes, by virtue of the fact that the musically knowledgeable listeners can instantly recognize and situate the setting.

Now, in "Circe" that will mean that they not only recognize the theme, but act it out as well. "Circe" is *Ulysses*'s "hallucinatory" chapter, compounded of hallucinations facilitated by drug- and alcohol-induced delirium and by mental derangement, hallucinations that to an extent still not widely recognized tend overwhelmingly to arise from the working of discernible external facts on those states, rather than from autonomous private fantasies or authorial caprice.[1] In the scene in question, which takes place in the music room of Bella Cohen's brothel, those external facts are especially abundant and exigent. Indeed we are given an account of the interior scene in detail more than adequate to meet the specifications of any operatic set designer who might be inclined to reconstruct it on the stage.

Let me review this setting, drawing mainly on the parenthetical catalogue of stage properties produced at the point when Bloom enters it (*U*, 15.2031–55). The flooring is of a multicolored oilcloth covered with footprints, probably tracked in recently by customers with wet shoes coming out of the rain that began falling about half an hour ago.[2] From the narrator's description of these prints as occurring in "*a morris of shuffling feet without body phantoms*" (*U*, 15.2045), we can surmise that in their shapes and placement they resemble the patterned footprint-shaped cutouts commonly laid down by dance instructors. (It is worth noting that although overall these prints appear "*all in a scrimmage higgledypiggledy*" [*U*, 15.2045–46], morris dancers move in circles.) The walls are covered with green wallpaper representing a sylvan scene of "*yewfronds and clear glades*" (*U*, 15.2047). Opposite the door is a fireplace, complete with brass fire irons (*U*, 15.2071), covered with a "*screen of peacock feathers*" (*U*, 15.2047–48), above whose mantle is a gilt-edged mirror (*U*, 15.2053). Before the fireplace is spread a "*hearthrug of matted hair*" (*U*, 15.2048–49). There is at least one window, which (as confirmed at line 2780) is opened— enough to let in the sound of a gramophone record (*U*, 15.2115) sending out its music through another open window in a nearby building (*U*, 15.605)—and will be opened wider in the course of the action, when things heat up, and when someone breaks wind. The weather outside has temporarily subsided into a drizzly mist but will soon return to the thunder and lightning that terrified Stephen Dedalus in the previous chapter. Hanging from the ceiling is a chandelier (*U*, 15.2041) of prismatically glinting cut glass (*U*, 15.3988), outfitted with a gasjet that is behaving erratically and will continue to do so throughout the chapter. This gasjet has a mauve tissue-paper lampshade (*U*, 15.2040–41). To one side is a brand new pianola (*U*, 15.2072), the pride of the establishment (see line 1991), so up-to-date that it boasts a Wonderlight, one of the Wurlitzer Company's latest and showiest gadgets.[3]

This Wonderlight, as described by Q. David Bowers in his *Encyclopedia of Automatic Musical Instruments,*

> consists of a rotating jeweled ball with a light bulb in the center. The
> swirling colors are reflected in mirrored glass petals which surround
> the center unit. Wurlitzer recommended the wonder light as being
> "ideal for dancing." (677)

Although alas I have so far failed in my efforts to get an adequate
photograph or videotape of one in action, I can at least report having
witnessed its operation firsthand, at the Musical Museum of Deansboro,
New York (Figure 13–1).[4] The jeweled lights are in all different colors,
and when a coin is dropped in the slot they flash brightly up in
synchronization with the music and send sparkles of rapidly circling
tints across floor, ceiling, and walls. The effect is similar to that
produced by a disco glitter-ball, only in color. (And the music is better.)
All in all it does indeed seem "ideal for dancing."

Action: Stephen Dedalus, dressed in black, is playing idly with the
pianola's keys, his hat and cane resting on its top. Vincent Lynch is
sitting by the fireplace, fiddling with the poker. The young men are
accompanied by two painted—as the saying goes—ladies, and are soon
to be joined by a third, escorted by Leopold Bloom. Apart from their
makeup the women are gaudily dressed, each with her own distinctive
color scheme: blue for Kitty Ricketts, sapphire for Zoe Higgins, red for
Florry Talbot. (Two of the men, by contrast, wear black.) When Bloom
and Zoe make their entrance to join the other two couples, the scene is
effectively set. Although smell, touch, and taste all come into play,
most of what transpires in this setting will be within the theatrical
modalities of sight and sound. And notice here how thoroughly, within
those modalities, has Joyce set up a scene conducive to something
theatrically phantasmagoric. In the modality of sight, he has stocked the
room with highly reflective surfaces and seen to it that all of his light
sources are changeable, multifarious, and variably chromatic. A similar
effect has already been established, if less elaborately, in the outdoor
scene, where shifting banks of fog expressionistically blur and refract
the streetlights and where there will soon be flashes of lightning, than
which of course nothing is more efficacious for purposes of dramatic
emphasis. Within, the prismatic chandelier flashes colored glints, as
does (we'll soon see) the Wonderlight when turned on. The
temperamental gasjet turns out to be an especially versatile piece of
stage machinery in the lighting department. Right at the start of the
brothel sequence, when by turning the gasjet full cock Kitty Ricketts

causes the shaft in Lynch's hand to flash into being as a brass poker instead of the "wand" it at first seemed in dimmer light (*U*, 15.2049, 2071), the gasjet's fluctuations are busily transmuting the scene's apparent reality.

To some extent Joyce's way with it here continues the long-standing convention that gaslight, in its mutable glarings and flickerings, is especially serviceable for setting almost any tone and establishing almost any mood desired. Of Mr. Pickwick, Dickens had written that,

> Like a gas lamp in the street, with the wind in the pipe, he had exhibited for a moment an unnatural brilliancy: then sank so low as to be scarcely discernible: after a short interval, he had burst out again, to enlighten for a moment, then flickered with an uncertain, staggering sort of light, and then gone out altogether. (23)

In many a novelistic interior after *Pickwick*—in Conrad, Wilde, and Doyle, among those of Joyce's day—both persons and the rooms they inhabit had been made to alternate between romantic glow and pitiless glare, fuzzy penumbra and harsh hard-edged anatomy, by means of the same handy mechanical effect. Joyce in his all-out way extends this convention to its logical extreme. First, his gaslight, prone as it is to malfunctioning, is exceptionally inconstant. It can flare blindingly one minute and cast the room into darkness the next; it can change color rapidly from white to mauve to green. Second, these changes, working on the hallucinatorily susceptible Stephen and Bloom, alter not only their moods but their perceptions of reality, and thus alter the reality presented to us, the audience receiving the episode's events through their eyes and ears as mediated by their more or less intermittently, variably delirious or transfixed brains.

So, to recount the transmutations of one sequence of thirty-six lines:

JOHN EGLINTON

(*produces a greencapped dark lantern and flashes it towards a corner: with carping accent*) Esthetics and cosmetics are for the boudoir. I am out for truth. Plain truth for a plain man. Tanderagee wants the facts and means to get them.

(*In the cone of the searchlight behind the coalscuttle, ollave, holyeyed, the bearded figure of Mananaun MacLir broods, chin on knees. He rises slowly. A cold seawind blows from his druid mouth. About his head writhe eels and elvers. He is encrusted with weeds and shells. His right hand holds a bicycle pump. His left hand grasps a huge crayfish by its two talons.*)

MANANAUN MACLIR

(*with a voice of waves*) Aum! Hek! Wal! Ak! Lub! Mor! Ma! White yoghin of the gods. Occult pimander of Hermes Trismegistos. (*with a voice of whistling seawind*) Punarjanam patsypunjaub! I won't have my leg pulled. It has been said by one: beware the left, the cult of Shakti. (*with a cry of stormbirds*) Shakti Shiva, darkhidden Father! (*He smites with his bicycle pump the crayfish in his left hand. On its cooperative dial glow the twelve signs of the zodiac. He wails with the vehemence of the ocean.*) Aum! Baum! Pyjaum! I am the light of the homestead! I am the dreamery creamery butter.

(*A skeleton judashand strangles the light. The green light wanes to mauve. The gasjet wails whistling.*)

THE GASJET

Pooah! Pfuiiiiiii!

(*Zoe runs to the chandelier and, crooking her leg, adjusts the mantle.*)

ZOE

Who has a fag as I'm here?

LYNCH

(*tossing a cigarette on to the table*) Here.

ZOE

(*her head perched aside in mock pride*) Is that the way to hand the
pot to a lady? (*She stretches up to light the cigarette over the flame,
twirling it slowly, showing the brown tufts of her armpits. Lynch with
his poker lifts boldly a side of her slip. Bare from her garters up her
flesh appears under the sapphire a nixie's green. She puffs calmly at
her cigarette.*) Can you see the beautyspot of my behind? (*U,*
15.2256–93)

Eglinton's shining lantern is "*greencapped,*" recalling and
summoning the "greencapped desklamp" (*U,* 9.29) accompanying his
earlier appearance in "Scylla and Charybdis," because the gasjet has
just flared to green, thus bathing the room in the snot-sea-greeny color
that helps turn Eglinton's accomplice in that earlier chapter, the
mystical, bearded, bicycle-riding AE, into a seaweedy, brine-encrusted
ocean god (see *U,* 9.30, 190–91). In "Sirens" a light-dimming dropping
of a crossblind, suddenly casting the barmaid Miss Douce in "cool dim
seagreen sliding depth of shadow" (*U,* 11.465), had helped establish
her, for Bloom and reader, as a kind of mermaid; here the process is
more drastic, a matter of hallucination rather than intimation, but
follows the same associative logic. When the gaslight then "*wanes to
mauve*" (an intermediary glow-phase is registered fleetingly by its
"*cooperative dial*" at line 2273), AE's domain glooms into that of a
"*darkhidden*" deity, just before a "*skeleton*"—or invisible—
"*judashand*" dims it down further to mauve, a color that may have
suggested the traditionally red-bearded Judas, who in any event is
Christianity's archetypal extinguisher of light. When Zoe Higgins then
adjusts the gasjet back to green, her flesh (passing through the brief,
probably disagreeable illumination of her hairy armpits, exposed by the
close vicinity of the brightened light) assumes the color of "*a
nixie's*"—that is, a sea-fairy's—"*green,*" as seen by a suddenly
ensorcelled Bloom.

As for the modality of the audible, in this same scene the sound of
the defunctive gasjet as it "*wails whistling*" accounts for the Mananaun
MacLir sound effects: with the cry of "*A cold seawind*" and the "*cry of
stormbirds,*" MacLir "*wails with the vehemence of the ocean*" and a
"*voice of whistling seawind*"; I would bet as well that his spluttery
monologue owes something to sputtering gas. As here, many of the
chapter's effects recall that imaginative "theater of the mind" invoked
by the BBC radio dramas of the '20s, '30s, and '40s, as reportedly

heard, in Paris, by the increasingly purblind James Joyce.[5] A staple of
the sound effects accompanying such performances was the sound of
silver foil being scrunched and twisted to produce various crackling or
rustling noises (cowboys ambling through sagebrush, rain on woodland,
etc.), and so Zoe Higgins is presented throughout the scene as
intermittently fooling with the silverfoil in which her chocolate has
been wrapped (*U,* 15.2708), in the process producing the *"silversilent
summer air"* (*U,* 15.3377) through which Bloom is envisioned to be
falling, Virag's tracker's tread through *"crackling canebrake over
beechmast and acorns"* (*U,* 15.3422), and the sound of the *"silverfoil of
leaves precipitating"* (*U,* 15.3453) contributed by the chorus of yew
trees accompanying Bloom's dialogue with the Nymph. Those yew
trees, to return to the visible, obviously derive from the room's
wallpaper.

To sum up: by and large, the hallucinations of "Circe" are
composites of determinable auditory and visual stimuli as noticed,
combined, and enacted in the inner theaters of the character's
consciousnesses, which consciousnesses fluctuate between more or less
passively registering these stimuli and absorbing and incorporating
them into some outwardly projected inner drama, a drama that in turn
will likely have been cued by something real.

Let me illustrate one such projected drama by turning to the
phenomenological events preceding Stephen's hurried exit from Bella
Cohen's establishment, and the way they have been conditioned by the
opera we know he knows, if only because everyone in Dublin knows it,
Amilcare Ponchielli's *La Gioconda.* The action in this sequence begins
at line 4000: Yorkshire-born Zoe Higgins, hearing soldiers outside
singing the song they may have perhaps picked up from today's band
concert (*U,* 10.1242), puts two pennies in the pianola slot and the
pianola, unaided, starts up a rendition of "My Girl's a Yorkshire Girl,"
a robust waltz. Frank Budgen records Joyce's reaction to a similar
sight: "'Look!' said Joyce. 'That's Bella Cohen's pianola! What a
fantastic effect! All the keys moving and nobody playing'" (228). Here,
the pianola's keys, uncannily playing with no one to play them,
summon the ghostly figure of the late music professor Goodwin, who
appears in order to beat *"handless sticks of arms on the keyboard"* (*U,*
15.4021), arms later described as *"vague"* (*U,* 15.4047). (Arms, that is,
which like the *"skeleton judashand"* of the earlier scene may plausibly
be considered to be invisible.) The Wonderlight's colored lights come

to life and send a wheeling rainbow kaleidoscope across the room's shiny surfaces. The lights are joined by the wheeling waltz patterns of Stephen and Lynch with their partners. As Professor Goodwin materialized to accommodate the pianola's handlessly moving keys, so the dance professor Maginni now appears (*U*, 15.4032) to choreograph the phantom dancers adumbrated by that morris of footprints on the floor.

The combination of automated music and the spinning of bright, many-colored lights reminds Kitty, she says (*U*, 15.4109), of the merry-go-round she saw at today's bazaar. That is one bazaar summoned to memory; another is the earlier one at which Bloom witnessed a performance of the famous "Dance of the Hours" (*U*, 4.525–26), from *La Gioconda*, in which the hours of the day, from dawn to nightfall, are acted out by a sequence of curvetting young women, each dressed in colors appropriate to her appointed time of day. Recalling it in "Calypso," Bloom had summed up thus: "Poetical idea: pink, then golden, then grey, then black" (*U*, 4.535–36). And so when the pianola is cranked up and its Wonderlight's array of "*Gold, pink and violet lights start forth*" (*U*, 15.4016–17) and begin spinning around a room of dancers, three of them dressed in brightly colored, distinctly colored outfits and themselves whirling around in waltz-step, the associative link for anyone familiar with the operatic scene is entirely natural. Which is why (starting at line 4054) the "Dance of the Hours" dancers join the spectacle, in what can probably best be conceived as an overlapping medley of the two tunes. Until, that is, the pianola finishing its rendition, Stephen launches into a dervishlike pas seul in which everything blurs vertiginously together:

STEPHEN

Pas seul!

(*He wheels Kitty into Lynch's arms, snatches up his ashplant from the table and takes the floor. All wheel whirl waltz twirl Bloombella Kittylynch Florryzoe jujuby women. Stephen with hat ashplant frogsplits in middle highkicks with skykicking mouth shut hand clasp part under thigh. With clang tinkle boomhammer tallyho hornblower blue green yellow flashes Toft's cumbersome turns with*

> *hobbyhorse riders from gilded snakes dangled, bowels*
> *fandango leaping spurn soil foot and fall again.) (U,*
> 15.4119–28)

To understand why that should happen when it does, it is necessary to refer to the music being played in Stephen's head; indeed the best advice I can give the reader is to go and find a recording of the opera and listen to the beginning of Act III Scene ii, where it occurs. "The Dance of the Hours" comes in two principal movements, both of them widely familiar. The first, repopularized some time ago as the melody for Alan Sherman's joke song, still sometimes played, entitled "Camp Grenada" ("Hello muddah, hello faddah," etc.)[6] is to say the least a stately, slow-moving piece (its tempo if not its beat at about that of "My Girl's a Yorkshire Girl"), conducive to the type of gradual procession, remembered by Bloom, designed to give the dancers plenty of leisure to show off their "Poetical" costumes. The second movement, obviously on purpose, is just the opposite: a deliriously fast-paced, rousing, soaring, whirling fandangolike revel. "Whirling" here should be taken quite literally: anyone who hears the piece will instantly recognize it as an invitation to whirl rapidly around the dance floor; the more energetic will feel like jumping and kicking too.[7] If the first half of "The Dance of the Hours" could be a slow march, the second half could be an unusually vigorous can-can: a dance that, as it happens, has just been mentioned by Stephen, recently back as he is from Paris (*U,* 15.3886).

So: Stephen is dancing and high-kicking in his frenzied way because of the music going on in his head, following in due order the operatic sequence that was established there by virtue of the associatively conditioned stimuli noted above. First *largo,* then *prestissimo,* just as in "The Dance of the Hours." He is playing out the story of *La Gioconda,* Act III, and the stage directions of "Circe" are, for now, following suit. To understand what happens next, we can therefore do no better than to consult Tobia Gorrio's libretto for the opera. As we join the action of Act III, "The Dance of the Hours" is being performed at a splendid Venetian ball held at the palace of Alvise, an official who, jealous of his wife Laura, has just, he thinks, had her poisoned in an adjoining room. (Actually she has taken one of those death-counterfeiting potions so useful for stories of this sort.) Also present are Laura's disguised lover, Enzo, and La Gioconda herself, a street musician in love with Enzo. Operating malevolently behind everything has been the villain Barnaba, a spy for the Inquisition, who in the pursuit of his beastly lust for La Gioconda has both brought about Laura's supposed poisoning and, falsely accusing her of witchcraft, seized Gioconda's old blind mother, the pious La Cieca (the blind one) who throughout the opera is forever praying for the dead. (In the one production of *La Gioconda* I have witnessed—a videotaped production by the Vienna Opera—La Cieca's affliction is conveyed mainly by heavy applications of eye shadow.) Immediately upon the conclusion of "The Dance of the Hours," Barnaba appears before the horrified assemblage with La Cieca, whom he will later murder—she has been caught praying for the dead again—accompanied by the sound of a death bell (*"The slow tolling of a bell is heard, indicating that someone is dead or dying"*) ringing for the supposedly dead Laura, whose laid-out body will shortly be revealed at the scene's climax (Gorrio, 36). Gioconda cries out at the spectacle of her poor mother, and various parties sing various duets about how terrible this all is (Figure 13–2).

It is of course a dramatically engineered plummet—Ponchielli is obviously partial to this kind of thing—from the heights of gaiety to the depths of misery. No wonder the chorus comments on how a fatal vampire—"un vampiro fatal"—has made all joy withdraw (Gorrio, 37). In the ensuing debacle, La Cieca accuses Barnaba of murder ("l'assassino sei tu!"), the distracted Enzo begs to be put to death, La Gioconda sings weepily, or perhaps weeps songfully—"Scorro il pianto a stilla a stilla" ("One by one, my tears are falling")—and Barnaba gloats about all the misery he has caused; the scene ends when Laura's body is revealed and Enzo, *"Lunging at Alvise with a dagger in his hand,"* exclaims "Murderer!" ("Carnefice!") and is stopped by guards as Barnaba spirits La Cieca away *"through a secret door"* (Gorrio, 38–39). The scene ends with the chorus going "Orror! orror!" (Gorrio, 39), and who can blame them?

Sure enough, in "Circe," as soon as Stephen rights himself from his dizzying spin who should appear to him, accompanied by a ringing bell and incantations from the burial service—and with the hollow eyesockets of the blind—but the specter of his afflicted mother:

(*Stephen's mother, emaciated, rises stark through the floor, in leper grey with a wreath of faded orangeblossoms and a*

> *torn bridal veil, her face worn and noseless, green with
> gravemould. Her hair is scant and lank. She fixes her
> bluecircled hollow eyesockets on Stephen and opens her
> toothless mouth uttering a silent word. A choir of virgins
> and confessors sing voicelessly.*)

THE CHOIR

Liliata rutilantium te confessorum ...
Iubilantium te virginum .... (*U,* 15.4157–65)

Combining the female roles, mainly those of dead Laura and blind La
Cieca, into one, she works the same kind of condensation on Stephen,
who acts out Enzo—he likewise will bring things to a head by lunging
forward menacingly with his own weapon, his ashplant—but, with the
Mulligan who accused him of killing his mother gloating in the
background, finds himself instead cast as a Barnaba, charged with
murder and ordered to beg forgiveness.

Again, much of the detail of this scene can be explained from
knowledge of its setting. That the mother is colored green—first from
gravemould, later as a green crab—suggests to me that the gaslight,
soon to be smashed, has turned green again. Stephen, terrified of
thunder, will testify in "Ithaca" that this crisis was precipitated by the
atmospherics outside,[8] and if with that in mind we take another look at
the text we may notice that there has been a sudden *"glareblarefare"*
(*U,* 15.4132) occurring just before the mother's appearance, followed
by the sound of *"Baraabum!"* (*U,* 15.4133), as in the flash of lightning,
the rumble of thunder. (The window, remember, is open.) The mother's
"scant and lank" hair, I suggest, originates in the *"hearthrug of matted
hair"* noted earlier, which might, logically, have become propped atop
her head at the moment that she *"rises stark through the floor,"*
assuming, that is, that this effect occurs in the vicinity of the hearth.
This assumption would also explain the smell of wetted ashes on her
breath (*U,* 15.4182).

And one more thing that may follow from that position. Above the
mantle of that hearth, remember, is a gilt-edged mirror. I think that
what is fundamentally happening in this sequence is that Stephen has
got the *La Gioconda* narrative running in his head and now finds the
visible occasion for this gruesome phase of it primarily in the image of

his own face, reflected in that mirror. Looking at his mother, conjured as "La Cieca," he is looking at himself, in that mirror. At the end of this chapter Bloom will remark on how much he resembles his mother (*U*, 15.4949). Here, in the reflection of that familial face, the mother's "*toothless*" grin gives back his own "toothless" state, real and contemplated, as established in the epithet applied to him by Mulligan in "Telemachus" (*U*, 1.708) and adopted by Stephen in "Proteus" (*U*, 3.494–96). The opened mouth gives back the image of Stephen's open mouth, which has just shouted, "Ho!" (*U*, 15.4156). Her La Cieca-like "*bluecircled hollow eyesockets*" reflect the shadows of his spectacle rims. The "*emaciated*" face reflects what we are told are his own conspicuously "drawn," indeed "*drawn grey and old*" (*U*, 15.4223) features. When he finds himself "*choking with fright, remorse and horror*" (*U*, 15.4186), it is from her mouth that a rill—again, green—of liquid drools. The "fire of hell!" (*U*, 15.4212) with which she threatens him comes from his own overheated state; like his fellow dancer Zoe Higgins, fanning herself and exclaiming, "I'm melting!" (*U*, 15.4206), he has worked up a sweat during the recent exertions. As for the mirror itself, I think we can discern its gilt frame in the "*wreath of faded orangeblossoms*" (*U*, 15.4158)—faded, presumably, to yellow—surrounding the mother's face. Delirious or not, he is therefore right—at some level he seems to know what is going on—when he thinks to end this horror show by smashing not the apparition before him but the gaslight above, the gaslight that has been showing him his face in the mirror and contributing to many of the vision's more vivid effects.

Those are some of the details, but the essential pattern into which they are made to fit, the essential story being acted out, originates in the *Gioconda* narrative, lodged in Stephen's mind by the sounds and sights around him, in a process variably receptive and projective, through the membranes of a selfhood whose unstable permeability seems to me Joyce's most distinctive contribution to fiction. Intellectually committed to the most stringent brand of realism but emotionally given over to the most florid extravagances of, above all, music hall and opera, Joyce contrived to have it both ways when he hit on the happy solution of realistically rendering the inner lives of people who like him loved, and sometimes lived, this music and the stories it tells. *Traviata* helped bring John and James Joyce back together; *Don Giovanni* helps condition Bloom's resignation toward Molly's adultery. The aria "Un bel dì" of *Madama Butterfly* was, as far as Joyce was concerned, his and Nora's song:

> I wanted to feel your soul swaying with languor and longing as mine did when she sings the romance of her hope in the second act *Un bel di:* 'One day, one day, we shall see a spire of smoke rising on the furthest verge of the sea: and then the ship appears'. I am a little disappointed in you. (*SL,* 174)

Disappointed in 1909 at Nora's reluctance to join him in the acting out, he was to make good the defect in *Ulysses,* where during the most romantic part of her story Molly plays Butterfly to the Pinkerton of her first lover, Mulvey, sailing away for good.

Molly is, after all, the book's most prominent singer, and an operatic singer at that. But in a way everyone in *Ulysses*—well, perhaps excepting Haines—is some kind of singer; everyone in the book is forever thinking or humming or dum-de-dumming some tune, often operatic in origin, and thereby letting into their consciousnesses the Trojan horse of the story it tells. It happens even at funerals, like the one at which Bloom catches himself: "The ree the ra the ree the ra the roo. Lord, I mustn't lilt here" (*U,* 6.640). But it is no use; as he remarks in "Sirens," "There's music everywhere" (*U,* 11.964): it will find its way into you and have its way with you, and in different ways and to varying extents take over and start telling the story you thought was your story. Because of his "hallucinatory" susceptibility in "Circe," Stephen's *La Gioconda*-governed encounter with his mother is an exceptionally vigorous—from a clinical view, virulent—instance of the condition. But in some degree or other, the condition is general all over Joyce's Ireland.

NOTES

1. For background on this statement, see my essay "Approaching Reality in 'Circe.'"

2. The rain came as the unexpected break in a long drought, therefore no one was prepared with galoshes or any other raingear (see *U,* 14.1442), and therefore the brothel's recent customers have probably been entering with wet shoes and leaving footprints.

3. This feature is not specified in the initial inventory. See *U,* 15.4016–17, and my commentary, below.

4. This was about fifteen years ago. Calls to the museum during the spring and summer of 1997 invariably got a recorded message advising that it was open "by chance." A friend in the area who kindly agreed to call it every day for weeks on end had no luck getting through. When I visited it personally in June 1997 it was still there but with no signs of habitation, present or in prospect. Letters sent to it have not been answered. When I last telephoned, in mid-September 1997, the message was that it was closed for the season.

5. For background on Joyce's radio listening, see Connor.

6. For those who delight in coincidence, it is perhaps worth noting that *Ulysses* makes an unexpected appearance in Alan Sherman's song: "And the head coach / Wants no sissies / So he reads to us from something called *Ulysses.*" "The Dance of the Hours" also makes an appearance, accompanied by alligators and hippos, in *Fantasia.*

7. Just before writing this, when I was playing a recording of the music to remind myself of how it went, my nine-year-old daughter ran into the room and began doing exactly that.

8. "Ithaca," lines 36–42:

> The collapse which Bloom ascribed to gastric inanition and certain chemical compounds of varying degrees of adulteration and alcoholic strength, accelerated by mental exertion and the velocity of rapid circular motion in a relaxing atmosphere, Stephen attributed to the reapparition of a matutinal cloud (perceived by both from two different points of observation, Sandycove and Dublin) at first no bigger than a woman's hand. (*U,* 17.36–42)

That is, Bloom blames Stephen's collapse, which will occur a few minutes after the scene under review, on Stephen's intoxication and dizzying dance, whereas Stephen remembers himself as having been affected by a change in the weather. He is afraid of thunder, and there has been thundery weather around since the middle of the chapter before "Circe." For the initial association between a small cloud—here imagined as the origin of one of the evening's thunderclouds—and Stephen's mother, see *U,* 1.247–79; the passage supplies much of the material for the "Circe" confrontation between Stephen and his mother. For a fuller treatment of this part of the subject, see my "Love in Bloom, by Stephen Dedalus," 247–49.

WORKS CITED

Bowers, Q. David. *Encyclopedia of Automatic Musical Instruments.* Vestal, N.Y.: Vestal Press, 1972.

Budgen, Frank. *James Joyce and the Making of* Ulysses. Bloomington: Indiana University Press, 1967.

Connor, James A., S. J. "Radio Free Joyce: *Wake* Language and the Experience of Radio." *James Joyce Quarterly* 31, 1 (1993): 825–43.

Dickens, Charles. *The Pickwick Papers.* Oxford: Clarendon Press, 1986.

Ellmann, Richard. *James Joyce.* Rev. ed. Oxford: Oxford University Press, 1982.

Gordon, John. "Approaching Reality in 'Circe.'" *Joyce Studies Annual* (1994): 3–21.

———. "Love in Bloom, by Stephen Dedalus." *James Joyce Quarterly* 27, 2 (1990): 241–55.

Gorrio, Tobia (pseudonym of Arrigo Boito). *Libretto for* La Gioconda. Trans. Walter Ducloux. New York: Ricordi, 1996.

Ponchielli, Amilcare. *La Gioconda.* New York: E. F. Kalmus, 1900.

Figure 13–1. The Wurlitzer Company's Wonderlight (Bowers, 679)

Figure 13–2. La Cieca (Alexandrina Milcheva, at right) and La Gioconda (Ghena Dimitrova) in *La Gioconda,* Metropolitan Opera, January 10, 1990. Photograph reprinted by permission of Winnie Klotz, Metropolitan Opera Association, Inc.

Section 3: *Finnegans Wake*

CHAPTER 14

Parsing Persse: The Codology of Hosty's Song

Zack Bowen and Alan Roughley

This essay explores the musical elements of "The Ballad of Persse O'Reilly," or "Hosty's Ballad," from *Finnegans Wake* (*FW*, 44.24–47.29; see Figure 14–1 for the music), and its relation to the song "Finnegan's Wake," as well as the literary and cultural aspects of its lyrics. To begin with the obvious, we will first consider the Irish-American song, "Finnegan's Wake," which provides the book with its modified title and the ur-text for its expanded meaning. "Finnegan's Wake" starts with Tim and his weakness for liquor, which accounts for both his demise—causing him to fall off a ladder—and his resurrection, as the whiskey scatters over the corpse like miraculous holy water, restoring life. The immediate clinical cause of Finnegan's death is a broken skull, linking him to Humpty Dumpty, the first of his many surrogates in Hosty's ballad.

Adaline Glasheen's several glosses of Hosty's name include *hostes,* "the plebs of the heroic peoples" (130), who become defenders of the homeland against the invasions of the rest of the human race, and thus the first sacrificial victims or the host of the mass. In the song "Finnegan's Wake" the collection of grieving, then increasingly rowdy mourners who initiate the posthumous proceedings are analogous to the crowd in Book I, Chapter 2, who insistently call on Hosty to articulate their hydra-headed identifications of Persse O'Reilly in Hosty's ballad. Tim Finnegan's mourners begin as an anonymous "they" who carry him home and lay him out for the wake, but a few are later specifically identified: Tim's wife (whose first name is suppressed), Biddy O'Neil, Judy Magee, Peggy O'Connor, and Mickey Mulvaney. There is a big enough crowd to start a row and a ruction (or "bloody" ruction in Ruth Bauerle's version [557]), whose combatants seem equally divided by sex. But the whole affair is vintage Irish, with initial sentimentality (Biddy's crying and traditional lament) followed by Judy Magee's querulous admonishment. The argument seems apparently about whether to voice the traditional laments, but could be based on how well the corpse looks. Either way, once the crowd squares off into an inebriated brawl, the outcome of the narrative is that Tim is resurrected, while in the novel the nay-singing Hosty declares that "not all the king's men nor his horses / Will resurrect" (*FW,* 47.26–27) the corpus of HCE. While Tim Finnegan's revival is in part due to the traditional whiskey/wake, ultimately it is immeasurably aided by the lively pugnacity of Tim's Irish friends. When he becomes Finn Again it is a celebration of Celtic behavior and the unique *hostes* who originated and continue to relive it down through Christian minstrelsy.

Glasheen sees Hosty, "the pleb who writes against H. C. Earwicker" (130), as a surrogate of Shem the Penman, and, by extension, of Joyce himself. In comic denigration/celebration of the ur-father/patriarch, he resurrects Ireland past, present, and future, identifying it with everybody and everything else it can stand for, warts and all.

Hosty's ballad is introduced by exhortations from the audience, in a sort of overture to the ballad-as-overture-to-the-book in its multifarious identifications of HCE from origins to conquering villain/hero to scapegoat. While the preamble to the ballad contains similarities to the overture of the "Sirens" episode in *Ulysses,* the comic emphasis is much more pronounced in the *Wake:*

> And around the lawn the rann it rann and this is the rann that Hosty made. Spoken. Boyles and Cahills [boys and girls], Skerretts and Pritchards [skirts and breeches] viersified [observed] and piersified [Persse/perceived] may the treeth [tree/truth] we tale of live in stoney [stone/story]. Here line the refrains of. Some vote him Vike[ing], some mote him Mike, some dub him Llyn and Phin while others hail him Lug Bug Dan Lop [Dunlop tires], Lex Lax [Ex-Lax],[1] Gunne or Guinn. Some apt him Arth, some bapt him Barth, Coll, Noll, Soll, Will, Weel, Wall but I parse him Persse O'Reilly else he's called no name at all. Together. Arrah, leave it to Hosty, frosty Hosty, leave it to Hosty for he's the mann to rhyme the rann, the rann, the rann, the

> king of all ranns. Have you here? (Some ha) Have we where? (Some
> hant) Have you hered? (Others do) Have we whered? (Others dont)
> It's cumming, it's brumming! The clip, the clop! (All cla) Glass
> crash. (*FW,* 44.7–20)

This elaborate introduction leads to a multilingual thunderclap, after
which the audience is commanded in Italian to listen ("Ardite") as
Professor Arditi ("dare" in Italian) lifts his baton to a clearly signified
Anglo-Saxon "Music cue" (*FW,* 44.23).[2]

Twice offered in the above introduction and then twice more
repeated during breaks in the ballad, the identification of ancient Celtic
rann versification with the St. Stephen's Day song, "The wren, the
wren, the king of all birds" or "The Wren-Boys' Song" (Bauerle, 515),
is linked to the song "Finnegan's Wake" in that the motivating behavior
in both the referents is strong drink. The wren, caught in a furze on St.
Stephen's Day and carried house to house in a cage by the singers, is,
according to the wren-boy singers, deserving of pity, and thus a
handout to buy a drop of booze for all concerned. While the trapped
wren itself is small, "his family's great" (like HCE's lineage and
associated surrogates) and his plight, like those of the singers, deserves
some sustenance. So Hosty's ballad, like the song, "Finnegan's Wake,"
and its counterpart, "The wren, the wren, the king of all birds," are
drinking songs about revival, a possibility of resurrection of the spirit as
well as the body:

> Sing hey! sing ho! Sing holly! sing holly!
> A drop just to drink, it would cure melancholy. (Bauerle, 516)

Hosty's ballad itself is about the fall and ostensible denial of
resurrection for a series of invading conquerors including Oliver
Cromwell, Lord Mountjoy, the allegedly cheating merchant/publican
HCE, the Ostman (Vikings), and, anomalously, the Italian tenor Enrico
Caruso. The last name on this list might sound a bit odd, but Ruth
Bauerle recounts an interesting, once celebrated but now nearly
forgotten story about how Caruso, on tour in New York, was arrested in
front of the monkey cage in the Central Park Zoo for groping a woman
in the crowd (Bauerle and Hodgart, 98–101). Hosty's relevant stanzas
are as follows:

It was during some fresh water garden pumping
Or, according to the *Nursing Mirror,* while admiring the monkeys
That our heavyweight heathen Humpharey
Made bold a maid to woo [...]

He ought to blush for himself, the old hayheaded philosopher,
For to go and shove himself that way on top of her.
Begob, he's the crux of the catalogue
Of our antediluvial zoo, [...]

He was joulting by Wellinton's monument
Our rotorious hippopopotamuns
When some bugger let down the backtrap of the omnibus
And he caught his death of fusiliers, [...]

For there's no true spell in Connacht or hell
        (bis) That's able to rise a Cain. (*FW,* 46.24–47.29)

Bauerle's account, in her and Hodgart's impressive *Joyce's Grand Operoar,* did not contain some interesting aspects of her earlier talk at the 1995 Joyce Providence Symposium. As we remember her talk, Caruso was accused of using a rent or opening in his overcoat to grab the woman. Bauerle later told us that Robert Day identified the monkeys as chimpanzees, accounting for one of HCE's middle names: Chimpden. After the incident, according to Bauerle, the monkeys physically exhausted themselves trying to perform for the enormous crowds attracted by the story to the site. The ensuing legal actions cast more than a little doubt on the plaintiff's story when one arresting policeman turned out to have been the best man at her wedding. The suspect policeman was "named James Caine or Kane (he used both forms of the name)" (Bauerle and Hodgart, 98). The slightly confused names give new meaning to both the biblical character and the conclusion of Hosty's ballad.

Joyce was much taken with the story, as his November 20, 1906, letter to Stanislaus attests:

I suppose you read about Caruso being arrested in the monkey-house at New York for indecent behaviour toward a young lady. [...] I wonder they don't arrest the monkeys in New York. It took three

N.Y. policemen to arrest Caruso. His impresario ridicules the charge
and says Caruso has to answer shoals of 'offers' from N.Y. women of
the upper classes. The papers are indignant. Do Americans know how
they are regarded in Europe? (*L*, II, 197)

Joyce had already made use of the incident in *Ulysses* during Bloom's
Circe trial (*U*, 15.1188–90), where he is condemned, like HCE/Humpty
Dumpty, to be "detained in custody in Mountjoy prison during His
Majesty's pleasure and there be hanged by the neck until he is dead"
(*U*, 15.1169–71). Bloom desperately answers the accusations,
parodying Caruso's appeal:

Innocence. Girl in the monkeyhouse. Zoo. Lewd Chimpanzee.
(*breathlessly*) Pelvic basin. Her artless blush unmanned me.
(*overcome with emotion*) I left the precincts. (*U*, 15.1188–90)

The oft-repeated but never confirmed Caruso allegations only add
to the grand parody of obfuscation in the shady business in the parks,
Phoenix and Central. However, it may be clearly and unequivocally
admitted that something may or may not have transpired; and whatever
it was, it is all fodder for Joyce/Hosty's accusatory ballad and the fun at
Finnegans Wake. As Bauerle points out:

Had he written this as fiction, Joyce could hardly have fitted it
better to his favorite themes: the tenor unjustly accused of some
vague sexual misconduct in the symbolic Eden of a municipal park,
the evil but aptly named policeman, the monkeys lending a jungle
quality to the setting, the confusion of the witnesses, and the
persistence of rumor. [...] Other allusions appear at 70.8 (one
monkey's damages), 139.31 (a magda went to a monkishouse),
193.32 (cannibal Cain), 491.12–18 (tryst, two a tutu, Ebell, Kane,
Mansianhase parak), 536.25–32 (Kanes nought, Zerobubble
Barrentone), and 611.10 (all him monkafellas). (Bauerle and Hodgart,
99–101)

But how do we know the song "Finnegan's Wake" was about a
happy time? Apart from the closing line of the chorus, "Lots of fun at
Finigan's wake" (Bauerle, 557), we have the assurance of it all being in
a major key, presumably happy music. Hosty's ballad, however,

undergoes a key change from A major to A minor when Hosty gets to the words *curled up*. Since there are no harmonic indications of chords in Joyce's rendition of the melodic line, the C natural or diminished third on *up* gives the song a turn to the minor. It was presumed, when Zack Bowen gave a sung rendition of the ballad at Zurich in 1996, that it stayed there in the minor, and became a tragedy; but it is possible that when returning to the final tonic resolution the concluding A might be chorded with a major instead of a minor triad. That is to say, the ballad might just as easily undergo a last note reconciliation with the major key, and be a happy rather than a sad song, even if happiness is denied by the permanent burial Hosty predicts for his fallen former tyrant/king/betrayer in the last two stanzas.

Of course the problem of the key evolves from the fact that Joyce didn't supply the chords, any more than he does with specific background material to make precise determinations of the setting/outcome/interpretation possibilities of the *Wake*. He offers only a single melodic line of narration from any number of sources about any number of things, infusing the hybrid result with the hope of an almost definable, pluralistic sense.

The major/minor key ambiguity at the end would complete the ambiguous story of a fall/resurrection. The last lines of the ballad, "For there's no true spell in Connacht or hell / [...] That's able to raise a Cain," could be read several ways. Besides the biblical/fraternal/Cromwellian/Carusoian sources and their related meanings, another interpretation might include puns on the words: in "no true spell," *true* might mean no straightforward way of spelling out/saying something that is always going to be ambiguous; or, no true *spell* or spelling according to one lexicon/language to represent the microcosmic history of Ireland/HCE in terms of its/his pluralistic nature. Therefore it would follow that only *Finnegans Wake* is capable of raising the dead by pouring into the ear(wig) the fluid languages of life in our time as well as the past. Enter the life-giving, resurrecting whiskey of the ballad of "Finnegan's Wake."

The construct of returns to the tonic in music also represents a variation on the return/resurrection motif, as Stephen pointed out in "Circe":

> The reason is because the fundamental and the dominant are separated by the greatest possible interval which.... [...] Is the greatest

> possible ellipse. Consistent with. The ultimate return. The octave.
> Which [...] went forth to the ends of the world to traverse not itself,
> God, the sun, Shakespeare, a commercial traveller, having itself
> traversed in reality itself becomes that self. (*U,* 15.2104–19)

The similarity between harmonics and the earth's daily and eternal life/death cyclical regeneration process lies in the return to the harmonic resolution/resurrection of the fundamental key.

In terms of the signature, there's no doubt of a major key and resurrection in the song "Finnegan's Wake," despite Tim's fall. In Bauerle's version of the song, the second stanza, fourth line, ends— "his corpse to wake" (557)—by plunging a major fifth to the tonic, sol do, instead of going up to it, sol la ti do, and the chorus ends with the same downward interval. However, each complete stanza ends going up to the tonic. Thus, the last and only words we hear from the dead and resurrected Tim, "'Bad luck till yer souls d'ye think I'm dead!'" (Bauerle, 557), occurring at the end of the fifth stanza, are also on their way up to a major key beginning. What difference does that make? We don't know, except that whenever one goes to resurrections one wants and expects them to be intellectually upscale, upbeat events, and Joyce at least leaves enough ambiguity for that kind of interpretation.

Returning to Joyce's musical composition of the ballad's melody enables us to see how Joyce has worked ambiguity, allowing for the dualities already discussed, into the very structure of the melodic line. The sort of ambiguity making it possible to harmonize the final notes with either a major or minor triad is also apparent in Joyce's use of accidentals: the sharps, flats, or naturals used in a musical composition but not included in the key signature. The first example, as noted earlier, occurs in the fifth full bar of the song (excluding the introductory, abbreviated initial measure) when Joyce uses a natural to lower the C sharp of the key to a C natural, thus modulating the ballad from A major to A minor. The eighth bar suggests that the ballad stays in the minor mode when Joyce again uses a natural to cancel the C sharp of the key signature. Before doing this, however, Joyce employs a sharp in an unlikely musical move when he places it before the G note with which the seventh bar begins. This is curious, to say the least, as the G is already sharp because of the A-major key signature that, by convention, makes all F, C, and G notes sharp unless the sharp is cancelled by placing a natural symbol in front of the note. Joyce had considerable knowledge of music, and his use of the natural to lower the sharpened C of the key signature in the fifth and seventh bars reveals his knowledge of this musical convention.

The possible logical explanations for the placement of the sharp in front of the G note that opens the seventh full bar of the ballad must include the possibility that Joyce simply forgot that the G was already sharp because of the key signature. This would be possible if, for example, Joyce, aware that he had modulated to the key of A minor, simply followed the convention by which the G note of the melodic A-minor scale is made sharp with an accidental. It does seem highly unlikely, however, that Joyce would not have noticed such an error when he composed the melody and later checked it through the various stages of publication. A less likely possibility is that Joyce, knowing the G was already sharp because of the key signature, decided that he wanted the G to be a double-sharp, thus making the note enharmonic, or a note with the same pitch as another note. In this case the G double-sharp would be enharmonic with the same pitch value as the tonic note of A. Playing the melody as this would dictate—with all of the double-sharp G notes in the seventh bar having the same pitch as the tonic A—produces a very acceptable melody line. This seems unlikely, however, unless Joyce is again letting us know that our "leg's getting musclebound from being too pulled" (*FW*, 64.32–33), but this time in a musical context. It seems improbable because the easiest way of notating the enharmonic pitch of the tonic A note would be to continue with the notation of the A note immediately preceding this ambiguous G. The sharp preceding the G may simply be redundant or it may sustain the sorts of ambiguities noted earlier in the paper.

Another intriguing ambiguity at work in the music of the ballad involves the paradox that, according to the traditional, theoretical musical conventions for setting lyrics to melodies, "The Ballad of Persse O'Reilly" is a song that cannot be sung. According to the common musical practice of matching melodies to lyrics, the syllabic structure of the lyric should be the same for each of the verses unless a different melodic pattern is provided in order to accommodate the different syllabic arrangement of the lyric. When there is only a slight difference in the syllabic pattern of the lyric, this is no problem. Most singers will be familiar with lyrics in which one verse will require two or three syllables to be sung along with a single note, while a different verse of the same lyric will require only one syllable. "The Ballad of

Persse O'Reilly" has great fun with this convention, reminding us once again that there's fun for all (including musicians) at *Finnegans Wake*.

Of course from a practical perspective, the paradox of the ballad as a song that technically cannot be sung makes little sense. Nevertheless, a comparison of the syllabic and melodic patterns from even a few of the ballad's fourteen stanzas indicates how Joyce pushes the musical conventions governing the relationship between music and lyrics to their breaking point if not beyond. The most convenient point of comparison is the first stanza, where the syllabic pattern from the four lines of the stanza proper and the two refrain lines exist in comfortable ratio with the notes of the melodic pattern. As the lyrics of this stanza and the provided score reveal, there is a one-to-one ratio between the syllables of the stanza and the notes of the melody. The rhythm (in 6/8 time) is as follows:

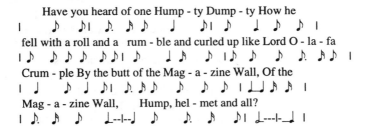

There are forty-nine syllables in the first stanza and the total number of articulated notes (excluding the notes tied to them) is the same. This is of course the most common note-to-syllable ratio in popular lyric settings because it is the easiest for the singer to articulate.

The second and third verses begin to strain this one-to-one ratio of the first stanza by gradually increasing the number of syllables to be sung with the pattern of forty-nine notes. The second stanza has fifty-four syllables, the third sixty-two. Following the refrain, and lines 25–27 (for which no music is provided), the fifth stanza has sixty-five syllables that the singer must try to fit to the forty-nine notes: no mean task. Only by repeating appropriate notes from each bar until there are enough to match the syllables can the singer produce a practical melodic structure to accommodate the extra syllables. Of course, this new comic melodic structure will not only be Joyce's creation, but also that of the singer who must engage in a re-creation of Joyce's melody

in order to render it vocally. The ambiguity produced by the gap
between the ballad's theoretical impracticalities and the practical
realization in performance is further illustrated by the two-line
"(Repeat)" and the "*Balbaccio*" lines, which presumably are
exhortations from the crowd, and a commentary on stuttering (*FW*,
45.25–27) to be discussed presently.

The tension produced between a song that may be impossible to
sing according to the traditional conventions governing the ways in
which lyrics are set to a musical score and then subsequently realized in
performance, and the attempt to sing that song in practical performance,
draws attention back to the *Wake*'s fundamental blurring of the
traditional categories of speech and writing. Stephen Heath suggests
that Joyce's "soundscript" is "not the reproduction of speech, but the
ceaseless confrontation of writing and speech in which reference is
involved in a tourniquet between the two, thus defining yet another
strategy of hesitation" (58). In "The Ballad of Persse O'Reilly" the
musical score that traditionally provides a notation for the music
against which the lyric can be sung with confidence and certainty fails
to provide the support for that certainty and confidence. Instead it sets
to work the thematic and tonal ambiguities explored in the first part of
this paper within the tension produced between the melodic score of a
ballad whose lyrics do not always match the melody provided for them.
This enforces the sort of hesitation described by Heath. With HCE, this
hesitation is realized, of course, in the hesitation of his stammering, a
hesitation signified in the ballad by the italicized "*Balbaccio,
balbuccio!*" that McHugh identifies with the Italian, "balbo," or
"stuttering," and the pejorative and diminutive Italian suffixes, "-accio"
and "-uccio" (45). In the middle of the ballad, following the hesitation
of the two "(Repeat)" lines for which there "may not or maybe a" (*FW*,
309.1) melody, these two italicized Italian words provide a small
hesitation in the progress of the ballad by provoking a rethinking of the
very relationship between a ballad's lyrics and its melody, the very
relationship Joyce's ballad is supposed to create and sustain.

Thus Hosty's song as musical paradigm creates more ambiguities
than it solves: as Joyce's reply to the book's title ballad, as parody of
actual contemporary history, as a score that cannot be performed with
any intentional accuracy, as a form of musical or lyrical order, or even
as a representation of itself. Like the *Wake* as a whole, it delivers so

much more than it would seem to promise: its plurabilities are its genius.

NOTES

1. Not an anachronism. Ex-Lax was introduced in 1906.
2. For details, see McHugh, 44.

WORKS CITED

Bauerle, Ruth. *The James Joyce Songbook.* New York: Garland Publishing, 1982.

Bauerle, Ruth and Matthew Hodgart. *Joyce's Grand Operoar: Opera in* Finnegans Wake. Urbana: University of Illinois Press, 1997.

Glasheen, Adaline. *Third Census of* Finnegans Wake. Berkeley: University of California Press, 1977.

Heath, Stephen. "Ambiviolences: Notes for Reading Joyce." *Post-structuralist Joyce: Essays from the French.* Eds. Derek Attridge and Daniel Ferrer. Cambridge: Cambridge University Press, 1984. 31–68.

McHugh, Roland. *Annotations to* Finnegans Wake. Baltimore, Md.: Johns Hopkins University Press, 1980.

Figure 14–1. "The Ballad of Persse O'Reilly" (*FW*, 44)

CHAPTER 15

Synthesizing "The Ballad of Persse O'Reilly"

Daniel J. Schiff

The following is the story of how I took "The Ballad of Persse O'Reilly" (*FW*, 44.24–47.29) from the page to the stage: the decisions I made in scoring the music and in vocalizing this song from *Finnegans Wake,* and the many problems that had to be solved in turning Joyce's words to song.

My interest in mixing James Joyce and song grew from reading aloud for the Tuesday night *Finnegans Wake* reading group in Berkeley, California. Experimenting with the voicing, I found that different voices were best for different characters: an echoing baritone for Humphrey Chimpden Earwicker, soothing watery feminine tones for Anna Livia Plurabelle, a radio evangelist rant for Shaun the Post, a high squeaky mincing lisp for Issy, a solemn creaky vacant drone for the Four Old Men, a grizzled Nordic growl for Sackerson, and so forth. When extended passages of rhyming text appeared, I would sing the words to tunes either composed for the occasion or provided in the text. The results were encouraging, and led to my performance, at the fifteenth International James Joyce Symposium in Zurich, of "The Ballad of Persse O'Reilly," live to a prerecorded tape of my synthesizer music.

I began my composing process by considering what aspects of *Finnegans Wake* might be incorporated or suggested by a musical score. The gossip motif, for example, was one aspect I could suggest in the music. The subject of the ballad concerns the "crime in the park" committed by the book's central character, HCE. The whole book is filled with gossip about this one event, and as is the nature of gossip, the story continues to grow and become distorted as it is passed down through the pages. I designed the musical score to resemble gossip in the following ways. First, the range of sounds starts out small and as the ballad progresses, the instrumental sounds grow progressively louder and have more of an echo effect. Second, I used the "call and response" structure to simulate the person-to-person nature of the transfer of gossip, so that for any given stanza, there is a "call" instrument, with a musical line that duplicates the melody of the lyrics of the stanza, and a "response" instrument, which comments or reacts to the melody, much as the second party listening to some gossip might interject "Do tell!" or "Go on!" in response to some juicy tale they were hearing. After the chorus of each stanza, when both instruments play with the singer, the response instrument switches to the call instrument, and a new response instrument reacts to this stanza's worth of gossip. In this way, the succession of instruments passes the musical story from one to the next.

Some further aspects of *Finnegans Wake* are illustrated by this structure. The succession of instruments suggests the passage of time and the progress of history: the ballad is scored with musical instruments that progress from classical music to jazz to rock and electronica. The combined effect was designed to move the listener from the classical to the modern age of music through melodic style and instrumentation. The musical arrangement also reflects the idea of circularity. There are allusions throughout the book to Giambattista Vico's three-stage theory of ages of civilizations, the Iron, Silver, and Golden ages, followed by a *ricorso,* returning to the start of the cycle. In my score, the same voice and flute instrumentation used for the first stanza of the ballad reappears for the final stanza, musically closing the circle. A final aspect of *Finnegans Wake* treated in the music is the way that chapters end. More often than not, a chapter's structure dissolves away, ending with more of a whimper than a bang. At the end of the eighth and last chapter of Book I, Anna Livia's voice gets tired and putters out into a final "Night!" (*FW,* 216.5). As the ballad also is placed at the end of a chapter (Book I, Chapter 2), and similarly sputters out in the final stanza, the music presents a breakdown of the established patterns of call and response—even the voice stops as the ballad moves into its final moments—to musically suggest a Wakean "fall-apart ending."

Figure 15–1 shows what sort of voice, and which call and response instruments, were used for each different stanza of the ballad. I would like to amplify that chart here, taking the ballad stanza by stanza. The spare beginning of the ballad features only my "normal" (unaccented) voice, singing according to Joyce's musical notation, with the flute supplying a very minimal response to the voice until the chorus, when it duplicates the vocal line. The second stanza brings a new meter: in fact, no two stanzas of the ballad have exactly the same meter, and thus, no stanza except the first matches the written music. By writing the ballad with this shifting meter, Joyce makes his musical notation not so much a template as a suggestion, and the singer is forced to fit the words around the melody. The flute is the response instrument to the call of my voice in the first stanza; in the second stanza it graduates to the call instrument and the violin gives the response, partly because of its classical associations and partly because the fiddle is a particularly Irish instrument. As for the voice, the phrase "kicked about like a rotten old parsnip" (*FW*, 45.8), brought to mind something a hillbilly might say, and so Local Yokel, a hick from the sticks, sings the stanza in a backwoods twang.

The hostility for "immaculate contraceptives for the populace" and "Openair love" (*FW*, 45.14, 16) in the third stanza suggested a Disgusted Matron singing the lines in a high-toned voice dripping with contempt, and the line "my fine dairyman darling" (*FW*, 45.20) in the fourth stanza yielded the baritone of the Stalwart Farmer. The fourth stanza contains the lines:

> All your butter is in your horns.
>   (Chorus)   His butter is in his horns.
>   Butter his horns! (*FW*, 45.22–24)

Although I was unsure that Joyce had this type of horn in mind, the triple repetition of the word "horns" was too good a musical cue to pass up. So the call instrument of the stanza became the concert brass (and thus also the response instrument for stanza three), and the response instrument the muted trumpet, together providing the stanza with buttery smooth horn music.

The next three lines of the ballad break from the established form, and have several quirks that beg for some sort of musical interpretation. The lines are as follows:

> (Repeat) Hurrah there, Hosty, frosty Hosty, change that shirt on ye,
> Rhyme the rann, the king of all ranns!
>
> *Balbaccio, balbuccio!* (*FW*, 45.25–27)

The problems with these lines start with the very first word, "(Repeat)." Repeat *what:* the first phrase, the first few phrases, the whole line, the next few lines, or the rest of the ballad? There is no way to be sure. By placing the instructions to repeat at the beginning rather than the end of a phrase, Joyce again forces the singer into the role of composer, for the singer must decide how much of the ballad to repeat, or perhaps to ignore the instruction altogether. I chose to repeat only the phrase "Hurrah there." In the larger structure of the song, lines like these appear after every four stanzas of "The Ballad of Persse O'Reilly." After the eighth stanza, we have "Lift it, Hosty, lift it, ye devil ye! up with the rann, the rhyming rann!" (*FW*, 46.23) and after the twelfth, "Suffoclose! Shikespower! Seudodanto! Anonymoses!" (*FW*, 47.19). My solution for them all was a musical vamp, a little repeating figure that orchestras play over and over between stanzas of a song until the singer steps forward to sing the next lyrics. The "oom pa-pa" beat resembles the generic tune of a merry-go-round, and so serves to emphasize the "circular" motif of the book. Since the voice seems to be obnoxiously asking Hosty to do things without offering to help, the character is made to sound weak and lazy: an English Fop.

The line *"Balbaccio, balbuccio!"* poses its own interpretive problems. Instead of being set flush left like all the other lines of the ballad, this verse is centered and set in italics. Should centered, italicized text be pronounced or sung differently from noncentered, nonitalicized text? Moreover, as there is no space between the *"Balbaccio, balbuccio!"* and "We had chaw chaw chops, chairs, chewing gum, the chicken-pox and china chambers" (*FW*, 45.28), should the two lines be musically connected? Since the following line was already eighteen syllables long, I detached the little centered italic phrase from the next line of verse, and wrote a unique snippet of music, a "flourish," or two-note trill played simultaneously by the concert brass and the muted trumpet, to accompany the words. It seemed natural, given the exclamation point and the italic nature of the two words, to sing the phrase in the voice of an Enthusiastic Italian.

The fifth stanza returns to the form of the opening four stanzas, and here, to slowly move the instruments from the classical music era to the jazz era, I chose a xylophone as a response instrument to the muted trumpet. The voice is the Gravel-Voiced Hipster, who sounds like a cross between Louis Armstrong and Tom Waits. The sixth stanza contains the phrases "hotel premises sumptuous" (*FW,* 46.5) and "trash, tricks and trumpery" (*FW,* 46.6), words that brought Las Vegas to mind, so the voice for the stanza is the Vegas Lounge Singer, a third-rate Frank Sinatra type, full of swinging, oozing sincerity. The xylophone sound moves into the call instrument spot and a saxophone provides the response, emphasizing the "bom" in the line "With the bailiff's bom at the door" (*FW,* 46.8) with a low, reedy note.

The words of the seventh stanza complain about seeing "his black and tan man-o'-war" (*FW,* 46.14), making the singer female emphasizes the sexual aspect of the phrase. Since a stand-up bass sound responds to the saxophone's call, the voice needs to be pitched very high to be distinct from the low tones of this instrumentation, leading to the high falsetto voice of Opera Lady. The eighth stanza begins with a mouthful: "Where from? roars Poolbeg. Cookingha'pence, he bawls Donnez-moi scampitle, wick an wipin'fampiny" (*FW,* 46.17). The lyrics mention "Poolbeg," a place known for its lighthouse, and "Norveegickers cod" (*FW,* 46.20): these phrases brought a Grizzled Salt Sailor to mind. For the next line, "Lift it, Hosty, lift it, ye devil ye! up with the rann, the rhyming rann!" (*FW,* 46.23), the vamp continues, but with different call and response instruments. Since I wanted to suggest a movement through the ages as the ballad progresses, the voice is transformed into a creakier Older English Fop.

The first line of the ninth stanza of the ballad mentions "fresh water garden pumping" (*FW,* 46.24). This phrase seemed to be begging for a little "water music" to accompany it, and as the call instrument, the "droppy" sound flows around the words of the stanza. To make the sound, the synthesizer is made to create a flanged envelope of sound around a note, so that it sounds like a drop of water from a dripping faucet, followed by some high ripplelike overtones. This sound also begins the movement of instrumentation toward the modern, synthesizer era, and takes the piece in the direction of increasingly echo-laden sounds; the response instrument is an electric organ. The matter-of-fact tone of the first few lines of this stanza, "It was during some fresh water garden pumping / Or, according to the *Nursing*

Mirror, while admiring the monkeys" (*FW,* 46.24–25), suggested an official report of the news (often the news is little more than gossip after all!). As vocals for this stanza, I decided that instead of singing, I would speak the lines in the manner of a Radio Announcer reading the evening news.

The angry speaker of the tenth stanza has a wide vocabulary— "hayheaded philosopher," "crux of the catalogue," and "antediluvial zoo" (*FW,* 47.1–4)—all of which brought the Pissed-off Librarian to mind. The eleventh stanza's second line mentions "Our rotorious hippopopotamuns" (*FW,* 47.8), leading to the voice of a Bass Hippo, with big, fat, rounded low tones. Continuing the march into progressively more echo-laden synthesized musical accompaniment, I picked a backward chorus sound for the response instrument to the space mandolin, introduced as the response in stanza ten. In the next few stanzas, I began to add dissonance to the echo that accompanied the music, for as gossip spreads, it frequently becomes distorted and ugly. I chose as a response instrument a sound I call "sinister chorus": a version of the backward chorus sound, but more melancholy and distorted. The vocal choice of the character of Bob Dylan's Nephew, nasal and off-beat, adds further dissonance, and keeps the musical styles of the ballad moving even closer to the present day.

The next line of the ballad, "Suffoclose! Shikespower! Seudodanto! Anonymoses!" (*FW,* 47.19), at first glance doesn't fit either the regular stanza pattern (it's too short) or the "oom pa-pa" pattern (it's still too short, and doesn't mention "Hosty" or "the rann"). So here is where the music begins to fall apart, with only the call instrument accompanying the text from here on. The line is made up of four words, each mentioning a great man from the past (Sophocles, Shakespeare, Dante, and Moses), which brought the characters of the Four Old Men from the *Wake* to mind: I sang this line as if an ancient barbershop quartet gave each of its members a name to sing, in alto, tenor, baritone, and bass tones.

The thirteenth stanza of the ballad has very aggressive lyrics—"to sod the brave son of Scandiknavery" (*FW,* 47.21) and "bury him down in Oxmanstown / Along with the devil and Danes" (*FW,* 47.23–24)— and so, in keeping with the desire for a modern dissonance, the Snarling Punker sings the lines with an off-key voice that howls, sneers, and drips contempt, with the sinister chorus doubling the vocal line. For the last stanza of the ballad, it was important to bring the piece back to where it began musically, and so the flute sound returns as the call instrument and the voice returns to normal. However, since Vico's idea of *ricorso* suggests *returning* back to the beginning, but not necessarily *duplicating* it, the sounds of flute and voice are slightly altered, with echo added to the flute, and vibrato removed from the voice.

My version of the ballad may run counter to listeners' expectations in at least two ways. To the charge that the ballad should be sung as a funeral dirge, with a sluggish, heavy tempo and a mournful, wailing vocal, I plead guilty, having chosen to err on the side of entertainment.[1] To the accusation that this musical version of "The Ballad of Persse O'Reilly" wanders into anachronistic musical territory, I again plead "guilty as charged," with the following justification: over the years of reading *Finnegans Wake,* I have come to the conclusion that Joyce was attempting to fully describe the human condition and the history of humanity in a cyclical series of rises and falls. And while the book was finished in 1939, the behavior that the book describes and the historical parallels mentioned continue to characterize the human condition up to and beyond the present day.

And now to the matter of voicing: whether the ballad was designed to be sung by one person or by many is an open question. Certain stanzas seem to be spoken with different accents: "You" is pronounced "you" in the first stanza (*FW,* 45.1), and as "ye" between the fourth and the fifth (*FW,* 45.25), while "my" in the fourth stanza (*FW,* 45.20) becomes "min" in the eighth (*FW,* 46.19). Either different people with different accents are singing different parts of the ballad, or one person is singing the ballad, imitating other accents in the process.

A look at earlier versions of "The Ballad of Persse O'Reilly" reveals that at one time Joyce actually named an individual singer of the ballad.[2] In early 1927, Joyce made two handwritten additions to the unnamed song in his typescript: "The Ballad of Persse O'Reilley" [sic] and "As sung by Poblacht" (*JJA,* 45.61).[3] In the next surviving manuscript version, dated "probably March 1927" (*JJA,* 45.45), Joyce changed the line to read "Ballad of Persse O'Reilley (as sung by Phoblacht)" (*JJA,* 45.71). And in the version of the ballad that appeared in the May 1927 *transition 2,* the words "BALLAD OF PERSSE O'REILLEY (as sung by Phoblacht)" appear in a decorative type in a larger typeface than the regular text (*JJA,* 45.110). When the *Finnegans Wake* typesetters set the first galleys, they did not include the musical notation; neither did they set the title "The Ballad of Persse O'Reilley" or the line about Phoblacht. In their place are the words "music block to come" (*JJA,* 49.57).[4] But the musical notation and the titles were slow in coming. The third and final existing galley proofs for the ballad are still missing them, although the words "music block to come" have been circled by Joyce, who wrote the twice underlined note "Printer wait for this please" (*JJA,* 50.65).[5] When the final version of the musical notation did show up, the title of the ballad did not show up with it. The typesetters reset the words "The Ballad of Persse O'Reilly" in nondecorative type, with the new spelling of the last name, and left out any mention of "Poblacht" or "Phoblacht." Joyce never reinstated Phoblacht back into the title of the ballad, and by eliminating all clues to the identity of the singer, it is now impossible to tell for sure how many voices sing in "The Ballad of Persse O'Reilly."

The issue of whether the ballad is more fittingly sung by one or by many remains up to the composer to decide. And while I'm sure that an impressive version of the ballad could be done with a full chorus, there is one aspect of the *Wake* that my vocalization underscores. While the book contains many characters, young and old, male and female, it appears that all the characters in the *Wake,* regardless of their age or sex, all spring from the mind of one person, the unidentified dreamer. Just as the *Wake* features many voices coming from a single source, my version of the ballad features many different voices coming from a single human being. Moreover, this "many-from-one" aspect of the *Wake* is also present in the musical score, where over a dozen different types of sounds emanate from a single instrument, a Korg M1 synthesizer.

There are many ways of performing the ballad: I envisioned flying to Dublin, combing through the bars and churches of Chapelizod, finding the best barroom and choir-loft singers I could, and assembling them under the Wellington Memorial in Phoenix Park at 11:32 in the morning to sing the ballad while I recorded the result using seven different microphones. But every version I could dream up suffered the fault of incompleteness. Although all the versions of the ballad I contemplated touched on different aspects of the *Wake,* none of them, including the version I performed in Zurich, comes close to fully describing the complexity of the ballad, let alone of *Finnegans Wake.* The process of composing my version of "The Ballad of Persse O'Reilly" taught me that a definitive version of the ballad is simply not possible.

Part of the complexity results from Joyce working up the ballad for two different publishing deadlines: the first for the May 1927 issue of *transition 2,* and the second for the 1939 publication of *Finnegans Wake.* The *transition 2* version of the ballad is an easier piece of music to sing than the *Finnegans Wake* version. True, there are still lines of verse that are jam-packed with many syllables to trip up the tongue, and there are still lines of verse that do not match up with the tune. But Joyce thoughtfully inserted an oversized dash and a space between the end of the fourth stanza and the start of the ill-fitting verse "Hurrah there, Hosty, frosty Hosty, change that shirt on ye" (*JJA,* 45.110). This helpful dash, while not providing the singer with the melody for the verse, at least alerts the singer of the ballad that *something* unusual is about to happen.

In the eleven years between first composing the ballad for *transition 2* and beginning the final corrections to it in the galley proofs of *Finnegans Wake,* Joyce had spent his time adding to other chapters of the *Wake;* he now made the singing of the ballad much more complicated. It is not entirely surprising that many of the parts of the ballad that are difficult to interpret musically—the "(Chorus)" command, the "(Repeat)" instruction, the centered line *"Balbaccio, balbuccio!"* and the line "Suffoclose! Shikespower! Seudodanto! Anonymoses!"—were among Joyce's additions to these galley pages (*JJA,* 50.64–67). And although the oversized dash after the fourth stanza made it all the way to the final galleys (*JJA,* 50.65), this helpful warning sign was removed by the time the book was printed, leaving the singer unaware that the strange lyrics that follow will be anything out of the ordinary.

All these changes that Joyce made, as well as the elimination of P[h]oblacht, add variety, ambiguity, and uncertainty to the act of singing the song. Confusing musical instructions, ill-fitting lines of verse, and a shifting rhythmic structure in "The Ballad of Persse O'Reilly" force those who sing it to improvise, adding their personal voice and song to all the other voices. "The Ballad of Persse O'Reilly" is a tune of uneasy listening music, and Joyce designed it so the uneasiness is felt by the singer as well as the audience. It is also a song of gossip that makes each singer throw a little of his or her own vocal styling into the telling of the tale. Joyce constructed the ballad in a way so that each singer is forced into the role of composer. As the complexities of the song unfold, all singers of "The Ballad of Persse

O'Reilly" end up synthesizing from their own wits, as well as from the pages of *Finnegans Wake*.

NOTES

1. Anyone interested in hearing a recording of my version of "The Ballad of Persse O'Reilly," as well as many other *Wake* tunes and James Joyce-related raps, can obtain a cassette tape from the author, D. J. Schiff, via The Wonderworker Press, 2636 Benvenue Avenue, Berkeley, CA 94704.

2. See also Bowen and Roughley, chapter 14.

3. *James Joyce Archive,* Vol. 45: *Finnegans Wake:* Book I, Chapters 2–3, Drafts, Typescripts, & Proofs.

4. *James Joyce Archive,* Vol. 49: *Finnegans Wake:* Book I, Galley Proofs, Vol. 1.

5. *James Joyce Archive,* Vol. 50: *Finnegans Wake:* Book I, Galley Proofs, Vol. 2.

CUE LINES OF VERSE	CHARACTER VOICE	CALL INSTRUMENT	RESPONSE INSTRUMENT
Have you heard	Normal Voice	—	flute
He was one	Local Yokel	flute	violin
He was fafafather	Disgusted Matron	violin	concert brass
Arrah, why,	Stalwart Farmer	concert brass	muted trumpet
(Repeat) Hurrah	English Fop	concert brass (oom)	muted trumpet (pa-pa)
Balbaccio	Enthusiastic Italian	concert brass (flourish)	muted trumpet (flourish)
We had chaw	Gravel-Voiced Hipster	muted trumpet	xylophone
So snug he	Vegas Lounge Singer	xylophone	saxophone
Sweet bad luck	Opera Lady	saxophone	stand-up bass
Where from?	Grizzled Salt Sailor	stand-up bass	droppy
Lift it,	Older English Fop	stand-up bass (oom)	droppy (pa-pa)
It was during	Radio Announcer	droppy	electric organ
He ought to	Pissed-Off Librarian	electric organ	space mandolin
He was joulting	Bass Hippo	space mandolin	backward chorus
'Tis sore pity	Bob Dylan's Nephew	backward chorus	sinister chorus
Suffoclose!	Four Old Men	backward chorus (oom pa-pa)	—
Then we'll have	Snarling Punker	sinister chorus	—
And not all	Normal Voice (with no vibrato)	flute (with more echo)	—
That's able to raise a Cain. (2nd time)	(chorus only)	saxophone, flute, violin, electric organ, droppy, xylophone, and backward chorus	—

Figure 15–1. The Vocalization and Instrumentation of "The Ballad of Persse O'Reilly"

List of Contributors

ZACK BOWEN is Professor of English at the University of Miami. He is editor of the University of Florida Press James Joyce Series, the *James Joyce Literary Supplement,* and the Twayne/Macmillan series, Critical Essays on British Literature. He is the author of six books, including *Musical Allusions in the Works of James Joyce* (1974), Ulysses *as a Comic Novel* (1989), and *Bloom's Old Sweet Song* (1995), and editor of three others; he has also published more than one hundred monographs, essays, reviews, and recordings. A former President of the James Joyce Society (1977-1986), he is currently President of the International James Joyce Foundation.

MURAT EYUBOGLU, a native of Istanbul, Turkey, earned his B.A. from Bennington College, Vermont, where he studied literature, philosophy and music. After some years in Paris, he started his graduate studies at the State University of New York at Stony Brook, where he is currently a Ph.D. candidate. Eyuboglu's dissertation explores the problems of subjectivity in the music of Gustav Mahler.

ANDREAS FISCHER is Professor of English Philology at the University of Zurich. He is the author of *Dialects in the South-West of England* (1976), *Engagement, Wedding and Marriage in Old English* (1986), and a variety of other publications, mainly on historical English lexicology. He is also interested in stylistics and has published several articles on Joyce. He is a member of the board of the Zurich James Joyce Foundation.

JOHN GORDON is Professor of English at Connecticut College in New London, Connecticut. He received his B.A. from Hamilton College and his Ph.D. from Harvard University. Besides teaching, he has also worked as a freelance writer and journalist. He is the author of two books on Joyce, *James Joyce's Metamorphoses* (1981) and Finnegans Wake: *A Plot Summary* (1986), in addition to the monograph, "Notes on Issy," and more than thirty published articles and notes. He has also published essays on T.S. Eliot and Hopkins. He is currently completing a book, to be entitled *The Somatic Muse,* tracing the influence of contemporary medical theory on English-language writers from Wordsworth to Plath.

ALLAN HEPBURN is Assistant Professor of English Literature at the University of Toronto at Scarborough. He has published articles on Edith Wharton, Joseph Conrad, contemporary Canadian literature, Louis Begley, Joan of Arc, and cultural studies. He reviews books regularly for *The Financial Post* in Toronto and serves as a co-editor of *Descant,* a literary journal. He is finishing a book, called *Spies and Traitors,* on cultures of espionage in the twentieth century.

SCOTT W. KLEIN is Associate Professor of English at Wake Forest University. He has published numerous articles and reviews in the field of Joyce and modernism in such journals as *E L H*, *Modernism/Modernity, James Joyce Quarterly,* and *Twentieth Century Literature,* and contributed to the MLA volume *Approaches to Teaching Joyce's "Ulysses."* He is the author of *The Fictions of James Joyce and Wyndham Lewis: Monsters of Nature and Design* (1994).

SEBASTIAN D. G. KNOWLES is Associate Professor of English at The Ohio State University. He is the author of *A Purgatorial Flame* (1990), a study of seven writers in the Second World War, and the co-author of *An Annotated Bibliography of a Decade of T.S. Eliot Criticism: 1977-1986* (1992). His lecture recital of songs in *Ulysses* has been heard in Vancouver, Dublin, Montreal, and elsewhere. He is currently at work on *The James Joyce Puzzle Book,* a study of ways in which to read *Ulysses.* He received his B.A. from Harvard University and his Ph.D. from Princeton.

PAUL MARTIN is completing his Ph.D. in Comparative Literature at the University of Alberta. A musician and composer himself, one of his chief areas of interest is the way that twentieth-century writers like Joyce, Mann, Butor, and Tournier attempt to use musical form in their fiction.

JOHN McCOURT, Ph.D., is a graduate of University College, Dublin. He has been living and teaching in Trieste since 1991. Founder and program director of the Trieste Joyce School and President of the Bottega Joyce, he has published several articles on Joyce and Trieste, and is editor of *Joyce in Svevo's Garden* (1996) and *Dubliners* (1998). His book *Joyce in Trieste: The Years of Bloom* will be published in 1999.

SUSAN MOONEY is a Ph.D. candidate at the Centre for Comparative Literature at the University of Toronto. She is currently writing her dissertation, "Censoring Bodies in Spain and Russia: Literary Censorship and Sexuality During and After the Regimes."

SEAMUS REILLY was born and educated in Ireland, and received B.A. (Hons) and M.A. degrees from The National University of Ireland (Dublin), and a Ph.D. from the University of Illinois in 1997. He is at work on a book-length project of Joyce and music, tentatively entitled *James Joyce, Music, and the Making of Modern Irish Culture.* He is currently a Visiting Assistant Professor at the University of Illinois, and Acting Director of Business and Technical Writing.

THOMAS JACKSON RICE, who received his Ph.D. from Princeton University, is the author of nearly a hundred essays and papers, and eight books on British and American fiction, including three books on Joyce: *James Joyce: A Guide to Research* (1982), *James Joyce* (1985), and *Joyce, Chaos, and Complexity* (1997). He is currently Professor of English at the University of South Carolina.

MARGARET ROGERS is a musician and composer who has written a series of choral pieces based on Joyce's works: "A Babble of Earwigs, or Sinnegan with Finnegan," which draws its inspiration from the general structure and the hundred-letter words of *Finnegans Wake,* "The Washerwomen Duet," which derives from the ALP sections of the work, and two works inspired by the "Sirens" section of *Ulysses:* "Sirens Fugue" and "Sirens Duet." She has written songs based on the writings of W. B. Yeats, and a satire on Swift's *Gulliver's Travels,* a musical setting from the Lilliputians' point of view.

ALAN ROUGHLEY is Research Fellow at the University of York, and a Lecturer at the Bolton Institute of Higher Education. His rendition of the ballad of "Finnegans Wake" is internationally renowned.

MYRA T. RUSSEL earned a B.A. in Music (Douglass '41) and, after raising a family, an M.A. in Literature (Sarah Lawrence '68). A professor for twenty-four years at Elizabeth Seton College (now part of Iona), she has published articles, given lectures and programs on *Chamber Music,* G. M. Palmer, and other topics at International Joyce Symposia, the MLA, and various other occasions. Her book, *James Joyce's* Chamber Music: *The Lost Song Settings,* was published in 1993 by Indiana University Press.

DANIEL J. SCHIFF is a long-time member of the Berkeley Tuesday Night *Finnegans Wake* reading group. In 1993, he was a Zurich James Joyce Foundation resident scholar. Through his Wonderworker Press, he has published *Let's All Chortle: A James Joyce Cartoonbook,* and two full-color art books, *Wather Parted from the Say,* and *The Ondt and the Gracehoper.*

Index

BORDER CROSSINGS
DANIEL ALBRIGHT, *Series Editor*